≈

Philo T. Farnsworth

The Father of Television

≈

Philo T. Farnsworth

Philo T. Farnsworth (1906–1971), circa 1926. Courtesy Elma G. Farnsworth.

Philo T. Farnsworth
The Father of Television

Donald G. Godfrey

Foreword by

Christopher H. Sterling

The University of Utah Press

Salt Lake City

ISBN 0-87480-675-5
Library of Congress Control Number: 2001089984

Dedicated to
Christina Maria Godfrey
and all who receive
“a great deal of satisfaction in seeing
the flights of imagination come true.”
(Farnsworth)

Contents

Illustrations

Foreword

Rescuing a Television Pioneer

It was while beginning graduate school at the University of Wisconsin–Madison more than three decades ago that I became fascinated with the development of American broadcasting and its audio and video technologies. Back then the relatively sparse published record of the pioneering days of television was dominated by accounts of John Logie Baird and Charles Francis Jenkins and their work with mechanical systems, as well as the work of Vladimir Zworykin's team at RCA. If Philo T. Farnsworth was mentioned at all, he was merely a footnote—one of many electronic media innovators who seemed only marginal to the main story.

Although the image of an Idaho farm boy conjuring up a workable electronic system of television in the 1920s could easily grab one's imagination, over the years Farnsworth's work faded into the background. Important to this disappearance was the lack of any corporate support to balance decades of steady propaganda from RCA praising Zworykin (on whose work RCA held the patents) as the real—and sole—father of television. About a year before Farnsworth died, I unfortunately passed up a chance to meet him when one of my graduate students interviewed him at his Salt Lake City home and obtained his shaky signature on the flyleaf of my copy of George Everson's *The Story of Television* (the 1949 biography that for 40 years was the only book-length study of the inventor's life).

As described in the pages that follow, Farnsworth's quest for success in electronic television was to be plagued by bad luck, sometimes poor timing, often impatient financial backers (who wanted vast and quick returns), and inadequate staff and research funding. Products using his name disappeared from catalogs and shelves years before he died. What remained was scattered and lacked any single sponsor interested in preserving and promoting what he had accomplished. Photos of Zworykin holding an old cathode ray tube became near icons of television's pioneering days, but pictures of Farnsworth were so rare he stumped a television quiz show panel in 1957. He died in 1971, worn out and ignored by the very industry he helped to create.

Luckily Philo Farnsworth was not doomed to permanent obscurity. Growing awareness of his vital role in the technical development of electronic television began in the 1970s. What had been forgotten over the years turns out to be a fascinating story, central to understanding the progress of electronic television. In 1977 a television magazine published a four-part biography of Farnsworth. He was also one of four electronics inventors featured in a set of U.S. postage stamps in 1983. The efforts of his devoted wife and family culminated in 1989 with publication of an informal memoir that helped revive our sense of who he was as well as what he accomplished. A statue of the young Farnsworth holding his pioneering television tube was added to the collection in the United States Capitol in 1990 after a statewide effort from Utah to recognize a favorite son.

A number of dedicated researchers have aided the effort to rescue the inventor's record and reputation from dusty records and archives so that Farnsworth is now more widely recognized than at any time since his exciting, innovative work in the 1930s. Descriptions and analyses of his role appear more prominently in the many published histories of television. A solid technical survey of Farnsworth's work graced the pages of the prestigious *SMPTE Journal* in the early 1990s. In a 1999 feature on the major American inventors of the 20th century, *American Heritage* included only two telecommunications pioneers—Edwin Howard Armstrong and Philo Farnsworth.

With this first scholarly biography of Farnsworth's life and times, Donald G. Godfrey has done the inventor and all historians (let alone watchers) of television a considerable service, by providing an appealing, balanced, and well-researched study of Farnsworth's life and work. Godfrey emphasizes the all-important context of the times—in terms of television developments elsewhere as well as, after 1929, in the investment-killing Depression years—to provide insight to what Farnsworth managed to accomplish against considerable odds.

Three decades after his death, the television and other achievements of Philo Farnsworth are finally plain for all to appreciate.

Christopher H. Sterling
George Washington University

≈

Preface

THIS BOOK PRESENTS A HISTORY OF THE MAN AND THE CORPORATIONS CARRYING HIS name. The challenges in writing this history were significant, some of which bear mentioning so that the reader may understand and profit more fully from the text as a historical resource.

The first challenge was Farnsworth himself. His work was his life. He did not care much for history; in fact, when approached during his lifetime about writing his history, he commented that he would leave that to others. This became an inspiration to his wife and family who have worked to get Philo Farnsworth credit for the invention of television. They have been largely successful in the popular literature, bringing attention to several historical sites, and have provided a perspective that was ignored by historians. The results of their efforts, however, have not been without controversy.[1]

The second challenge was that Farnsworth worked in different laboratories and with corporations across the country—California, then Pennsylvania, Maine, Indiana, and Utah. Because of his many moves, important corporate records have been lost. For example, Farnsworth worked for the Philco Corporation during his career; but Philco has been sold several times since then, and historical records were rarely retained with the change in corporate ownership. Thus, there are no easy answers to some intriguing questions.[2] The story of Farnsworth's involvement with International Telephone and Telegraph (ITT) is similar. ITT's office in Fort Wayne has retained some of Farnsworth's commercial newsletters and brochures. There are a few papers and some tubes at the Allen County–Fort Wayne Historical Society, but again corporate records are sketchy.

Fortunately, the available resources allowed me to sustain historical integrity. The family papers and many of Farnsworth's original records have been deposited at the J. Willard Marriott Library at the University of Utah. This critical collection contains not only Farnsworth's daily log books and related records but also the daily logs of the individual engineers who worked and moved with him to different locations. Papers, professional correspondence, corporate records, and selected papers of Elma G. Farnsworth are all part of this collection. The University of Utah Farnsworth Collection is complemented by the George Everson papers housed at the Charles Trumbull Hayden Library, Arizona State University.

Throughout the research, many papers were graciously provided from various sources, which have been donated to Arizona State University and are now contained under the title Godfrey Papers. These contain photocopies of corporate and family records, publicity scrapbooks on pre-1929 television, technical papers, and correspondence. There are two of Farnsworth's notebooks detailing his technical work and a mention of Farnsworth in the George Clark and Allen B. DuMont collections located in the Archives Center of the National Museum of American History, Smithsonian Institution, Washington, D.C.[3] The television station records for the two stations Farnsworth used during experimental broadcasts are housed with FCC records at the National Archives. Finally, there are a number of engineers and colleagues in Fort Wayne and across the country who worked with Philo. These and small collections scattered across the nation provided the foundation of the present study.

In *Media History Digest,* Thomas Ropp called Farnsworth the "forgotten father of television."[4] His colleague and biography George Everson described him as a "genius."[5] Journalist Kenneth Kistler concluded that "Philo T. Farnsworth gave to the world the most powerful communications form of [the] century . . . unparalleled in scientific development."[6] To date, only one article on Farnsworth has appeared in the scholarly journals. In that significant work, Stephen Hofer provides a sketch of Farnsworth's early life combined with a focus on Farnsworth's battle with RCA.[7] Hofer concludes, "Philo Taylor Farnsworth successfully conceived, developed, and ultimately realized his youthful idea of an electronic television system and therefore should be known in history for that accomplishment."[8] Kenneth Bilby, describing the inception of television from the RCA point of view, concurred that there was "[one] American inventor who I think has contributed, outside RCA itself, more to television than anybody else in the United States, and that is Mr. Farnsworth . . . Farnsworth succeeded in creating a profitable enterprise."[9]

Eckhardt's *Electronic Television,* published in 1936, was important to this book because it was written at the time of the events under discussion and it focused on Farnsworth's work. Eckhardt detailed the emergence of television and compared the differing technologies of the time crediting Farnsworth, along with Zworykin, as being the two "pioneers in electronic television."[10] Albert Abramson's works provide us with a technical history of television and its pioneers. In his *The History of Television, 1880 to 1941,* he chronicles television's prehistory through 1941. Abramson, citing primary materials, patents, and technological data, traced the technological development of television.[11] His work on Zworykin mentions Farnsworth, but Abramson discusses Zworykin as the "father of television," stopping just short of awarding him the title.[12] R. W. Burns's *Television: An International History of the Formative Years* is the most recent definitive work.[13] George Everson's *The Story of Television*[14] and the recent *Distant Vision* by Elma G. Farnsworth[15] are important biographically—Everson was the first and longtime financial associate of Farnsworth, and Farnsworth's wife, Elma (Pem), worked in his laboratories.

In recent years Farnsworth has received attention. The San Francisco *Examiner* called him the "father of video."[16] A magazine article noted that the "television inventor was finally getting the public's respect."[17] There is even an author who has hinted that the idea of television belongs totally to Farnsworth.[18] Frank Lovece charged that RCA and Zworykin conducted a massive misinformation campaign, the results of which appear to have altered the facts and directed the credit for the invention of television away from Farnsworth and toward RCA[19] (these publications are based primarily on family interviews).

In more recent scholarship, Christopher H. Sterling and John M. Kittross hint at the significant challenges in Farnsworth's career in listing his name among the great inventors of the time. They also note that he was one who "never had enough good fortune or entrepreneurial skill to innovate successfully."[20]

This book is not intended to argue technology or to trace Farnsworth's technological developments in television, although while writing about Farnsworth one cannot totally avoid these topics. This is a biography of a man whose life was inseparable from his work. Using business and family records, my purpose is to document, not editorialize on, the development of Philo T. Farnsworth's life so that we might conceptualize his involvement in television history and the events underlying his career. Most of what has been written about Farnsworth deals with his youthful genius and his technical innovativeness. Forgotten in the literature is that Farnsworth was an independent inventor, and his businesses grew parallel with the size of his patent portfolio.

The evolution of Farnsworth's business ventures provides the basic outline for this work. His technical achievements are noted throughout the manuscript, as well as in the "Technical Progress" sections that appear at critical points in the text. Each chapter, except 4 and 9, is prefaced with a chronology providing the reader a comparative historical context. The endnotes, as well as providing documentation, also expand the details of this story. Chapter 1 chronicles Farnsworth's formative years. Chapter 2 sets the stage for the career of an inventor and an entrepreneur. Chapter 3 reflects an independent

Farnsworth as he struggles during the height of the Depression to establish himself in the race for television. Chapter 4 steps back somewhat from the chronological order of events and examines solely the Farnsworth versus RCA legal challenges. This was an important legal challenge, but not the only one. The competitiveness of Farnsworth versus RCA is a thread appearing within almost every chapter. Chapter 5 displays Farnsworth at the pinnacle of his career. He's won his battle against the giant RCA and his business ventures have grown to include television manufacturing. Chapters 6 and 7 chronicle Farnsworth during World War II. Chapter 8 describes how Farnsworth's corporation became a division of ITT, with Farnsworth one of the only corporate leaders to make the transition. At ITT the Farnsworth Corporation became the foundation for today's ITT Aerospace/Optical Industries. Chapter 9 summarizes Farnsworth's legacies and his contributions to humanity.

≈

Acknowledgments

MY APPRECIATION GOES TO ALL WHO HAVE CONTRIBUTED TO THIS WORK. I EXTEND special thanks to scholars and colleagues; my wife, Christina, who patiently works as I write; to Christopher H. Sterling of George Washington University, and Albert Abramson, author and retired CBS engineer, both of whom read and reviewed preliminary manuscripts and provided valuable insight; to Kevin Knight, who acted as a research assistant throughout the project; to Steven C. Runyon of the University of San Francisco, who assisted in gathering materials from the San Francisco era of Farnsworth's work and who facilitated the donation of the Philo T. Farnsworth Foundation files to the project; and to Lew Klein, executive director of the NATPE Foundation, who networked resources on the Philadelphia period for me. Thanks to all my colleagues at Arizona State University's Walter Cronkite School of Journalism and Telecommunication and especially to Douglas Anderson and Joe Foote, directors, who provided inspiration, editing advice, and financial assistance throughout the process.

I owe a special thanks to Elma G. Farnsworth and the Farnsworth family, who not only permitted access to primary family papers, but also provided time for manuscript reviews, personal direction, and assistance. They have all been more than cooperative in this research. They may not concur with all that is written, but they have provided support as well as access to materials and people.

Marilyn Wurzburger, curator of Special Collections at the Arizona State University Hayden Library, assisted in the establishment of the Farnsworth-Everson Papers and the Godfrey Papers; and her enthusiasm for the topic was great. Stan Larson, curator at the J. Willard Marriott Library at the University of Utah, assisted in the Farnsworth papers recently placed there.

Special thanks to the people at ITT, Fort Wayne; the Indiana State Library; Indiana State Archives; the National Archives; the Museum of American History; University of California, Berkeley; the Farnsworth Museum; San Francisco Public Library; Sarnoff Corporation Library; Brigham Young University

Archive; and the Church of Jesus Christ of Later-Day Saints Archives and Historical Department.

Without the computer support from Janet Soper of the Publication Assistance Center, College of Public Programs, Arizona State University, this book would not have been possible. My thanks to Mary Fran Draisker, who aided in the proofreading process and other phases of production, and to Chrys Gakopoulos, Vic Garman, Julie Patch, and Roisan Rubio who worked on various stages of the manuscript.

≈

Philo T. Farnsworth

The Father of Television

Caricature of Philo Taylor Farnsworth (1906–1971). Courtesy ITT.

"Beetle Bailey" July 17, 1981. Reprinted with special permission of King Features Syndicate.

1
Youthful Genius
1906–1926

Chronology

Farnsworth	Electronic Media
	1837 — Samuel F.B. Morse applied for first patent on telegraph system (received 1840). 1873 — James Clerk Maxwell puts forth modern concept of electromagnetic energy. 1876 — Alexander Graham Bell applies for first telephone patent. 1887 — Heinrich Hertz discovers he can project a magnetic field into the air. 1892 — Nathan B. Stubblefield begins broadcasting speech and music. 1894 — Charles F. Jenkins begins mosaic television system experimentation. 1895 — Guglielmo Marconi begins experimenting on his father's farm. 1897 — Marconi forms the Wireless Telegraphy and Signal Company in England. Cathode ray oscilloscope is developed by Braun. 1899 — Marconi Wireless Company of America is formed. 1900 — British Marconi Company is founded. • U.S. Weather Bureau hires Reginald A. Fessenden. 1901 — Marconi sends signal across Atlantic, from St. John's,

Farnsworth

1906 — Born the son of Lewis Edwin Farnsworth and Serena Amanda (Bastian) Farnsworth. Philo's grandfather, Philo T. Farnsworth Sr., was a prominent Utah settler.

1914 — Moved to father's farm near Vernal, Utah, and again to Washington, Utah, near mother's family.

Electronic Media

Newfoundland, to Cornwall, England.

1902 — Fessenden forms his own company, National Electric Signaling Company.
• Lee de Forest creates the De Forest Wireless Telephone Company.

1903 — First world Radio Conference conducted in Berlin to discuss control of broadcasting.

1906 — Fessenden transmits the human voice.
• Lee de Forest patents the audion tube.
• Second world Radio Conference conducted in London.
• David Sarnoff hired as office boy working in Marconi stations.
• Farnsworth born.

1907 — De Forest begins radio broadcasting in New York.

1908 — De Forest broadcasts music from Eiffel Tower in Paris.

1910 — First *Wireless Ship Act* passed; requires passenger vessels to carry radio equipment.

1911 — Marconi contracted with Wanamaker in New York and Philadelphia to install wireless.

1912 — *S.S. Titanic* sinks, and the value of wireless is proven.
• *Radio Act of 1912* passes; places Secretary of Commerce in charge of regulating radio; station licenses now required; Secretary to assign wavelengths.

1913 — De Forest sells patents to AT&T.
• Feedback circuit developed by Edwin H. Armstrong.

1915 — San Francisco World's Fair features demonstrations of de Forest's radio.

Farnsworth

1918 — Philo at age twelve drives one of the family's covered wagons in their move from central Utah to southern Idaho.

1920–21 — Family purchases farmland near Rigby, Idaho. Philo's teenage years combine farm work and scientific curiosity as the "chief engineer" on the farm.

1922 — At age fifteen, Philo describes his ideas for television to his high school teacher, Justin Tolman (Tolman's oral testimony of these experiences would later be instrumental in Farnsworth's legal

Electronic Media

• Charles D. Herrold's radio broadcasts received from San José.

1916 — De Forest radio broadcasts the first presidential election returns in New York.

1917 — The United States enters World War I; the Navy takes over all wireless installations.

1919 — Following the war the Navy returns control of radio to private sector.

• General Electric (GE) forms the Radio Corporation of America (RCA) to protect against a foreign monopoly in radio (Marconi).

• RCA acquires the rights/assets of American Marconi; enters into cross-license agreements with GE.

1920 — Westinghouse radio KDKA, the first commercially licensed radio station in the United States, broadcasts Cox-Harding election returns.

• CFCF radio, Canadian Marconi station, broadcasts historic program.

• AT&T goes into a cross-licensing radio group.

• American Marconi corporation dissolved.

1921 — Westinghouse joins patent pool group. In cross-licensing agreements, GE and Westinghouse have the exclusive right to manufacture radio receiving; RCA, the right to sell the sets; AT&T, the right to make and lease transmitters.

1922 — Herbert Hoover conducts first Radio Conference.

• The AT&T radio station WEAF broadcasts first commercial program called a toll broadcast.

Farnsworth

struggles with RCA). Earned his electrician's license certificate through National Radio Institute correspondence course.

1923 — The Farnsworths moved to Provo to enhance their children's educational opportunities, and Lewis, their father, dies.

1924–26 — Farnsworth meets Elma Gardner. The family struggles for employment and education.

1926 — Philo meets George Everson and Leslie Gorrell. His description of electrical television captivates these promoters.
• Philo and Pem are married.

Electronic Media

• Inventor Edwin H. Armstrong demonstrates superheterodyne receiver.
• ASCAP (American Society of Composers, Authors and Publishers) wants music royalties for music used on the air.

1923 — Hoover conducts second Radio Conference.
• National Association of Broadcasters (NAB) formed.
• First radio network experiment links AT&T stations.
• Federal Trade Commission (FTC) begins radio patent and monopoly investigations.
• Wallace H. White drafts first radio bill.
• Everready (batteries) launches radio program, *Everready Hour.*
• Jenkins performs a shadowgraph demonstration.
• Zworykin files for patents on iconoscope camera tube.

1924 — AT&T experiments with first national radio network hookup.
• Competition between AT&T stations and the Radio Group (RCA, GE, and Westinghouse) stations becomes heated.
• Hoover conducts third Radio Conference.
• FTC issues report critical of radio monopoly.
• AT&T experiments with facsimile by wire.

1925 — Hoover conducts fourth Radio Conference.
• Scopes trial broadcast by WGN-AM.
• Zworykin works with mosaic screens in color system.
• Baird demonstrates mechanical system.
• Jenkins demonstrates "mechanical system."

1926 — Congress begins serious debate on radio legislation.
• Zenith Radio Corporation challenges Hoover's regulatory authority; U.S. Attorney

Farnsworth

- Farnsworth receives first underwriting from Everson and Gorrell, experimentation begins in Hollywood and later San Francisco.

Electronic Media

Donovan suggests Hoover seek new legislation.
- AT&T withdraws from the business of broadcasting, and RCA purchases radio interests.
- RCA forms two radio networks: NBC Blue and NBC Red.
- NBC inaugural radio broadcast conducted.
- WEAF carries Jack Dempsey–Gene Tunney fight.
- Father Charles Coughlin begins his radio career.
- Baird demonstrates mechanical system for the press; licenses first British experimental stations.

Philo Taylor Farnsworth is easily cast and too often dismissed as one of the last of America's independent electronic media inventors. He struggled against the growing corporate communications empires and was a fascinating character in American history. He was a man whose life and character were indivisible from his work. He was not just a scientist working in the laboratories of various East Coast manufacturers. He was a Utah farm boy with a creative mind and will to work who saw his creations as both landmarks and profitable to humankind. His dream of "capturing light in a bottle"—the phrase he first used to describe his idea to his family—we now call television. *Media History Digest* called him the "forgotten father of television." "One of the great minds of the century," *Time* magazine said, "he was an American original, brilliant, idealistic, undaunted by obstacles."[1]

Farnsworth was described as a genius from birth by those who knew him. At age fifteen he drew a rough schematic for electronic television on a blackboard for his high school teacher. In 1929 he demonstrated publicly the first electronic television pictures, leading to San Francisco's claim as the birthplace of television. Three years later he had an experimental television station on the air for the Philco Corporation and shortly thereafter created a second station for the Farnsworth Television Corporation. It would be Farnsworth's inventions that were "so important [to television] that they blocked RCA's efforts to obtain patents on a completely electronic system."[2] Farnsworth achieved an extraordinary victory in winning his patent interference case over RCA.[3] Four corporations bearing his name conducted groundbreaking research, manufactured television and radio sets, and contributed significantly to the world around us.

ITT Aerospace/Optical Industries, Fort Wayne, Indiana, is built upon the Farnsworth foundation. Farnsworth was an inventor who imagined a world based upon his discoveries. But all of this came much later.

FARNSWORTH HERITAGE

The story of Farnsworth's heritage and his youthful genius has been the focus of considerable attention. He was a Utah farm boy whose formal education was limited to high school and a little college training. But he possessed a humanitarian spirit and an enthusiasm for constant learning, work, and invention. These characteristics motivated his life.[4]

Philo Taylor Farnsworth was born August 19, 1906, at Indian Creek, Utah (today known as Manderfield) on the family farm in central Utah, seven miles west of Beaver.

Philo's family history includes a rich religious heritage. Philo's grandfather, Philo T. Farnsworth Sr., was a native of Burlington, Ohio, and joined the Church of Jesus Christ of Latter-day Saints when he was seventeen.[5] These were turbulent times in church history as the church's members, including the Farnsworths, were driven from settlement to settlement and exposed to mobs and persecution.[6] Philo Sr. endured these experiences and was among the earliest pioneers to migrate to Utah; he arrived in 1848, one year after the first settlers entered the Salt Lake Valley.[7]

In Utah Philo Taylor Farnsworth Sr. (the grandfather) helped establish the settlement of Pleasant Grove. He also lived in Filmore (later Utah's first capital) and, in 1856, was asked by church leadership to take some families and establish a town on the sagebrush flats, later called Beaver. There he served as a church bishop, a member of the Utah territorial legislature, and a probate judge. He also acted as an interpreter between the Native Americans and the new central Utah settlers. His family included four wives and 30 children—20 boys and 10 girls.[8]

Philo's father, Lewis Edwin Farnsworth, was the son of Philo, Sr. and Agnes Ann (Patterson) Farnsworth, third in a family of ten children. Life was not easy on a farm subject to drought and famine; at times, they dug sego bulbs for food.[9] Restlessness seemed to be a part of the Farnsworth heritage. Lewis and his family were always on the move, searching for more productive land. Lewis married Serena Amanda Bastian, December 28, 1904, and they moved their family no fewer than eight times, finally ending up in Provo, Utah.[10] Each move was meant to be the last in their search for family prosperity, and each of the children was born at a different location.[11] Philo described his mother as of "sturdy build [and] golden brown hair, which was naturally wavy and blue eyes." She had, "known nothing but hard work." His father he described as,

Philo Taylor Farnsworth
Born: 21 January 1826
Died: 30 July 1887

Lewis Edwin Farnsworth
Born: 30 July 1865
Beaver, Utah
Married: 28 December 1904
Died: 8 January 1924

Agnes Ann Patterson
Born: 10 April 1844
Died: 1 May 1909

Philo Taylor Farnsworth

Agnes Farnsworth Lindsay

Laura Farnsworth Player

Carl W. Farnsworth

Lincoln B. Farnsworth

Jacob Bastian
Born: 14 March 1835
Died: 22 April 1924

Serena Amanda Bastian
Born: 21 January 1880
Washington, Utah
Married: 28 December 1904
Died: 22 May 1960

Christina Hansen
Born: 11 October 1845
Died: 18 March 1929

Philo (called Phil) Taylor Farnsworth
Born: 19 August 1906
Indian Creek, Utah
Married: 27 May 1926
Provo, Utah
Died: 11 March 1971
Salt Lake City, Utah

Elma Gardner
Born: 25 February 1908
Jensen, Utah
Still living

Philo (called Philo) Taylor Farnsworth
Born: 23 September 1929
San Francisco, California

Kenneth Gardner Farnsworth
Born: 15 January 1931
San Francisco, California

Russell Seymour Farnsworth
Born: 5 October 1935
Philadelphia, Pennsylvania

Kent Morgan Farnsworth
Born: 4 September 1948
Fort Wayne, Indiana

Lewis Edwin and Serena Amanda Farnsworth family. From the family records of Elma G. Farnsworth. See also the Church of Jesus Christ of Latter-day Saints, Family Group Records, Ancestral File, AFN: 6B4X-K3.

"stern, yet kind and sensitive. He was a rather larger than average build, and had sandy-brown hair and blue eyes. He had the sensitive soul of dreamer," a characteristic he passed on to his son.[12]

During the Indian Creek venture, which lasted four years, Philo was born. Here, according to the family records, he exhibited his first genius at age three when he sketched in detail a locomotive he had seen while with his father.

Indian Creek was to have been the center of the family, and Lewis, along with his wife's brothers, had invested in 1,000 acres of land there. The soil was good, but the winters were too long and harsh. The family had to raise all their own food, including enough to survive through the winters. Crops consisted largely of hay, grain, some potatoes, and vegetables; the season was too short for fruit or much else.

GROWING UP ON THE FARM

In spring of 1918 Lewis decided to move his family to Idaho. They had relatives near Blackfoot, Idaho, and farming was more successful there. It took three covered wagons and five weeks to travel the more than 500 miles. Philo, at age eleven, drove the third wagon.[13] When they arrived in Idaho, Lewis took a job with the Utah-Idaho Sugar Company near Ucon, and all the family helped support the farm. Philo worked in the fields thinning and topping sugar beets for

The log cabin where Philo was born. This photo was taken in Indian Creek, Utah, near Beaver about 1907. From left: Ronald Farnsworth, about ten years old; Lewis Edwin Farnsworth (father) holding Philo, age one; Serena Farnsworth (mother), age approximately twenty-seven; Lewis Franklin Farnsworth, about age sixteen; man in doorway is unidentified. Photo courtesy of Agnes Farnsworth Lindsay.

harvesting. He trapped muskrats and sold their fur for extra cash.[14] In 1919 they moved to the Bungalow Ranch owned by their uncle Albert Farnsworth, which was a few miles north of Ucon and not far from Rigby.[15] The Bungalow Ranch was different than other ranches in the area because it had electricity—powered by its own generator. When 40 acres became available in Bybee, west of the Bungalow Ranch, the Farnsworths bought it and worked it to pay off their debts before making one final move.[16]

These were difficult years for the family. Agriculture in eastern Idaho was suffering a severe depression following World War I. Sugar beets that had sold for $12.03 in 1919 were selling for half that only two years later. Potatoes once at $1.51 were selling at $0.23.[17] Oblivious to the family difficulties, Philo began to explore a world far from agriculture. Here in the attic of the Rigby farmhouse, he found and studied the electrical magazines of the era and learned about "pictures that could fly through the air."[18] The magazines aroused his imagination,[19] a fact not always appreciated by his mother as she worried that his boyhood enthusiasm for electricity "interfered with his violin practice."[20] The young Philo confided to the family that "he would one day be an inventor."[21]

The subject of radio and "radio vision" was a popular science magazine topic. Many writers described John Logie Baird's and Charles Francis Jenkins's ongoing experiments with mechanical television systems.[22] This material was likely a part of what young Farnsworth was digesting. As his knowledge grew he developed a special interest in Albert Einstein's theory of relativity.

At the age of twelve, Philo was repairing the electrical machinery around the ranch. One day, as his father and others were trying to figure out what had gone wrong with the power generator, Philo stepped in and repaired it. From that time forward at the Rigby farm, Philo was the chief engineer of the Delco generator that provided light and energy to the houses, barn, granary, and automatic elevator. Philo's imaginative use of electricity amazed his family, "He was always occupied with the problems of more interest to him than farming."[23] "Always fixing things," recalled a close high school friend, Vernal T. Sorensen.[24] Philo even constructed an electric washing machine for his mother with parts he found around the ranch. He wound the motor's electrical coils himself.[25]

Farnsworth later wrote that the "solitude of the open country was most conducive to thought and reflection."[26] One day Lewis found Philo relaxing from his assigned farmwork, with one of the reins of a three-horse harrow team dragging in the dirt field where Philo was supposed to be plowing. The three horses were just plodding along in what was a dangerous situation. His father was angry at first, but dared not shout at Philo before he or Philo had control of the team. As Lewis approached the team, the daydreaming Philo shouted, "I've got it. I really think it will work."[27] This incident, depicted in the film documentary *Big Dream Small Screen,* implies the conception of electrical image scanning. His father recognized an inspirational moment in his son's life and did not reproach him. Philo had been thinking about television and the challenge of an engineering contest offered in one of the science magazines. Shortly thereafter, Philo sent in a plan for a "thief-proof ignition switch for automobiles" to Hugo Gernsback's *Science and Invention* and was awarded $25 and first prize for his work.[28] With his winnings, Philo purchased his first pair of long pants.[29] According to Philo's younger brother, Lincoln, Philo was "obsessed with the invisible force" of electricity and was known to "read a book in a night."[30] He remained an avid reader throughout his life.

Farnsworth was not only an inquisitive inventor but also an accomplished musician; he was a member of his high school dance orchestra and later the Brigham Young University chamber music orchestra. He loved music, and later in life music was one of the few ways he could relax. But science was his overriding youthful motivation. He was an impatient student, wanting his science education all at once. He took the regular courseloads at school and then supplemented his learning with reading material borrowed from his teachers and the work in his attic laboratory. But there were not many people to whom he could talk about his inventions. A younger sister, Laura, remembers Philo gathering his brothers and sisters around to show them his experiments: "He'd put us in a line and start electricity down the line to show us how it traveled."[31] Philo's father apparently discouraged his son from sharing his ideas with too many people, feeling someone might steal them. In the 1920s, his father felt Philo's ideas were "too valuable and fragile, and could be pirated easily."[32] Farnsworth's wife wrote later that "father Farnsworth . . . [taught Philo] the lessons of self-reliance."[33] His father even tried to help his son patent a fine-tuning radio dial. He sent $200 to an attorney who had advertised in *Science and Invention,* but the family never heard from him.[34]

HIGH SCHOOL WITH AN INSPIRATIONAL TEACHER

It was a Rigby, Idaho, high school chemistry teacher, Justin Tolman, who made the greatest early impression on Philo—and vice versa. Tolman was someone Philo could talk to about science and inventions. Their relationship started when Philo, at fourteen, asked if he could sit in on Tolman's senior high chemistry class. "I looked at him and laughed," Tolman reported.[35] However, Farnsworth was persistent and kept coming back day after day with the same request. Finally he asked that if he could not get the class for credit, could he just "come to class and absorb? Under these conditions I gave him permission to come in."[36] Tolman was reluctant, but Farnsworth wasn't interested in the credit, he wanted the education, and Tolman introduced him to a wide variety of scientific literature. "I do not think a day ever passed that he did not come to me with from one to a dozen questions on science," Tolman commented. "We would make drawings on the blackboard, scraps of paper, or anything we had handy as we tried to explain to each other what we meant."[37]

Tolman notes that "the custodian of the [school] building called Farnsworth the laboratory pest. He complained that I let him stay so late at night that they never had a chance to clean it up, and if they did, he came so early the next morning the place never looked clean. Philo's questions were apt to come at any time and any place."[38]

Justin Tolman, Rigby High School teacher. Courtesy Thomas Tolman Family Genealogy Center.

Farnsworth and Tolman became good friends, and the young student was given access to the teacher's own library, and, according to Tolman, "he devoured electrical encyclopedias like other students wolfed down popcorn."[39] Lincoln described his older brother as having "a photographic memory . . . what he didn't know, he learned quickly."[40] As a result of Farnsworth and Tolman's close association, Tolman put Philo in charge of one of the school's study halls. One day when Tolman passed by, he reported finding Philo lecturing to the students on Einstein's theory of relativity.

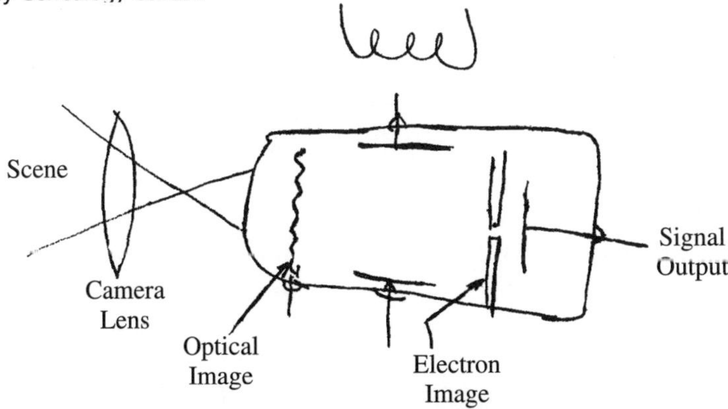

Graphic based on a photo of a drawing made by Farnsworth in 1922 for his high school teacher Justin Tolman. Tolman later reproduced the original drawings he had kept to be used in the Farnsworth/RCA patent infringement hearing. Photo courtesy ITT, Fort Wayne Div., reorder number M4 4 14.

An afterschool session in 1922 has historical significance. Tolman entered his classroom one day to find fifteen-year-old Philo at the blackboard. "What's that?" he asked. "It's an electrical system for projecting an image," responded Philo. "But what does it have to do with our chemistry assignment?" "Oh, nothing," Philo said. "It's my new invention."[41] Philo then went on to explain how his invention could create electrical pictures. It was Tolman's detailed recollection of the conversation that later played a part in the patent interference hearings between the Farnsworth Corporation and RCA (see Chapter 4).

During one year at Rigby High School, Farnsworth completed two years of algebra and a year of chemistry, as well as National Radio Institute correspondence courses.[42] The next year, while working as an electrician's assistant in Idaho, he took an additional four correspondence courses from the University of Utah. At the end of the school year, Philo borrowed a few more books from Tolman. As the two parted, Tolman gave him advice that underscored his father's early teaching. "He [Philo] asked if I could not give him a suggestion that would help him realize his ambition of television. Looking him in the eyes, I replied, 'Study like the devil and keep mum.'"[43]

Rigby High was a memorable experience not only for Philo but also for Tolman, who captivated his later students with stories of young Farnsworth. He told them about young Philo's drawing diagrams for his image dissector on the blackboard and about his own 1934 testimony before the patent hearings.[44]

FARNSWORTH AT BRIGHAM YOUNG UNIVERSITY

In 1923 the Farnsworth family moved from Rigby, Idaho, to Provo, Utah, hoping to take advantage of the educational opportunities they felt a university town had to offer their children. They purchased a large home near Brigham Young University and rented the upstairs to eight students. The rent money supplemented the income Farnsworth's father made from working the Idaho farm and in road construction.[45] Farnsworth attended Brigham Young High School, 1923–1924, and enrolled in Brigham Young University in 1924.[46] He was still in a hurry and, according to Everson, acquired "the run of the [Brigham Young] university research laboratory."[47] However, BYU science professors were unimpressed with the youthful farmboy and, when he asked to attend advanced classes, he was told an exception could not be made (the class he wanted was actually a physics course that his cousin, Arthur Crawford, was taking).[48]

Being told "no" was motivation for Philo: He studied science on his own and earned his Junior Radio-Trician in 1924 and his Certified Radio-Trician in 1925 from the National Radio Institute.[49] He also took part in the school plays, learned to play the piano, and was first violinist in the BYU chamber music orchestra. It was during his days at BYU that Philo met the woman who would play a central role in his life—Elma "Pem" Gardner, then attending Provo High School. Their courtship included dances and going to radio parties at BYU.[50]

Living in Provo also provided work opportunities. Farnsworth asked to hang around the local power plant. According to the *Deseret News,* the plant foreman approved as long as

> he didn't meddle with anything. One day a mysterious trouble stopped the plant's operations. Experts were unable to solve the trouble. Philo stepped forward, asked permission to fix the machinery, and set to work. Soon everything was running smoothly, and the offer of a job followed immediately.[51]

The year 1923 was important to another television pioneer—the man who would become Philo's chief competitor. While Philo was still in high school drawing his schematics on the blackboard, Vladimir Zworykin was well into his career in electricity and television.[52]

DEATH SETS A NEW COURSE

Tragedy struck in January 1924. Philo's father caught a cold while returning home to Provo from a construction job in Idaho. The cold turned to pneumonia and he died at the age of fifty-eight on January 8, 1924.[53] His father's death was catastrophic for Philo. He felt that the obligation for sustaining his family had fallen upon his shoulders because he was the oldest son, yet he still had six months of high school left before graduating. According to Laura, he felt "responsible for his brothers and sisters . . . he had such a paternal feeling about us that sometimes it felt like he wasn't letting us make up our own minds."[54]

Farnsworth's anguish was understandable. He and his family had left a supportive family and teacher in Rigby. When tragedy struck, it evoked a spectrum of emotions and unanswered questions—why would God take a father when he was needed most? Philo did not understand, and he would not return to the church of his heritage until the final years of his life. The death of Philo's father challenged his faith yet at the same time strengthened his independent spirit. He later said, "My father's death was a great shock to me . . . I was extremely unsettled."[55]

After graduating from high school, Philo had a difficult time finding work, so he and a friend signed up to attend the U.S. Naval Academy in Annapolis, Maryland. Here, Philo reasoned, he could continue his work in electronics and support his family. Hofer claims that on his entrance test Philo "ranked second in the nation."[56] It was here too that Philo became Phil—the name all his friends and associates called him—dropping the "o" from Philo because he didn't want to be called Fido.[57] However, his Navy experience did not last long.

According to the family records, a chaplain encouraged him to get out of the Navy: "You don't want the U.S. government to own your patents, do you? That's not the education you want."[58] Farnsworth realized he was in the unexpected position of turning over his ideas to the Navy or developing them himself. He decided upon the latter. He was honorably released after only a few months of attending classes based on his mother's request made through a U.S. Senator that he needed to return to his family as the chief breadwinner.[59] They needed his help after his father's death.[60]

Farnsworth moved back to Provo and enrolled at BYU for another year. BYU seemed more receptive after his short stay in the Navy, and Farnsworth took several science classes.[61] However, finances were still a problem, and he worked odd jobs to stay in school. During the semester he worked as a custodian at BYU and, in the summer, with his brother in a lumber mill in Payson Canyon, southeast of Provo. He worked as long as he could to keep himself in school, hoping that the profits from the sales of his television system would someday support the family. Finally, however, he was forced to leave BYU and seek full-time employment in Salt Lake City.

After moving to Salt Lake City in 1926, he set up a radio repair shop, making small radios with Cliff Gardner, who later became his brother-in-law. There were only twelve radio stations in Salt Lake City at the time, and radio repair was not demanding, so Philo registered with the University of Utah employment agency and continued his research work at the university library. The shift to a larger city proved beneficial.

2
The Experimentation Stage of Farnsworth's Career

1926–1931

Chronology

Farnsworth

February 25, 1926 — Farnsworth proposes marriage to Elma "Pem" Gardner on her eighteenth birthday.

Spring 1926 — George Everson and Leslie Gorrell come to Salt Lake City to conduct a Community Chest fund-raising drive. Everson, Gorrell, and Farnsworth soon form a partnership to develop electronic television—initial funding $6,000.

May 27, 1926 — Farnsworth and Pem Gardner are married. Farnsworth tells Pem on their honeymoon that "there is another woman in his life and her name is television."

Summer 1926 — The couple makes their first home in Hollywood. The first TV experiments take place in their apartment.

Fall 1926 — Additional funds are needed to continue experiments, so Farnsworth and Leslie Gorrell write up a prospectus and, along with Pem Farnsworth, create the drawings that are shown to area engineers. Officers of the Crocker First National Bank, San Francisco agree to fund continued research privately and set up a lab at 202 Green Street.

January 7, 1927 — First four patents filed including the one for the P. T. Farnsworth Television System.

Electronic Media

1927 — *Radio Act of 1927* becomes first comprehensive commercial radio legislation.
• Federal Radio Commission (FRC) created to regulate radio.

Farnsworth

September 7, 1927 — Important experiments on this day produce a single line of light.

1928 — Five more patents are filed and demonstrations for public and corporate interests begin.

May 7–12, 1928 — Experiments are conducted using photographs.

September 3, 1928 — Farnsworth gives first demonstration to the San Francisco press.

May 1929 — Farnsworth Television Laboratories Inc. is formed to develop invention. Finances are a strain at the bank and in the lab.

June and August 1929 — The first broadcast transmission of an all-electric television system.

July 1929 — In his laboratory, Farnsworth first operates all parts of his all-electric television system.

October 1929 — Stock market crash increases financial pressures from the investors as efforts intensify to sell. Farnsworth is ever optimistic about the potential of his system.

April and May 1930 — Zworykin, and RCA engineers visit Farnsworth's Television Laboratories in San Francisco.
• Farnsworth works on improved image dissector and 300-line narrow-band system.

Electronic Media

• United Independent Broadcasters (UIB) organized to supply talent at a network level; UIB struggles and seeks financial assistance from Columbia Records, thus creating the Columbia Phonograph Broadcasting System.

1928 — William S. Paley family comes to the aid of the struggling Columbia system, and CBS is created.
• Baird transmits mechanical image across the Atlantic.
• Jenkins transmits movies on his station with experimental call letters 3XK.

1929 — Quality Network begins (later to become Mutual).
• Stock market crash leads to global Depression.
• Zworykin hired by RCA.
• FRC limits television transmission, grants limited experimental licenses.
• RCA broadcasts from W2XBS.
• Westinghouse broadcasts from W8XAY.
• Baird conducts demonstration in New York.

1930 — RCA unification takes over GE radio engineering and manufacturing interests.
• Census reports 14 million radio receiving sets.
• Raymond "Gram" Swing begins his broadcast career with the British Broadcasting Corporation.
• David Sarnoff appointed president of RCA.
• The Federal Radio Commission denies station license for Dr. Brinkley.
• Zworykin works on improved photoelectric mosaic.
• Jenkins and Baird work on mechanical receivers.

Farnsworth

May 1931 — Sarnoff visits Farnsworth's Television Laboratories.

July 1931 — Farnsworth proposes a new experimental television station for San Francisco.
• Farnsworth moves to Philadelphia to work with Philco in establishing a research lab and station.

Electronic Media

1931 — Gabriel Heatter begins on station WMCA.
• NBC radio reports having 1,359 employees; CBS radio has 408 employees.
• CBS radio begins series *The March of Time.*
• Jenkins advertises its receiver kits; conducts numerous mechanical demonstrations.

≈

THE RADIO SET SALES AND REPAIR BUSINESS FARNSWORTH AND CLIFF GARDNER HAD started in the spring of 1926 was slow. Few stations were on the air in Salt Lake City, and the households able to receive radio were limited.[1] Farnsworth and Gardner were able to sell the sets they made, but parts were difficult to obtain, profits went right back into the business, and the cash flow was slow. There were also several companies manufacturing sets in Salt Lake City, and free sets were being given away. There was little money to meet family needs. As a result both worked odd jobs to supplement the radio business. Farnsworth considered writing up his ideas for television and selling them to a science magazine. Cliff said, "He thought he might be able to get $100 if he worked it right," but encouraged him to hold off on publication.[2]

Meanwhile, George Everson and Leslie Gorrell were on their way to Salt Lake to organize the Community Chest fund drive when car trouble forced them to leave their car in St. George, Utah.[3] They continued via bus and train. After they arrived in Salt Lake City, their first task was to set up an office, initiate staffing, and retrieve Everson's car. As was their usual procedure in hiring, they contacted the local university, seeking temporary office help. Farnsworth was one of those who interviewed and was hired for the job.[4]

This connection with George Everson would prove vital to the development of Farnsworth television. Everson was a professional fund-raiser working for the Community Chest, a public financial organization much like today's United Way. The annual drive was held in communities across the nation, and the funds raised went to local welfare and institutional agencies.

Farnsworth began work as the office survey manager. Although he was not interested in door-to-door solicitations, he knew the Salt Lake territory and drew up maps of business districts, laying out the geography of the campaign so that the businesses could be canvassed.[5] As work started, it soon became apparent that additional office help was needed, and Farnsworth volunteered his friend Cliff Gardner. The jobs of clerical assistants were filled by another of

Philo T. Farnsworth at nineteen, the age at which he first met George Everson. Courtesy Elma G. Farnsworth.

Farnsworth's references, his sister Agnes and young Pem, by this time Farnsworth's fiancée.[6]

Pem Farnsworth described Everson as "a congenial fellow with an average substantial build . . . in his early forties who enjoyed good food and spent his weekends playing golf to keep fit . . . Above all he was good at business and at judging people."[7] Everson described Farnsworth as "a hard-working boy."[8] Everson, Gorrell, the Gardners, and Farnsworth worked closely during the fund drive.

One evening, after working late on a mailing, Farnsworth introduced Everson to television. While relaxing after their long day, Everson asked Farnsworth if he was going to continue his schooling. He was surprised when Farnsworth answered, "No, I can't afford it." Farnsworth told Everson he could not afford college because he was "trying to find a way to finance an invention of mine."[9] In fact, he and Gardner had often even gone without meals in order to purchase parts for their radio business.[10] It was a business they did not want to give up, and they continued to assemble radios in the evenings while temporarily employed elsewhere—all in search of both finances to support their respective families and to underwrite Farnsworth's invention.

Everson and Gorrell did not say much after that first conversation. Farnsworth was somewhat hesitant to continue, this having been the first time he had expressed his ideas outside of his family and a close circle of friends. Gorrell, however, encouraged Everson to talk to Farnsworth about his ideas and discuss television further.[11]

George Everson (1885–1982) was born in Brighton, Ohio. He graduated from Oberlin College in 1908 and did postgraduate work at Columbia University. His career included work at the New York City Committee on Criminal Courts, the Page Commission, the U.S. Army Cavalry, the National Tuberculosis Association, and the Community Chest. He was a major fund-raiser for Farnsworth from 1926 through 1938 and worked as an ITT Farnsworth advisor. He was employed from 1942 through 1958 as director of scientific and engineering personnel for Dr. Ernest O. Lawrence's radiation laboratories in Berkeley, California. Courtesy ASU Library Special Collections.

Farnsworth was nineteen at the time. Everson described him as looking older than his age, "moderate height and slight build and gave the impression of being undernourished . . . There was a nervous tension about him."[12] Everson was skeptical, but his doubts soon vanished:

> As the discussion started, Farnsworth's personality seemed to change. His eyes, always pleasant, began burning with eagerness and conviction; his speech, which usually was halting became fluent to the point of eloquence as he described with the fire of earnestness this scheme . . . He became a super salesman, inspiring his listeners with an ever-increasing interest.[13]

Everson thought that surely General Electric or Bell Laboratories had the lead in developing television. However, with each question, Farnsworth responded with a knowledge of the scientific journals and the experimentation of John Logie Baird and Charles Francis Jenkins and concluded "they are all barking up the wrong tree."[14]

It is likely that Everson understood little of Philo's technical explanations, but he was impressed with the phenomenal knowledge of his young man who had so little formal education. Farnsworth answered each of Everson's questions, illustrating his own understanding of technology and how he would overcome the challenges. However, as Farnsworth noted, the idea was not yet patented; he was still looking for the finances to conduct the experiments and patent the system. Throughout the weeks of the fund-raising campaign, Farnsworth took every opportunity to explain and promote his ideas with Everson. "He . . . snatched every opportunity . . . Any scrap of paper would suffice for him to draw out scratchy designs of some part of his system."[15]

The conversations continued during the Community Chest campaign. Late one evening after extended discussion, Everson asked the bottom-line question: How much would it cost to prove Farnsworth's system? The response was a total guess on Farnsworth's part. He could not foresee the time and effort that would be involved but knew the necessity of experimental proof of his ideas and the royalties that would result from the sale of television sets. "About $5,000," was Farnsworth's response. Everson was willing to take a chance on the young man.

> I have about $6,000 [$58,000][16] in a special account in San Francisco. I've accumulated it with the idea that I'd take a longshot chance on something, hoping to make a killing. This is about as wild a gamble as I can imagine. I'll put that up to work this thing out. If I win, it will be fine, but if we lose I won't squawk.[17]

Farnsworth, Everson, and Gorrell formalized their agreement. Farnsworth was to retain control and fifty percent ownership, with Everson and Gorrell sharing the remainder. They agreed that Gorrell would repay Everson from his

The original three investors (left to right): Leslie Gorrell, Philo Farnsworth, and George Everson. Courtesy Arizona State University Library Special Collections.

own pocket if the venture failed. Gorrell, who was a Stanford University graduate, had more of a grasp of the technical information than Everson. He took the agreement to San Francisco, where it was formalized as Everson, Farnsworth, and Gorrell—a simple alphabetical listing of the principals.[18]

The early association with George Everson reveal several of Farnsworth's personality characteristics. His commitment to work and achievement is illustrated in his constant struggle to fund his own projects. His commitment to family and those closest to him is seen in his first and continued business ventures. Building radios was a partnership with his future brother-in-law, and it was his family and friends who were hired to work in the fund drive. His nervous tension, created by family finances and underwriting pressures, was generally subdued except when he talked about his television ideas. Then he changed from a shy and introverted youth to a man with the eloquence of conviction and scientific knowledge. He was a charismatic salesman when he needed to be. He was convinced of the strength of his own ideas, and he had a natural talent for science and discovery.

FIRST EXPERIMENTS FIZZLE IN LOS ANGELES

The Community Chest fund drive was over in a few weeks, and Everson's next assignment was in Los Angeles. He wanted Farnsworth's experiments to take place there, but Farnsworth did not want to leave his bride-to-be. He liked the idea of being near the resources of the Los Angeles libraries and the California

Institute of Technology. So the decision was either to postpone the wedding or to move up the date.

Their wedding would be a little earlier than the couple had anticipated, but Farnsworth was adamant about getting married. His mother and Pem's parents were surprised at the quick announcement and a bit reluctant because of the couple's age[19]—Farnsworth was only nineteen and Gardner eighteen—as well as financial worries, but the wedding took place on May 27, 1926.[20] The couple was married by a local church authority, President J. William Knight.[21] Everson volunteered his car for the trip to Provo for their marriage, and the newlyweds planned on returning to Salt Lake in the evening for their honeymoon and the train to Los Angeles. After the ceremony the young couple returned to Salt Lake, but Farnsworth decided he must return Everson's car and make preparations for the morning. He was concerned he did not have the money to make the trip to Los Angeles. Philo returned the car and got his first loan so the couple could get to Los Angeles. He also left Pem alone on their wedding night as he and Everson got into an extended conversation about television. It was after midnight when Farnsworth returned to the hotel room. He apologized, but told Pem that there was another woman in his life, and "her name was television."[22] Recalling the events later, Pem commented that "if he [Farnsworth] had said he was going to fly to the moon the next day, I would have believed him."[23]

The train ride to Los Angeles, which took thirty hours (two days and one night), was the first time Pem Farnsworth had been out of Utah. They settled into a small four-room apartment in Hollywood, which also housed their first laboratory.[24] Farnsworth appropriated the dining room for his work. He put an electrical generator in the garage, and tube equipment was set up in a closet adjoining the dining room. The Farnsworths, Everson, and Gorrell worked through the summer. It was not an easy task; everything—even the tools necessary—were constructed to meet specific tasks. Glass blowers doubted they could produce the tubes Farnsworth wanted, but he eventually found one who could. Everson, who was enthusiastic about having things move along, took over the job of winding the first focusing and reflecting coils. During the day the curtains were drawn so that the experiments could be conducted under controlled light. The neighbors grew suspicious of all this strange activity, and someone complained of interference with their radio reception. As a result, one day at noon, they were visited by the local police. A neighbor had reported that the Farnsworths were brewing alcohol behind those curtains (these were the days of prohibition). The police searched the house and left confused with the explanations they heard, but they were assured there was no brewery at the residence.[25]

Farnsworth's own journal describes tests on the electro-light relay, the magnetic image builder, the dissector-cell combination, and the magnetic image dissector.[26] Pem Farnsworth described the very first experiment, humorously as, "Bang! Pop! Sizzle!"[27] Apparently, after Farnsworth had hooked everything up and started the generator, an electrical surge blew up everything, including his new image dissector, before the generator could be cut off.

THE SEARCH FOR FUNDS

By the end of the summer a few of Farnsworth's theories had been worked out. Time was of the essence, as Everson and Gorrell had Community Chest fund-raising activities scheduled in other cities, and personal funds allocated for television experiments were running out. In order to expedite future financing, Farnsworth and Gorrell prepared a prospectus to present these materials to associates who might provide funding. Farnsworth's sketches were rough, so Gorrell made the drawings for the first investment brief and taught Pem how to formalize drawings for records and presentations. These drawings, along with Farnsworth's narratives, were the foundation for enlisting additional adequate support for the earliest experiments.[28]

The next move for the group was to acquire authoritative testimonial as to the merits of the system, as well as patent protection. Gorrell suggested some old college friends, Leonard and Richard Lyon, lawyers from Los Angeles who agreed to hear Philo's proposal. Richard Lyon, a graduate of the Massachusetts Institute of Technology, arranged for Dr. Mott Smith from the California Institute of Technology to attend the presentation. Dr. Smith was a nationally known authority on electrophysics.[29] A meeting was set with the Lyons, Smith, Farnsworth, Everson, and Gorrell in the attorneys' office. The outcome of the meeting, which took all afternoon, was encouraging. Dr. Smith declared, "I am pretty well acquainted with the literature on the subject of electronic developments, and I know of no research that is being carried on along similar lines."[30] The Lyons suggested the materials be forwarded to Washington, D.C., for a patent search.

The topic of discussion then turned from scientific theory and patent rights to the plausibility of an operating unit. Each visit brought about more enthusiasm from Smith for the Farnsworth system. "In his opinion the television system was scientifically sound," and it appeared that at least it was reasonably probable that the system could be successfully completed.[31]

The next step was to acquire stable financing. This time when Farnsworth was asked how much it would take to get the system running, his quote was $12,000 and a year's time—$1,000 a month for twelve months. However, they had spent Everson's $6,000 in just three months, so again his estimate was optimistic. Discussions among the group over the next few weeks led to the decision to seek $25,000 [$241,800] to finance one more year of experimentation.

Farnsworth began writing the patent claims, and Everson took the prospectus papers, along with the testimonials, and approached people Everson knew as a part of his Community Chest work. He contacted associates in southern California, but the scheme of electronic television seemed beyond their interest and understanding. As he talked to his banker friends, Everson was discouraged by information they relayed about Westinghouse having control of television development as a result of patent pool agreements.

THE PATENT POOLS AND PROGRESS

These pool agreements were a part of the outcome of World War I as radio patents were returned from Navy control to private enterprise.[32] Major corporations were making broad claims about who had the rights to what developments. The patent pools, as they are often called, were more influential during radio's development in the early 1920s.[33] Most television experimentation at this time was mechanical. The Bell Laboratories and General Electric were working on television systems by 1925, systems based on mechanical rotating parts.[34] Zworykin was employed by Westinghouse Electric, in east Pittsburgh. He was working with a cathode ray tube, but Westinghouse was not pleased with the results, and he was discouraged from further work on his television project—Westinghouse was more interested in radio.[35] In March 1925, John Logie Baird presented his first public demonstration in London.[36] Charles Francis Jenkins was not far behind, giving his first public demonstration in Washington, D.C., in June 1925.[37] Jenkins was well known as a cofounder of the Society of Motion Picture Engineers. In January 1927, AT&T exhibited a crude television system with the ability to send still pictures over their phone lines.[38] Farnsworth was aware of these mechanical experiments, but they only fostered his enthusiasm for his own work.

These earlier experiments generated a good deal of scientific journal literature as well as popular literature, read anxiously by the young Farnsworth.[39] Television had indeed reached a critical point in its development; it was growing beyond the experimental stage and being recognized by the major corporations as well as individual inventors as a potentially profitable technology. Farnsworth's timing was ideal, but the financial foundation for his experiments was minuscule in comparison to that of the large American corporations.

It took Philo several days to overcome Everson's discouragement after he learned about mechanical television systems and the major competitors. But the young inventor was an enthusiastic communicator of his own inventive scheme and had Everson feeling that just as he had raised millions for charity surely he could raise a little more for television.

FINANCING FROM SAN FRANCISCO INVESTORS

Everson's search for finances next took him to San Francisco to meet with Jesse B. McCargar, vice president of the Crocker First National Bank. McCargar, too, had worked with Everson as a part of the community fund-raising campaigns, and they had a good relationship.[40] As it turned out, McCargar was out of town on vacation and not expected to return for several weeks. So Everson, who was preparing to leave for Texas for another Community Chest campaign, presented the prospectus to James J. Fagan, executive vice president of the bank. Fagan was the most conservative banker on the West Coast at that time. Schatzkin reports that Fagan had the reputation of being a "cold-hearted, glassy-eyed guardian of the money bags," as well as a trusted banker whose roots brought him through the California bonanza era.[41] William H. Crocker (president of the bank) was also president of the local San Francisco Community Chest.[42] Crocker, who had been a Community Chest president since 1923, was known for his interest in science.[43] He had established the small Crocker Radiation Laboratories, where scientists he supported worked on the x-ray and cancer research.[44] The Crocker Bank officials saw Farnsworth's television experimentation as a complement to the existing work at the Crocker Radiation Laboratories.

Everson's first meeting with Fagan led to another. Fagan wanted to meet Farnsworth and have him present his ideas to others with a more technical understanding. He was interested, but skeptical. Television seemed a good idea for an investor who had enough money that "he could afford to lose it."[45] Two engineers, Roy Bishop and Harlan Honn, were asked to look at the Farnsworth plans. Bishop was a San Francisco engineer of independent financial means, and Honn was an engineer at the Crocker Laboratories.[46] The report from these two engineers to McCargar, Fagan, and Crocker was positive and, as a result, another meeting was set up with the banking executives in what Everson called the "throne room" of the bank—the boardroom.[47] Present at the meeting were Farnsworth; Everson; McCargar; Crocker; his son (William W.); James J. Fagan, executive vice president; R. J. Hanna, vice president of Standard Oil of California; and Roy Bishop, consulting engineer. It was a prestigious group of San Francisco capitalists.

Bishop conducted the meeting and led the questioning. Nineteen-year-old Farnsworth, who had dressed in a new suit for the presentation, addressed all their questions. He gave them a history of television and how his proposed system was different from those currently under development because it was all electric. Bishop pressed for detail, and Farnsworth explained the process in his usual youthful eloquence. Although Bishop felt the idea was sound, he doubted Farnsworth's ability to work it out commercially; however, after listening to

Farnsworth's presentation his response was enthusiastic.[48] The venture capitalists would underwrite the work.[49]

WORK BEGINS AT THE GREEN STREET LABORATORY

Experimentation began in the laboratory facility where the Crocker Research Laboratories were already working—202 Green Street at the foot of Telegraph Hill.[50] Everson indicated "the word laboratory was a flattering name for a large second-story loft over a garage."[51] The location was surrounded with electrical interference problems emanating from nearby industry and subject to the whims of weather. A carpenter shop and garage occupied the ground floor. Years later Farnsworth described it as "a big old loft . . . the floors weren't too good . . . no water, no sanitary facilities of any kind just a roof and a floor."[52] The space given to Farnsworth was approximately 20 feet by 30 feet, the ceiling was high, and there were tall windows along two of the walls. It looked like anything but a scientific laboratory. But Farnsworth was satisfied: He was a young, self-educated inventor with a goal.

During negotiations for financing, one of the banking executives suggested that a consulting engineer be hired to supervise the work, but Farnsworth took great encouragement from Jesse McCargar's reply that this was "Farnsworth's show."[53] It was Farnsworth's inventive ideas they saw as profitable, not his engineering.

The first three people on the list of early television laboratory personnel were Farnsworth, B. Clifford Gardner, and Pem Farnsworth—husband, brother-in-law, and wife.[54] Gardner had been living in Baker, Oregon, with his

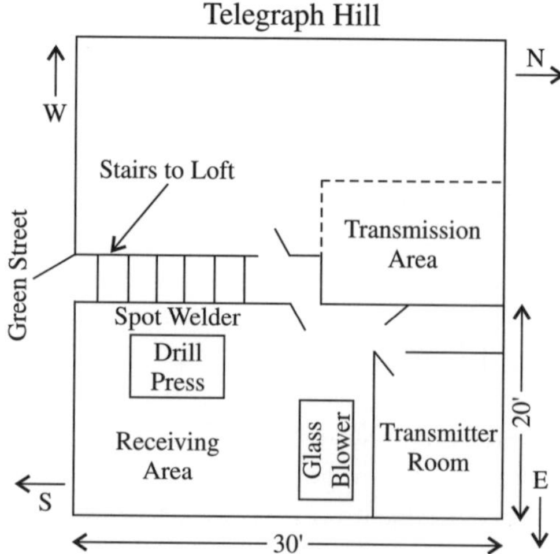

Floorplan of Farnsworth's first lab from a sketch by Elma G. Farnsworth.

sister and working at a lumber mill. He was sent a telegram and told to meet Farnsworth in San Francisco. The three met at the Green Street laboratory September 22, 1926. Getting settled and organizing the laboratory were immediate priorities. For Farnsworth the priority was reversed as he, Pem, and Cliff Gardner first visited the lab to discuss layout, leaving the lab only as the evening approached and they realized they had nowhere to stay. Their first home was in Oakland, not far from the University of California at Berkeley.

Farnsworth and Gardner began setting up the lab immediately, which required constructing several benches for parts assembly and glass blowing. Farnsworth reported that "at the end of six months we had something that resembled a lab."[55] Equipment used in the Los Angeles experiments, left over after the explosion of the first test, was shipped to the new lab. The labwork began with intensity, each experiment growing in complexity. Work progressed quickly, and Farnsworth and Gardner learned as they went. Pem's job was keeping the journal of daily activities.[56] She was added to the payroll in January 1927, as secretary, and paid ten dollars a month for her services.

The year 1927 was a landmark year for Farnsworth. On January 7, the all-important first patent was filed for the television system.[57] It related to electronic scanning and "the broad idea of image dissecting."[58] Three other patents were filed the same day for the light valve, electric oscillator system, and the

Green Street Laboratory, 1997. Farnsworth was in the upper left of this building. The entrance and stairway were from the south, just in front of the automobiles. Note tourists reading the plaque on the corner. Marker and Laboratory photos by Donald G. Godfrey.

television receiving system.[59] Of these patents, the television system and television receiving system were of unusual importance.

FIRST TRANSMISSIONS—LINES AND PHOTOGRAPHS

The first patent, based on Farnsworth's work in San Francisco, was filed by the lawyers Lyon and Lyon from Los Angeles,[60] and Farnsworth left San Francisco for a few days to facilitate the paperwork.[61] However, the move to San Francisco

Historical marker at the corner of the Green Street building. It reads: "Farnsworth's Green Street Lab. In a simple laboratory on this site, 202 Green Street, Philo Taylor Farnsworth, U.S. pioneer in electronics, invented and patented the first operational all-electronic 'television system' on September 7, 1927. The twenty-one-year-old inventor and several dedicated assistants successfully transmitted the first all-electronic television image, the major breakthrough that brought the practical form of this invention to mankind. Further patents formulated here covered the basic concepts essential to modern television. The Genius of Green Street, as he was known, died in 1971. California Registered Historical Landmark No. 941. Plaque placed by the State Department of Parks and Recreation in cooperation with the Philo T. Farnsworth Foundation, Inc., September 15, 1981."

necessitated a change from Lyon and Lyon to the law offices of Charles S. Evans, who signed for the patent on the television receiving system.[62] Evans's law office referred Farnsworth to Donald K. Lippincott, a former lead engineer for the Magnavox Company and an employee at the Evans law firm. Farnsworth and Lippincott formed a friendship that continued for years, and it was at Farnsworth's urging that Lippincott started his own business, which handled future Farnsworth patents.[63] However, filing the applications, getting the patents granted, and preparing a demonstration of the Farnsworth system were all separate challenges.

Everson reported that by the fall of 1927, after they had moved to San Francisco, a crude television image was created.[64] Actually, images came later. The September 7, 1927, experiments produced a one-dimensional vertical line swinging back and forth.[65] Among these first transmissions were black lines, a triangle, and a dollar sign painted on a sheet of glass.[66] The words *radio news* were used with various line widths, and movement of the lines was easily recognized.[67] Line experiments continued, and as they improved, photographs were added.[68] The first images of human beings transmitted were those of Pem Farnsworth and Cliff Gardner. The image of Pem with her eyes closed was viewed on a screen approximately 3½ inches square and was transmitted the week of October 19, 1929.[69]

BROADCAST TRANSMISSION

The first line experiments might have been demonstrated earlier. Farnsworth was ready in February 1927, but when an investor learned he was going to show

Donald K. Lippincott (1886–1958) was a 1913 electrical engineering graduate of the University of California, Berkeley. He worked as engineer and chief engineer at the Magnavox Corporation until 1927. His legal education was from the Hastings College of Law, San Francisco Law School, and George Washington University. He was president of the Patent Law Association of San Francisco, 1934–35. He then developed his own patent law office where he worked until the beginning of World War II. He served as a colonel in the U.S. Army, 1941–46, where he continued work as a patent attorney. Photo courtesy of ASU Library Special Collections.

Technical Progress to Date: 1927

Patents. In 1927 Farnsworth filed for four patents (see Appendix A). Two of these earliest patents would be his most important: Television System (no. 1,773,980) and Television Receiving System (no. 1,773,981). These were the patents that would be challenged by RCA. More important they contained the design claims for a working camera tube. In 1927 Farnsworth had an electronic tube . . . and it worked. [Note the spelling of dissector in the log with only one "s."]

I spent some time thinking about the work that should be done now before trying to offer any of our equipment for sale. The research to be done might be outlined as follows:

LINES OF RESEARCH

I - Image Disector
II - Amplifier
III - Special Oscillograph
IV - Sources of oscillating currents
V - Transmission method and apparatus
VI - Receiving Equipment
VII - Misc. Equipment
VIII Power production Receiving

The image disector needs to be generally improved in order to use it to the best advantage. It should be improved improved along three lines.

1- Photo Electric Sensitivity
2- Fineness of Disection
3- Ease of use.

The amplifier problem must be investigated fully with the point in mind of simplifying and making it more fool proof. It will be well to investigate this with the thought in mind of using the high frequency type.

The special oscillograph will have to be developed nearly from the ground up.

August 24, 1927, entry from Farnsworth's daily log highlights his thinking and technical research lines. National Museum of American History.

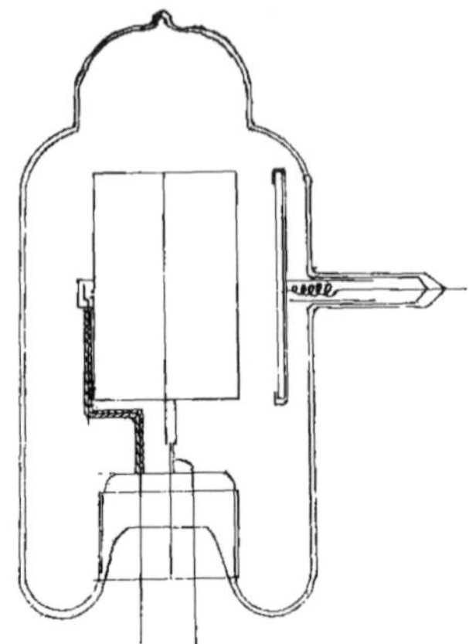

October 25, 1927, entry from Farnsworth's daily log shows a sketch of the image dissector. National Museum of American History.

Technical Progress to Date: 1927 (continued)

Dec 29, 1927 Gardner worked on another Cathode Ray oscillograph. An attempt was made to secure better grid control and this attempt succeeded perhaps too well because a brilliant spot could be obtained only by the use of a positive bias on the grid.

I continued experiments on Television and arrived at the following conclusions:—

The image dissector in use is of the smaller type. We have not as yet been able to secure one of the large type as shown in figure 4, which has a uniform surface.

It is required that a grating of at least 50 or 60 lines be placed over the image being transmitted in order that the frequencies of the signal be of the requisite nature to be transmitted by the amplifier. Now the present tube in use will not clearly transmit this number of lines, it will accordingly be necessary to build a larger tube before good pictures can be transmitted by this method.

December 29, 1927, entry from Farnsworth's daily log discusses Gardner's work on a cathode ray oscillograph and Farnsworth's experiments with the image dissector. National Museum of American History.

≈

the system with only a line picture of a triangle and a dollar sign, he persuaded Farnsworth to wait until a real photograph could be utilized. According to Everson, the photographs "televised much better than the solid black triangle and dollar sign."[70] The first transmissions progressed from single-dimension lines to the photograph, and finally motion. Radio Telephoto (today called motion picture film) was accomplished on January 23, 1928.[71] The first transmission of motion was that of cigarette smoke in the laboratory.[72] These images were all within the laboratory.

The first broadcast transmission was from the Green Street lab to the top of the Merchant's Exchange Building.[73] Little is known of these tests. According to Abramson, the experiments were conducted between June and August of 1930. Unfortunately, the cost for continuing over-the-air tests was high, and, because the results produced a picture showing multiple reflections, they were discontinued. They do represent, however, the "first transmission of an all electric television signal by radio."[74]

Rutherford described the intensity of those early days.

> We had two great big klieg lights and a chair that the secretary was going to sit in . . . everything was adjusted, of course without her there, when someone touched one of the arms [of the stainless steel chair], they were red hot. But everything had to go [forward], so we told her to sit down there, but don't let your arms touch the chair.[75]

FARNSWORTH GOES PUBLIC: TELEVISION INC.

The work continued with increasing pressure for a public demonstration. Everson and Gorrell, who were still traveling for the Community Chest, dropped in to check progress periodically, as did Fagan and other financial investors. One day, Fagan asked Farnsworth if he "saw any dollars in that pick-up tube yet," and that was when Farnsworth responded by "televising a dollar sign painted on a sheet of glass."[76] Lubcke, one of the engineers working in the laboratory, reported that the bankers were coming down "every few weeks . . . to see what was happening [and] where their money was going."[77]

As work progressed, the lab staff and expenses grew. By the end of 1927 there were seven full-time lab employees, and applications had been filed for four patents.[78] Each member of the staff was working on different components of the system as well as on drafting patent materials with Philo, who encouraged those who worked around him. Everson indicated that Farnsworth "enjoyed enlisting the interest of people . . . There was something of the evangelist and propagandist in his makeup."[79] This characteristic, however, was apparent only to those around him.

The growing number of experiments moved Farnsworth into the limelight. Up to this point most demonstrations had been in-house and primarily conducted for the investors.[80] However, the investors were growing uneasy and, at a meeting presided by Roy Bishop, Farnsworth presented an excellent demonstration; but Bishop had more than technical success on his mind.[81] After the demonstration and the appropriate accolades Bishop became quite formal, expressing doubt as to the feasibility of financing. He said, it would take "a pile of money as high as Telegraph Hill to carry this thing on to a successful conclusion."[82] The cost of the laboratory, personnel, and research had reached $60,000 by late summer 1928 [$600,700]. Bishop said that investors had lived up to their part of the contract, Farnsworth had lived up to his part of the agreement, and now the question was how to fund continuing development. For Bishop the options were clear—he wanted to sell to one of the established manufacturing companies. They had conducted public demonstrations, and the "modest sum . . . would ensure them a profit on their original investment."[83]

Farnsworth was conscious of the financial burden. In his daily logs, there is early mention of spending time "thinking about the work that should be done before trying to offer any of our equipment for sale" and holding demonstrations for interested investors.[84] On March 1, 1928, a demonstration of the Farnsworth system was presented to Dr. L. F. Fuller and James Cranston of General Electric.[85] They were shown only a part of the system, and Farnsworth, being a perfectionist, was not satisfied with the results; so he immediately wrote up his report, providing a complete description for the system and prepared another "television demonstration . . . for the purpose of interesting G.E. in our ideas."[86]

It was a time of conflicting emotions for the young Farnsworth. Finances remained tenuous, but tests and experimentation continued. Quietly, inside the privacy of the lab, experimentation had progressed to include motion.[87] The motion had grown from the laboratory cigarette smoke to film. A darkroom was constructed to work with film—"rapid telephoto work" and moving film.[88] Cartoons of "Felix the Cat" and a clown were used, as well as a film segment featuring Mary Pickford from *The Taming of the Shrew,* who combed her hair "a thousand times for Farnsworth Television." Reels of film including material from the famous Dempsey-Tunney fight were worn out in the continual testing.[89]

Farnsworth's outlook remained optimistic. On July 28, 1928, he recorded, "very good pictures could be transmitted," and by August 11, "the pictures are infinitely better."[90] However, only two months later a fire broke out in the lab, hindering progress and requiring reorganization of the testing.[91] While the lab was being put back together, the employees went without work and Farnsworth worked from home.

The key to raising money and interesting buyers was publicity. The first public demonstration, for the San Francisco press, was held September 1, 1928.[92] The *Chronicle* headlined it as "S.F. Man's Invention to Revolutionize Television . . . New Plan Bans Rotating Disc in Black Light . . . W. W. Crocker, R. N. Bishop Head Local Capitalists Backing Genius." The article described the general differences between the mechanical system and the new electronic system. "The system is . . . simple in the extreme and one of the major mechanical obstacles to the perfection of television is thereby removed."[93] The *Christian Science Monitor* described the experiments as a "radical step toward eliminating the problems inherent in the "mechanical scanning disk now used in television."[94] The publicity attracted a good deal of national and international attention to the Green Street Laboratories. The programming for these exhibitions could hardly be considered entertainment—it was the miracle of transmitting pictures through the air that attracted attention.

The 1928 demonstration prompted the beginning of a stream of visiting engineers; some merely curious, others invited as potential sales opportunities. It is interesting that the September 1 experiment was not mentioned specifically in the daily log. Farnsworth indicated merely that between the end of August and the first of October, "we have spent the time in demonstrating and numerous small experiments, which . . . have been worth while . . . [but] are not of a nature as to be worth recording."[95] Farnsworth cared little for publicity.[96]

On the other side of the country, mechanical television was still being demonstrated and drawing crowds. In 1928 the Federal Radio Commission licensed W3XK to the Washington, D.C.–based Jenkins Laboratories, which began regularly scheduled programming in May 1928. It was not the programming, however, that interested the audience, it was the marvel of Jenkins's Radiovisor.[97] Most experimental transmissions at this time were scanning less than fifty lines, and the picture was a blurred image.

TELEVISION LABORATORIES INCORPORATED IS ORGANIZED

A key change in Farnsworth's organization took place in 1929 when Farnsworth formally incorporated as Television Laboratories Incorporated. The first partnership had been an agreement drawn up by Everson, Farnsworth, and Gorrell in 1926. In the second agreement, between 1926 and 1928, Farnsworth conducted his experiments at the Green Street Laboratories in San Francisco. Everson raised the initial funds, and capitalists associated with the Crocker Bank extended their personal funds, investing in the initial operations. Jesse B. McCargar was the first president of the Laboratories, Farnsworth was vice president, Everson was secretary/treasurer, and W. W. Crocker and Roy N. Bishop were the trustees. McCargar, by this time had resigned from the Crocker

Bank and was making his living as an independent financial consultant.[98] The new Television Laboratories was one of McCargar's clients. Farnsworth was now salaried. Everson was still involved in Community Chest activities, but was spending increasing amounts of time in Farnsworth's enterprises—he and McCargar now had duties of selling stock and raising operation funds. Crocker and Bishop's only interests were financial backing and return. The agreement was signed, and 10,000 shares of stock were approved for sale to investors for support of the new company.[99] Farnsworth remained the largest stockholder controlling fifty percent.[100] The articles of incorporation were filed with the State of California on March 29, 1929.[101] Television Laboratories was the most formal of the organizations surrounding Farnsworth's work established thus far.

The breadth of Farnsworth's inventive and business vision was described in the 1929 articles of incorporation. It was to "deal in discoveries, inventions, trade names, trademarks, labels, and brands . . . To apply for, obtain, hold, own, use and acquire, sell, lease, and license . . . patents and patent rights in all countries of the world."[102] The object was to operate the laboratory, engaging in electronic media experimentation, "for the purpose of making discoveries and inventions of all kinds."[103] The business was to use the inventions in manufacturing and establishing a chain of stations and to manufacture electrical supplies for use in the assembly of radio and television operations.[104] It was to be a large undertaking.

The corporation authorized 20,000 shares of capital stock.[105] McCargar, Bishop, and Farnsworth had the controlling percent of stock shares and options on the holdings of other investors. The organization and options were established to provide stability during financially difficult times when some of the original capitalists who had invested were desiring to simply sell the company for a profit.[106]

WORK PROGRESSES IN THE LAB

In direct contrast to the foreboding picture of the financial Depression, the records of the laboratory reflect progress and optimism for each scientific development. Work had progressed to include a talking movie system, and the pictures produced were satisfactory.[107] Farnsworth was comfortable in this environment and very much in control. The handwritten portion of the 1929 journal record is drafted in first person and reflects the active mind of a young man very much in charge: "I have decided . . ."; "I have spent some time thinking about idea #20 . . ."; "It has occurred to me . . ."; "work has been completed and the most important conclusions reached are . . ."[108] Journal entries from the week of March 23, 1929, provide a glimpse of the daily work within the lab.

Technical Progress to Date: 1929

Patents. Farnsworth filed for ten patents between 1927 and 1929 (see Appendix A). The "Television System" was the archetypal patent, which included the camera tube (image dissector). Several among these first ten patents included improvements on the image dissector tube. Others in this group included specifications for electronic circuits for the transmitters and receivers. The most important patents up to this time were the "synchronizing system" (no. 2,246,625) and the "slope wave generator" (no. 2,059,219), patented with Lubcke. The electrical scanning generator produced enhanced scanning and "gave Philo Farnsworth the first all-electric television system in the world." In just a few short years he had developed the dissector tube (a camera tube), the cathode ray tube for viewing, and the pulse generator. See Abramson, *History of Television,* p. 131; "New Television Systems," *Radio News* 10 (January 1929), p. 637; also see S. R. Winters, "Radiovision," *Science and Invention* 16 (January 1929), p. 840.

Comments. By 1929 Farnsworth had made remarkable progress with technical advancements that had provided him with national publicity.

The daily Farnsworth journals indicated differing line experiments at this time, ranging from 60 to 250 lines. Farnsworth talked about high-definition images scanning 250 lines. Any new system to be effective, "must transit a person's face . . . with sufficient detail to make the features readily discernible and sufficiently clear to 'entertain' the viewer." (P. T. Farnsworth and Harry R. Lubcke, "Transmission of Television Images: Intimations of How It Can Be

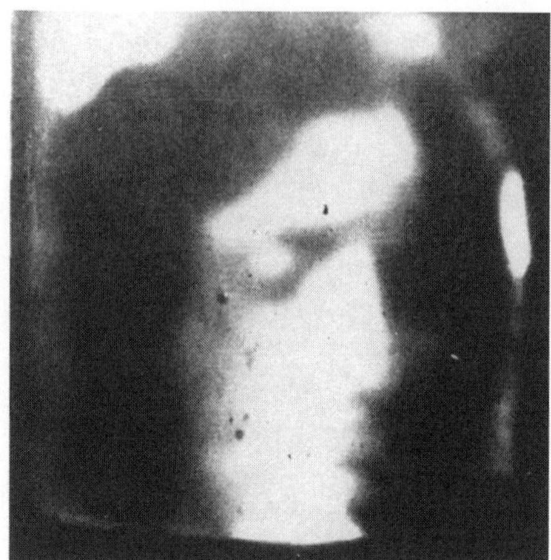

One of Farnsworth's first transmissions, October 19–21, 1929. On the left is the original photo of Elma G. Farnsworth taken with the Farnsworth camera. On the right is the image transmitted, "much better than any which we have previously been able to handle," wrote Farnsworth. See Farnsworth Notebook, no. 2, week ending October 19, 1929, National Museum of American History.

Technical Progress to Date: 1929 (continued)

Ultimately Accomplished in Practice." *Radio* 11 [December 1929], pp. 36, 85–86.) The number of lines in any given experiment was not critical to Farnsworth because as he progressed, he could produce whatever line number he wanted. In later demonstrations it was common for him to crank the number of lines scanned up to 600, simply by making calibrated adjustments. There were no standards; they were experimenting.

Preface

The journal system used during 1928 has proved quite satisfactory and will therefore be continued for 1929. Under this system, this record is journal # 1. Journal # 2 consists of an abstract of this journal together with an account of all important experiments, written by the experimenters performing them.

During the coming year, I shall write an account every week, at least as a rule. For periods warranting it, I shall write every day and for periods of relative inactivity, only as often as I think necessary.

One change which I believe will be helpful is to adopt a number system for ideas. I shall also refer to old ideas by the numbers designated below.

Idea # 1 - Electro-Light Relay - General
" " 2 - Image Dissector - General
" " 3 - Oscillight or Receiving Oscillograph - General
" " 4 - Synchronizing System - Aug. 27, 27 -
" " 5 - Change in General Construction Image Dissector (Figure
" " 6 - Magnetic Focusing (Figure 8 etc, 1928) (7. vol II, 1928)
" " 7 - Improvement of Idea # 4 (Page 88-9 J. 1 vol # 2)
" " 8 - Relay within Dissector (Figure 12 - journal 1, vol 2
" " 9 - Flat end Dissector (journal 1 vol 2 Figure 13)
" " 10 - Narrowing of Wave Band (J 1, vol 2 June 4-7)
" " 11 - Compound Aperture for Image Dissector
Idea # 12 - Dissector Improvement, Lead out of front end. (Figure 20, journal 1, vol II)
" " 13 - Neutralization of dissecting current induction - (Oct 1, 1928, J. # 1 vol II)
" " 14 - 10 ~ Generator (Oct. 1, 1928, J. # 1 vol II)
" " 15 - New Cathode Ray tube (Figure 27, Jo # 1 vol. II page 129)
" " 16 - Admittance Neutralization - (Dec 31, 1928)
" " 17 - Correcting focal Surface in Magnetic focusing System (Page 142-4 J. 1 vol # II)

This Preface to the Farnsworth Notebook no. 2 reveals the progress of research and the direction of future research for 1928 and 1929. National Museum of American History.

≈

> Rutherford worked on the television amplifier . . . Lubcke continued on the deltatron experiment . . . This is idea #26 . . . Lyman spent most of his time this month working on a special sound measuring device . . . Gardner has been kept busy this week building special radio tubes and working on the new special oscillography idea #22 . . . Rutherford and I have spent the greater part of this month working on television amplification. The result of our work will be given fully as experiment #2.[109]

Farnsworth was confident his work would produce results. He even purchased a home for his family in the Marina District—he was soon to be a father.[110] He was optimistic and in "high hopes of paying the mortgage when his invention brought him a fortune."[111] Everyone in the lab was excited about their accomplishments. Everson reported to Lowsley, of the First National Bank of Santa Barbara, that

> the developments in the laboratory are going on very satisfactorily and Farnsworth feels that practical television is not far off. We are developing a Movietone set-up for demonstration, which will be ready within a short time and everyone seems to be quite happy about the way things are progressing.[112]

Years later Farnsworth described the San Francisco lab as "a handful [of people] with limited funds pitted against the world," a condition that never discouraged him. "What we lacked in number and dollars we made up for in zeal and perseverance. Without the unstinting effort of every man, our venture could not have possibly succeeded."[113]

Only Farnsworth and Zworykin were thinking electronic television at this time.[114] In 1930 Farnsworth is reported to have declared, "I have abandoned the old idea of a whirling television disk with its motor and other contraptions. A simple beam of light does the trick."[115] Publicity was growing for the young "Mormon inventor," as the New York City *Mirror* called him.[116] At this time, "Phil would gladly have settled for . . . a license under his patents that he expected to be worth millions."[117] He was convinced as to the value of his system, but the financial backers were concerned with the experiments returning immediate profits.

THE DEPRESSION, TELEVISION, AND FARNSWORTH

The stock market crash in late October 1929 brought an abrupt end to the rapid expansion and optimism of the 1920s. Investors were wiped out, and those remaining panicked. During the 1930s, small media companies disappeared or merged with larger companies. RCA and Victor merged and Columbia Phonograph joined with the American Record Corporation, later to become CBS. Television, a new phenomenon still in the laboratory, was threatened as the

Depression resulted in most investors rechanneling their money. In England, Baird Television fell on hard times and was about to declare bankruptcy.[118] In other countries television experimentation was severely limited. According to Abramson the only "significant research being conducted [was in the United States] by Zworykin, in Camden, and Farnsworth, in San Francisco."[119] Zworykin had the financial advantage, however, in that he had the stable funding of RCA and radio during these critical years. As Barnouw noted in *Tube of Plenty,* the foundations "of television were strengthened by events in radio."[120] More accurately he could have said that the foundations for RCA television were strengthened by events in radio, because RCA's investment in radio was paying dividends that provided substantial money for RCA television experimentation.

This financing gave RCA the strength to fight legal and public relations battles, whereas Farnsworth and others struggled for existence. Jenkins Laboratories, for example, had opened a second television station in Jersey City by 1929 and was selling receiving sets and providing instructions on how to build a mechanical television receiver for those who could not afford to purchase his. But the Depression hurt sales and Jenkins Television was sold to the De Forest Radio Company. Unfortunately, De Forest was also experiencing hard times and was forced in turn to sell to RCA.

It is important to note that with these sales went all of the related patent rights. De Forest had the audion tube still under patent, and Jenkins had a patent on a charge storage device, both important for the transmission of sound and the storage of electrical energy. Buying out the competition was a way of eliminating it.

Farnsworth encountered these same pressures. His financial backers were eager for a return on revenues, but his own desire was more long term—to perfect his electronic television devices. The Depression years turned Farnsworth's backers from skeptical dreamers who were willing to risk their investments provided they could see hope for a financial return into panic-stricken investors who were more interested in selling out to one of the established manufacturers.

OPTIMISM DURING THE DEPRESSION

Despite the Depression, the years 1926 to 1931 were important in the development of the Farnsworth television system. Abramson states that while working in San Francisco, Farnsworth had "the only operating camera tubes in the world," and between January 1, 1927, and July 22, 1931, Farnsworth filed twenty-one different television system patent applications.[121] In 1930 three were granted, followed by a fourth in 1931.[122] This was encouraging news. Now that television was nearly finished, the question was, what are we going to do with it? How can it be made to pay its way without sacrificing its possibilities?"[123]

Farnsworth's business plans were clear. First, the Television Laboratories were to "retain control of our television, and to act as a parent organization, directing the general scheme." Second, negotiations would begin with "ten representative radio manufacturing companies . . . and licenses granted to them to manufacture, on a royalty basis." Third, in order to provide programming a "television broadcasting company [would] be organized to establish a chain of shortwave stations throughout the U.S." Fourth, revenue was to come from two sources, advertising and "directly from the consumer, as a monthly service charge." And finally, the Television Laboratories was to retain the job of doing research. Farnsworth's estimate for establishing the stations was $15,000 per station plus another $15,000 [$155,770] for the first year's operations. The company "would have to be capitalized for around $250,000 [$2,568,000] at the outset."[124] His outlook was progressively optimistic.

PROPOSED WEST COAST TELEVISION STATION

The optimism generated by publicity and patent development led to Farnsworth's announcement that San Francisco was to have the first television station on the West Coast. Tests were scheduled to broadcast from the lab to "downtown," as early as June 1930.[125] By July of the following year, Farnsworth's Television Laboratories had made an application with the Federal Radio Commission (FRC) relating to "our developments to radio and telephotography."[126] It was merely awaiting approval. Visiting the Bay Area, FRC Commissioner Harold A. Lafount praised Farnsworth's work as making television possible. Speaking before the San Francisco Junior Chamber of Commerce, Lafount "told his . . . audience how Farnsworth had astonished the eastern radio technicians at a recent Washington Radio Commission Conference." According to Lafount, Farnsworth's work was expected to result in the "commercial use [of television] within the next three years." Apparently, what had astounded the radio engineers was Farnsworth's claim that he could transmit pictures on a bandwidth of 20 kilocycles—when the width accepted by the eastern authorities was 100 kilocycles. "When the technicians scoffed at his claim, Farnsworth demonstrated his contention.[127] The proposed station was to begin construction in San Francisco as soon as the FRC granted the permit.[128] The station was to broadcast outdoor sporting events. The Farnsworth television receiver, "tested in local shops, gives an image of 12 x 14 inches in size and may be clearly enlarged to three square feet." Radio pioneer, Lee de Forest visited the lab in the summer of 1930 and declared Farnsworth, "the coming man in radio."[129]

REALITIES OF THE DEPRESSION KILL STATION IDEA

The proposed station was not a vision shared by everyone. To the investors, expensive station construction, camera tubes, and filing patent applications did not equal financial return. As always, finances were the major challenge—they caused contention between those working in the lab and those underwriting the costs. Few were willing to extend more money in the midst of a Depression, and expenses were constantly mounting: experiments conducted from 1926 to 1929 had run more than $100,000 [$1,001,160].[130] Everson was critical because he felt frustrated; nevertheless, his relations with Farnsworth were always strong (Pem described Everson as their guardian angel).[131] But Jesse B. McCargar was described in Everson's unpublished autobiography as turning into "a mean SOB."[132] He'd come down to the lab and fire all the employees, trying to hold down the costs. Lubcke later reminisced that after "the crash of '29 had come and gone, the Crocker interests had found out they'd rather not have the considerable monthly expenditure of the television laboratories as an outgo on their corporate funds, so we were all taken off salary."[133] Russell Varian reported that work continued despite the fact that "[t]he television labs have shut down completely and are awaiting developments on their negotiations for sales . . . No one is getting paid at present."[134] The listing of lab personnel footnotes people who were hired by Farnsworth, fired by McCargar, and rehired by Farnsworth, so work could progress. It was a difficult time.

By the end of 1931, pressures were mounting, and the lab still had not demonstrated a market-ready product by which investors would reap a return. Everson tried to keep the Television Laboratories solvent, but raising investment money was difficult. Everson wrote to McCargar: "I have a total of $850 [$9,574] to cover salaries and other laboratory expenses with three men on the payroll at $225 [$2,534] per month, there is not much leeway."[135] He added, "I am not getting panicky . . . but I am naturally a little nervous and concerned; however, I feel confident . . . I'm having a devil's own time . . . the whole trouble seems to be the lack of cash." The financial records for 1931 reflect the sale of 1,012 shares to thirty-seven people.[136]

DEMONSTRATIONS FOR POTENTIAL INVESTORS: RCA

The financial efforts of both Farnsworth and Everson were not limited to the sale of individual shares. Farnsworth's work was demonstrated to a number of potentially larger investors whom he hoped would underwrite his work. Years later Farnsworth noted that these visitors seemed primarily interested in parts rather than his entire system. But he was not interested in selling parts or individual patents; he had that broader vision of the future and wanted solid financial underwriting. This he would seek from a general underwriter or from the financial return for sale of his patent rights to other manufacturers.[137] Farnsworth and Everson were in communication with Philco, AT&T, Western Electric, the Canadian Pacific Railway (which played a part in Canadian radio), the International Standard Electric Corporation, ITT, Atwater Kent, and RCA. The Farnsworth Papers leave the impression that all of these corporations were felt to be potential parts of a Farnsworth organization. McCargar described RCA as potentially good for Farnsworth: "I felt RCA later would have to get aboard, but if they waited long enough, they might wake up to find themselves just another radio manufacturer."[138] So RCA was invited to visit Farnsworth's Television Laboratories in San Francisco.

It was this meeting that set the stage for a twenty-year running conflict. RCA was interested in Farnsworth's work, and initially he and his backers were certainly interested in RCA's money. However, RCA, assuming they were true to form, was interested in purchasing Farnsworth, thus eliminating the competition. In contrast, Farnsworth wanted royalties and investment capital to continue his work.

The people at Television Laboratories were excited about the first pending visit with Zworykin and the prospects of working with RCA. Everson writes that when he dropped into the lab one morning he "found Farnsworth in a most jubilant mood because he had just received word that Dr. Vladimir Zworykin, of Westinghouse and RCA, was shortly to visit his laboratories." Farnsworth was familiar with Zworykin's work and apparently felt that "there was no engineer in the country he would rather have view his results."[139] Zworykin's actual visit occurred April 16, 1930.[140] Zworykin was shown the complete laboratory while Farnsworth answered all his questions. There is considerable controversy surrounding this first visit: Clearly Zworykin was head of RCA's newly established laboratories in Camden, New Jersey (his report was addressed to Dr. Alfred N. Goldsmith, chief engineer of RCA).[141] Nineteen years later, writing the first Farnsworth biography, Everson records the visit of Dr. Zworykin "of Westinghouse and RCA."[142] Pem Farnsworth reports that, as far as they all knew, Zworykin was still at Westinghouse.[143] The Daily Log book entries surrounding the date record little of this visit. Lubcke and Gardner make no reference to Zworykin in their reports. Farnsworth himself records only that he was working on the voltage wave, synchronization, and target design. Doris E. Haggerty simply noted that "a demonstration was given for Dr. Zworykin, which was very successful."[144] Russell Varian supports Pem Farnsworth's contention, indicating that Zworykin did represent himself as being from Westinghouse and that rumors spread throughout the lab that "Westinghouse might be interested [in underwriting the experiments]."[145]

All descriptive accounts agree that Zworykin was treated with kindness and hospitality. He was even invited to Farnsworth's home for an evening supper where the conversations continued.[146] Lincoln Farnsworth reported that "Phil was quite verbal in answering questions he shouldn't have answered," and it was later quite clear that "Philo good-naturedly talked too much to one whom he considered a scientific colleague."[147]

According to Pem Farnsworth this proved to be a disastrous mistake.[148] Zworykin was shown the process for optical sealing and the dissector tube. He watched as Cliff Gardner constructed the tube and commented, "This is a beautiful instrument. I wish I had invented it myself."[149] Farnsworth was flattered. Zworykin was impressed with the sealing of the tubes and the Pyrex glass disks Farnsworth Television was using, because he had been told that such disks could not be created. One of Farnsworth Television's investors and a consultant, Albert Mann, fearing Zworykin might have ulterior motives for visiting the lab, wrote Farnsworth asking for a report of Zworykin's visit. He wanted to know where Zworykin had spent his time, what tests he had observed, what photos and apparatus were given. He also wanted Farnsworth's report notarized.[150] Nothing appears to have come from the inferences of this letter, but it does reflect an important concern: It was not that they were afraid he would steal their ideas, but that Farnsworth's work would "spur Dr. Zworykin on to intensive work that would be highly competitive."[151] RCA was interested. Zworykin's report to Goldsmith rejected the idea of purchasing Farnsworth, calling his work "clever," but doubting that television was "going to develop along these lines." Farnsworth was declared more valuable as a competitor, because if RCA were to purchase the Farnsworth patents, the costs of continued experimentation along Farnsworth's theoretical lines would be high. On the other hand, if Farnsworth were right and he were allowed to continue, he would have to bear the costs and RCA could still at a later time afford the purchase of his patents. RCA president David Sarnoff, however, was not convinced.[152]

On May 10 there was another visit from RCA by G. Harold Porter.[153] As a result, two more demonstrations were provided for Porter and W. W. Crocker along with a Lt. Highleyman, U.S. Department of the Navy.[154] In the summer there was yet another visit from two more RCA officials—the head of RCA/Victor's Advanced Development Division and an RCA patent attorney.[155] RCA was genuinely concerned about Farnsworth's ability to be competitive.

Work continued in the lab despite the visits and demonstrations. Later in 1930 there was an experiment in transmitting pictures via telephone lines, and a broadcast transmitter was set up on the roof of the lab. *Radio News* touted the Farnsworth system—"scanning without a disc," the article declared, "probably offers television experimenters more food for thought and study than any of the other systems to date."[156]

A year later Farnsworth's Television Laboratories received a visit from David Sarnoff.[157] Farnsworth's work was beginning to attract publicity, and RCA set its public relations machinery into motion to counter the publicity. Almost immediately following Sarnoff's visit to San Francisco, RCA prepared a press release for the Associated Press (AP) touting their "television set was entirely electrical and much better than the Farnsworth system."[158] Everson suggested that Television Laboratories contact the AP and counter the RCA story. "I thought it would be a good idea to spike their campaign of misrepresentation of our system."[159]

Sarnoff's visit took place in early May 1931,[160] but Farnsworth and McCargar had left San Francisco for Washington to testify at Senate hearings concerning radio monopoly and negotiations with Philco Radio.[161] Since Farnsworth was gone, Everson was left to conduct the tour. Sarnoff was shown a demonstration and seemed particularly impressed with the seven-inch picture. Everson described "the most outstanding feature of the conference was the seeming anxiety of his [Sarnoff's] over the possibility of our having anything to do with IT&T." "You know," Sarnoff reportedly said, "IT&T and the Radio Corporation are like the proverbial 'cat and dog' and it will be difficult to deal with both of us."[162] Sarnoff was worried about the competition and was not convinced by Zworykin's report to Goldsmith that Farnsworth would be more valuable as a competitor paying his own expenses during developmental experimentation. Sarnoff was there to evaluate the Farnsworth operations for himself.[163] This was an unusual visit for the head of RCA. He was concerned about competition and, in true business form, he offered to buy the competition.

As a result of Sarnoff's visit to the Farnsworth labs, Farnsworth was offered $100,000 [$1,126,310] for his services and his patents.[164] Much to Sarnoff's surprise Farnsworth said no. If Sarnoff had offered a royalty on Farnsworth's patents, television history might have been different. RCA, which to that point had paid royalties to no one, was ready to buy the competition as it had done before, but Farnsworth wanted a royalty for use of his patents. Farnsworth began to feel that RCA was campaigning against him. Everson called it a "campaign of misrepresentations" conducted by RCA.[165] It was obvious that RCA would not be a Farnsworth investor.

The competition between RCA and Farnsworth moved into the courts and the public relations field, as well as in the lab. Farnsworth would win the court battle with RCA, but RCA won the public relations contest hands down.

3

Implementation: TV Station and Public Demonstration

1931–1934

Chronology

Farnsworth

July 1931 — Farnsworth's Television Laboratories moved to Philadelphia to work with Philco Radio in establishing their television laboratory. San Francisco remained company headquarters until it was reorganized in 1938.

June 1932 — Station W3XE is granted an experimental broadcast license and goes on the air for Philco. Experimental programs include a Mickey Mouse cartoon. Farnsworth monitors RCA broadcasts, and RCA monitors the Philco-Farnsworth W3XE experiments.
• RCA issues an ultimatum to Philco—get rid of Farnsworth or Philco's license to use RCA patents would not be renewed.

September 1933 — Farnsworth leaves Philco. Television Laboratories is restructured; the designation "Laboratories" is dropped and the firm becomes Farnsworth Television Incorporated with offices in San Francisco and Philadelphia.
• Signals transmitted and received from San Francisco laboratories to facilities more than a mile away.
• Farnsworth continues experimentation with Philco W3XE, then resigns to develop his own lab.

Electronic Media

1932 — RCA becomes independent of GE and Westinghouse.
• Don Lee system experiments transmit to airplane.
• RCA sues Farnsworth for patent interference.

1933 — Press-Radio War begins as press restricts radio news.
• President Franklin D. Roosevelt begins Fireside Chats, the first dealing with the national banking crisis.
• Vaudeville comes to radio programming.
• Hitler comes to power in Germany.
• RCA sees Armstrong's demonstration of FM.
• Zworykin and RCA experiment with 240 scanning lines at 24 frames; German systems scanned 180/25.

Farnsworth	**Electronic Media**
	• Baird demonstrates color transmission.
August 1934 — Farnsworth provides the world's first public demonstration of an all-electronic television system. The demonstration ran for ten days at the Franklin Institute. October 1934 — Farnsworth demonstrates his system before the British Television Advisory Committee that would decide British standards. Farnsworth demonstration conducted with 220-lines at 30 frames. December 1934 — Farnsworth and Baird enter into license agreement. Farnsworth negotiated $50,000 cash payment plus royalties for use of his electronic television system patents by Baird Television.	1934 — *Communications Act of 1934* replaces the FRC with the Federal Communications Commission; powers of the Commission are extended beyond radio to include wire and wireless communications, both interstate and foreign. • Mutual Broadcasting System begins operations. • Jack Benny begins on radio; Upton Close first appears on NBC.

≈

THE PHILADELPHIA STORAGE COMPANY (PHILCO) WAS THE FIRST MANUFACTURING company to enter into a formal agreement with Farnsworth's Television Laboratories. The alliance provided Farnsworth with the opportunity to move to the East Coast, which he felt was the center of experimental television. The new arrangement also gave him stable funding, with royalties paid by Philco. He in turn was to give Philco what it needed to enter the television market. Philco wanted a television lab, an experimental television station, and the ability to manufacture TV equipment using Farnsworth's patents.

THE AGREEMENT WITH PHILCO

In Philadelphia, Farnsworth faced the same challenges as in San Francisco: converting his ideas into a commercial reality while under continued financial stress and competition from RCA and other corporations.[1] At Philco, however, there were differences. For the first time, Farnsworth worked directly with other scientists from the nation's leading radio manufacturer. On the East Coast he could better monitor competitor's activities and become more directly involved with the scientific and governmental communities affecting his work. Most importantly, he could acquire sufficient funding and thus stabilize his development base. Philco was the nation's largest manufacturer of radio sets in the 1930s—they had established a modest television laboratory in 1928—and their primary interest remained in radio, even as Farnsworth was hired to organize the Philco lab.[2]

The competitive atmosphere between RCA and its rivals was ever-present at Philco. Philco "resented being subservient" to RCA, according to Abramson.[3] The resentment was, in fact, more than from subservience, it was also from the pressure of paying patent royalties to RCA for every radio set Philco manufactured. But Philco had a plan for reducing these fees, which included hiring Farnsworth.

Philco split into the Philadelphia Storage Battery Company—the manufacturing arm—and the Philco Radio and Television Corporation, where Farnsworth worked—the research and sales operation. RCA's fees were based on the sale of receiver chassis. So to lower the fees the Philadelphia Storage and Battery Company sold its chassis to its own Philco Radio and Television Company, which packaged them for the consumer. Philco was in effect selling to itself in order to offset costs and make itself competitive. The reorganization was only on paper, but it had the desired effect.[4]

In the depths of a Depression economy, Philco reorganized and reached out to Farnsworth as a means of catching up with RCA's dominance in television.[5] Farnsworth had the only U.S. electronic system to rival that of RCA. Philco expected that Farnsworth would make them more competitive.[6]

On June 3, 1931 Farnsworth and Philco reached a formal agreement that called for a nonexclusive arrangement allowing Farnsworth to retain patent ownership, with royalties paid to the Farnsworth company, whereas Philco had the rights to manufacture and sell equipment using the inventor's patents.[7] Specifically, the license agreement allowed Philco the right to manufacture and sell tubes as well as radio and television receivers. The sale of these receivers was directed to amateur, experimental, and broadcasting reception users; the market for transmitter tubes was aimed at users licensed by Farnsworth.[8] Royalty payments on the first 22,500 television sets was exempt from the agreement, and the expenses of the Farnsworth lab, paid by Philco, were charged against future royalties. The term of this license allowed Philco to use Farnsworth's patents under royalty until August 26, 1947. In addition to paying royalties to Farnsworth, Philco agreed to finance him for one year; an extension for a second year was later amended to the agreement. The agreement allowed Farnsworth to maintain the San Francisco television laboratory, which remained Farnsworth's fund-raising center.[9]

The Philco-Farnsworth agreement seemed promising to both parties. Philco wanted Farnsworth to establish a position of competitive strength in television against RCA. Farnsworth had proclaimed commercial television to be only a few years away and saw Philco's royalties as a means of financing his work.

Technical Progress to Date: 1931

Patents. By the end of 1931, Farnsworth had filed for twenty patents (see Appendix A). The patents reflecting the most important progress, filed since 1929, include: Television scanning and synchronizing system, which provided picture quality; pulse transmission system, which resulted in wave form generation.[a]

Farnsworth holding his image dissector. In the foreground is an early lab camera, circa 1929. Green Street lab. Courtesy Elma G. Farnsworth.

Technical Progress to Date: 1931 (continued)

Mobile camera developed 1930, Green Street lab. Courtesy Elma G. Farnsworth.

Comments. By 1930 Farnsworth was transmitting 300-line pictures and claiming his cathode-ray tube system, "would require frequency bands no wider than those used for broadcasting."[b]

An independent report written by the Robert W. Hunt Company of San Francisco was conducted for the News Projection Corporation of New York, March 16, 1931. The report was drafted after demonstrations were witnessed, May 13, 1931, by representatives of the Hunt and News companies, M. H. Merrill and L. K. Irvin. The purpose of the report was to assess technical progress and commercial viability of Farnsworth's work.

Television demonstrations conducted for the report consisted of pictures of Lee de Forest and Mary Pickford, both stills and head and shoulder shots, and a film showing a football game at Stanford University. The demonstration was closed circuit, although Farnsworth indicated during the presentation that "equally good results are obtained by wireless transmissions. The practical limit of wireless transmission is at this time about fifty miles," Farnsworth declared, "by line wire it is unlimited."

The fact that Farnsworth had eliminated mechanical scanning is an important factor in the superiority of the Farnsworth system. Mechanical scanning disks at the time were 36 to 72 lines, in comparison with Farnsworth's electrical scanning tests at 200 lines. "Work is now being done on 400 lines and this will doubtless be utilized in the Farnsworth commercial installations."

Comparing Farnsworth's work the report indicates, "improved picture details . . . are very noticeable," when comparing Farnsworth's 200-line system to the "RCA broadcast at 60 lines, and Bell at 72 lines."[c]

a. Everson, *Story of Television,* pp. 106–09.

b. "Declares New Tube Solves Television," *New York Times* 24 (December 4, 1930), p. 2. See also "A Radio Idea from the West," *New York Times* 24 (December 14, 1930), pp. 6–8.

c. Report on the "Farnsworth Television System," by F. M. Randlett of the Robert W. Hunt Company Engineers, San Francisco, March 16, 1931, Farnsworth Papers, Box 1, File 3.

≈

Farnsworth's last San Francisco demonstration took place on July 12, 1931, just before the move to Philadelphia. United Press reporter, Carle H. Bennette described the San Francisco event in a story printed in the Salt Lake *Tribune.*

> Motion pictures were transmitted on the television set for today's demonstration, the final showing by Farnsworth before he began dismantling the machine. The radio-transmitted "movies" were shown on a screen eight by twelve inches. Two subjects were projected: the heavyweight championship fight between Jack Dempsey at Chicago, and a woman combing her hair. In the fight picture, faces of men three or four rows back from the ringside could be seen. Each punch could be followed from the start until it landed.[10]

Immediately following the showing, Farnsworth, his wife, their two children, five staff members, and the contents of the San Francisco lab were loaded onto the train.[11]

Coinciding with the move, Everson, who was still with the Community Chest, began to spend more time on Farnsworth fund-raising and took up a temporary residence in New York. He traveled back and forth to Philadelphia several times each week, usually bringing potential investors to see television in operation.[12]

WORK BEGINS AT PHILCO

Farnsworth was twenty-seven when he moved to Philadelphia. Always optimistic, he rapidly gained a reputation as an inventor with a technologically competitive edge. He had addressed the Federal Radio Commission, was receiving a good deal of publicity because of his experiments, and was drawing scientific visitors from every major electronics manufacturer to his laboratory. Independent consulting engineers witnessed a 200-line demonstration and deemed his system ready for commercial use.[13]

The move to Philadelphia took place in the summer, and for those engineers used to the cool San Francisco breeze, Philadelphia's heat and humidity were unbearable. Philco had arranged for Farnsworth to set up his laboratory on the top floor of their plant; the broadcast operation was on the roof. The room was even smaller than the San Francisco lab, and there was personal friction from the beginning. William Grimditch, Philco's director of research and overseer of Farnsworth's work, was immediately antagonized by the Farnsworth group. The informal work atmosphere of San Francisco was much different than the dress code Philco required of its employees. In the "oven on the roof" of the Philco factory building, the Farnsworth engineers were often too casual to suit the straightlaced supervisor. According to Pem Farnsworth, one day when

Grimditch visited the lab and found two engineers without their shirts, he flew into a rage. It did not seem to matter that there were no fans, no air conditioning, or that it was summer, and the two were working with welding torches making TV tubes. The Farnsworth group refused to wear the required suit and tie and simply rolled up their sleeves.[14] This perceived rebelliousness of the engineers earned them a description as "mavericks, a gang of crazy cowboys from California."[15]

Despite these differences the work proceeded steadily. The mavericks continued their work for Philco, in preparation for their independence and the establishment of a Philco experimental station. Three patents were filed in July 1931.[16] In 1932 two more were filed, as the picture quality improved with each experiment.[17]

RESTRUCTURING FARNSWORTH BEGINS

In preparation for the end of their contract with Philco, Everson explored his California connections.[18] He communicated with Antoine De Vally, who was encouraging Farnsworth to work with Hollywood film distributors as well as eastern manufacturers in the new medium of television. It was his belief that both distribution and manufacturing were essential to television's future. De Vally suggested two primary divisions for the Farnsworth company: The first would produce television sets and technical equipment for both commercial and public consumption; the second would handle program distribution. De Vally suggested that television entertainment products be distributed through a system of broadcasting stations that would be supported by sustaining, sponsored programs, and advertising agencies.[19] This was the direction RCA had taken and was in fact already there in terms of radio; television would follow.[20] De Vally's vision was not new. The financial support remained a major challenge for Everson, who would work continuously to keep Farnsworth progressing.

Farnsworth worried that RCA was catching up technically. He attended a 1932 RCA demonstration for its licensees. Afterward he reported to Everson, "The picture which we saw was extremely good . . . the best television picture I have ever seen."[21] The transmission from the Empire State Building was at 120 lines. He said:

> I was afraid, when I went to the meeting, that RCA was ahead of us. I still believe that they are in many respects, but in others we are miles ahead of them, particularly as regards [to] detail and the amount of equipment which we require in our receiver. Also, our sound work has progressed further than theirs, in that we are able to put it over a single channel, while they are broadcasting from entirely different broadcast stations. Also, since our system makes use of the present radio for its

> sound, I feel confident that we shall be able to convert everyone to our way of doing at least this part of it, as it is so simple and effective. There are various points of technique in which they have completely outstripped us, and other places where, I think, we are considerably ahead of them.[22]

However afraid Farnsworth might have been, his emphasis was still positive. He encouraged Everson to continue thinking about commercial manufacturing of broadcast equipment and the program film supply. He said, "The sale of broadcasting equipment is going to be equally profitable to that of receivers . . . since the margin of profit will be tremendously higher. . .. And this film problem is not one which can be handled simply by starting up [a station] and attempting to do it."[23] At this time Farnsworth was estimating home receivers to be on the market within a year or two, while RCA was estimating that public distribution would not be available for a number of years.[24]

Competitive forecasts aside, Farnsworth's priority was putting Philco on the air. Although working under a tight schedule, he hoped to have the station in shape by June 1, 1932. He reported to the San Francisco office that they would make that deadline "by the skin of our teeth."[25]

W3XE: THE PHILCO-FARNSWORTH STATION

The application for the experimental station was first drafted during the late summer of 1931. It requested a license for Television Laboratories Inc. to experiment over the air with the Farnsworth television system for a period of one year.[26] W3XE was constructed for Philco and granted a license by the FRC on June 28, 1932, for experimental broadcasting (it would later become WPTZ and today is KYW-TV).[27] The Farnsworth engineers, in conjunction with Philco, set up a television control room and a transmitter. William N. Parker described the early studio as "a complete TV control-room . . . in operation, but the only signal source was from 35-mm film."[28]

In Farnsworth's first experiments programming consisted primarily of cartoons. Later it would include Hollywood films, sports, and local talent. Farnsworth's first son, Philo III, was described as the "first charter member of the television generation."[29] This was accomplished when his father set up a prototype receiver in his own home, and W3XE began programing Mickey Mouse cartoons, including "Steamboat Willy," and Mary Pickford film segments.[30] Parker confirms that this was a typical procedure at Philco: "Any new Philco radio [and in this case television] being developed was taken . . . [to the] home [of a supervising engineer] for a shakedown run, along with its development engineer."[31] These were the final equipment tests prior to marketing.[32] W3XE underwent these same tests, with the receiving equipment in Farnsworth's home.

W3XE's hours of operation were intermittent, as they were with all early experimental stations, but they grew with regularity. There is no mention of specific programming in the FCC records. They merely report that in 1933, after its first full year of operation, W3XE had been on the air for 150 hours.[33] The usual hours of operation reported to the FCC were 9:00 A.M. to 5:00 P.M. and 7:00 P.M. to 9:30 P.M., not extensive by today's standards. But 150 hours is a lot of cartoons.

The most significant audiences for W3XE were likely RCA and the Farnsworth/Philco engineers themselves, as each group struggled to improve the image with each transmission. Farnsworth described the Mickey Mouse programming in a letter to his mother in December 1933, just four months after leaving Philco, as "awfully good and has perfect sound along with the picture." He predicted, "These cartoons are going to be very popular over television—they are so easy to transmit that they come over perfectly and are most entertaining."[34]

Programming these early years was limited to tests with no pretense of appealing to a general audience. The FCC reports contain what seems like every breath of a technological achievement with little mention of business, programming, or operations—technology was the emphasis of the time.[35]

Being on the air, however, even with just a test pattern and its accompanying audio, was not without its hazards, primarily because the competition could see what you were doing. RCA and Farnsworth were transmitting in the same market (Philadelphia and Camden) and they were monitoring each other. Farnsworth was monitoring RCA signals from Camden and the Empire State Building in New York where RCA had established an experimental station transmitter, and RCA was monitoring W3XE's signal from Philadelphia. Camden, New Jersey, at that time the location of the RCA experimental laboratories, is across the Delaware River from Philadelphia.[36]

Scanning experiments, January 25, 1933. Farnsworth is experimenting with differing black-and-white shading and their differences in reproduction. From Daily Notes, Television Laboratories Ltd., Farnsworth, Vol. VI, p. 194, University of Utah, Box 54, Book 1.

PHILCO AND FARNSWORTH VERSUS RCA

While Farnsworth was setting up the new experimental television station for Philco, the tensions increased between Philco and RCA. These two corporations had a long history of competitive rivalry; in fact, in the late 1920s it was thought that Philco "could become a permanent casualty" of RCA's actions.[37] RCA was not happy when, to avoid RCA fees, Philco formed the Philco Radio and Television Corporation, the organization under which Farnsworth worked. RCA tried to cancel Philco's license, and as a result, Philco filed suit against RCA.

Even the radio industry in general was not happy with Philco, feeling that its reorganization resulted in a pricing war.[38] Farnsworth no doubt felt the pressure of competition. In fact, the *RCA vs. Farnsworth* patent interference case also began this same year, 1932 (see Chapter 4). If the Philco reorganization was abandoned, because of the threat from RCA, there was the question as to what would be done with Farnsworth. Rumors were abundant. Farnsworth had the impression, according to Pem, that RCA gave Philco an ultimatum: "either it dumped Farnsworth Corporation forthwith or its [Philco's] license to use RCA's radio patents would not be renewed."[39] The RCA-Philco battle over royalties and license fees would be settled in court.[40] Varian reports the competitive pressure was to begin manufacturing. If Farnsworth was not ready, then RCA systems would have to be used. The pressure to begin production of home and industrial equipment was building.[41]

Farnsworth knew his contract with Philco was coming to an end. Originally intended to last for one year, it was extended to two. At the same time, he was feeling the pressure from Philco to get the experimental station on the air. He knew that the agreement would not be renewed for a third year and had plans under way to reorganize an independent East Coast operation. He had established a television lab for Philco and put a station on the air for them, but he was merely a part of their larger picture to enter television.

It is unlikely that RCA actually would have cut off the patent rights to Philco. First, they were a source of income; second, the patent licenses were standard and the same requirements applied to everyone; and, third, the growing threat of antitrust actions from the federal government against RCA would have dissuaded them from any overt action against the smaller company. The pressures Farnsworth felt were likely from both the ongoing battle between RCA and Philco and the maverick westerners' behaviors aggravating Philco management.

PHILCO AND FARNSWORTH SEPARATE

The separation of Farnsworth and Philco was based as much on planning and personal motivation as it was professional and competitive fear. The Farnsworth team had not complemented the more straightlaced eastern engineers from Philco; they were independent thinkers not used to the protocol of the larger eastern corporations. They all looked forward to returning to the West Coast.

Perhaps the most devastating blow to the relationship between Farnsworth and Philco occurred in March 1932, just three months before W3XE went on the air. On March 6, Farnsworth rushed his second son, Kenneth, to the hospital. He had developed a streptococcal infection in his throat. Since there were no effective medicines at the time, the doctor at the hospital performed a tracheotomy on the young boy to allow him to breathe. The anxious parents were at the hospital from the early morning and on into the late evening. The boy died shortly thereafter.[42] This personal tragedy was compounded by the insensitivity of Philco management. As the distraught parents made arrangements to have their son's body returned to Utah for burial, Farnsworth was informed by his superiors at Philco that he could not leave. "He was too essential to their investment [in television] and could not be spared."[43] Farnsworth was forced to stay in Philadelphia while Pem Farnsworth made the train trip back to Provo, Utah, alone.

The death of his son drove Farnsworth inward. He seemed unable to share his feelings with anyone, including, for a time, his wife. She pleaded with her husband to rest. While on the train to Provo she wrote to Philo: "It seems so unfair to take our baby away . . . Phil, dear, please don't work like you have been doing for a while."[44] But Philo wasn't listening. He lost himself in his work.

Philco's insensitivity left Farnsworth highly suspicious of their motives, and he began to dissociate himself from them. He began removing his equipment, which had been brought from San Francisco, and put it into storage in preparation for the separation.[45] Schatzkin and Kiger state that Farnsworth "could stand the strain . . . no longer, [he] called Jesse McCargar in San Francisco and told him that he was leaving Philco."[46] Varian reports that in March 1933, "something [was] brewing in way of a change in Philco." And by June 27, the crew was "all packed up and out of Philco."[47] Even before the official announcement of their parting, Farnsworth was in New York looking for underwriters. No one in the Farnsworth lab knew where they were going (the crew suspected back to San Francisco), but Farnsworth wanted to remain in the East.[48] Varian said that "Philco [was] taken aback by our [Farnsworth's] leaving. It is likely that they were bluffing to make us tie up to RCA and didn't expect us to pull out rather than knuckle down."[49]

It was an uneasy time. In addition to RCA and other industry pressures, Philco engineers were on strike, and Farnsworth's engineers were not sure if they had a job, let alone a laboratory. Documents from the Philco Radio and Television Corporation indicate that for the "period ending September 30, 1933 . . . P. T. Farnsworth left Philco."[50] The initiative for leaving was Farnsworth's. However, it is obvious that Philco did not object. Farnsworth had put a station on the air for them—the contract had been completed.

Television work would continue at Philco, but under new leadership. The engineer Philco hired to continue research had been the head of RCA engineering, Albert F. Murray. Murray would now be working to produce a system compatible with RCA, and he would have the benefit of Farnsworth's work as he took over the Philco television station.[51] From Philco's point of view, it is not hard to see why they were impatient with Farnsworth. Even though Philo put them on the air, Murray brought to Philco all the secrets of the RCA operation in Camden, New Jersey, including the iconoscope, the kinescope, and Randall C. Ballard's interlaced patent. Philco wanted to move ahead at a faster pace, and Farnsworth, not trusting Philco's motives, was anxious to be independent once again.

The philosophical difference between Philco and Farnsworth, according to Hofer, was that "Philco wished to pursue a production program of television [sets]," and Farnsworth's aim was the establishment of a broad-based patent structure whereby manufacturers would pay him for the use of his patents.[52] The practical differences in the competitive corporate world were that Philco and RCA were fighting for market dominance while Farnsworth was fighting for his continued independent existence.

FARNSWORTH TELEVISION INCORPORATED IS FORMED

Farnsworth Television Incorporated was the structure formulated following Farnsworth's severance from Philco.[53] The new company had dropped the designation "laboratories" from its title and had plans to manufacture and distribute. It was up and running by December 19, 1933.[54]

In their business license application to the State of Pennsylvania, the principal offices listed were San Francisco and an office at 127 Mermaid Lane, Chestnut Hill, Philadelphia, Pennsylvania. The purpose of the new corporation was to operate an experimental and developmental laboratory for television. The actual value of the equipment and machinery, the only items listed in the application, was $5,000 [$65,846]. There were 20,000 authorized shares of capital stock and 10,371 aggregate shares, both listed without par value.[55] Farnsworth Television Incorporated was the trade name that would accompany Farnsworth for the next five years.[56] Major funding came from the Frank

Turner family of San Francisco. The Turner family had been among the larger investors since the 1929 reorganization. A son, Seymour (Skee) Turner, took more than a financial interest in the lab; he wanted to move Farnsworth's work into commercial operation and as a result came to live and work with Farnsworth. According to Skee, his family was willing to build and was not looking for as quick a financial turnaround as the San Francisco bankers had been.[57]

Seymour (Skee) Turner, circa 1936. Courtesy University of Utah Archives, P0437 1:7:2.

FARNSWORTH COMPETITIVE IN CONTINUED EXPERIMENTATION

Several events focused the attention of Farnsworth Television over the next five years. Continued experimentation led to the nation's first public demonstration of electronic television, and Farnsworth was attracting international attention. The Farnsworth television business, although comparatively small, had grown in competitiveness and notoriety right alongside the major corporations. At the same time, his conflict with RCA was moving into the courts.

To place these events in context, it must be remembered that television in the 1920s was experimental—laboratory-based with experiments conducted before dignitaries and investors using the mechanical systems of television. This had led Jenkins, Baird, and others to establish businesses in the hope of selling their manufactured television products. As electronic experimentation replaced these mechanical systems at the end of the decade, experimental stations ushered in the next phase of television's growth. RCA, CBS, Philco, Farnsworth, and others established experimental stations. DuMont Laboratories were organized in June 1931.[58] At the same time, the Depression hit banks and these smaller radio operations hardest. The larger companies had the profits of radio—a still-maturing industry—to support the growth anticipated in television and other technologies, including FM radio. In the mid-1930s, Farnsworth's television faced the same trials of any small business in the Depression.

By 1933 Farnsworth had set up independent Philadelphia operations with the equipment he had brought from San Francisco, along with his equipment removed from the Philco labs. The engineering staff was still small, and the new equipment he had developed for Philco would have to be rebuilt, because much of it was left behind. Their only source of funding was the Turner family and whatever Everson could raise from investors. The new laboratory, however, was sophisticated in comparison with the former facilities. The system experiments had incorporated all of the earlier enhancements and was producing 220 lines per frame.[59] In 1933 Farnsworth Television filed for five more patents,[60] the first of which was filed while Farnsworth was still at Philco, but with Farnsworth retaining the rights. Meanwhile, in San Francisco, work continued, as transmission tests received signals from "more than a mile away."[61]

By 1934 the real competitors were Farnsworth and RCA, with Philco not far behind. Because Farnsworth had set Philco's course of action, the similarities between the continuing Philco system and Farnsworth's are apparent. But Philco's experimental station had gone off the air after Farnsworth left, and their lab was working hard to maintain competitiveness. *Electronics* magazine also included J. V. L. Hogan in its 1934 television systems comparison, but

Hogan appears only briefly in the history of television (see Technical Progress to Date: 1934).[62] His work was with mechanical and electronic systems, but he was far behind the leaders. The three leaders were all working in studios, using a form of the cathode ray tube as a display device. There were variances in design that were at the root of picture quality debates. The number of scanning lines used by the competitors varied almost with each report. As improvement was sought with each test, Farnsworth also explored differing projection systems to increase the size of the overall viewing screen. When interviewed for the article, Farnsworth's proudest achievement was his ability to produce the clearest pictures in outdoor sunlight.[63]

WORLD'S FIRST GENERAL PUBLIC DEMONSTRATION

Farnsworth's greatest triumph was yet to come. It was not in amassing his constantly growing list of patents, the sophistication of the picture, the cabinetry or laboratory experiments, but rather the world's first general public demonstration of an all-electronic television system.

Philo T. Farnsworth at the controls during the Franklin Institute demonstration, August 1934. Permission to publish from *The Historical Society of Pennsylvania* (HSP), "P. T. Farnsworth at Franklin Institute, August 31, 1934," *Philadelphia Record* Morgue Collection [Accession #V7:2272].

In the year following Farnsworth's departure from Philco, he set about to develop a portable television unit that he could transport to various locations for demonstration. The plan was to conduct a series of dramatic expositions that would help pull things together technologically as well as attract public attention and more investors.[64] There was talk of taking the Farnsworth system on the road to the Chicago Century of Progress exhibition. Farnsworth invited Franklin Institute officials to his lab to see his work. As a result, he was invited to provide a general public demonstration.

The demonstration took place at the Franklin Institute on August 25, 1934. It was reported in the *New York Times,* as "Tennis Stars Act in New Television."[65] The headline referenced the appearance of two athletes—Frank X. Shield, New York, and Lester Stoeffen, Los Angeles, who swung their rackets around, talked, and demonstrated their techniques while audiences in an adjoining room watched in amazement.

Other newspaper headlines appeared throughout the country: the *Philadelphia Record* heralded the first day of these public demonstrations with "Television on a 4-Foot Screen Demonstrated for 200 Here"; the *Philadelphia Inquirer,* "Scientists See Exhibition by Super-television Device"; and the Salt Lake *Telegram,* "Home Television Due in 10 Years, Utahan Says."[66] There were 200 scientists and others in the audience amphitheater the first day, and a small studio was set up in the institute for inside demonstrations. Nathan Hayward, president of the Franklin Institute, and Mayor J. Hampton Moore of Philadelphia praised the system, and Farnsworth explained its workings to celebrity

Marion Kingston of Anchorage performs at the Franklin Institute Farnsworth television demonstration, August 1934. From *Philadelphia Record* Morgue Collection [Accession #V7:2272].

figures who were paraded before the camera. Farnsworth touted the system as capable of all kinds of sports broadcasts—football, baseball, and tennis. He claimed it was capable "not only of close-ups, but entire . . . games . . . as well as news shots." Outside the building there was football action: Coach Lud Wray and Philadelphia Eagle players Dick Lackman and Roger "Red" Kirkman explained plays. Inside, the museum viewers saw the close-ups of the players acting out the coach's calls, "tackling, punting, and passing while Coach Wray's image and voice thrilled the observers as the pictures were recorded on a flourescent screen."[67] The demonstrations were not limited to athletics and speakers—nighttime views of the moon were also "televeyed." "The Man-in-the-Moon posed for his first radio snapshot," was the *Christian Science Monitor*'s description of the nighttime experiments as Farnsworth included the "first recorded use of television in astronomy," in his Franklin Institute experiments.[68] Vaudeville acts were also a part of the program demonstration line up. Perhaps the most dramatic to those attending was the placement of one camera at the door entering the exhibit so that as people came in, "the power of the invention was instantly driven home . . . for they were immediately confronted by their own disembodied image."[69] Farnsworth was no doubt pleased at the

Farnsworth demonstration at the Franklin Institute, August 1934. Camera operator Tobe Rutherford is at the left standing on a box, and Seymour Turner is at the far right with his hands on his hps. Courtesy Elma G. Farnsworth.

publicity generated. The *Times* generously wrote that "some of the scientists who watched declared it the most sensitive apparatus yet developed."[70] Reporting at the 25th Annual Pacific Coast Electrical Engineering Convention in Salt Lake City, September 3, 1934, A. H. Brolly, a Farnsworth engineer, told the audience that the "practical demonstrations of television . . . now being made at the Franklin Institute in Philadelphia [are] with perfect synchronization of sound and pictures."[71]

> Soon the world will be able to see and hear style shows, motion pictures and world events as they occur many miles away and while they are seated in a comfortable rocking chair in their homes.

Philo Farnsworth, twenty-seven-year-old inventor, demonstrates at the Franklin Institute, August 1934. Farnsworth watches a televised picture of Joan Crawford as it appeared on the cathode tude. Courtesy of UPI/Corbis-Bettmann Photo Archives.

> The Farnsworth system brings television within the reach of millions and is so simple it requires no more than a turning of a dial to place it in operation.
>
> It is now possible, engineers estimate, to manufacture a combined television and sound receiver for $250 [$3,194] which will give perfect reception.[72]

At the Franklin Institute demonstrations Farnsworth recalled that the auditorium would be filled with people every twenty minutes every day until 11:00 P.M.[73] According to Pem, there was so much interest that the exhibitions were extended another week. Reporter C. William Duncan asked Farnsworth if people would be able to sit at a telephone and see the persons to whom they are [were] talking. Philo replied, "That is years and years away."[74] Farnsworth envisioned a wired telephone system as being too limiting for television. Television was an adjunct to radio delivering broadcast "news events . . . dramatic skits . . . and good movies," via the thousands of stations that would be in operation.[75] The institute published a technical explanation of the system in the *Journal of the Franklin Institute,*[76] but the simplest answer to the question "how does it work?" comes from the Duncan interview with Farnsworth:

> Just what have you done? [Duncan asks]. We have eliminated mechanical parts . . . We use only tubes . . . In televising an image it has to be dissected and transmitted a point at a time . . . If transmitted in pieces, this image must be dissected into many parts . . . Each picture must be transmitted thirty times per second. That means we have to assemble 60,000 elements thirty times per second . . . [The] Electron image is a special name we have given to the electrical picture. That is produced by focusing an optical image on to a very sensitive photo-electric surface. Then we pull the electrons away from that surface with an electrical potential, which is simply voltage. Then we focus those into an electrical image by means of a magnetic lens.[77]

The attending scientists were interested in the latest developments and their own competitive edge, but most people were attracted by the novelty.

Just a few days after the Franklin Institute demonstrations a cold-cathode tube was announced by Farnsworth experimenters in San Francisco. The new tube was under tests at the Heintz and Kaufman Limited laboratories in south San Francisco. Kaufman laboratories were licensees of Farnsworth Television Inc., who successfully transmitted radio shortwave signals from the lab to New York, Hawaii, and ships in the Pacific.[78] The tube used a conventional radio circuit, but in the studio it was the "rays of light" that set the electrons in motion; in daylight the rays of the sun would do the same. Several messages of differing lengths were sent and received by the participating stations. "Young Farnsworth planned to make tests later for transmitting pictures over similar facilities."[79]

Farnsworth was in the middle of the Franklin Institute demonstration and planning for the Century of Progress when a call came from Baird Television of

Technical Progress to Date: 1934

Patents. By the end of 1934, Farnsworth had filed for thirty-two patents (see Appendix A). The patents reflecting the most significant progress were the Scanning Oscillator (no. 2,059,683), which was a scanning generator for magnetic deflection; the Electron Multiplying Device (no. 2,071,515), which along with several other patents to date refers to the improved image dissector; and, "scanning means," referring to interlaced scanning and film transmission. Farnsworth had also developed several film projection apparatus during this time period and was continuously improving his image dissector.

Comment. By 1927 Farnsworth had a camera tube system with an electric optical receiver, demonstrated privately in 1928, then for the press in 1929. By December 1930 he was working on a new 300-line narrow-band system. In

Period Caption: "Televising football maneuvers at Franklin Institute. The latest system of television demonstrated football action today for the first time at the Philadelphia Franklin Institute Museum, when Philo T. Farnsworth, young 28-year-old inventor of Chestnut Hill, focused his camera on Dick Lackman and Roger 'Red" Kirkman, star Eagle gridders, as Coach Lud Wray explained the plays. The scenes were outside the big museum building. Within the spacious lecture hall hundreds of visitors saw clearly the 'close-up' images of two players tackling, punting and passing while Coach Wray's image and voice thrilled the observers as the pictures were recorded on a fluorescent screen." Permission to publish from *The Historical Society of Pennsylvania* (HSP), August 31, 1934, Photo by Gladys Mller, *Philadelphia Record* Morgue Collection [Accession #V7:2272].

Technical Progress to Date: 1934 (continued)

August 1934 Farnsworth conducted the world's first public demonstration of a completely electrical system. It was scanning at 220 lines and 30 frames per second. Note scanning line demonstration numbers vary over differing reports. While the general direction was always to scan as many lines as possible for improved picture quality, there is significant variance between demonstrations and experiments. Note Farnsworth's remote system enabled a growing number of public demonstrations. "Remote" simply connoted a separate demonstration unit, which was dismantled and reconfigured for each public display conducted outside the laboratory.[a]

a. Philo T. Farnsworth, "Television by Electron Image Scanning," *Journal of the Franklin Institute* 218 (October 4,1934), pp. 411–44.

Representative Electronic Television Systems: 1934

Company	Type of subject	Method of scanning	No. of lines	No. of frames	Type of light-sensitive device	Audio synchronization	Receiving light source (color)	Method of light modulation	Method of image recreation	Screen type
Philco Radio and Television	studio film outdoor	cathode-ray "camera tube"	240–360	24–60	mosaic plate	separate signal	fluorescence (green)	control electrode	cathode-ray tube	fluorescent
RCA-Victor Co.	studio film outdoor	cathode-ray "iconoscope"	240–360	24–60	mosaic plate	separate signal	fluorescence (green)	control electrode	cathode-ray tube	fluorescent
Television Labs (P. T. Farnsworth)	studio film outdoor	cathode-ray "image dissector"	240	30	uniform plate	separate signal	fluorescence (green)	control electrode	cathode-ray tube	fluorescent
J. V. L. Hogan	studio film	mechanical (not disc)	120–60	20–24	photocell	transmitted signal; also power system	glow-lamp (white)	direct	mechanical (not disc)	projection & direct
		cathode-ray	300–60	20–24–30			fluorescence (green) (white)	control electrode & special	cathode-ray tube	fluorescent

Source: Adapted from *Electronics* 7 (October 1934): 305. John V. L. Hogan (1890–1960) is mentioned only briefly in the literature as a broadcast inventor. See endnote 62.

London.[80] The invitation from Baird to demonstrate electronic television in London seemed more suitable than the Century of Progress exhibition. It would generate good publicity that in turn could produce licensing agreements with greater cash flow and extend Farnsworth's reputation internationally. Thus, the group turned their emphasis toward going overseas.

FARNSWORTH DEMONSTRATES FOR JOHN LOGIE BAIRD

Baird Television was a well-known British company. John Logie Baird was one of the pioneers of the mechanical television systems.[81] His work dated back to the early 1920s, and at the end of that decade there were mechanical sets available for sale; however, they were not producing satisfactory pictures. In Britain the Television Advisory Committee (appointed by Parliament) was established to review technical and operational aspects of television, including standards, and make a recommendation to Parliament. Because the electronic systems were producing far superior pictures, the committee seemed to be leaning that way. This left Baird in a difficult position. Despite years of work, if an all-electronic standard were adopted, Baird would be left out in the cold. Baird's chief competition was from Marconi-EMI (Electric and Music Industries Ltd.). The alliance between Marconi and EMI, formed in May 1934, left Baird's company with "General Electric of Great Britain (not connected with GE in the USA) . . . and Fernseh [Aktiengesellschaft] A.G. in Germany as its only allies."[82] As EMI was somewhat dependent on RCA patents, Baird felt EMI was nothing more than an RCA subsidiary. Baird Television, in reaching out to Farnsworth, was working to cover its bases. Arrangements with Farnsworth's electronic system would make Baird more competitive in Britain. Hence, Farnsworth was invited to provide Baird with a demonstration of his electronic system of television.[83]

In October 1934, Farnsworth and three engineers—Seymour Turner, Tobe Rutherford, and Arch Brolly—boarded the *S.S. Bremen* and headed for London. Farnsworth, Turner, and Rutherford were in Philadelphia, and Brolly came from the San Francisco laboratory. The equipment for the demonstration came from Philadelphia.[84] All of the Farnsworth equipment was declared "luggage." However, when they reached Britain, the customs people were highly suspicious, and there were a few problems checking everything through, including dropping a crate in which the tubes had been packed. However, the equipment passed customs and sustained only slight damage. It was easily repaired for the demonstrations to follow.[85]

Time was of the essence in setting up the demonstration. As the Farnsworth engineers ran preliminary tests prior to the presentation before the committee, Farnsworth recalled the Baird engineers passing by the door seeking a glimpse of the electronic picture. While the engineers were setting up,

Farnsworth "went off in search of Mr. Baird to show him the happy results." Having found him,

> All the way back to the studio Mr. Baird was busily extolling the virtues of his mechanical system over Farnsworth's. As they came to the door, Mr. Baird, still in his argument, caught sight of the picture on the monitor and became silent. He advanced slowly, as if hypnotized, until he was standing directly before it. He stood there for a time; then breaking the spell with visible effort, he turned without a word and left.[86]

Seymour Turner says, "I could have cried for the poor guy."[87] What Baird had shown Farnsworth had "big lines" going through it, and in comparing the two systems the difference in clarity was obvious.

The actual demonstration for Baird Television was conducted at London's Crystal Palace, where the Baird laboratory had been established. Farnsworth's demonstration consisted of a signal that was transmitted across metropolitan London to a receiver, which had been placed at Potter's Bar, twenty-five miles north of the palace.[88] Brolly notes: "The signal was received on a superheterodyne receiver. Very good results were attained. . .. Interferences from auto ignitions from the street in front of the house was [sic] eliminated with a dipole antenna in back yard, feeding [the] receiver through a twisted pair feeder."[89] According to Abramson, this demonstration consisted of a film image and included no live coverage.[90] But this was more than a demonstration for the Baird company officials, it was attended by members of the Parliament committee including Sir Harry Greer, who was also chairman of the board of directors for Baird Television.[91]

The demonstration was a success, and financial negotiations to license Farnsworth equipment for Baird's use were the next step. The negotiations were handled by Farnsworth and Turner.[92] The Baird officials presumed there would be a patent exchange between Baird and Farnsworth, but Farnsworth had no interest in anything in Baird's mechanical patent portfolio, and back home they were in need of cash. The asking price was $50,000 cash, plus royalties [$638,800]. Baird agreed to the cash advance and royalties. According to Everson, "The Baird laboratories [would be] enlarged immediately for manufacture of high definition television receiving sets using Farnsworth patents."[93] The sets were to be ready for the public within six months, just about the time a new broadcasting station was to be completed.

The future looked bright for Farnsworth. Baird officials touted their arrangements: "This company [Farnsworth] had developed . . . [electronic television research] which we consider to be much superior to the many other types of electric eye . . . This has very great possibilities."[94] Farnsworth had his first international agreement, a cash advance, a vision of new stations, and continuing royalties.

Following the successful negotiations, Brolly stayed in England to assist Baird Television personnel in adapting the Farnsworth electronic "methods and build[ing] equipment [for them] similar to ours [Farnsworth's]."[95] Dr. Szegho, a Baird Television scientist, worked closely with the Farnsworth engineers in making the transition from Baird's mechanical system to Farnsworth's electronic one.

The Baird agreement was the first real financial return for Farnsworth Television Incorporated—finally there would be a positive cash flow. Farnsworth's vision was to take the new finances and establish a U.S. television station as he had done for Philco. Farnsworth wanted another station on the air so that program distribution could begin, and, as he had described in the Duncan interview following the Franklin Institute demonstrations, he felt manufacturing would follow naturally. However, the former San Francisco banker, Jesse B. McCargar, had other ideas for the money. He was still the president of Farnsworth Television, he had been a key figure in organizing Farnsworth's Television Laboratories, and he had raised the funds for its continued operation. As the president, he held the controlling financial strings.[96] He "demanded" the money be forwarded to San Francisco where it would be used to pay lab debts, stockholder dividends, and defense lawyers now engaged to do battle with RCA.[97] The idea of another experimental station was tabled by McCargar. Back in San Francisco, the board of directors sided with McCargar, and Farnsworth lost one of the best opportunities he had had to fulfill his vision.

4
Farnsworth versus RCA
1932–1939

THE LEGAL BATTLES BETWEEN FARNSWORTH AND RCA DO NOT FALL EASILY INTO THE chronology of Farnsworth's corporate history. The most significant conflict actually began shortly after RCA officially visited the San Francisco labs. Then it quickly evolved into a legal case in 1932, when Farnsworth was still working at Philco. It no doubt contributed to the RCA versus Philco versus Farnsworth rumors and tension that was evident during the Philco period of Farnsworth's work, as noted in Chapter 3.

After RCA filed its case, Farnsworth's patent attorney, Donald K. Lippincott, organized Farnsworth's response. It would take two years from the actual filing in 1932, until it was heard in 1934. Three years after the case began, the patent hearing examiner ruled in favor of Farnsworth; however, it took another four years before RCA and Farnsworth reached an operable agreement. By this time, Farnsworth had purchased manufacturing plants and was distributing a line of radio and combination radio and phonograph sets. Throughout this extended process Farnsworth's financial backers, led by McCargar, were more interested in seeing an end to the RCA litigation and a positive cash flow than they were in developmental research or creating another experimental station. Understandably, the competition between Farnsworth and RCA presented a situation that was difficult for McCargar to comprehend, since he had little technical knowledge of television. It was a vitally important battle for Farnsworth because a negative outcome would have meant disaster. In contrast, it was merely a part of daily business for RCA.[1]

PATENTS AND THE INVENTOR'S ROLE

To better understand these struggles, one must look at the inventor's role. The inventor or company creates an apparatus and seeks a patent on it. A *patent* is the legal means whereby the inventor of the apparatus is guaranteed exclusive right of ownership and revenue generation for 17 years. The patent rights provide the inventor time to get the apparatus into production and profit from it. If the inventor does not want to go into the manufacturing business, he or she can *license* those rights to a manufacturer in exchange for financial *royalties* (monies paid the patent holder in exchange for the rights to use the invention). An inventor's portfolio of patents is a potential source of income. Patent interference cases involve one inventor or patent holder challenging another's patent.

Farnsworth was working to achieve a broad patent base (a series of related patents) that would mean a substantial income in royalties and provide a financial foundation for growth. However, establishing this foundation was not without its struggles from within, as in the case of McCargar, as well as without, as with RCA.

Historic Patent Challenges

Lee de Forest, the self-proclaimed father of American broadcasting and the inventor of the Audion tube, was constantly tied up in legal battles over patent rights. The purchase of some of de Forest's patents enabled AT&T to move into long-distance telephone service from coast to coast in 1915. These rights eventually ended up with RCA in 1926 when AT&T sold most of its radio interests.

Acquiring patent rights not only allowed technological expansion, it was profitable. Following World War I, the Navy relinquished its wartime control of radio, and cross-licensing agreements between General Electric, RCA, AT&T, and Westinghouse brought almost 2,000 patents into a cross-licensing patent pool. The profits from these royalties and cross-licenses is hinted at by Barnouw: "sales of over $5,000,000 in any one year would be subject to a 50 percent royalty to the others of the patent group."[2] It was a profitable arrangement. However, in 1923 the Federal Trade Commission investigated radio to determine "whether patents were being used to gain control over reception and transmission" of radio and thus were in violation of the antitrust laws. The FTC's report charged that indeed there had been a conspiracy to "restrain competition and create monopoly" in radio manufacturing.[3]

The size and influence of these larger companies at the time made them no stranger to patent suits. General Electric was involved in patent disputes with AT&T; AT&T was in dispute with others who were trying to manufacture transmitters; and RCA was in dispute with manufacturers that it felt were infringing on patent rights of its receiving sets. Many of the cases centered on RCA because of its dominance in the industry (through a large patent portfolio). The radio manufacturers were paying RCA royalties for patents used in manufacturing radio sets. It was, at least at first, a government-sanctioned business monopoly.

One of the more interesting patent cases that sheds some light into the behind-the-scenes negotiations of such cases was the 1926 challenge brought by the Splitdorf Radio Corporation against RCA. The suit contends that RCA infringed on a Splitdorf patent.[4] Douglas suggests the legal negotiations created an unexpected settlement that led to a personal gain for the Splitdorf executives, a free license for RCA, and, as usual for them, no royalty payments. RCA's philosophy was that it collected royalties, it did not pay them. Even some management felt Splitdorf could have won the case, but to win would have meant a prolonged and costly litigation that it could not have afforded.[5]

Armstrong v. RCA

The most famous of the RCA suits concerned Edwin H. Armstrong. Armstrong was granted four patents in 1933 for his FM radio system. During the early 1930s, he worked with the support of his friend, David Sarnoff, using the RCA facilities in New York to conduct his tests. But his continued insistence that FM would replace AM led to a parting of ways.[6] RCA's financial resources allowed them the luxury of waiting and battling it out in court, but this was not the case for Armstrong. When Armstrong was asked to vacate the RCA facilities, he went across the Hudson River to Alpine, New Jersey, and developed his own station, where he continued experimentation. When RCA engineers began testing their own version of FM, Armstrong sued.[7] The suit dragged on; RCA offered to purchase his patents for $1 million, but Armstrong refused. He became ill, his once considerable resources were exhausted, and the Armstrong story ended in tragedy—in 1954 he took his own life.[8] According to Bilby, "Sarnoff was stunned by the tragedy."[9] RCA quickly settled with the Armstrong estate for the same amount it had offered previously.

Barnouw surmises that when Armstrong made the decision to sue RCA, he may have been encouraged by Farnsworth's successful patent-interference case against RCA. The only exception to the RCA rule that it did not pay royalties, it collected them, was Philo T. Farnsworth.[10]

RCA V. FARNSWORTH

Harold J. McCreary brought the first patent-interference case against Zworykin on November 25, 1927.[11] His claim was simply that the Zworykin system did not work. The case, spearheaded by McCreary of Associated Electric Laboratories, included four other inventors against Zworykin:[12] Philo T. Farnsworth, Frederick W. Reynolds, Theodore Willard Case, and Camille A. Sabbath.[13] This case dragged on from November 1927 to February 1932 before the hearing examiner declared Zworykin the winner. The first hearing held April 15, 1929, actually declared Zworykin's patent as the one having priority. However, McCreary appealed the decision of the examiner to the Board of Appeals (April 1, 1930) and the United States Court of Custom and Patent Appeals (February 8, 1932). At each stage of appeal the authorities ruled in favor of Zworykin. It had taken McCreary almost four and one-half years and he never did prove that Zworykin's system was inoperative. His supporters withdrew throughout the appeal process, but the issue of Zworykin's patent primacy would resurface.

The primary patent-interference case between Farnsworth and RCA was brought by RCA on May 28, 1932. It claimed that Farnsworth's 1930 patent for a television system (patent no. 1,773,980) was infringing on a patent filed by Zworykin on December 29, 1923 (patent no. 683,337).[14] This most significant case was actually the second of many cases between Farnsworth and Zworykin.[15] The patent included the formation of an "electrical image" and was something RCA wanted under its control.[16]

The legal experience was grueling and expensive. According to Everson, attorneys made trips to New York, Salt Lake City, Kansas City, and Washington, D.C., in order to gather information in support of Farnsworth's position.[17] Testimony was gathered from Justin Tolman (Farnsworth's high school teacher); Dr. Leonard B. Loeb, a professor of physics at the University of California; and people associated with the Farnsworth's Television Laboratories including Donald K. Lippincott, Leslie Gorrell, George Everson, Archibald H. Brolly, Clifford Gardner, and Arthur Crawford.[18] The Farnsworth group claimed that "since he [Zworykin] had shown no conception of an operative device prior to Farnsworth's patent . . . [h]is application does not constitute a reduction to practice."[19] Tolman surprised RCA by producing portions of Farnsworth's old student notebooks, which were dated 1922 and contained original sketches.[20] Farnsworth was subjected to days of grueling cross-examination by RCA attorneys and technical experts. The money to support not only experimentation but also defense of such litigation, was raised, Everson said, by "McCargar and me."[21] To lose the case would have been disastrous for Farnsworth.

Zworykin countered Farnsworth's presentation with his own battery of experts: Colonel Ilia E. Mouromtseff; Professor Joseph Tykociner, University of Illinois; George F. Metcalf; Dr. Dayton Ulrey; and Samuel Kintner. Zworykin claimed he had shown Mouromtseff his idea for television in 1919 and Tykociner in 1921. Metcalf, Ulrey, and Kintner were said to have witnessed the Zworykin device in 1923.[22]

The issues in the case revolved around three primary contentions: the conception date, when the apparatus under question was reduced to practice, and when it was put into operation. These, along with pointing out the flaws in the competing applications, were the key elements of the arguments. The legal briefs were delivered to the United States Patent Office in Washington, D.C., in April 1934, the month the final hearing took place.

Farnsworth based his claim on drawings dated between January 1, 1922, and April 30, 1922, "a written description [produced] on August 4, 1926, and on a reduction to practice on January 7, 1927."[23] Zworykin claimed that this "unsupported testimony of an inventor is insufficient to prove conception" and that the testimony of Tolman was "vague and incomplete."[24] The term *electrical image* seemed to be a major point of contention related to reducing the apparatus to practice. The Farnsworth patent clearly defined a term that was heretofore nonexistent.[25] The examiner commented that such a term could not be "extended [at a later date] to have a broader and different meaning,"[26] as apparently Zworykin's lawyers were implying.

Zworykin's own testimony was not too helpful. Abramson said it, "did little to enhance his reputation" as Zworykin appeared vague and evasive in his testimony and cross-examination.[27] The hearing examiner felt Zworykin's disclosures and his collaborating witnesses were "not convincing." It was "entirely oral and is given some ten to fourteen years after the alleged events."[28] According to Abramson, Zworykin did not hold up well under cross-examination from Farnsworth's lawyers. Zworykin was said to have shown "that he is perfectly ready to make any statement on the stand which he believes, at the moment, will be to his advantage. His memory is alternately superactive and distressingly vague, and throughout his cross-examination he was so evasive as to make the elicitation of any fact whatsoever extremely difficult."[29]

Another issue surrounded Zworykin's apparatus—it was never produced for the hearings.[30] Farnsworth's lawyers pressed for the tube to be presented as evidence, and Zworykin's lawyers offered no explanation as to why they did not present it. Abramson suggests that, although the tube existed, it was probably different "from those described in the 1923 patent application in construction and perhaps even in operation."[31]

On July 22, 1935, the hearing examiner ruled in favor of Farnsworth, stating:

> Zworykin has no right to . . . [claim] the specific definition of the term "electrical image" given in the Farnsworth patent.
>
> Zworykin has no right to . . . [claim that] because it is not apparent that the device would operate to produce a scanned electrical image unless it has discrete globules capable of producing discrete space charges and the Zworykin application as filed does not disclose such a device.
>
> Zworykin has no right to . . . [claim] even if the device originally disclosed operates in the manner now alleged by Zworykin because this alleged mode of operation does not produce an electrical image that is scanned to produce the television signals.[32]

In other words the examiner ruled that Farnsworth had produced the electrical image as he had defined it, and Zworykin's system did not produce a scanned electrical image. It produced a different kind of electrical image not germane to the patent question under consideration.

The San Francisco newspaper heralded the victory with the headline: "S.F. Inventor's Claims Win."[33] But the battle was not over: RCA appealed the examiner's ruling. The appeal was heard on January 31, 1936.[34] Both parties submitted motions to dismiss the interference case. Zworykin claimed that his winning the earlier case against McCreary (case number 54,922) gave him priority with the patent and that his appeal should be awarded based on that precedent. Farnsworth countered that Zworykin could not produce an electrical image with the system described. The examiner denied the motions for dismissal. Zworykin was unable to convince the appeals board of his position. Farnsworth on the other hand had a working system and won the appeal.

On March 6, 1936, the case closed with a significant victory for Farnsworth. Although he won, the lawsuits had cost him time and money. Indeed, RCA would tie up the patent for yet another three years in more appeals. McArthur and Waddell, writing the John Logie Baird story, reported that "RCA has spent more than 2 million dollars in legal wrangles, and another 7 million in developing television equipment, in attempts to overcome Farnsworth's patents.[35]

In 1939 an agreement was reached between what was then the Farnsworth Television and Radio Corporation and RCA. Signed by E. A. Nicholas, president of the Farnsworth Corporation, and Otto S. Schairer, vice president of RCA, it stated that $1 million would be paid over a ten-year period, and RCA was licenced to use Farnsworth's patents.[36] The agreement paved the way for continued development of television in the United States.

Even though he had won his most prominent case, the effect of the patent interference suits on Farnsworth was significant. In testimony before the Federal Monopoly Committee, he later commented that "the patent system has cost his company heavily in suits to defend its rights, diverting money from important research work." While basically a supporter of the U.S. patent system as "the best in the world," he felt it needed streamlining for "greater speed and efficiency" and suggested it provide "greater protection for individual inventors, to enable them to compete with the companies that have already arrived." Farnsworth wanted "special protection . . . [a]fforded to young and inexperienced inventors with small means."[37] The legal battle with RCA had cost Farnsworth seven years out of the seventeen-year life of the patent—four in the courts (1932–1936) and three in appeal.

The victory was an appraisal of Farnsworth Television and his personal work. The lawsuits cost them money they could not well afford. It diverted finances from research and corporate development. The patent system itself was slow to react, which was especially difficult for the smaller operations that had few resources with which to lobby established regulatory controls and compete with existing companies. There was, in Farnsworth's opinion, a special protection needed for the small entrepreneur.

5

Farnsworth Television Incorporated

1935–1938

Chronology

Farnsworth

1935 — Baird Television, under contract with Farnsworth, and Marconi-EMI are the primary competitors to supply electronic television apparatus for the coming electronic standards.

June 1935 — Farnsworth Television reaches patent-licensing agreements with the Fernseh A.G. company of Germany. These cross-license agreements extended to most European countries.

July 1935 — Farnsworth Television conducts live studio and film demonstrations in Philadelphia.

December 1935 — Farnsworth provides a bid to the Army Air Corps for airplane surveillance equipment.

1935 — Farnsworth files for seventeen more patents.

March 1936 — Farnsworth demonstrates "cold" tube power at New York Radio Engineers meeting.

August 1936 — Farnsworth camera and equipment are used by Fernseh A.G. at 1936 Olympic Games, the first Olympic games to be televised.

October 1936 — Farnsworth receives an urgent request for help from Baird in Great Britain. He is shocked upon his

Electronic Media

January 1935 — The British Television Advisory Committee recommends electronic as opposed to mechanical standards for television in the United Kingdom.

1935 — Armstrong demonstrates FM at Radio Engineers Convention.

• Press-Radio War ends as the Associated Press and United Press International agree to provide stations with news service.

• The first recording device, the magnetophone, is demonstrated at the German Annual Radio Fair.

• Edward R. Murrow joins CBS as director of talks and education.

• RCA announces planned tests with 343 lines of interlaced scanning and a million-dollar, television-research program.

1936 — FCC conducts conference on FM and television.

• BBC compares Baird mechanical system with EMI-Marconi electrical system.

Farnsworth

arrival in England to find Baird still using mechanical scanning.

November 1936 — McCargar moves to reorganize the Philadelphia laboratory while Farnsworth is in Great Britain working with Baird. Contention is seriously undermining the work in the lab, and finances are frustrating McCargar.

November 30, 1936 — The Crystal Palace burns in London, destroying Baird's facilities and the newly constructed electronic system Farnsworth had set up for more demonstrations before the parliamentary committee making television standards decisions in Great Britain.

December 1936 — Farnsworth visits the Fernseh A.G. company in Germany. He tours the plants and tries to collect royalties owned him by Fernseh A.G.

• The Federal Communications Commission grants Farnsworth's application for an experimental station in Philadelphia, W3XPF.

1936 — Twenty-two more patents are filed.

February 4, 1937 — Great Britain adopts the Marconi-EMI system of electronic television, thus rendering Farnsworth-Baird agreements of limited value.

April 1937 — Farnsworth sells television equipment to CBS.

• Talk of corporate reorganization begins in earnest as the situation between McCargar and Farnsworth worsens.

July 27, 1937 — AT&T and Farnsworth reach a cross-licensing agreement in exchange of patent rights. Agreement opens the door to manufacturing for Farnsworth.

1937–1938 — Nineteen more patents are filed.

Spring 1938 — A vacation in Maine provides Farnsworth some needed rest and marks a change in life and corporate direction.

Electronic Media

1937 — Philco demonstrates 441-line picture.

• FCC allocates more channels for experimental television.

Farnsworth

December 1938 — Farnsworth Television and Radio Corporation is created.

Electronic Media

1938 — Orson Welles's famous *War of the Worlds* radio program creates panic.
• Mutual Broadcasting System requests investigation of radio monopoly.
• Armstrong establishes first FM station, W2XMN, in New Jersey.
• Columbia Records purchased by CBS.

THE HISTORICAL ENVIRONMENT OF TELEVISION

THE FEDERAL COMMUNICATIONS COMMISSION WAS SLOW IN REACTING TO TELEVISION. Initial rules and regulations pertaining to "visual broadcasting" were first adopted on February 18, 1929, and clearly protected existing radio stations. Experimental television stations were granted licenses for only six months at a time with "transmitters to be located outside the city limits and sufficiently distant from important receiving centers to avoid interference." Following each six months of operation, the stations were required to report to the Commission.[1]

Television by the mid-1930s had passed the stage of laboratory experimentation and progressed to experimental stations, but the government was not keeping pace with the industry. The FCC had no established procedures for introducing a new medium. The Commission moved slowly in determining television frequency allocations and technical standards. Television entrepreneurs, including Farnsworth, were anxious to move television in the same direction as radio and to position themselves competitively in the corporate race to bring television to the American public. But FCC rules strictly forbade commercial programming, limiting it solely to experimentation. Not until 1941 would the FCC allow the launch of commercial television. This frustrated leaders involved, as it allowed time for those behind in experimentation to catch up.

By the 1930s, television engineers knew that they could produce electronic pictures. The chief challenges were in improving the quality of the pictures and transmission methods. Early demonstrations had created a growing public interest in television as a novelty, but this interest was commercially insufficient. Hollywood motion pictures already enjoyed a quality far superior to the early 60-line television experiments, so the experimenters were working continually to improve. The number of scanning lines tested during the mid-1930s ranged up to 400.[2] Questions of transmission frequency allocation were yet to be resolved by the industry or the FCC.

By 1937 interest and development in television had grown to the point where the Commission held initial frequency-allocation hearings to determine where this new technology might best be placed on the spectrum. However, it was not until 1939 that the Commission set two station classes: experimental and commercial. There were no transmission or reception standards; the FCC left those to the manufacturers—at least temporarily.[3]

The lack of technical standardization left manufacturers and research engineers developing differing systems, each of which could be described with glowing reports in the popular press. Those watching the Farnsworth system were supplied receivers constructed by Farnsworth for experimental purposes. To pick up an experimental signal one had to have a set that would tune to the frequency being used and was complementary to the system being tested. So it was with all the developing American television systems: RCA, Philco, DuMont Laboratories, Farnsworth Television, General Electric, the Don Lee Broadcasting System, and "to a limited extent Zenith."[4] Even considering the limited number of receivers available, the audience watching and listening to television was composed of one's competitors, engineers who had the systems that could tune in differing signals, and a mix of selected homes that had been furnished sets for experimental purposes. In Philadelphia no fewer than three companies, Farnsworth, RCA and Philco, were broadcasting from experimental stations. Collectively they shared an audience measuring only a few dozen receivers.

The lack of agreed industry standards, the slowness in any governmental regulation movement, and the power of the radio industry were setting the timetable in the development of television. While the government dragged its feet, companies with the leading edge were at a disadvantage because, given time, their competitors would naturally catch up.[5] This process was happening in Farnsworth's case. At one time he had the leading edge in electronic television, but that edge was eroded by time spent in legal decision making, litigation, fund-raising, patent litigation, the legal processes, and waiting for industry-designated and/or government-dictated standards.

Farnsworth was becoming discouraged. His belief that he held the leadership position in electronic television development was wavering. With its patent cases against Farnsworth, RCA had gained years to catch up technologically. Farnsworth knew he would never have the reserves to compete successfully. Though discouraged, he remained determined. He established yet another corporation and put another station on the air.

FARNSWORTH TELEVISION INCORPORATED: PUBLIC DEMONSTRATIONS

The new television research laboratory, located in Chestnut Hill, outside of Philadelphia, was still small in comparison with the manufacturing and research facilities of RCA or Philco. This first independent Philadelphia lab was more like the old Green Street facilities. It was a space above a two-story garage that was connected to a home owned by the Andrew O'Neill Construction Company. O'Neill used it for his construction office until the Depression affected the construction industry. Farnsworth Television moved in, using it as laboratory space.[6] It was from this location that the remote equipment was created for use in the Franklin Institute and Baird demonstrations. It was from here in 1934 that four more patents were filed.[7] The facilities were small, but that didn't inhibit the work, which was actually picking up in pace.

In an attempt to broaden television's public support, Farnsworth was accommodating an increasing number of requests for demonstrations. In February 1935, he addressed another audience at the Franklin Institute, declaring the "art [of television] in America has progressed to a point where very satisfactory television service is possible if suitable transmitting stations were to be erected."[8] He hinted that business problems were the chief hindrance to the development of a commercial television system. In July he invited the press to Chestnut Hill for a demonstration. A photo was staged in front of the home, providing a beautiful stone backdrop. It featured a talent model coming from the house in the background, with Farnsworth inspecting the camera. The actual demonstration included "a group of chorus girls, an orchestra, and [again] Mickey Mouse."[9] The chorus girls and Mickey Mouse were provided from film. The "William Eddy Orchestra" (made up of community volunteers) and the announcers were live from the Farnsworth studio.[10] A small-screen television was inserted into a radio cabinet for the reporters and invited guests. The screen was 5½ x 7 inches, but it produced a "clarity and sharpness of definition that surprised many of the observers," according to the *New York Times* and *Newsweek*.[11]

Abramson indicated that Farnsworth was fundamentally scanning 240 lines at the time of these demonstrations. The Farnsworth engineers were working at 343 lines by December, and his competitors were scanning between 240 and 360 lines.[12] Farnsworth was also working on a projection system in which the picture would be reproduced on a small tube and then optically projected onto any size screen desired. When reporters asked about the future of television—"would it be available in the next two, three, or five years?"—Farnsworth humorously responded, "Some of my predictions haven't turned out too well."

Philo T. Farnsworth and Mable Bernstein inspect one of his first portable television cameras, built in 1934. Courtesy Farnsworth-Everson Papers, Arizona State University.

He followed this reference to his previous optimism by another optimistic prediction: He hoped it would be available within a year.[13]

Not all of the laboratory demonstrations were formal. The people of Chestnut Hill performed, schoolchildren were invited to the studios, and members of the O'Neill family acted as talent for some of the experiments. In 1935 Leon and Josephine O'Neill performed a duet in the office and were thrilled, O'Neill reported, "when Farnsworth was able to transmit pictures of people performing before his camera on the first floor of the garage to a receiving set on the second."[14] According to O'Neill, within a few months of experimentation, his duet was transmitted into New York. Children and faculty from the Chestnut Hill Academy, where young Philo Farnsworth III attended, also made trips to the studio. All the speeches and demonstrations—formal and informal—focused around the construction of a new television station, W3XPF.

PREWAR MILITARY INTEREST

Not all of Farnsworth's activity during the mid-Depression years concerned public demonstrations. Bids for equipment were coming in. Farnsworth Television Incorporated was selling private stock offerings at $425 per share [$5,311]. The Corporation Commission of California authorized the sale of 230 capital stock shares. A 1935 letter to stockholders noted the worldwide attention Farnsworth inventions were getting, along with the agreements with Baird Television Limited.[15]

In December 1935 the first military interest in Farnsworth's work surfaced when the Navy requested information for an airplane television transmitter. According to lab notes labeled "confidential," the request was for a "compact camera for use in scouting . . . sufficient to distinguish battleships, cruisers, and destroyers in mixed formation at a distance of 5,000 yards . . . [with] sensitivity good enough to give clear images under all conditions of reasonably clear visibility."[16] There was little detailed information provided in Farnsworth's daily log books relative to the bid or its fulfillment, but the bid request illustrated the beginning of a changing international environment in which industry would make a transition from experimental equipment production to wartime support.

COLD TUBE DEMONSTRATION

Farnsworth's renown increased with each experiment and the resulting publicity. He was constantly being asked to publicly demonstrate his work. Even though he was not favorably disposed to all these public showings, he always accepted the invitations that included an engineering audience and generally deferred those for the more general audiences.[17] According to Everson,

Farnsworth considered the latter "a waste of time and a tax upon his energies."[18] Nevertheless, he was obviously persuaded by Everson, Turner, and his backers that the publicity his appearances generated promoted the acceptance of his system. So he gave these demonstrations the same detailed preparation he gave his scientific experiments.

One of Farnsworth's most challenging presentations took place on March 4, 1936. The audience was the New York chapter of the Institute of Radio Engineers. Farnsworth spent weeks in preparation. Although indifferent to a general audience, if the attendees were scientists, he held them "by the brilliance of the subject matter of his presentation."[19] The subject of the demonstration before the New York Radio Engineers was power generation. He used a cold tube to amplify and create more power for both radio and television systems. "Using a tube about the size of a quart container, fitted with a cylindrical cold cathode rather than the usual hot filament, Mr. Farnsworth produced 1,000 watts of power," reported the *New York Times.*[20] The multipactor, as the tube was called, would become patent no. 2,071,517, one of seventeen Farnsworth filed in 1935.[21] Everson reported that the engineers were crawling all over Farnsworth's equipment before they arrived and that "the entire stage was overrun."[22] Farnsworth was initially worried that the equipment would be damaged and the experiment upset. However, the demonstration went off without a hitch. Everson reported that his appearance before the New York Radio Engineers was too technical for the layman who would not understand the scientific details of the lecture that Farnsworth read from his notes, but that Farnsworth delighted the audience during his question and answer period. Mixing humor with science, "Farnsworth came off very much the victor."[23]

At a dinner presented for the Forman's Club in Germantown, Pennsylvania, Farnsworth reported that England and Germany were ready to begin the sale of household television receivers, "but American manufacturers prefer to wait until the sets are more nearly perfected."[24] Farnsworth's remarks were beginning to show an international flavor as was his reputation.

FARNSWORTH'S EUROPEAN FRONT

Farnsworth's agreements with Baird Television, Limited, Britain, and the German corporation Fernseh A.G. were significant achievements. The basic agreement between Farnsworth and Baird was that Baird had the exclusive licenses to "manufacture, lease, use, and sell" Farnsworth equipment in the British Commonwealth countries, with the exception of Canada.[25] The agreement with the German corporation, Fernseh A.G., reached June 26, 1935, also gave both parties a cross-license to each other's patents. The territory of the Fernseh A.G. agreement covered much of Europe—Germany, Austria, Hungary,

Czechoslovakia, Poland, and Switzerland. As had Baird, Fernseh A.G. also agreed for a cash payment of $10,000 [$124,963] plus royalties.[26] These agreements meant that Farnsworth's inventions should "dominate in television throughout the world."[27] Unfortunately for Farnsworth, the success of Baird was short-lived and World War II was about to interfere with the German arrangements.

FARNSWORTH AND BAIRD TELEVISION (BRITAIN)

By the fall of 1936 it was evident that television standards in Britain would be the Marconi-EMI electronic system. Although with Farnsworth's 1934 assistance Baird had been able to remain in the competition, unfortunately for Farnsworth, Baird made a significant error. In his continuing work, he had held on to his own system of mechanical television, merely integrating Farnsworth's electronic components system into what remained a largely mechanical set-up. Baird was still using a disk scanner, a mechanical film scanner, and only the Farnsworth electronic camera.[28] The Baird engineers were mechanically oriented in their thinking and seemed to have constant problems with the Farnsworth electronic camera, which was working well in the United States.[29] But without Farnsworth's supervision, the Baird engineers did not do well with the electrical television system. Farnsworth was called again for help.

Farnsworth, however, did not want to leave his Philadelphia lab or the experimental station he was about to put on the air. Besides, he had other problems: He was in the middle of his most significant differences with McCargar; and he was struggling for continued financial backing. He was engaged in a string of public demonstrations as well as being in the middle of negotiations with both CBS and AT&T; and he wasn't feeling well. After ten years of working almost around the clock, at times with a complete lack of concern for food and sleep, his work schedule was taking a toll on his health.

Still, it was decided that Farnsworth would make the trip. After all, if Baird was successful, it would mean millions. However, there was a condition attached to Farnsworth's traveling to England—that his wife would accompany him. Farnsworth put his brother-in-law Cliff Gardner and Arch Brolly in charge of watching over the laboratory. Along with Everson, they would protect the integrity of Farnsworth's work and maintain his direction during his absence. After ten years of marriage, the Farnsworths would be able to enjoy the honeymoon they never had. They were on a slow boat to England. For the first time in years, Farnsworth relaxed.

Upon arriving in England, work began immediately. Farnsworth was shocked to discover that Baird was still using mechanical components and discouraged to find that projects and parts that had been started by him and his engineers during the earlier visit were left incomplete.[30] However, once at the Crystal Palace, Farnsworth went to work with his usual dedication. He set his system in order and conducted another demonstration before the parliamentary committee. Baird was back in the electronic business, with a clear picture reflecting "crisp detail and subtle contrasts."[31] Following the demonstration's success, the Farnsworths left England for the beaches of south France.

They were vacationing on the French Riviera when they received a cable informing them of the final blow to the Baird Television system. A fire destroyed the Crystal Palace (November 30, 1936) and with it the studio, laboratories, and research facilities. The fire was devastating and could be seen for miles around.[32] Farnsworth returned to England to help Baird sift through the rubble, but there was little left he could do for the Baird company. There was nothing left of his work except for the charred remains.

Only two months later, February 4, 1937, Britain adopted the Marconi-EMI system.[33] Marconi-EMI received the credit in England, and RCA took the credit in America. The system was based "upon the electronic television system developed by RCA and, through an exchange of patent licenses with Electrical & Music Industries Ltd. of England."[34] Baird's mechanical television was dead.[35] The agreements between Farnsworth and Baird were still legally in force, but now they carried little dollar value or hope for financial return. The rights to sell equipment negotiated in the agreements were worthless. There was nothing left to sell—an alternative system had been adopted by the British government.

FARNSWORTH AND FERNSEH A.G. TELEVISION (GERMANY)

The Fernseh A.G. company of Germany gave Farnsworth notoriety during the 1936 Olympic games, when a Farnsworth camera was used. Held in July and August, the 1936 Olympics were the first covered by television, provided by Fernseh A.G. and the German Post Office. Because Fernseh A.G. had the Farnsworth license, they were using a Farnsworth camera as well as Farnsworth equipment in the studio and the remote van. The *Wall Street Journal* described the cameras as "placed about the stadium at vantage points to pick up various events. Cables from these cameras led into a distributor so that always the most interesting event or view of an event may be selected for broadcast."[36] The broadcasts were seen by audiences in several theaters in Berlin.[37] Following the Olympics, Fernseh A.G. showed the Farnsworth camera at the Berlin Radio Exhibition, August 28 through September 6, 1936. These events served once again to focus attention on Farnsworth's achievements. So, following a disappointing trip to England, Farnsworth decided to visit Germany in hopes that he could capitalize on his success and collect the royalties due from Fernseh A.G.

Captain A. G. D. West, a former chief research engineer for the BBC and engineer at the Baird corporation, advised the Farnsworths against the trip to Germany because he was concerned for their safety as a result of rising political tensions. Although Farnsworth was anxious to find out what was happening with his license agreements and collect royalties, he also wanted to stay away from a volatile political situation. Dr. Paul Goerz, president of Fernseh A.G., arranged for the travel so as to avoid the military and politics.[38] As they toured Fernseh A.G., security was tight. At the conclusion of the visit, Dr. Goerz quietly escorted the Farnsworths out of the country during the night.

Farnsworth was able to relax only temporarily on this working vacation, and from a business perspective, it had not been a successful trip. The trip was a precursor to his upcoming confrontation with McCargar, who in Farnsworth's absence was again trying to reorganize the lab, bring in new management, and fire the Farnsworth engineers.

FARNSWORTH VERSUS MCCARGAR

The refusal by McCargar and the San Francisco Board of Directors to fund the experimental station with the first Baird payment caused a great deal of friction within the company. McCargar had suggested Farnsworth move his experiments back to San Francisco following the Philco separation, but Farnsworth declined. He wanted to remain where he was, close to the center of

1936 Farnsworth Television Incorporated cameras. The camera on the left is the model used by Fernseh A.G. in the 1936 Olympic games. Courtesy Al Abramson and Elma G. Farnsworth.

experimentation. RCA research facilities were still in Camden, and New York and Washington, D.C., were within driving distance. Farnsworth was where he wanted and needed to be; but McCargar was a banker. Noted Seymour Turner, "He thought like a banker. I can hear him talking now . . . how he was going to walk into Sarnoff's office and ask for $5 million."[39] McCargar's financial worries inhibited operations. The confrontations between McCargar and Farnsworth were difficult for Farnsworth personally, as well as affecting the personnel negatively.

Farnsworth had a strong personality: quiet yet self-directed and stubbornly determined. He was an idea person working with a close-knit group of engineers who had been with him for a long time. Working for the Farnsworth group was like working with family. "Once accepted, a new employee found himself welcome into . . . one big happy family . . . I'm building men, not gadgets, was a part of Farnsworth's working philosophy."[40] He encouraged those who worked around him. They, too, were developing patents for the Farnsworth television system. Farnsworth was the undisputed leader, but McCargar held a tight rein on the financial operations. By 1936 the time was rapidly approaching when Farnsworth's vision would be pitted squarely against McCargar.

Farnsworth's vision of television's future was to have his own network of stations and a research company supported by royalties on his patents. The television laboratories at Chestnut Hill were for "operating an experimental and development laboratory for television."[41] The station itself was to be supported by income from licenses and royalty contracts.[42]

In contrast to Farnsworth's inventive vision, McCargar's aim was for commercial profit. He was willing to sell the station and the laboratory. He constantly antagonized the lab with his worries over financing, which he and Everson always seemed to raise. He fired engineers to cut down on expenses, but Farnsworth would rehire them because of their value to the work. Writing years later, when McCargar was finally forced to resign from the Board, Pem Farnsworth described him as the one individual who had "caused Phil more headaches than any other person."[43]

McCargar had refused to allow the money from Baird to develop a new station, so funding for construction of W3XPF was put up by Seymour Turner's family. In a brief discussion about his work with Farnsworth, Turner refers to the station as "the studio I built."[44] It was up the road from the laboratory in Wyndmoor. This station was supposed to have been Farnsworth's "stepping stone . . . into the commercial broadcasting field."[45]

The tension between McCargar on the West Coast and Farnsworth on the East Coast is best illustrated in McCargar's writing. In a letter to George Everson, McCargar rages, "Now for God's sake George, don't toss this off with the expression that I am having a pathological outburst" (McCargar, then fifty-six, was short-tempered).[46] This plea was in a cover letter to Everson and included a letter McCargar addressed to Russell G. Pond, a stockbroker McCargar had hired to manage the Philadelphia operations while Farnsworth was in England.[47] McCargar had sent not only Pond to Philadelphia, but also his son-in-law George Sleeper. As usual, McCargar's decisions caused a great deal of dissension in the studio.[48] Engineers, knowing McCargar's reputation and the history of his hiring and firings, were leery of the two new McCargar appointees. They refused to work with them, which infuriated McCargar:

> I think it is a terrible state of affairs when any of the men in the laboratory have the effrontery to say that they do not want to work with George Sleeper because he is my son-in-law. It seems to me that I am entitled to some consideration and respect, particularly in view of the fact that Phil has had most of his family and in-laws in the lab at various times since the thing started . . . The only reason I am backing George [Sleeper] . . . so strongly is because I have confidence in their work, which I haven't [in] any of the rest of the crowd.[49]

McCargar moved to put Everson in the role of peacemaker, declaring that he and Pond needed to work this situation out. McCargar wanted the engineers

Jesse B. McCargar (1880–1954) was president of the Farnsworth corporation's board of directors from 1929 to 1938. He served thereafter as a member of the advisory board to the new Farnsworth Television and Radio Corporation and chair from 1939 to 1948. He was associated with the Crocker First National Bank, San Francisco, from 1906 to 1928 and a vice president and director at the time of his resignation. After leaving the banking industry, he worked as manager of the George G. Irwin estate and, in addition to his work with Farnsworth, served as a director for several corporations including American Trust Company, Pabco Products Incorporated, Moore Dry Dock Company, Pacific Securities Company, Pioneer Kettleman Company, Honolulu Oil Corporation, and the Pacific Transportation lines. Photo courtesy San Francisco History Center, San Francisco Public Library.

who would not cooperate to be fired. A follow-up letter to Everson a few days later reflects McCargar's rationale as he seeks to explain further that "I did not know that George Sleeper was going to marry my daughter until after it had been decided that he was to go to the laboratory in Philadelphia."[50] Those afraid of Sleeper, "are afraid someone is going to show them up, because as you know they have been working for years and years to get a picture and never have succeeded. They are pursuing a course that will wreck us unless we stop them," McCargar declared. McCargar knew successful pictures had been produced, and numerous public presentations conducted—he had witnessed some of the earlier ones himself—but this was an emotional plea, not a logical one, and it was followed with more threats of firings and accusations of the opposing engineers being "petty, short-sighted professional jealousy or it is a frantic cooperation with our competitors."[51]

Everson was the mediator and had personal interests in both Farnsworth's success and in supporting McCargar. He rationalized that McCargar was trying to help the Philadelphia lab produce the same quality picture as that made by engineers in San Francisco (he'd sent two engineers from California to Pennsylvania).[52] McCargar knew what was going on in San Francisco because that lab was close by, but he was frustrated by what he did not know about the lab in Philadelphia. The result, Everson reports, was friction. In describing the friction, however, Everson overlooks McCargar's emotional state and is critical of Farnsworth for his inability to turn his research more quickly into a commercial advantage. Everson was a confidante who would "drop [into the Philadelphia lab] . . . at least twice a week" and must have known that there were open communications between East and West Coast laboratories.[53] Regular weekly reports by the engineers from both labs were sent to Farnsworth. Thus, ideas were exchanged to ensure progress and coordination on any experiment. Occasionally, a Green Street engineer would visit the East Coast lab, and Brolly was even transferred by Farnsworth to work in Philadelphia.[54] These were Farnsworth's labs, his life's work: "This is my laboratory. Neither you [Everson] nor anyone else is coming in here giving orders as to what is to be done," he declared.[55]

The differences between McCargar and Farnsworth put Everson in a difficult situation. He had discovered Farnsworth, and had acquired underwriting from his friend McCargar. He did not want to frustrate or alienate either man. He was hopeful that his personal investment in Farnsworth would pay financial dividends, and he needed McCargar for continued success in his other ventures. Farnsworth was not Everson and McCargar's only investment. They were not employees of Farnsworth Television; they were primary investors, and although they were members of the corporate board of directors, only a portion of their working day was related to Farnsworth interests. Everson worked in cities across the nation, continuing to raise funds for local Community Chest organizations, though as the years progressed more of his time was spent on Farnsworth Television. McCargar's influence as a banker was important to Everson's overall success, as Everson was always on the lookout for investment opportunities.[56]

This was a clash of two personalities and ideological purposes. Understanding these characters and views during an emotionally-charged period is difficult. Everson described the engineers as "temperamental . . . as prima donnas" working to reconcile "every problem by invention" and bankers, whose only interest in research was to turn a commercial advantage.[57] According to Everson, "This assignment of reconciling the purposes and the will of an inventor to those of a banker, with the latter's practical and realistic outlook on our development, was not an easy one."[58]

Formal correspondence focused on concerns about sale of stock to support the lab with few begrudging emotions displayed over the laboratory controversy. The only written response as to why McCargar's actions were irrational comes from Donald K. Lippincott, Farnsworth's patent attorney. In communications with George Everson, Lippincott mentions "a letter concerning a lot of intangibles [that] . . . in the aggregate, [have] given us a very definite opinion as to his [McCargar's] attitude and what it means."[59] Lippincott wrote that he

> really felt sorry for Jesse. Although many of his [McCargar's] troubles are imaginary and have been brought on by his own stubbornness, it is evident that he feels very strongly and is hurt by the fact that he has lost a close personal touch and complete concord which he used to have with the whole crowd. I believe that he is definitely determined to shed the whole thing as soon as he possibly can . . . A visit to his office these days is depressing. He worries over everything and predicts disaster . . . His attitude now is that Farnsworth will never actually produce anything and that our best move is to make the best deal that we possibly can with RCA, AT&T or anyone else that will take over the burden.[60]

In a handwritten note appended to the letter, Lippincott confided in Everson: "This . . . is intended primarily for your own eyes . . . I am leaving [it] entirely up to you how much, if any, you pass on."[61]

It was clear McCargar wanted out of the fund-raising end of the corporation. The financial pressures, especially during the Depression, were more of a burden than he could now tolerate. In contrast, the engineers shared Farnsworth's vision and remained loyal to him. McCargar had lost control, but not influence. He pressured the company for yet another reorganization that would place an engineer in the executive role. He wanted someone who would communicate with the technical staff and a name that would be recognized within the industry. The unsettled internal operations, financial difficulties, and competitive pressures were felt by Farnsworth as well as McCargar. Forever the optimist Farnsworth could not relax, he just kept on working.

EXPERIMENTAL TELEVISION STATION: W3XPF

Farnsworth Television Incorporated filed a construction permit for station W3XPF on May 2, 1936.[62] The Federal Communications Commission, which was moving slowly in all matters concerning television, and considering experimental TV licenses on a case-by-case basis, declared that it was unable to determine whether the application would "serve the public interest, convenience, or necessity"; therefore, a public hearing on the application was designated.[63] The hearing was to determine if Farnsworth had "a program of research and experimentation which indicates reasonable promise of a substantial contribution to the development of the visual broadcast art," whether research would be conducted by qualified engineers, and whether Farnsworth was "legally and financially qualified" and possessed the technical facilities.[64] As was common practice, public input was solicited, and notices of the hearing were sent to both Philco and RCA.

At the hearing on August 20, 1936, there was no opposition or public comment. Farnsworth's response to the Commission constituted a very good showing in support of his application, according to the *New York Times.*[65] Farnsworth testified to his achievements and, according to FCC engineer James P. Buchanan, Farnsworth's research "promise[d] a substantial contribution to the art of television." Buchanan specifically cited improvements between two recent experiments, conducted a year apart, noting that the scanning had improved the detail and that the flicker had been eliminated from the picture.[66] Farnsworth said there was absolutely no flicker.[67] Picture specifications, according to his testimony, included 341 lines with an image of 5½ x 7.[68] The hearing recorded that Farnsworth had complete control of the activities of twenty-five to thirty engineers employed at the laboratory and the station, some of whom had worked with him ever since his days in San Francisco.[69]

As to the question of financial qualifications, the license records lack specific detail. However, press reports concerning the questions of Farnsworth's financial support are interesting. The *New York Times,* reported that $700,000 to $800,000 [$8,261,500 to $9,853,200] had been spent during the last eight years of experimentation.[70] The FCC application seemed purposefully vague so as not to disclose its limited resources to competitors. It outlined the capital stock at $10,000 [$1,231,650], "divided into one hundred shares having no par value." The funds for the station operations were reported as being "taken from income from licenses and royalty contracts," and if those were insufficient to keep the station in operation, "the stockholders are men of large means and have here-to-fore advanced sufficient funds to carry on the work and defray the cost."[71] This is as it had been to that date; it was how Farnsworth had always been financed. Philo's testimony at the hearing for the station reflected a little more financial detail. He noted the "book value of the . . . assets [was] $500,000 [$6,158,200]. Liabilities do not exceed $35,000 [$431,070]" and, according to him, the "actual value is much greater than book value," suggesting his perceived value of his patent portfolio.[72] When Farnsworth was asked during the hearing about the specifics of the financial support for the station, he stated that the company at this time was "not going to attempt to make money through commercial sponsors" and added again that royalties from licenses and contracts should be sufficient, "[i]f not, stockholders would supply the deficit as they have done in the past."[73]

Under cross-examination, Farnsworth's lawyer objected to the publishing of the company finances. They did not want to reveal details to their competitors, but they did indicate a willingness to allow the Commission to examine it. Farnsworth admitted that based on current resources it would be likely that "stockholder[s] will have to advance additional funds."[74] The general intent of Farnsworth's comments on his finances and commercial television was to assure the FCC that he was financially stable. He knew the FCC was not ready to approve such commercial operation. However, his statements illustrate the comparatively minuscule state of financial affairs, Farnsworth's own attitude toward finances, and his future. He'd had financial problems from the beginning, but his supporters had always come to his rescue.

The technical facilities of the proposed station were described as "well-equipped laboratories," "a television studio," having "three separate camera channels, with provisions for showing both outdoor and indoor television 'shots,'" and engineers "capable of making the equipment needed."[75] The studios were almost complete at the filing of the application, and work was beginning on the transmitter. However, completion and continued experimentation depended on FCC approval.

The evidence presented in the August 20 hearing was taken under consideration by FCC examiner Rosel H. Hyde, with the granting of the license still pending.[76] On October 30, 1936, Hyde recommended Farnsworth receive permission to construct the station.[77] The Commission accepted the recommendation, December 1, 1936, granting Farnsworth's application for a new experimental visual broadcast station, effective January 5, 1937.[78] Farnsworth's first wholly owned station, W3XPF, became the sixteenth experimental television station in the United States to begin operation.[79]

W3XPF: EXPERIMENTATION AND PROGRAMMING

W3XPF was the flagship station of Farnsworth Television Incorporated. With the construction permit granted, engineers worked long hours to put the station on the air. George Jenkins and William C. Eddy drafted the station design. Initial plans included a studio, offices, a transmitter room, and monitor space.[80] All studio and transmission equipment in the station was manufactured by Farnsworth's engineers or purchased through license agreement. The studio had two cameras and a telecine channel for transmission of motion pictures.[81] Schatzkin credits the Farnsworth engineers with developing the first video switcher to accommodate the two camera set-up in the studio.[82] This "video fader" was being developed by two of Farnsworth's engineers, Frank J. Somers and B. J. Herbert.[83] It allowed for "smooth fading from the closeup to the long shots and reverse."[84] Eddy worked on indicator lights so that people would know "if their program was being fed to the transmitter."[85] In addition to warning and studio lights, Eddy worked on other experiments concerning the interlace scanning pulse, interlace scanning generator, transmitter RF, and the transmitter tower. The 774-foot tower still stands. At each stage the experiments and results were submitted to Farnsworth for approval and/or modification. He was in charge.[86]

The station was granted authority to operate with one kilowatt of power with frequencies from 42,000 to 56,000 KHz visual and from 60,000 to 86,000 KHz aural,[87] but it actually signed on the air at 62,750 and 66,000 KHz, respectively.[88]

Plans were to have three hours of daily programming. The Farnsworth crew decided that the programs for television had to be shorter than radio's in

W3XPF facilities and lab crew, 1936. Courtesy Arizona State University.

Farnsworth Television experimental station, W3XPF, studio building. Courtesy University of Utah Archives, P0437 1:20:4.

Farnsworth Television experimental station, W3XPF, transmitter building. Courtesy University of Utah Archives, P0437 1:20:5.

order to hold and maintain audience interest, "which is admittedly more difficult to hold for both visual and auditory media than for auditory alone."[89] Eddy was in charge of programming.[90] His challenge—to arrange a continuing program schedule—was more complex than a single demonstration. The station simply didn't have the funding to engage in commercial program experimentation in competetion with RCA, which already had a commercial radio network and experience with the entertainment industry.[91] Programming was necessary to illustrate technical progress, however, so Eddy lined up local talent, skits, playlets, song and dance materials from radio, films of sports figures, and animated cartoons.[92] In general, the first broadcasts originating from the studio were all live. Pem Farnsworth described some of the humor of these live events.

> The bright red trunks of one boxer were not visible on the monitor; he seemed to be boxing in the nude . . . A similar incident [occurred] when a professional ballet dancer came to perform for a special group, only this time the problem was that the material from which her costume was made was invisible to the camera.[93]

The events all originated in the studio where Eddy had arranged several different stages to facilitate the live activities. Makeup for performers proved to be

Demonstration features Nick Ross and his orchestra and "Smiles" Blum (age eleven) and Baby Doloras (age four) who sang and tap-danced. Two Farnsworth camera operators (center and right) focus on the children performers while technicians work around the perimeter. This photo is from the Philadelphia studios. Courtesy ITT.

Early 1936–1938 receiver prototype. Note the period caption describing television makeup. Courtesy Arizona State University.

Period Caption: Before making up his subject with revolutionary television makeup, **Max Factor, Jr.** views the televised image of **Elaine Sheppard** in this television receiving set, with **Bart Molinari**, Farnsworth technician, operating the controls. Tests also made with motion picture makeup resulted in similar poor results. Filtered through television equipment, all of the natural and makeup shadings have vanished from Miss Sheppard's face. Note that there is no clear definition on any of her features, such as the eyes, nose, and lips, which "wash out" completely. The effacement of lip and cheek rouge are particularly obvious, clearly demonstrating why a completely different type of makeup, than that used for either street or screen, is necessary for the reception of a clear defined image in television. A television receiving set of this type operates on ordinary house current much the same as a radio. When commercial production on these sets is reached, they will sell for $250 to $450 [$3,079 to $5,542].

a bit different for television than it was for film and stage performances, so a representative from Max Factor was brought in to work with Laura Player (Farnsworth's sister) and develop proper makeup for television.[94] Eddy described the excitement and the pressures of the Philadelphia lab:

> We knew nothing about what was going on at RCA. They were able to keep their work under wraps because they had all the financing they had . . . we were forced to make every move we made very obvious to the public in the hopes of getting new investors and new money. If we didn't have money we didn't get paid. Phil would sometimes give us fifteen dollars or twenty dollars and a couple of shares of stock . . . To eat, we'd go to the Italian market in South Philadelphia and buy a gunnysack of week-old bread for one dollar. Bread, and rabbits that I raised on our farm in Philadelphia, constituted my family's menu. Still, there was no lack of enthusiasm. We were either naive or crazy. If morale dropped, Phil would get up on his platform and start spouting his ideas, and we were back in the battery again. He was a world class promoter and P.R. man.[95]

Newspaper and magazine reports of the period make it sound like television coverage was universal. However, as noted, few people had receiving sets. Farnsworth rallied his men, conducted the demonstrations, and often appeared in publicity photos. He answered questions and directed the technical aspects of the exhibits. Farnsworth's programming orientation seemed to surround the idea that sight and sound would allow "spot coverage of news events" and sports. He envisioned the day when the public would be able to see an event as "soon as we can get our trucks to the scene."[96]

The station was not without its trials, both personal and financial. Farnsworth's brother Lincoln had an accident while working on a television chassis in the studio that cost him his sight in one eye.[97] On the one hand, Farnsworth felt he had in place the best team of engineers in the world, all coming into focus at the station and agreements with CBS and AT&T were in the works. On the other hand, the continual struggle to raise funds led to increasing clashes between he and McCargar.

CBS-FARNSWORTH SALES CONTRACT

One proposal providing optimism for Farnsworth Television was an invitation to bid for work with CBS in establishing a studio, cameras, and transmitting facility. McCargar, of course, saw CBS as an opportunity to free himself of his responsibilities and generate "a lineup with Columbia, Philco, or some other manufacturer."[98] However, Farnsworth was working on a separate deal to design the studio, sell transmitters, and license his system to CBS. According to the 1937 report to the stockholders of Farnsworth Television Incorporated, the deal included an order for the "manufacture of television studio equipment comprising of two complete camera channels."[99] The catalyst in the negotiations was the idea that CBS was looking to expand into television.

At this time, there were only four primary radio networks: NBC Red and Blue (both owned by RCA/NBC), the Mutual Broadcasting Company (which was not moving into television), and CBS. *Business Week* described the negotiations as the "CBS-Farnsworth Deal," but their headline was premature.[100] No deal had been reached. Everson reports that Farnsworth held numerous demonstrations for CBS.[101] The plan, according to *Business Week,* was to have a transmitter installed at the top of the Chrysler Building in New York City and allow independent inventors, such as Farnsworth, "a chance to test and prove their sending and receiving equipment."[102]

A letter from Ed Cohan, CBS director of general engineering, seems to suggest that negotiations were serious. He was leaving town and referred communications between CBS and Farnsworth to Paul Kesten, vice president of CBS.[103] If Farnsworth was willing to test his system at CBS, CBS could gain access to competitive technical information and compete with RCA. CBS was particularly interested in Farnsworth because he was "the biggest independent interest in the field [and] boasts basic patents to rival RCA's own."[104] To Farnsworth's advantage, the move would have extended his work actively into New York and aligned them with CBS, a growing company with a progressive radio network.

But a critical view of the CBS proposal suggests an RCA advantage. It was rumored that RCA might have engineered negotiations between Farnsworth and CBS to force Farnsworth to reveal his position just before the inevitable RCA patent settlement. RCA and Farnsworth were still disputing patents (see Chapter 4).

Farnsworth did demonstrate his system for CBS; however, the deal, no matter what the motivation from CBS or RCA, included only the sale of Farnsworth equipment to CBS. In other words, the arrangement boiled down to a sales contract for specific electronic devices. Lippincott commented on the Farnsworth and CBS agreement indicating it was his feeling, "that the way the Columbia deal is working out is probably the best for all concerned."[105] He questioned Seymour Turner's ability to handle both studio equipment and transmitters, then concluded that RCA's "getting the transmitter job . . . [would] modify their hostility."[106] Putting the CBS arrangements in a positive light, Everson reported that Dr. Peter Goldmark, the key CBS engineer looking to move his company into television, was a regular customer for the Farnsworth dissector tubes. This had a wholesome effect on the tube department of Farnsworth Television.[107]

Seymour "Skee" Turner and Philo Farnsworth in front of W3XPF studio. It was the Turner family of San Francisco who largely funded the studio. Courtesy Elma G. Farnsworth.

The CBS-Farnsworth association generated more favorable publicity. Abramson reported that CBS was experimenting with the Farnsworth image dissector tube and electron multiplier.[108] Although there was no big contract for a studio or joint transmission experiments, Farnsworth television equipment was sold to CBS.

AT&T-FARNSWORTH PATENT AGREEMENT

By the mid-1930s, Farnsworth had license agreements with Baird Television of Britain and Fernseh A.G. of Germany (the Marconi-EMI system would not be adopted until 1937); CBS was using the Farnsworth dissector and electron multiplier and Farnsworth had a station on the air. At the same time, with Farnsworth Television in the middle of patent litigation with RCA and the differences with Jesse McCargar at an all-time high, an agreement with AT&T appeared the most promising development.

The negotiations with AT&T came about through Donald Lippincott's association with AT&T's chief patent attorney, George Folk, who asked Lippincott to suggest a cross-licensing arrangement with AT&T.[109] Two other names important to these negotiations were Hugh Knowlton and Carl Christensen. Conversations between Knowlton and Everson included Farnsworth and Farnsworth Television financing. Christensen had worked for Farnsworth before being employed by Bell Labs.[110] As a result of these associations, a series of meetings was set in motion between AT&T and Farnsworth.

AT&T technical personnel were invited to the Philadelphia lab for demonstrations and meetings with Farnsworth and Dr. Herbert E. Ives, who was Bell Telephone's chief television research scientist.[111] At these meetings Everson reported on Farnsworth's charm: "I was proud of Phil in his conference with them [AT&T]. As always, he was modest in his presentation, but I could see that they were impressed with the brilliance and originality of his conceptions."[112]

Formal meetings were followed by inspections of patent portfolios.[113] Everson noted that Farnsworth's disclosure was not without its dangers. Farnsworth had heretofore been careful in revealing proprietary research. He was persuaded to reveal his materials openly to AT&T, as earlier communications between Hugh Knowlton and Frank B. Jewett, a vice president of AT&T, had created a degree of trust between them. In meetings between Jewett, Knowlton, and Farnsworth on the CBS-Farnsworth contract, Jewett reported there would be no "difficulty in our extending a license to Mr. Farnsworth for the experiments he has in mind."[114] Farnsworth wanted to use AT&T lines between Philadelphia and New York. AT&T reasoned that it had licensed other manufacturers and could surely license Farnsworth. The cross-licensing of patent agreements, however, was not as simple as providing wired connections between cities. The Bell engineers examined Farnsworth's patent portfolio for four months, an anxious time for Farnsworth.

As the communication between Farnsworth and AT&T scientists progressed, McCargar continued his push to sell Farnsworth Television. He wanted more meetings so he could attend to take advantage of a situation that was "hotter than ever." He was still seeking to sell out but was also working for another reorganization plan for Farnsworth Television. He had "ideas . . . about a lineup with AT&T."[115]

A patent cross-licensing agreement between Farnsworth Television and AT&T was announced July 22, 1937.[116] It gave each the right to use the other's patents and showed AT&T's recognition of the value of Farnsworth's work. It was an agreement with as much psychological importance to Farnsworth personally as it was legally and technically important to Farnsworth Television. "Farnsworth had such high regard for Bell Laboratories [AT&T] that it seemed to him almost too good to be true that they should give formal recognition to the fruits of his years of research and effort."[117] The signing of the agreement was an emotional moment for Farnsworth; it represented a respected peer's acceptance of his life's work.[118]

But the agreement was more than an acceptance of his work. For Farnsworth, it created access to some 6,000 AT&T patents in a nonexclusive agreement.[119] It also gave him a "strong trading position."[120] Farnsworth's access to AT&T patents enabled him to "compete with RCA on more equal terms."[121] According to *Business Week,* "[t]he deal means the grip which the Radio Corporation of America was generally assumed to have on the future of American television was relaxed."[122] Donald Lippincott reflected Farnsworth's interests when he declared that the agreement "clears the path for cooperation between the Bell System, Farnsworth, and certain Farnsworth licensees, helps to clarify a difficult patent situation, and brings one step nearer the broad use of television and other advances in communication."[123] The agreement was a major coup for Farnsworth Television.

Headlines in the Beverly Hills *Citizen,* where Everson was seeking publicity and capital, clearly placed Farnsworth in control. A nearly full-page article with photographs mentions RCA as having only an alternative system.[124] The publicity sought to spark increasing interest for consumers while raising money from investors. Television was to be the industrial boom and Farnsworth was to be at the forefront.[125]

FARNSWORTH TELEVISION REORGANIZATION PLANNED

Overriding the favorable publicity, the program experiments, and the CBS and AT&T agreements was the continuing conflict between Farnsworth and

McCargar. It would be the catalyst for Farnsworth's most important corporate endeavor—manufacturing.

Reorganization of the Farnsworth Television company was made possible through Hugh Knowlton, a partner in the investment banking firm of Kuhn, Loeb and Company. They would finance Farnsworth in exchange for modest compensation and "an option on a limited block of Farnsworth stock."[126] This would relieve Everson and McCargar from the task of raising funds and allow Farnsworth to create a chain of stations, extend his experimentation, and, a step he'd resisted previously, get into manufacturing.

McCargar and Everson saw Farnsworth as an opportunity in a highly speculative venture when they first decided to invest. As costs and demands grew on this investment, however, McCargar tired of the responsibility of raising the money for a growing and expensive television laboratory (see table of laboratory expenses). He wanted relief, and Farnsworth wanted out from underneath McCargar. Everson claims, "neither McCargar nor I ever received any salary or fees as compensation from the [Farnsworth] company."[127] Between 1929 and 1938, it was reported that McCargar spent "in excess of one-half of his time" working for Farnsworth, "for which he has never received any salary or other compensation."[128] Although this statement was literally true, it would be incorrect to assume there were no profits. When the Philco agreement was reached to support Farnsworth research in 1931, McCargar received $112,500 [$1,365,909]; and he profited additionally between 1930 and 1938 when he sold shares in Farnsworth Television for a value of $222,000 [$2,695,400], "a portion of which was used for [his] corporate purposes."[129] Working with Farnsworth was a profitable activity.

Farnsworth returned from his trip to Europe at the height of McCargar's frustration. He found McCargar's men, Pond and Sleeper, and an engineering crew frustrated and unwilling to continue work with the McCargar personnel. So Farnsworth immediately fired Pond and Sleeper. Just days later, McCargar appeared at Philo's office door and demanded he fire the whole engineering

Farnsworth Television Incorporated Laboratory Expenses

1929:	$15,484.17	[$154,980]	1934:	$47,183.87	[$602,770]
1930:	16,228.92	[166,380]	1935:	70,631.55	[882,610]
1931:	59,287.06	[667,740]	1936:	126,870.90	[1,562,900]
1932:	93,182.50	[1,164,400]	1937:	143,299.55	[1,703,600]
1933:	54,524.48	[717,980]	1938:	109,406.28	[1,328,300]

Source: "Registration Statement," Development Expenses for Farnsworth Television, Securities and Exchange Commission, p. S-13. Donald K. Lippincott Papers.

Technical Progress to Date: 1938

Patents. Through 1938 Farnsworth had filed for a total of ninety-one different patents. Primary patents involved improvements on the image dissector and film transmission. The "scanning means," and "projection apparatus" (patents no. 2,280,572 and no. 2,091,705) combined the outputs for interlaced scanning and film transmission. The "photoelectric cells" (patent BR no. 468,333 filed March 13, 1935) detailed the manufacturing process for the image dissector tube. Patent no. 2,155,478 details a picture tube with an incandescent screen. The "electron image amplifier" (patent no. 2,292,437 filed July 1, 1935) modified the image dissector. His most important patents of the period

P. T. Farnsworth with the Wyndmoor Studio monitor, 1936–1937. Courtesy Elma G. Farnsworth.

Technical Progress to Date: 1938 (continued)

were his "means of electron multiplication" (no. 2,143,262), the "charge storage dissector" (no. 2,140,695), and the "scanning current generator" (no. 2,214,077). The electron multiplication took a small output and built up the current, thus improving the picture. The charge storage dissector enhanced photocell storage. The scanning current generator provided a means of capturing high-voltage surplus scanning energy and returning it to brighten the picture tube. This was an important Farnsworth patent. Numerous patents were improvements on earlier ones and thus simply divided from the originals.

Comment. Between 1934 and 1938 Farnsworth had put another experimental television station on the air in Philadelphia, W3XPF. In 1936 he demonstrated the "cold" tube power concept before the New York Radio Engineers meeting. His latest television camera was used to televise the 1936 Olympic games. By 1937 he had started field tests at 441 lines.

a. See Appendix A. Also George Shiers, *Early Television: A Bibliographical Guide to 1940* (New York: Garland Publishing, 1997). Shiers indexes the U.S. patents issued Farnsworth including those divided and filed in Britain. Also see interview with Albert Abramson, July 16, 1999.

b. "Television News Shorts," *Radio-Craft* 8 (April 1937: 583.

Farnsworth Television broadcast equipment.
W3XPF Philadelphia, 1937–1938.

crew. Farnsworth refused, so McCargar walked out into the lab and yelled, "You're all fired!" The men left, even though Farnsworth tried to assure them they were still employed. Everson was summoned from New York and worked again to calm McCargar, but many of the men refused to return as long as McCargar was there. Any tolerance and compassion by Farnsworth and the laboratory personnel that might have existed for McCargar's service in the past was gone.[130] McCargar had become an "unpredictable threat to the entire enterprise."[131] Farnsworth decided to take some time off to gather his thoughts. A short trip to Bermuda allowed the family to relax and Farnsworth to reflect upon his situation.

When they returned, Farnsworth took action. A meeting of Farnsworth loyalists on the board was called in early 1937 to discuss how the company might be reorganized and get funding sufficient to enter into manufacturing.[132] McCargar was not invited to the meeting. He knew his influence was slipping, and one of the goals in the reorganization was to diminish his direct intervention. Farnsworth described the meeting in a letter to his mother. "Business matters have gone from bad to worse . . . The Board of Directors [met] here at home on Saturday." Farnsworth went on to describe the results of the meeting.

> We will manufacture both receivers and transmitters. We will erect and operate television broadcasting stations. We will modify our licensing policy to provide the

Philo and Pem Farnsworth pose for photo on the beach of Bermuda, November 1937. From left to right: Mr. and Mrs. Fred Lambert, New York; Mrs. Richard Hoyt, Danbury, Connecticut; Mr. and Mrs. Philo T. Farnsworth. Foreground: Lois Gardner, Pem's sister and Philo Jr. Lifeguard in rear. Courtesy Elma G. Farnsworth.

> greatest use for all the radio industry. We will negotiate all the cross-licensing necessary to permit us to enter the entire radio and television field. [McCargar will resign] from the company in favor of a highly paid technical executive.[133]

Everson supported this expansion plan as an opportunity to "have a proving-out field for the use of our patents in a production plant."[134] He arranged the meeting with Hugh Knowlton and his partners at Kuhn, Loeb and Company, but it would take several years to reorganize the company as a manufacturing entity. Financial arrangements had to be solidified; the organizational and operational structure had to be redeveloped; and a facility had to be built or bought. It would be almost two years before the new Farnsworth Television and Radio would be a reality. Bartley C. Crum, a legal representative of the Farnsworth Television stockholders and soon-to-be member of the new board of directors, expressed the sentiment that "with Hugh and his partners in the picture I think we may all feel and know that the Farnsworth interests will be adequately protected against the attacks that will undoubtedly come."[135] During the transition period, Farnsworth busied himself in the laboratory, and nineteen more patents were filed for 1937 and 1938.[136]

In spring 1938, Farnsworth took another vacation to Everson's property east of Brownfield, Maine. It was so enjoyable that the family bought the land. With the purchase came grand plans to build a home and another lab. Pem Farnsworth describes the joys and challenges they all faced in a letter to Everson:

> I can hardly tell you what acquiring this place in Maine means to us. This summer we kept Phil going at the lab by spending roughly a third of our time fishing . . . I was terribly worried because he hadn't been able to build up any reserve energy . . . When we left Phil was all upset and nervous and hadn't eaten in two days . . . [H]is nerves [are] better than they had been for years.[137]

6

Farnsworth Television and Radio Corporation

1938–1942

Chronology

Farnsworth

Spring 1938 — Laboratory work slows as reorganization plans begin, and Farnsworths head for Maine to relax.

December 13, 1938 — New Farnsworth Television and Radio Corporation organized. Edwin A. Nicholas becomes the president and begins immediately to organize manufacturing and distribution. Farnsworth becomes vice president in charge of research.

1939 — Seven more patents filed this year.
• Farnsworth Television and Radio begins a cross-country promotional tour featuring their mobile television units.

January 1939 — Farnsworth appears before the National Temporary Economic Committee investigating the patent office and monopoly questions. Farnsworth's testimony gains him allies in the patent office and with AT&T and RCA.

February 1939 — Farnsworth Television and Radio purchases Capehart Corporation plant in Fort Wayne, Indiana.

Electronic Media

1938 — Orson Welles's famous *War of the Worlds* radio program creates panic.
• Mutual Broadcasting System requests investigation of radio monopoly.
• Armstrong establishes first FM station, W2XMN, in New Jersey.
• Elmer Davis begins broadcasting just before the Germans march into Poland.
• Norman Corwin's *The Plot to Overthrow Christmas* airs.
• Columbia Records purchased by CBS.
• CBS radio inaugurates *CBS News Roundup* as fighting escalates in Europe.

1939 — Broadcast Music Incorporated (BMI) formed as a competitor to ASCAP.
• RCA inaugurates regular television programming at New York World's Fair.
• Armstrong establishes FM station in New York.
• RCA agrees to pay Farnsworth for use of patents.
• RCA and others put television receivers on the market.

Farnsworth

March 1939 — Farnsworth Television and Radio purchases General Household Utilities Company plant in Marion, Indiana.

April 1939 — New York World's Fair used by RCA to launch their system of television.
• Financially unable to participate in the World's Fair, the Farnsworth Corporation remote vans tour nationwide with demonstrations.

May 1939 — FCC's Advisory Committee recommends delaying establishment of final television standards.

June 1939 — N. W. Ayer & Sons Inc. contracted to handle Farnsworth Corporation advertising and public relations.

Summer 1939 — Farnsworth suffers nervous breakdown and is hospitalized in Boston. Returns to Maine.

August 1939 — First dealer sales distribution meeting held for Farnsworth Television and Radio to promote radio models available. Dealers told television sets would be available December 1939.

September 1939 — Farnsworth and RCA reach patent agreement. RCA pays $1 million in royalties for use of Farnsworth's patents.

February 1940 — Farnsworth and corporate representatives testify before Senate committee appearing to defend RCA and recommend adoption of the Radio Manufacturers Association's (RMA's) television standards.

April 1940 — David Sarnoff testifying before the Senate Interstate Commerce Committee notes that 1936–39 British Broadcasting Corporation (BBC) television operation was based on both RCA and Farnsworth's research.
• Farnsworth supports RMA standards along with RCA.

Electronic Media

July 1939 — RCA and other manufacturers place initial 441-line television receivers on the market.

1940 — Census figures indicate 44 million radios in America (1935 figures indicated 33 million radio homes).
• Listening hours reported at five hours per day.
• One world versus isolationism becomes the focus of radio discussion.
• FCC temporarily approves 441-line system.

May 1941 — FCC adopts RMA television standards, but hopes are quickly dashed for television

Farnsworth

Electronic Media

as President Franklin D. Roosevelt declares a state of emergency and redirects raw materials necessary for radio and television manufacturing to war materials.

1941 — FCC issues *Chain Broadcasting Report*, NBC forced to give up one of its networks.
• FCC authorizes commercial FM operations. Also issues first Mayflower Decision, which forbids station editorializing.
• FDR's declaration of war produces a radio audience of 90 million, 79 percent of all American homes.
• Howard K. Smith, Charles Collingwood, and Cecil Brown join the CBS network.
• FCC adopts 525-line standard.

1942 — Office of Censorship opens; censorship to be voluntary to assist in war efforts.
• Elmer Davis heads the Office of War Information.

May 1942 — War Production Board officially orders a halt to further construction of stations so materials can be directed toward the war.
• American Armed Forces Radio begins.
• FCC bans construction of new stations due to war efforts.

≈

THE CREATION OF THE FARNSWORTH TELEVISION AND RADIO CORPORATION IN LATE 1938 was the pinnacle of Philo's life and career. During the previous decade, Farnsworth had risen from obscurity to become an important figure in television history; he was counted among America's Top Ten Young Men of 1939 and one of the world's greatest scientists.[1] He controlled a growing list of important television patents; he had reached cross-licensing agreements with Baird Television in Britain, Fernseh A.G. in Germany, and Philco and AT&T in the United States; and he was about to reach a historic settlement with RCA. He had publicly demonstrated electronic television in San Francisco and in Philadelphia, all before the 1936 BBC inauguration of regular television service in London and RCA's demonstrations at the 1939 New York World's Fair. He had put two experimental television stations on the air—one for Philco and a second for Farnsworth Television. Farnsworth had grown to become a presence even RCA could not ignore. Equally important, the Farnsworth name had market value.

Until 1939, the family name of Philo Farnsworth and the corporate entities of Television Laboratories and Farnsworth Television were synonymous. Although the corporate names reflected different eras within the growth years—talking about Phil Farnsworth the person was the same as talking about his companies. He was effectively the individual in charge. He was the heart of the operation—full-time inventor, engineer, entrepreneur, the chief stockholder, the corporate vice president, and, most importantly, the catalyst. His activities in the laboratory were paramount to the organization, and his decisions established the firm's overall direction. Now, all of this was about to change.

The new Farnsworth Television and Radio Corporation separated the direct influence of the man from the corporation that still bore his name. Farnsworth, the man, would continue his developmental role, but the Farnsworth corporation would now be under the leadership of others.

ORGANIZING FARNSWORTH TELEVISION AND RADIO CORPORATION

Farnsworth had led the operation into its strongest position. The Farnsworth company had a portfolio of seventy-three patents issued, with another sixty pending. Of those granted, Farnsworth was the inventor or coinventor of forty-nine.[2] Of the patents pending, he was the inventor of forty-six.[3] The list of his patents was his base for the future, and it was an impressive one. He had patents registered not only in the United States, but in European and Commonwealth countries as well.[4]

The new corporation would use the Farnsworth name and reputation to become a manufacturing and distribution entity as well as to continue as a research organization. The credit for its creation is as follows: Farnsworth contributed his inventive genius; Everson his tireless fund-raising efforts; and Knowlton assembled the financial package.

The Farnsworth Television and Radio Corporation was first organized December 13, 1938, under the laws of the State of Delaware, where it was more easily organized, and was temporarily titled the Farnsworth Television and Radio Distributing Corporation.[5] This temporary name hailed its new direction, and Farnsworth Television Incorporated as a California corporation was effectively dissolved.[6] The official nature of the corporation's business was listed as retail radio.[7] The plan called for continued research as well as the manufacture and sale of radio, phonograph sets, television receivers, transmitters, and special [television] apparatus.[8] The first officers were old names: McCargar, Everson,

Edwin A. Nicholas, president, Farnsworth Television and Radio Corporation, 1939–1949. Courtesy ITT.

Lippincott, Crum, and Farnsworth. These were transitional officers; only Farnsworth and Everson would be formally employed full-time by the new corporation.[9]

The first order of business was to hire management. An executive search led to Edwin A. Nicholas, a veteran of wireless engineering and one of the vice presidents of RCA.[10] Nicholas had three characteristics that made him attractive to the corporation: He knew the workings of RCA; he had an engineering background; and he had sales and distribution experience. Nicholas was wooed with a salary of more than $35,000 [$424,964], 5,000 shares, plus stock options on 50,000 shares.[11] He agreed to take the helm as soon as finances were organized.

The financial agent in the company was Hugh Knowlton, who suggested that, in order to finance the business, the corporation float 2 million shares of common stock, at a par value of $1 per share.[12] The first shares were distributed to existing stockholders, who received forty-six shares for [every] one held, in the old company.[13] Once the reorganization became effective, these shares were distributed to the directors and stockholders of the original Farnsworth Television.[14] In all, the assets of the old company were basically transferred to the new company for 690,000 shares of its stock.[15] Then, more importantly, the sale of the 2 million shares was promoted to underwriters and offered on the open market.[16]

Farnsworth Television and Radio Corporation Initial Stock Distributions

Farnsworth (the Farnsworth family held 10.7% of the shares)	65,377.5 shares
Kuhn, Loeb and Company (8.78%)	38,778.0 shares
Everson (3.37%)	23,253.0 shares
McCargar (3.29%)	22,781.5 shares

Each share had a par value of one dollar. However, the price per share on the market was six dollars. For total assets see "Registration Statement," p. S-5, Donald K. Lippincott Papers.

Three million dollars was netted.[17] It was the financial foundation for a company evolving from the Depression.[18] The *New York Times* described the first budget in broad terms as providing $2 million [$24,633,000] for "working capital and inventory requirements [with] other portions of the proceeds . . . for research and development activities and for plant improvements."[19] The *Times* estimated a "capitalization consisting of 1,401,007 shares of common stock, including 690,000 issued to its predecessor company . . . 600,000 shares presently offered to the public, and 111,097 shares" issued in connection with the purchase of two manufacturing plants.[20]

NEW MANUFACTURING CAPABILITY

Plant operation was the next priority for the reorganization. The question was whether to buy or build a manufacturing facility. The Depression had produced difficult times for many smaller radio manufacturers, so there were a number of plants available. The two acquired, Capehart Incorporated and the General Household Utilities Company, were located in Fort Wayne and Marion,

Period photos from a Farnsworth newsletter illustrate the plants' size and layout. The top photo is of the Fort Wayne plant, and the second photo is of the Marion plant. Courtesy ITT.

Indiana—a long way from Philadelphia. Capehart had a reputation for building quality phonographs.[21] By the end of the 1930s, the Depression had taken a heavy toll and Homer Capehart was ready to move on to other business ventures—a great opportunity for the Farnsworth organization.[22] On February 28, 1939, Capehart "real estate, plants, factories . . . all patents, patent licenses or other patent application rights . . . and all trade marks [and] trade rights" were purchased for $261,586.48 [$3,222,000].[23] The plan was to combine the quality brand of Capehart with the Farnsworth name to market a prestigious line of radio and television receivers.

The General Household Utilities Company was purchased on March 30, 1939.[24] It had suffered the effects of the economy and had closed its doors in 1937.[25] Plants of both firms would be activated, retooled, and become the headquarters for the Farnsworth company.[26]

The new Farnsworth Television and Radio Corporation joined a large and growing number of receiver manufacturers.[27] RCA, DuMont, General Electric, Philco Radio and Television, the American Television Corporation, and the Andrea Radio Corporation had all announced plans to begin selling television receivers by 1939.[28] RCA was well ahead because it not only operated research laboratories and manufacturing plants, it also had entertainment radio networks that would help support television financially and eventually give them access to a programming base for commercial television. RCA's line of television receivers, which went on sale in July 1939, included four different models (only Philco had more), with the size of the screen ranging from five to twelve inches and a retail price of $150 to $600 [$1,847 to $7,390].[29] There was little profit from these early sets because, with no FCC-approved standard, there was little market demand and only limited programming was available.

Philip Kirby provides an interesting financial insight of television in 1939. He estimated that approximately $25 million was spent on television research and experimentation between 1919 and 1939, with two-thirds of that coming between 1934 and 1939. The corporate shares of this investment, according to Kirby, were RCA and subsidiaries, $10 million; CBS, General Electric, Farnsworth, Westinghouse, and the Don Lee System investments together totaling $4 million; and $9 million spent in Britain. The figures are generalized, secondary information, but still provide an interesting competitive perspective.[30] The financial figures for RCA and Farnsworth, from about the same time, dramatically reflect the size difference. RCA's net income for 1940 was reported to its stockholders at more than $17 million with its assets totaling almost $104 million.[31] Just prior to the organization of Farnsworth Television and Radio Corporation, Bartley C. Crum, a San Francisco attorney, calculated Farnsworth Television's total assets at just over $1 million [$207,885,000 for RCA and $12,228,500 for Farnsworth].[32]

FROM MANUFACTURING TO SALES

By March 1939, just one month prior to the New York World's Fair, Nicholas had appointed Ernest H. Vogal as vice president in charge of sales and merchandising.[33] In May, J. P. Rogers and B. R. Cummings were named vice presidents. Rogers, who was imported from the Crosley Radio Corporation, brought manufacturing experience.[34] Cummings came on board as the vice president of engineering.[35] In June, N. W. Ayer & Son was contracted to handle advertising and public relations from their Chicago office.[36] Handling the sales was Pierre Boucheron, another management executive imported from RCA. As general sales manager, he supervised direct sales, merchandising, advertising, and promotion.[37] Each corporate executive was given stock options in addition to salary.[38]

The two plants were retooled and readied for manufacturing by April 1939 (the month of the New York World's Fair).[39] In August a sales and distribution plan recruited franchised, territorial sales distributors and directed sales to the nation's largest retailers. The plan divided the country into geographic sales territories with distributors that handled wholesale marketing within each.[40] The direct sale of radio and television sets to major retailers was to be handled out of the Fort Wayne office. The "Farnsworth Radio Book of Facts" provided information, sales hype, and details regarding the specific new radio and phonograph models manufactured.[41]

The first Farnsworth dealers were organized in August 1939. At the meeting in New York, they were promised twenty-eight different radio models with a large national newspaper and magazine advertising campaign for sales support, along with "billboards and point-of-sale materials," followed by initial television receivers to be available by December 1939.[42] In San Francisco the Frank Edwards Company invited dealers from California to an exhibit of the 1940 Farnsworth line of new radios.[43] Dealers in Fort Wayne were given a demonstration of television that included still photograph shots, a singing group, dramatic skits, and the invitation for the audience to come forward and be televised. Vogal assured the distributors that television was not intended to replace radio. He said: "We take our radio programs as an incidental part of our life . . . We listen to a radio while playing bridge, reading the paper or even while conversing. In television our habits must change . . . We must sit for an hour . . . or two hours whatever the length of the program we wish to see. And we can do practically nothing else while that is going on. In other words we will attend our television programs as we now attend moving picture shows."[44]

The first receivers off the Farnsworth manufacturing line were radios.[45] Among the brand names used were Farnsworth, Capehart-Panamuse, and Capehart. The Farnsworth, which was the least expensive set manufactured,

The "Farnsworth Radio Book of Facts" was a 1939 booklet distributed to dealers. This twelve-page promotion chronicled the history of Farnsworth and provided details on specific models.

..The Genius of Television

Modern television— employing the electronic principles of image transmission — starts in story-book fashion as the dream of a high-school boy — Philo T. Farnsworth.

How for many ambitious years this dream was shaped by heroic struggle, force and circumstance, laughter and tears, is a story that some day will take its place with others which have made names like Bell and Marconi immortal.

No great invention is ever wholly the story of one man. But out of the story of television emerges the giant figure of Philo T. Farnsworth, guiding genius, lonely experimenter, scoffed-at dreamer — history already has a page reserved for this man who, convinced that mechanical principles were wrong, held fast to his theories and made television a practical reality—today's front-page scientific discovery.

"HE PROFITS MOST WHO SERVES BEST"

You have chosen to sell the new Farnsworth Radio. You, therefore, have a great opportunity and a great responsibility. This book is designed to help you make the most of this opportunity — and to assist you in discharging your responsibility honorably.

Farnsworth—television's greatest name—enters the radio industry with no past to live down. Its name is unsullied. In the building of Farnsworth Radio great care has been taken to give the public the greatest dollar value that engineering skill, experience, and resources make possible. There is no place in such a background for exaggeration or misrepresentation — nor is there a need for any other policy than one of truth and honesty.

Farnsworth believes that in the values it offers, in its respected name, in its emphasis upon straightforward dealing — lies the formula for your success as well as its own. To depart from this policy would be folly — and it is the purpose of this book to tell you — in a language uncolored by false claims —what Farnsworth brings to radio and why Farnsworth represents the logical choice of consumers eager to get the most for their money!

FARNSWORTH TELEVISION & RADIO CORPORATION

Fort Wayne, Ind.

F
Farnsworth
THE HOME OF TELEVISION
FARNSWORTH TELEVISION & RADIO CORP.
FORT WAYNE, INDIANA
Form No. 106

sold for between $15 and $275 [$184 to $3,363]; the Capehart-Panamuse was the midrange set priced between $150 and $300 [$1,834 to $3,669]; and, the Capehart was the prestige instrument selling from $500 and $2,500 [$6,114 to $30,571].[46] The price depended upon the combination of radio and phonograph equipment within the set. These were the options with which Farnsworth hoped to capture the consumer market.

The advertising campaign promoted a number of different Farnsworth radios. In October the *Saturday Evening Post* carried a two-page advertisement emphasizing "The Greatest Name in *Television* Is the Newest Name in *Radio*—Farnsworth." The first-page pictorial was a laboratory setting featuring Farnsworth at work on a dissector tube. A third of the page gave the Farnsworth story, "Out of America comes another name . . . [t]o take its place with Fulton, Bell and Edison. Eighteen years ago, when radios still had headphones, an earnest Idaho farm boy . . .," and the famous story is romanticized for its commercial value.[47] The second page featured eight different models for sale—two tabletop and six consoles with prices ranging from $9.95 to $99.95 [$122 to $1,223]. All of the consoles were captioned as having a "television bridge," which would allow the consumer to adapt an audio hookup for their television set when it became available. The small print at the bottom of the page invited dealers to telegraph "for full information about the most important franchise since 1930."[48]

Everson reported that initial sales were very successful. "By the middle of August [1939] the company had a complete line of radios ready for the market . . . 75 percent of the . . . United States covered with excellent distribution [and] . . . approximately $1,000,000 worth of radios were sold [$12,316,500]."[49]

FARNSWORTH AND THE NEW YORK WORLD'S FAIR

Had the Farnsworth Television and Radio Corporation chosen to participate in the 1939-1940 New York World's Fair, television history might have been written a little differently. According to Everson, however, the Farnsworth group decided they could not afford to demonstrate at the World's Fair because they were preoccupied with reorganization, structural and financial decisions, retooling plants, staffing, and initial manufacturing.[50] Money would be forthcoming shortly for Farnsworth Television's own promotion using nationwide touring vans.

Public relations was a one-person effort for the early Farnsworth corporations. As one reads the press attention Farnsworth achieved over the years and compares differing releases, it is evident that Everson is the primary author of most of the early public-relations activities. This changed under Farnsworth Television and Radio Corporation. RCA, by comparison, had an active in-house public relations and press organization that worked constantly to portray the multiple dimensions of RCA in a favorable light.[51] It was no secret that RCA was participating in the fair—David Sarnoff had been contemplating the

Farnsworth

1 *The show begins! The Farnsworth Television Camera picks up the actions of the speaker and converts them into electrical impulses.*

has brought half a million people their first sight of television

Control Board of the Farnsworth Mobile Unit . . . which amplifies the video impulses from the camera, injects blanking and synchronizing pulses and feeds the composite signals to the receivers. 2

3 *Crowds watch . . . as these signals are reconverted into moving images on the Farnsworth Television Receivers.*

From Portland, Oregon, to Portland, Maine . . . in little villages and in towering cities . . . the nation-wide Farnsworth Television Tour has given half a million men and women a wholly new experience in their lives . . . *actual television!*

Every show in Farnsworth dealers' stores has been packed and jammed with people. The demonstrations of the Farnsworth Traveling Unit have awakened keen public interest in television . . . the new art in whose development Farnsworth has played a major role. *And enormous store-traffic has been created through the radio departments where Farnsworth radios are sold.*

The Farnsworth Television Tour is another of the many spectacular Farnsworth promotions to help Farnsworth radio dealers move more Farnsworth merchandise. From coast to coast, it has helped dealers establish the fact that Farnsworth is the greatest name in television and the rising name in radio. In the months ahead, Farnsworth dealers will profit from many new aggressive promotional activities. Get the complete story from your Farnsworth distributor. *Your future is with Farnsworth!*

WATCH FARNSWORTH FOR '40!

Farnsworth Television & Radio Corporation, Fort Wayne and Marion, Indiana

4 *Philo T. Farnsworth, Director of Research of the Farnsworth organisation, is generally recognised as the man who has done more, perhaps, than any other to make television a vital, living reality. For Mr. Farnsworth conceived, pioneered and developed many of the basic principles of the electronic system of television . . . the practical modern method for this new art.*

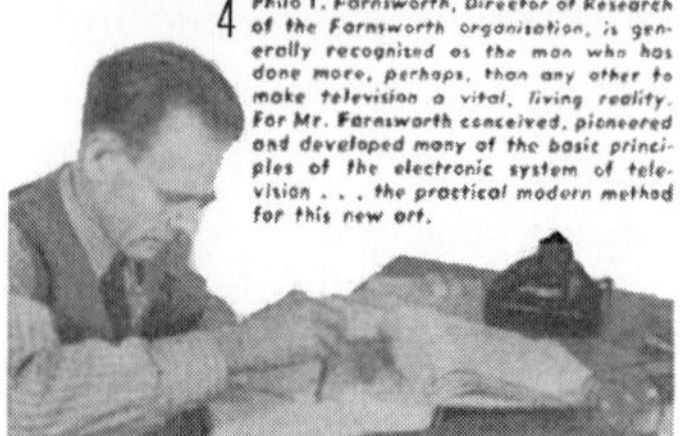

Farnsworth April Trade Paper Ad

Farnsworth Television and Radio trade paper ad. Courtesy Arizona State University.

World's Fair for quite some time. As a member of the fair's planning committee, he arranged for RCA's public "launch" into commercial television with regular program offerings.[52] As a result, the fair turned out to be a bonanza for RCA, with historical declarations and information that would stand uncontested for years that gave RCA credit for developing television.[53]

RCA's demonstrations at the New York World's Fair were similar to Farnsworth's 1934 demonstrations. The descriptions reflect the same types of programming and audience interaction that Farnsworth staged five years earlier at the Franklin Institute in Philadelphia. The New York *World-Telegram* labeled the RCA display as largely a research exhibit.[54] The fair was a promoter's event with all of the publicity, credit, and advantages reaped from it going directly to RCA.

FARNSWORTH REMOTE VANS: TRAVELING PROMOTIONAL EXHIBITS

The Farnsworth corporation decided to conduct a nationwide traveling exhibit.[55] "From Portland, Oregon, to Portland, Maine," the advertisements read,

Mayor Rossi with the mobile unit crew and George Everson, San Francisco, September 23, 1939, just before the start of the caravan. Left to right: Arthur Halloran, Bud Gamble, Mayor Rossi, Bart Molinari, John Stagnaro, George Everson. Courtesy Arizona State University.

Farnsworth demonstration tour in Flint, Michigan, illustrates tour activities with opening ceremonies, local dignitaries, and auditorium demonstrations for the crowds. Courtesy University of Utah Archives.

Farnsworth remote vans toured and put on television demonstrations. Caravan and unidentified crew pose in San Francisco. Courtesy Arizona State University.

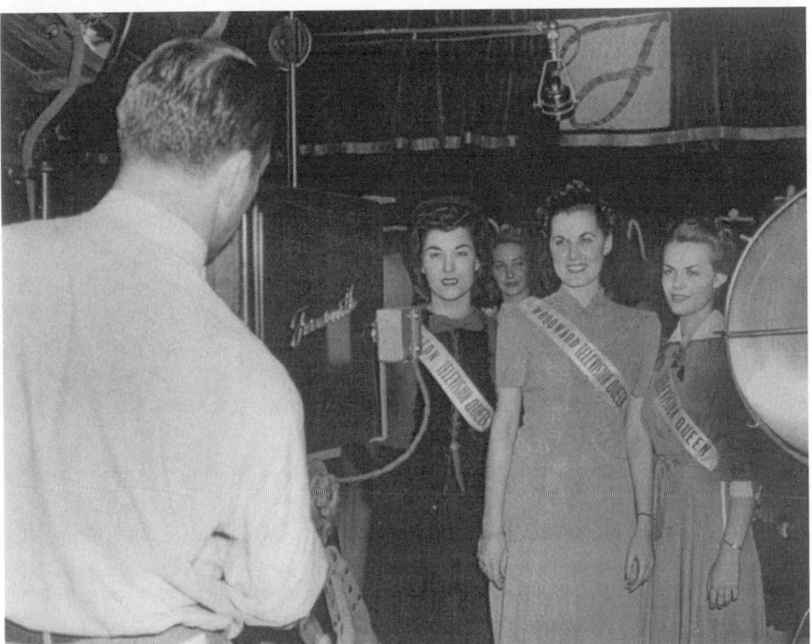

Television Queen Contest, September 24, 1940, Oklahoma City. Miss Woodward was queen, accompanied by Miss Enid and Miss Lawton as assistants. Man at the camera is John A. Stagnaro. Note the Farnsworth logo on the camera and at the top of the photo. Courtesy Arizona State University.

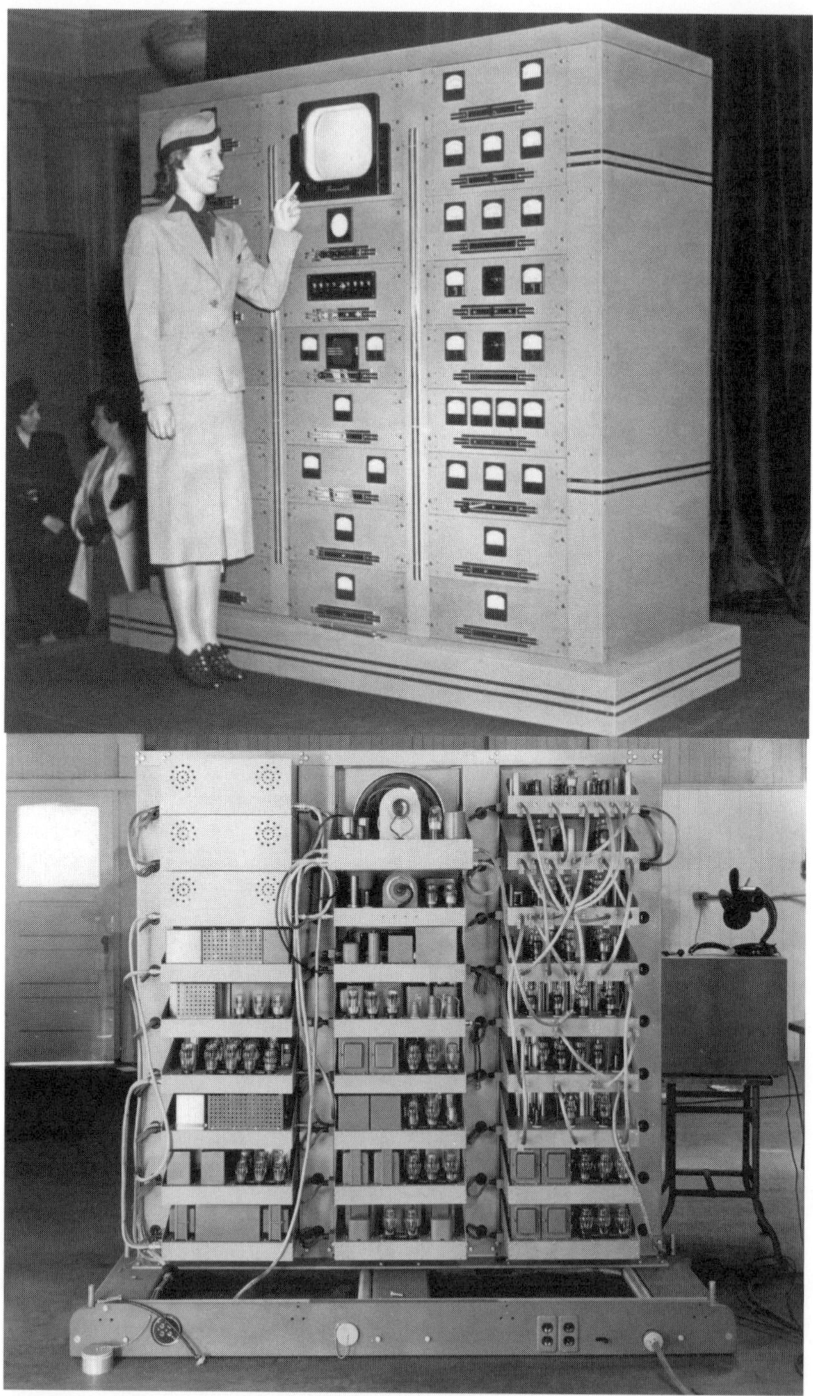

Front/rear views of mobile caravan equipment racks. Courtesy Elma G. Farnsworth.

"in little villages and in towering cities . . . the nationwide Farnsworth Television Tour has given half a million men and women a wholly new experience in their lives . . . *actual television!*"[56] For a year, beginning in the fall of 1939, the tour featured the Farnsworth Mobile Television Units driving from city to city and conducting live demonstrations.

The mobile-unit presentations lasted from several days to a week in each city. As a van arrived, local celebrities, beauty contestants, and Farnsworth dealers were on hand to attract attention. Morning and afternoon demonstrations were conducted in a local auditorium or a dealer's store. Admission was free and everyone was invited.

George Everson kicked off the tour on September 23, 1939, in San Francisco, and in Seattle a local comedian performed before the cameras. Unfortunately, all the publicity in Seattle went to the comedian, who wrote the newspaper article describing himself as a "pioneer of new art." The only way

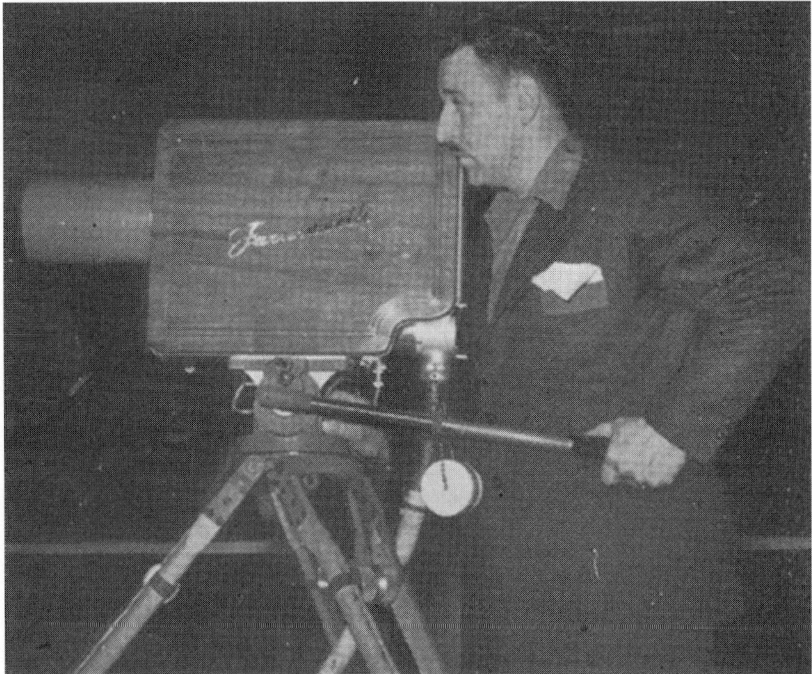

Period caption: John Stagnaro, considered the dean of television cameramen, will operate the Farnsworth dissector camera at the demonstration of television at the Brown-Dunkin store, October 1, 2, and 3. The camera is the "heart" of the electronic television system. The camera converts the light picture into an electrical picture. It is valued at $12,500, and is the first television camera in the nation that has a special coating on the lens developed to increase the speed of the lens to do away with glare. This camera was first used in Hollywood in photographing *Gone with the Wind.* Courtesy Arizona State University.

one could identify the Farnsworth participation in this demonstration was by the pictorial captions that identified the mobile crew member, John Stagnaro.[57] In Tulsa it was a beauty queen contest that provided the program demonstration. "The mobile unit arrived [in Tulsa] September 24, 1940. The unit, valued at $110,000 [$1,345,140] in equipment, was to be used in demonstrations here [Tulsa]." The demonstration was conducted with a "complete television transmitting studio installation on the fifth floor of the Brown-Dunkin company store. There will be no admission charge to see it."[58] Here the local talent and event publicity were provided by a television queen contest.[59] In Richmond, October 22, 1940, "the first demonstration in Virginia of the scientific marvels of television" was conducted at the Hotel John Marshall.[60]

The touring promotions campaign crisscrossed the country and although well intended, they clearly did not generate the publicity of the World's Fair activities.

THE FARNSWORTH-RCA AGREEMENT

The foundation of the Farnsworth organization had always been the man, his patent portfolio and his name Farnsworth. These gave the corporation the "strongest patent position in television outside of RCA."[61] *Time* magazine reported that "no television sender or receiver can be made without using some of his [Farnsworth's] patents."[62] The reverse was also true: Farnsworth needed access to RCA's Zworykin patents.

A precedent-setting agreement between Farnsworth and RCA was reached in the fall 1939. The credit for the agreement belongs to Farnsworth's lawyer, Donald Lippincott, who defended Philo through almost a decade of challenges (see Chapter 4). The credit for negotiating payment goes to Edwin Nicholas. Nicholas was the former head of the RCA Patent License Division, and he knew the strength of both companies' positions.[63] At Farnsworth Television and Radio as president, he was the one who put into motion the final negotiations that resulted in RCA's payment of $1 million to the Farnsworth company [$13,451,400]. The terms were spelled out in a document dated September 15, 1939, with Nicholas and Edwin M. Martin representing Farnsworth and Otto S. Schairer and Lewis MacComnach representing RCA. RCA received a license to use Farnsworth's patents in the manufacture of television sets and transmitters and "other radio and sound recording and reproducing apparatus."[64] Farnsworth in turn acquired a license to use RCA patents for television, phonographs, and transmitters. Under the agreement, publically announced October 2, 1939,[65] RCA paid their first royalties to an outside company.[66]

The agreement was historic: It forced RCA to pay out royalties, and was a "seal of recognition on Farnsworth's inventive genius and the patience and persistence of his backers."[67] Within the industry, the agreement was critical to the continued development of television in the United States. The agreement was of pivotal importance in reaching an industry-wide television standard agreement. The *New York Times* reported, "The radio industry sees peace and no patent war ahead to mar the progress of television."[68]

The Farnsworth operation was a growing multimillion-dollar manufacturing and distribution entity.

FARNSWORTH: IN THE NEW FARNSWORTH TELEVISION AND RADIO CORPORATION

Philo Farnsworth was active in restructuring his corporation. But he was personally moving along a different path. During the reorganization (fall 1938 to fall 1939), he was busy with his work at the Philadelphia lab, which continued until his equipment was crated for the Indiana move. In 1939 he filed for six more patents.[69] These were improvements on existing equipment and thus filed and divided from previous patents.

Farnsworth appeared before several congressional committees reviewing the status of television. His testimony before the Senate Monopoly Investigation Committee coincided with the FCC's investigation of network monopolies.[70] Although the two were separate government investigations, the subject of monopoly was a common thread providing discussion and newspaper headlines. The FCC was concerned about the growing strength of the radio network monopoly—specifically the practices of CBS and RCA.[71] The Senate committee was concerned about the practices of AT&T (based on FCC telephone investigations from 1936 to 1939) and the patent office and about whether these entities were encouraging monopolistic practices, thus negatively affecting the national economy. Farnsworth appeared on January 19, 1939, and denied the radio industry had attempted to suppress the new art. His testimony was complimentary to RCA; he told the committee that RCA would have a television set in April (a reference to the New York World's Fair festivities) that would sell for approximately $125 [$1,540]. According to Farnsworth, the consumers would benefit shortly through the RMA's work with the FCC regarding standards and commercial broadcasting.[72] He had complete confidence in as well as respect for the patent office, which he felt was slow at times in their processing, but scrupulously honest and fair.[73] He would have favored streamlining filing and processing of patents and patent interference cases, but his experiences with the patent office had helped him create a program of research and a corporation that would not have been possible without patent protection, without which, he told the committee, "he never could have obtained the money to carry forward his television research."[74]

In the fall of 1939, Farnsworth moved his family to Fort Wayne. The personal contract between Farnsworth and the corporation set in motion a new role for him. Farnsworth Radio and Television was becoming a national manufacturer. Philo was a member of the board of directors, held for a time the title of vice president, and was in charge of research—operationally he was the director of research, but his corporate influence was diminished by a new layer of corporate management.[75] In examining the early records of the corporation, it was apparent that Farnsworth was active as a member of the board of directors. He attended the meetings and spoke up. It was now a large corporation, however, and he placed his faith for manufacturing and distribution in the management the board had hired to direct the company. Farnsworth's personal time remained primarily devoted to directing laboratory research, and his contract spelled this out. It called for him to "determine the nature, extent, and general fields of research."[76] In other words, he had free reign on what projects he would undertake and was to dedicate his exclusive service to the company's electronic-media research program. Despite freedom in research, there was a string attached in the same paragraph that described his services: The contract noted that although Farnsworth was free to undertake any related media research, the company officers were to determine the direction of the research of his subordinates. So, although he finally had a well-funded laboratory, other officers could influence the direction of the research. No doubt Farnsworth reasoned that he would have the same autonomy as he had always had — after all, he was still one of the "officers" who would determine the work as well as the officer in direct charge of the laboratory. His salary started at $8,000 [$98,532] per year and was increased to $15,000 [$184,748] in April 1939.[77]

The value of the name Farnsworth is seen clearly in the contract. All of his patent portfolio became the exclusive property of the corporation along with use of his name. "The Corporation shall have the right to use the name and likeness of Farnsworth . . . in connection with manufacturing, advertising, selling or distributing . . . such right to include the use of Farnsworth's full name or the name of Farnsworth in any corporate name."[78] His personal reputation had grown to be of marketable value.

FARNSWORTH: CAUGHT IN "TELEVISION'S FALSE DAWN"

Unfortunately, the reorganization of the Farnsworth corporation could not have come at a worse time in history. The late 1930s was a period of economic instability and the unfolding of critical world events. The economy was still slowly emerging from the worst of the Depression, and any business—let alone a large new one—was in for a difficult time. Political tensions were high. The Second World War was spreading. For the first time the American public heard

Farnsworth Radio and Television Corporation executives display prototype receiver, Fort Wayne, 1939. E. A. Nicholas (left) with George Everson (right) and unidentified executives (center). Courtesy Elma G. Farnsworth.

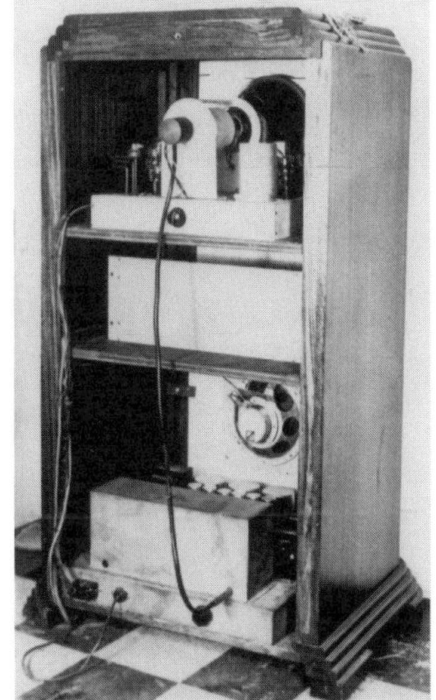

Front and back views of this set were used in home and studio demonstrations beginning 1936 to 1938. At this time Farnsworth was experimenting with 441 lines and this screen was nine inches. Courtesy Elma G. Farnsworth (left) and University of Utah Archives (right).

the sounds of war broadcast from radio networks. These factors converged on television's development in 1939 and 1940, which Sterling and Kittross labeled, "television's false dawn."[79]

This false dawn was launched by the industry's optimistic outlook for television's immediate future versus the realities of a slow-moving Federal Communications Commission. The manufacturers, chiefly RCA, tried to rush commercial distribution by freezing a 441-line standard. The television and radio manufacturers expected to market television sets soon. Those first 1938 and 1939 sets were designed to get a competitive edge in a new market.[80] But the sales were also intended to force the FCC's hand to accept the system of 441-line standards.

The process of defining the technical standards of monochrome television had been under way since the early 1930s. With each experiment, picture definition improved, but the standards varied according to each manufacturer. RCA was pushing for its standards, while Farnsworth, Philco, DuMont, Zenith, and the others were different. As a result, the Radio Manufacturing Association (RMA) organized a National Television System Committee (NTSC).[81] The job of the committee was to see an industrial compromise and advise the FCC. The group was representative of the industry and it included both RCA and Farnsworth Television and Radio, with Farnsworth himself a member. Complicating an industry compromise, the industry was forging ahead.

The patent agreement between Farnsworth and RCA, reached in 1939, paved the way for RCA to push strongly for RCA standards. The Farnsworth and RCA standards merged through their joint patent agreement, and these two entities held the most important patents. In May 1939, however, the FCC's advisory committee recommended delaying selection of final television standards. Given the pace of television development, the FCC felt it was premature to pick a final standard.[82]

The NTSC meetings were not without controversy and led to further accusations of RCA's monopolistic approach to television. Appearing before the Senate Interstate Commerce Committee, DuMont television representatives charged RCA with dominating the NTSC. Farnsworth and Edwin M. Martin attended the meetings to represent their corporate interests, and again allied with RCA. It was at these meetings where the Farnsworth group first heard RCA's Sarnoff acknowledge Farnsworth's personal contributions to television. Speaking about BCC television standards, Sarnoff declared, "The English system, as a matter of fact, was based on the American inventions primarily the invention of our [RCA] iconoscope and the inventions of Farnsworth."[83] Following the DuMont charge of RCA's control, Martin refuted it, asserting that the proposed standards were not RCA standards alone. He declared the Farnsworth company a supporter of the recommended NTSC standards and stated that the DuMont company had nothing worthwhile.[84] Farnsworth Television recommended the endorsement of the NTSC standards and also limited commercialization for television licensing. "The public is ready . . . the service is ready . . . the sponsors are ready."[85] While seemingly expressing allegiance to RCA, however, Martin also took steps to distance Farnsworth from RCA.

> We do not belong to RCA . . . We do not go so far as to say there is a Farnsworth system, but we do say, and it is recognized generally in the art, that Philo T. Farnsworth did probably more than any other man in the United States to invent what we call electronic television . . . I think Mr. Farnsworth's word, said through me, should have a little weight with this committee. Mr. Farnsworth had a part in the drawing up of those standards and he was at the hearings . . . The Farnsworth Company had never been controlled or influence in any way by RCA . . . we are distinctly a competitor of RCA.[86]

It would take until May 1941 for the FCC to adopt the NTSC's standards.[87] By this time RCA was the industry leader. The lead Farnsworth had held in technological research was closed by 1941—RCA was at the head of the pack. The first of Farnsworth's most important patents had only a few more years before they would expire and become public property.

World events brought an end to the optimism of television's false dawn. In May 1941 President Franklin D. Roosevelt declared a state of national emergency, which redirected most raw materials necessary for the manufacture of television and radio sets to military needs. According to Abramson, "RCA's television receiver production line had been closed for over a year, and other companies had been forced to drop their work on television in favor of research for national defense."[88] A year later on May 12, 1942, the War Production Board officially ordered a halt to further construction of broadcast stations so that building materials could also be directed toward the war effort.[89] Before the war, the FCC had authorized the operation of thirty-two experimental stations, and these were permitted to continue limited construction.[90] Abramson reports that there were only seven stations on the air at the time. "They included NBC, CBS, and DuMont in New York City, General Electric in Schenectady, Philco in Philadelphia, Don Lee in Los Angeles, and station WBKB in Chicago."[91] Programming at these stations was minimal — merely a handful of hours per week.

Farnsworth's experimental station was caught in the middle. W3XPF, Philadelphia, was being dismantled and carted away to Fort Wayne as world peace unraveled. The license for Philadelphia expired with the plan to create a new station in Fort Wayne. Although Farnsworth filed for another experimental license, W9XFT in Indiana, the war was approaching rapidly. The Farnsworth Television and Radio Corporation, like all others across the nation, moved from manufacturing, research, and development of television to wartime production of electronic communications equipment. Abramson describes best this national industry transition:

> American television, which had finally reached a goal of technical excellence, was suddenly given the lowest priority . . . The infant television industry, which had suffered many false starts in the past, was once again put under wraps to await a brighter tomorrow.[92]

7

Farnsworth Television and Radio, Wartime Success

1939–1948

Chronology

Farnsworth

September 1939 — Farnsworth moves to Fort Wayne.

October 1939 — Farnsworth corporation announces decision to discontinue station W3XPF in Philadelphia.
• RCA agrees to pay Farnsworth for use of patents, thus systems become generally available to the industry.
• Farnsworth corporation purchases manufacturing plants: Capehart and General Household Utilities.
• Farnsworth corporation remote vans tour the country.

1940 — Farnsworth supports RMA standards along with RCA.

Electronic Media

1939 — Broadcast Music Incorporated (BMI) formed as a competitor to ASCAP.
• Armstrong establishes FM station in New York.
• RCA and others put television receivers on the market.

April 1939 — At the New York World's Fair, Sarnoff exhibits RCA television.

1940 — The FCC approves 441-line television standards, but then suspends that decision.
• Census figures indicate 44 million radios in America (1935 figures indicated 33 million radio homes); listening hours reported at five hours per day. One world versus isolationism becomes the focus of radio discussion.

Farnsworth

January 1941 — Marion and Fort Wayne Farnsworth plants are retooled for wartime manufacturing.

1941 — Farnsworth contract is signed with the Civil Aeronautics Administration and the Signal Corps to produce airport landing equipment.

June 1941 — FCC staff visits Fort Wayne station development.

December 1941 — Amateur radio stations close due to the war.

February 1942 — Farnsworth takes a leave of absence from the corporation and moves to Maine where he establishes a small laboratory close to home and Farnsworth Wood Products, Fryeburg, Maine.

April 1942 — Corporation announces it is now 100 percent into wartime manufacturing.

March 1943 — Farnsworth corporation employees are given the Army-Navy Production Award.

June 1944 — The Farnsworth corporation's radar-jamming device is reportedly instrumental in D-Day success.

July 1944 — Farnsworth purchases WGL-AM, Fort Wayne, Indiana, from Westinghouse, upgrades power of

Electronic Media

1941 — FCC issues *Chain Broadcasting Report;* NBC forced to give up one of its networks.
• FCC authorizes commercial FM operations. Also issues first Mayflower Decision, which forbids station editorializing.
• FDR's declaration of war produces an audience of 90 million, 79 percent of all American homes.
• Howard K. Smith, Charles Collingwood, and Cecil Brown join the CBS network.
• FCC adopts 525-line standard, July 1941.

1942 — Office of Censorship opens; censorship to be voluntary to assist in war efforts.
• Elmer Davis heads the Office of War Information.
• Radio and television manufacturing turns to manufacturing war communications materials.
• American Armed Forces Radio begins.
• FCC bans construction of new stations due to war efforts.

February 1942 — FCC halts construction on all new stations. Only a few TV outlets are left on the air. The freeze is to conserve materials for wartime use.

1943 — RCA Blue Network purchased by E. J. Noble.
• Wire recorders used in reporting war efforts.

1944 — Disc jockey programming appears.
• FCC holds hearing on television spectrum applications.

Farnsworth

the station, and promotes it as a centerpiece in a new communications system.

June 1945 — The board of directors is concerned about Farnsworth's extended absence from Fort Wayne.

August 1945 — Farnsworth Corporation announces the purchase of Traffic Communications Corporation.

September 1945 — Farnsworth resigns as vice president of the corporation and becomes a full-time consultant.

October 1945 — A new plant in Huntington, Indiana, is added to corporation's manufacturing capabilities.

January 1946 — Farnsworth corporation files application with the Securities and Exchange Commission to issue more common stock. Capital is raised to pay for a new radio and television center.

May 1946 — FCC grants Farnsworth corporation an application for a TV station in Fort Wayne—W9XFT.

September 1946 — Nicholas issues a memorandum to management calling for financial cuts, assisting the company into postwar competition.
• The purchase of the Thomasville Furniture Company is announced to build cabinets for receivers.
• Carl (Farnsworth's brother) is killed in a plane accident.

November 1946 — Two-way tests are conducted in conjunction with railroad communication interests. A larger railroad test sponsored by the Ford Motor Company is repeated in February 1947.

January 1947 — Farnsworth utiliscope, a closed-circuit camera setup, is unveiled and is marketed for industrial surveillance.

Electronic Media

1945 — RCA Blue Network becomes the American Broadcasting System.
• Edward R. Murrow reports from Buchenwald, a German concentration camp.
• Audience hears funeral of FDR via radio.
• Radio set manufacturing begins again as war ends.
• FCC reassigns FM broadcasting to 88 to 108 MHz, where it remains today.
• FCC allocates thirteen UHF channels for television.
• The war ends and the FCC begins consideration for license applications for television stations.

1946 — FCC issues a memorandum titled, "Public Service Responsibility of Broadcast Licensees," more commonly called the Blue Book.
• Dr. Frank Stanton becomes president of CBS.
• Tape recorder appears.
• RCA demonstrates color system.
• BBC renews television broadcasting following the war.
• RCA demonstrates color television.

1947 — Cold war feeling erupts between United States, WWII allies, and Russia.
• Television systems begin interconnection.

Farnsworth

March 1947 — Fort Wayne plant is expanded to accommodate more research and engineering functions.

May 1947 — Television demonstration is conducted in Fort Wayne for International Harvester.

August 27, 1947 — The first Farnsworth television patents expire.

September 1947 — The first postwar Farnsworth television receiver is introduced to the officers of the D. W. May Corporation.

October 1947 — The board of directors entertains takeover offers from ITT, RCA, and General Electric.
• A forest fire sweeps through the Brownfield, Maine, area destroying Farnsworth's home and laboratory.

November 1947 — McCargar is replaced on the board of directors of Farnsworth Television and Radio Corporation, and the board is reorganized.

December 1947 — Farnsworth attends his first board meeting in several years. In meetings with Everson, Nicholas, and Martin, he is asked to return to Fort Wayne as vice president and a member of the board.

August 1948 — Farnsworth is officially welcomed back to the corporation after his leave of absence. The new 1949 Farnsworth television sets are introduced.

Electronic Media

1948 — CBS offers NBC talent differing contract and succeeds in talent raid on the competing network.

September 1948 — FCC issues a freeze on all applications, needing time to study issue of frequency allocation, interference, education, and television development.
• Fred Allen program ratings at high of 28.7.
• Vinyl records, 33⅓ and 45 rpm, appear.
• First African-American radio stations established.

≈

World War II halted television station development and the manufacturing of consumer radio and TV equipment. Television technology was directed toward military applications as well as postwar industrial uses in rail and air travel, industrial surveillance, and weather forecasting.

Thirty-two experimental TV stations were authorized before the war, but many never reached the air, and of those that did, few remained on the air into 1942.[1] Stations went off the air because there were no parts to repair transmission equipment or receiving sets; besides, there were very few TV sets, and the audience was tiny. By the end of the war, those stations still operating were serving New York and Philadelphia. Programming was a necessary means for testing a system, and many of the wartime experiments supported what manufacturers hoped would become a peacetime fortune in television.[2]

World War II equipment demands would bring both prosperity and challenge to the Farnsworth Television and Radio Corporation. Prosperity came from government defense contracts; challenge came from the rapid expansion necessary for meeting the military production orders and the eventual postwar transition back to commercial production.

CASUALTIES OF FARNSWORTH TELEVISION IN WARTIME

Farnsworth moved his family to Fort Wayne early in the fall of 1939, and work in the laboratory began almost immediately.[3] Looming concerns of war delayed the construction of the new TV station in Fort Wayne and increased the pressure on Farnsworth's deteriorating health.

Farnsworth TV: Off the Air

Farnsworth's experimental station W9XFT, Fort Wayne, had been granted a license prior to the war; unfortunately, it was not on the air when the war began.[4] The intention of the corporation was simply to move the Philadelphia station facilities to Fort Wayne. But after a year, the FCC inquired about the lack of progress of the experimental station in Fort Wayne.[5] The corporation had let several construction permits expire without action. Nicholas declared that "it was the intention of this Company to continue its television development and research program, which includes the construction and operation of an experimental transmitter in Fort Wayne."[6] However, Nicholas, who at this time was more concerned about establishing manufacturing facilities than the station, was apparently too slow in responding, and the Commission was pressuring the corporation for information. Nicholas told them that the research work was continuing, and he reminded them that the Farnsworth corporation did not need a license because they were not then transmitting a signal beyond the confines of the laboratory.

In June 1941 the FCC sent Inspector Ernest J. Galins to Fort Wayne to find out exactly what was happening. Galins reported that the "aural" [audio] transmitter was ready for operation, but the "visual" [television] transmitter was still under construction. Work was progressing, however, as cameras were being upgraded to comply with present standards, and while the "studio equipment [was] under construction, no antenna [had been] erected."[7] The corporation was progressing in terms of studio facilities, but slowly, in terms of any transmitter station license.

The 1941 construction permit, granted to W9XFT, was canceled because of the corporation's inaction. The corporation had also failed to file extensions of the license prior to the FCC's halting all new television construction; therefore the file on the Farnsworth station was "closed and the call letters deleted."[8] B. Ray Cummings, vice president of engineering, reported to the FCC that the experimental applications were "not carried through because of the war situation."[9] The corporate newsletter repeated Cummings's explanation.[10]

But the inaction was not entirely the fault of the station; the Commission was not always responsive. Fred A. Barr from Farnsworth's patent department complained that he could not file the reports the Commission had requested "due to the fact that the FCC will not supply this corporation with the proper forms. Please consider this an urgent request for a supply of form no. 730."[11] The construction permit was granted for Fort Wayne station W9XFT, but the Farnsworth corporation did not act upon it, so it was canceled as of December 31, 1941.[12] The corporation would wait until the end of the war before starting another television station. W9XFT became the first Farnsworth casualty of war.

Farnsworth's Health

Farnsworth's personal history from 1929 to 1939 provides insight as to the second Farnsworth casualty of this wartime period—his health. Continuous round-the-clock workdays, sometimes not even stopping to eat or sleep, and corporate challenges affected the inventor's vitality and well-being.[13] Even positive developments such as agreements with Philco, Baird Television, Fernseh A.G., and the victory over RCA came at a heavy personal cost. The parting between Philco and Farnsworth was traumatic, coming at the same time as the death of his son. Both incidents drove him inward and created a distrust for doctors. He really wanted to be working on the Philadelphia TV station when he went to help Baird Television in London, only to see his work turned to ashes in the Crystal Palace fire. The trip to Europe designed in part as a restful vacation was exhausting. Farnsworth came home sick only to return to a lab McCargar had turned to chaos by hiring and firing engineering staff. After the move to Fort Wayne, W9XFT was off the air.

Perhaps professionally most devastating of all these events over the years was Farnsworth's realization that by 1939 he'd lost his competitive edge over RCA, which at that time had successfully tied up Farnsworth's patent for almost ten years of its seventeen-year life.

It was not surprising that Farnsworth was not well. It was difficult for him to relax, and the constant pressures took their toll. He sought help from doctors and psychiatrists who urged him to slow down and regenerate his body. They even recommended alcohol and tobacco, and finally gave him a prescription for chloral hydrate, but these drugs were addictive. Pem Farnsworth later wrote that the treatment "was bad advice . . . Had they known then what they do now about treating depression, they could have saved us both years of pain and anguish."[14] Family records describe Farnsworth as a man with a mind so full of ideas that he had trouble letting go, and doctors seemed unable to help.[15] Farnsworth's health would have its ups and downs for the remainder of his life.[16]

Critics of Farnsworth imply that his addictions were of pivotal importance in his career failures, but this is not true.[17] He was in and out of hospitals as a result of a perforated ulcer, a hernia, seizures, and pneumonia. He suffered a nervous breakdown. Just before the move to Fort Wayne, he was hospitalized in Boston, not far from the farm in Maine. To relax he spent parts of spring and summer 1939 on the farm property in Maine. Unfortunately, even there, relaxation was not part of his character.

After the move to Fort Wayne, Farnsworth became something of a celebrity, but felt self-conscious in the role. Pem described his feeling as "something like a show fish in an aquarium—a role in which he was very uncomfortable." She recalled the gist of a conversation one day when he came home from the lab. "Pem, I just can't go on like this . . . I've trained my brain too well, now I have a hard time turning it off; I think I'm going crazy . . . It's come to the point of choosing whether I want to be a drunk or go crazy."[18] In 1940 his brother Carl wrote: "Phil is fine now and when he's fine, you know how things pop—gosh he's got an idea every minute. But boy it's fun—it's worth a million to have him this way again."[19] But in spring two years later, Carl wrote to his sister, "Phil stays about the same, he hasn't showed any marked improvement for ages. It's very discouraging for Pem, but she's sure a brick."[20] By Christmas of that year, Farnsworth was feeling better again. "My strength is returning rapidly now, and I am gradually gaining weight."[21]

At the height of his personal achievements, with "the constant overdraft on his energies . . ., [Farnsworth] was call[ed] for payment and with interest . . . he lay desperately ill, at one time [Philo] was at the point of death."[22] By 1942 he had lost considerable weight and was down to just a little more than 100 pounds. The turning point in this crisis was when his wife threatened to leave him unless he sought help.[23] At her insistence, medical attention was obtained, and Farnsworth again was hospitalized. Here he began the slow recovery process.[24]

WORK ON THE FARNSWORTH FARM

In February 1942, Farnsworth formally left all management of the company in the hands of people who had manufacturing and distribution experience, people he had helped hire. He was given a leave of absence from his Fort Wayne responsibilities with a salary of $8,000 [$84,024] per year and a small corporation-funded laboratory "to facilitate my personal research program for your corporation" in Maine.[25] Writing a letter of appreciation to Nicholas, Farnsworth noted, "I think that a summer spent in outdoors work, minus responsibility, will permit me to be on my toes by fall."[26] The leave lasted six years.[27] It was not until 1948 that Farnsworth returned to Fort Wayne, when the company was struggling to get back on its feet after the war.

In Maine, Farnsworth spread his time across three matters: regaining his health, immersing himself in his home lab, and starting a business with his brothers—Farnsworth Wood Products Incorporated.[28]

Farnsworth relaxed by keeping busy. The word "relax" was probably not in his vocabulary—it was certainly not an ability within his character. Upon returning to Fernworth Farm[29] east of Brownfield, Maine, he found a dam he had constructed had broken and decided to rebuild with something that would last. The result created a four-and-one-half-acre trout pond. Its construction was something of a community effort that involved the building of a large cement dam. After the dam came additions to the house and the building of the laboratory and the lumber business—all his way of forgetting about the pressures of commercial television.

Labwork on the Farm

The personal challenges Farnsworth faced in Maine were really not much more relaxing than the pressures of Fort Wayne—just different. Working on the farm did help take the stress and pressures of television out of Farnsworth's mind. He wanted to be working, searching for those new ideas, and he was in the lab at every opportunity, never quite giving his body time to heal fully before he was back at it again.[30]

In Maine Farnsworth's work supported corporate research directed toward wartime needs. Everson notes: "He kept the research engineers [in Fort Wayne] well supplied with ideas for new inventions and ways of perfecting earlier discoveries." He adds that Farnsworth was missed as a member of the board of directors, and "the laboratory staff also missed his leadership and inspiration.

am construction on the Farnsworth property, Brownfield/Fryeburg, Maine. Courtesy Elma G. arnsworth.

However, all understood his inability to be with us and looked forward to the day when he would return."[31]

The board of Farnsworth Television and Radio grew uneasy about Philo's extended absence. Early in 1945 they questioned his participation in Farnsworth Wood Products as a conflict of interest. His letter to Edwin M. Martin, Farnsworth Television and Radio's corporate secretary, described his role as president of the wood production business as nominal, but he wasn't

Farnsworth's home (above) and personal lab in Maine. Courtesy Elma G. Farnsworth.

convincing.[32] The Farnsworth television company was running into financial trouble, and the board wanted Philo to return to Fort Wayne. When he declined, the corporation pulled its support for the Maine lab, forcing two of his associates, Cliff Gardner and Harold Bernhardt, to resign. Gardner took employment with the Raytheon Manufacturing Company, and Bernhardt went to work for MIT.[33]

Without corporate support, Farnsworth sold portions of his stock to support the Maine lab.[34] As a result of his activities, he was asked by the board to resign his position on the board of directors and accept appointment as a consultant. In a handwritten response to the "gentlemen of the Board," his reaction was strong. "I am not only bound by my contract with you, but I also am personally a party to an agreement with AT&T, whereunder I agreed not to sever my connection with you." As to the matter of the lumber business, Farnsworth reminded the board that he was making a contribution to the war effort and that they had been fully apprized of all his activities, adding that raising "the question at this late date implies strongly that you are merely seeking an excuse to void a contract which is unsatisfactory to you for other reasons." In conclusion, Farnsworth declared that if the board found his contract unsatisfactory, perhaps he could be released and become a free agent.[35]

Though displeased with Farnsworth's absence, the board needed the man and his name. It was a difficult situation for all parties, but the board compromised. Just a few months later—September 19, 1945—Farnsworth agreed to resign as vice president and accept the position of consultant.[36] He was not cut loose, as he had suggested, to a freelance status but given a reduced salary along with his continued commitment to support the Fort Wayne company. He did not return from Maine, in any formal management position until 1947, when as a result of the corporation's weakening position, he was asked to help restore wartime losses. Philo Farnsworth was still the chief asset of the Farnsworth Television and Radio Corporation.

FARNSWORTH TELEVISION AND RADIO AND FARNSWORTH

E. A. Nicholas was at the corporate helm. There was regular communication between Nicholas (in Fort Wayne) and Farnsworth (Maine), but Philo's participation in the corporate operations was limited to helping organize the corporation, initiating the first manufacturing, and what was most important, inventing. From 1942 to 1946, his major contributions were from research conducted in Maine. He had little knowledge of overall operations or finances, other than the generalized published reports, which were calculated to emphasize the company's strengths and goals.

· LOOK TO THE FUTURE

They were veterans when they joined Farnsworth 5 years ago! These *21 men* in the Farnsworth headquarters organization are today all in the same important positions they took in 1939 when Farnsworth expanded its research laboratories and began also to build radios, phonograph-combinations and special television equipment!

That's a record of stability with a very real value to Farnsworth distributors and dealers. It means sound policies and steady, healthy progress.

These men are planning post-war policies and products *now*—to help you plan *your* future. . . . Restricted dealerships for Farnsworth instruments—to produce volume at fair prices and profits. . . . The finest merchandise in every price range. *Quality at popular prices.* . . .

Distinctive cabinet designs with assured sales appeal. Improved reception for broadcast and shortwave. Radio-phonographs with time-proven record-changers—simple in construction and operation—*service-free in performance.* Advanced FM . . . and modern television, the result of 19 years of pioneering.

Farnsworth accomplishments in the past have received high recognition. Farnsworth possibilities in the future are unlimited.

FARNSWORTH

Television · Radio · Phonographs

Farnsworth Television & Radio Corporation, Fort Wayne 1, Indiana • Farnsworth Radio and Television Transmitters and Receivers • Aircraft Radio Equipment • Farnsworth Television Tubes • The Farnsworth Phonograph-Radio • The Capehart

Primary Farnsworth management team, 1939–1949. Farnsworth was in Fort Wayne until 1942, after which these people provided for the leadership of the company. Courtesy ITT.

ERNEST H. VOGEL
Vice President—Sales

E. A. NICHOLAS
President

J. P. ROGERS
Vice President—Treasurer

B. RAY CUMMINGS
Vice President—Engineering

FARNSWORTH EXECUTIVE MANAGEMENT COMMITTEE

...with these men

W. J. AVERY
Export

MADISON CAWEIN
Research

J. C. FERGUSON
Chief Engineer Fort Wayne

JOHN S. GARCEAU
Advertising

PAUL H. HARTMANN
Assistant Treasurer

E. J. HENDRICKSON
Sales

E. M. HOEY
Order Service

I. C. HUNTER
Sales

R. C. JENKINS
General Superintendent

GLENN KELSO
Superintendent Fort Wayne

REESE KENNAUGH
Superintendent Marion

H. J. MYERS
Controller

E. S. NEEDLER
Purchasing

F. B. OSTMAN
Service

J. H. PRESSLEY
Chief Engineer Marion

A. E. SIBLEY
Credit

WHAT WILL YOU DO IN TELEVISION?

Write for copies of "The Story of Electronic Television"—a prevue of what you'll sell.

The management of Farnsworth Television and Radio used Farnsworth's patent inventions, along with his name, as their foundation for the move into commercial manufacturing. However, as the war began, they moved directly into military production.[37] Plants were added to meet the demand for armed service contracts. At its apex, the Farnsworth corporation had four plants in Fort Wayne and one each in Marion, Huntington, and Bluffton, Indiana. It owned radio station WGL-AM, Fort Wayne and the Thomasville Furniture Company, in North Carolina. In addition it supported Farnsworth's personal lab in Maine. Philo was particularly pleased with the 1944 purchase of the radio station and the declarations by Nicholas that this station would become a focal point of the Farnsworth corporate broadcast center. The plans included AM-FM and television stations. It was reminiscent of Farnsworth's earlier forecasts envisioning a chain of stations that would cover the nation like those of RCA and CBS.

FARNSWORTH RETURNS TO THE FARNSWORTH CORPORATION

During Farnsworth's stay in Maine, the Farnsworth Radio and Television Corporation financially overextended itself. Following the war, military contracts were canceled and the corporation was in trouble. It had accumulated a $3 million [$21,311,200] war debt, and, although banks had extended payment deadlines, shortages in manufacturing supplies were inhibiting the corporation from filling its orders. The expected sales were not producing the cash flow necessary to overcome the debt.

Nicholas and Everson called for Farnsworth's return to Fort Wayne because he was a significant corporate asset. Philo did not like the limelight, but he was an effective interactive leader. His presence would aid in negotiations and perhaps attract new contracts.

Farnsworth's return could not have come at a better time for both the corporation and Philo. Just as the corporation needed Farnsworth's presence, Farnsworth needed a new laboratory. A forest fire that swept through Brownfield, Maine, had destroyed everything in its path, "except for a few scattered houses . . . and standing chimneys."[38] The Farnsworths lost almost everything—home, laboratory, research notes, and most of their household belongings. The estimated value of the loss was $50,000, a significant sum for 1947 [$383,856].[39] The family didn't know where their next home or lab would be.

In December 1947, Farnsworth attended his first board meeting in years. In a meeting with Everson, Nicholas, and Martin, he learned how bad finances were in Fort Wayne and agreed to resume his duties as vice president and director of research and advanced engineering.[40] Farnsworth faced a company in trouble. He would end up once again working in the lab as well as dealing with company reorganization and public relations.

The first evidence of Farnsworth's renewed corporate involvement was the development of the new research facilities and his public appearances at the dealer meetings held across the country in late 1947 and 1948. In an August 1948 meeting in New York, he was officially welcomed back by Martin, who introduced him as the "father of television," and then noted that "Phil Farnsworth is neither too old nor too young to be father of anything he wants to be."[41]

Following the conferences, Farnsworth relocated his family to Fort Wayne.[42] Philo was himself again, busy at work and at home, and with an addition—son Kent, born September 4, 1948.

Corporate reorganization began almost immediately following Farnsworth's return. In writing to her father, Pem described the times as "hectic days for us—Phil especially . . . He had to fight too many people to get the policies under way to make the company pay its way."[43]

Farnsworth could not understand why such a heavy debt had not been paid during the prosperity of the war and worked to establish new policies in relation to television and defense "so the company could make some money . . . and the prospects looked very good—but our bankers made it impossible to raise enough funds to operate on until our new program started off."[44] In effect, the company was going to be forced to sell "unless they, the other Directors, would agree to new policies."[45] In November 1947, several key board members resigned: Nicholas replaced McCargar as chair of the board;[46] Farnsworth replaced Martin as a vice president and board member; Abe Fortas was appointed as a new member of the board;[47] and resignations were accepted from several others.[48] Farnsworth went to a Washington meeting with Charles Stec, who had worked for him in the lab at Philco and who was now in charge of nonmilitary contracts for the Bureau of Shipping. In Washington Farnsworth attracted new business for the struggling corporation.

CORPORATE RESTRUCTURING OR SALE

Board resignations, budget cuts, and talk of selling the corporation contributed to an atmosphere of instability. In 1948 a business management counsel was hired to assist in restructuring the corporation. As a result, one of the factories was sold, excess equipment liquidated, operations consolidated, the payroll reduced, and the price for receivers lowered in hope of attracting working capital. Lowering prices was not enough though: the larger customers such as Sampson Company of Chicago were rapidly losing faith in the Farnsworth corporation

Technical Progress to Date: 1939–1948

Patents. By 1939 Farnsworth had amassed ninety-seven patents. Between 1939 and 1942, he filed for nineteen more. These were primarily further improvements on the image dissector and various reproducing devices. There were

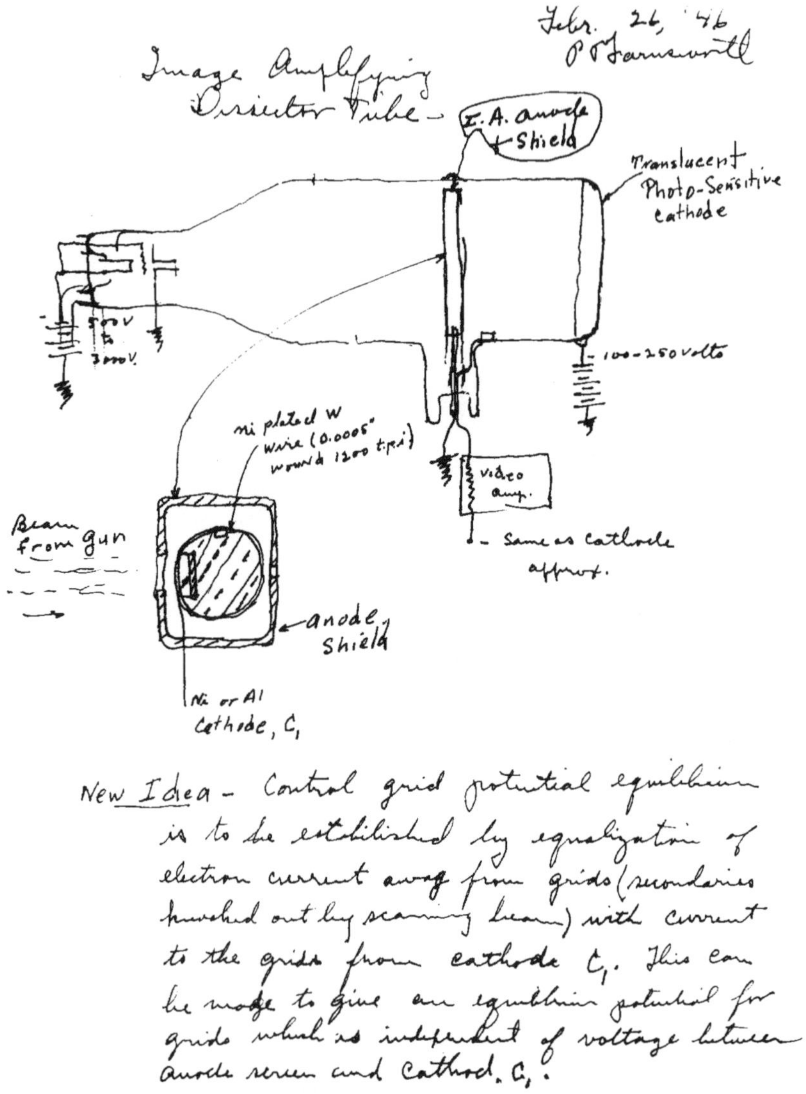

Improving the image dissector tube was a continual task. Experiments to improve this tube appear constantly throughout the logs. Note the new idea to establish equilibirum.

Technical Progress to Date: 1939–1948 (continued)

three patents reissued, all relating to the image amplifier and dissector (RE 22,009, RE 21,504, and RE 21,818; see Appendix A). Between 1941 and 1948 he filed for only one new patent, this one for an image-reproducing device (no. 2,355,212). His research log books indicated he was working with 441 lines on

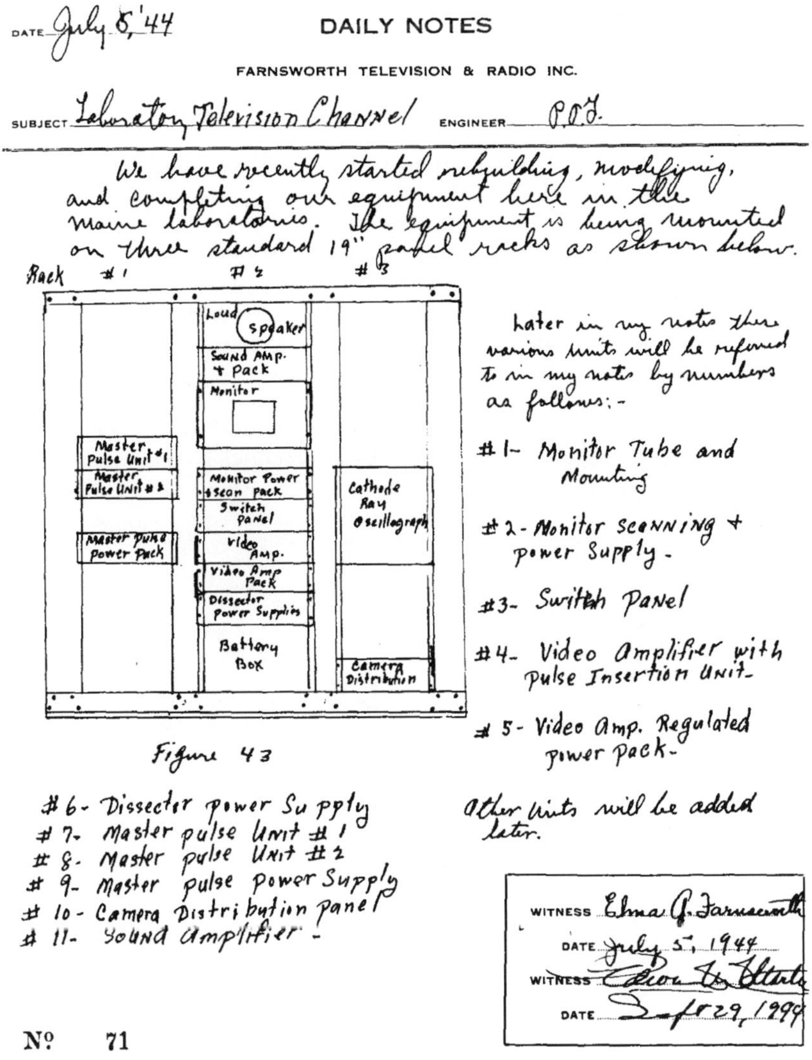

DATE July 5, '44

DAILY NOTES

FARNSWORTH TELEVISION & RADIO INC.

SUBJECT Laboratory Television Channel ENGINEER P.T.F.

We have recently started rebuilding, modifying, and completing our equipment here in the Maine laboratories. The equipment is being mounted on three standard 19" panel racks as shown below.

Rack #1 #2 #3

Loud Speaker
Sound Amp. + Pack
Monitor
Master Pulse Unit #1
Master Pulse Unit #2
Master Pulse Power Pack
Monitor Power + Scan Pack
Switch Panel
Video Amp.
Video Amp Pack
Dissector Power Supplies
Battery Box
Cathode Ray Oscillograph
Camera Distribution

Figure 43

Later in my notes these various units will be referred to in my notes by numbers as follows:-

#1- Monitor Tube and Mounting

#2- Monitor Scanning + power Supply-

#3- Switch Panel

#4- Video Amplifier with Pulse Insertion Unit-

#5- Video Amp. Regulated power pack-

#6- Dissector power Supply
#7- Master pulse Unit #1
#8- Master pulse Unit #2
#9- Master pulse power Supply
#10- Camera Distribution panel
#11- Sound Amplifier-

Other Units will be added later.

WITNESS Elma G. Farnsworth
DATE July 5, 1944
WITNESS [illegible]
DATE Sept 29, 1944

№ 71

Here we see Farnsworth's sketch for his closed-circuit television laboratory in Maine. Note his initials as each engineer was required to sign the daily notes and have them witnessed. One of the witnesses here was Elma G. Farnsworth.

Technical Progress to Date: 1939–1948 (continued)

a 14-inch tube. During this time his patent list tells only a part of the technical story. Work projects include continued image dissector and projection tube improvements. He saw projection experiments as a means of increasing screen size. Work also included tungsten velvet screen (1940), a method for making condensers (1940), frequency modulation recording (1940), a video radio transmission system (1943), color television (1944), suspended reflection (1945), electron acceleration (1946), and objective mirror lens systems (in both 1947 and 1948).[a]

Comments. Farnsworth's personal contributions to the war effort came from the lab in Maine, where he directed the research work for the corporation. His ideas were credited with the developments surrounding a guided bomb, telemetering, and a weather sleuth.

The television-guided bomb used Farnsworth's image dissector tube so the image of a target could be transmitted from the bomb to the plane or ground control stations that in turn could direct the bomb to the target with "terrifying accuracy."[b] The television-telemetering device provided the aircraft pilot with warning of things he could not see from the vantage point of the plane. The weather sleuth was an airborne camera in weather balloons to improve weather tracing.[c]

Although these were wartime mechanisms, Farnsworth was quick to point out the peacetime applications. The television-guided bomb (camera), he commented was so small "it fits into an eighteen-inch cylinder, [and] is ideal for spot[ting] visual hookups of newsworthy occurrences, such as parades, fires [and] sporting events."[d] The weather tracker could, of course, improve peacetime weather reporting.

a. See Research Notebooks for the 1939–1948 period in the Farnsworth Papers, Box 61, Book 3; Box 62, Book 2; Box 37, File 2; Box 65, File 4; Box 66, File 2. These are highly theoretical notes with massive mathematical calculations logged and witnessed.

b. Norman Carlisle, "Farnsworth of Television," *Coronet* (October 1946), p. 126. The armed services ordered military equipment from many manufacturers; RCA's iconoscope, the orthicon, and image orthicon were also used in guided missiles.

c. In drafting a bicentennial presentation for ITT, W. J. Williams indicated that Farnsworth, "was one of two manufacturers that supplied television equipment," during the war. See "From Capehart to Farnsworth to ITT," W. J. Williams, March 18, 1994, ITT Library Papers.

d. Carlisle, pp. 126–27.

because of its inability to supply a steady inventory.[49] Merchandising chains were interested in the low-priced units, and when they were unavailable from Farnsworth, they simply switched producers. The Farnsworth corporation was also having trouble with its own local distributors because it was paying too much attention to the larger retailers, who in fact were undercutting the local Farnsworth corporation dealers. In other words, according to Freeman "Customers . . . [doing] comparison shopping saw the same units at the chain stores they saw at their local service sales dealer and the small retailer's price was always higher, so they couldn't move the merchandise."[50] As a result neither the local nor the large retail distributors were happy with the Farnsworth corporation.

In the winter of 1949, a rapid succession of events led to the sale of Farnsworth Television and Radio Corporation to International Telephone and Telegraph (ITT).

The process actually began with stock purchase and merger discussions, which had been going on between the two corporations for two years, but an attractive offer had never been forthcoming.[51] The sale had to be mutually beneficial—ITT was interested in increasing its presence in the United States, and Farnsworth needed cash to pay its debts.

During discussions with ITT, there was another attempt at a financial rescue through a stock sale. In January 1949, the corporation filed with the Securities and Exchange Commission to sell additional commodities. The financial pictures were confusing. The *New York Times* quoted the debts reported in the Securities and Exchange Commission prospectus to be "a $140,000 [$1,007,050] inventory loan and a $300,000 [$2,157,980] mortgage loan."[52] Corporate losses from the end of the war through October 1948 were reported at $10,590,000 [$76,176,800].[53] The publication of conflicting information produced a one-hour halt to the trading of Farnsworth stock on January 14, 1949. There was a discrepancy between losses reported to the Securities and Exchange Commission (SEC) and published losses for the same period. The Commission was told the loss for the first six months of 1948 (April 30 to October 31, 1948) was at $3,100,000 [$22,299,100]. However, the Farnsworth corporation had earlier reported a loss for the same period at only $724,000 [$5,207,930].[54]

Whatever the cause of the SEC discrepancies, Nicholas quickly dispelled any misgivings or misrepresentations. On January 14 he indicated that the deficit was increased in the SEC report "because of an additional provision of $1,765,000 [$12,696,100] for inventory reserve and write-downs and another reserve of $396,000 [$2,848,530] to cover a possible loss on the investment in an affiliate. Other audit adjustments account for an additional $233,000 of the loss."[55] Two weeks later he added that it was the "downward trend in prices of television receivers . . . and a realistic appraisal of trade conditions together with other audit adjustment[s] produce the loss figure," reported to the SEC.[56] Whatever the reasons for the differences, the contradictions created confusion and added to the mistrust in the consumer as well as the exchange market.[57]

At the same time the proposed new stock issue made news, the corporation was undergoing a business and legal affairs analysis by Roy D. Jackson, a business management counsel from Columbus, Ohio. The beginning reports were optimistic, but they ended with little hope of reestablishment. Jackson's first report filed October 27, 1948, was positive. "It is our opinion, at this writing, that the business can be made profitable." Noting that "hundreds of thousands of dollars have been unwisely spent," the final recommendation was "that the business not be liquidated or merged. In either case the moneys realized would be but a fraction of the company's true value."[58] Jackson suggested trimming the expenses by selling radio station WGL, valued at $215,000 [$1,527,300], and transferring corporate operations from Fort Wayne to Marion. As a result, the station was sold to the News Sentinel Broadcasting Company Incorporated.[59] The money from the station could be used for working capital, and the move to Marion would save in labor costs.[60] The next month, in his November 11 report, Jackson reversed the recommendation that the operations move to Marion, and said they should be consolidated in Fort Wayne.[61] Jackson's January 14, 1949, report sounded optimistic. He recommended a business marketing plan, dividing the country into geographic areas with regional sales departments representing different products.[62]

The reports held out hope, but they changed tone suddenly, likely due to the confusion on the stock exchange. Less than one month after the January report another was subtitled, the "Good News, Bad News Report." The good news was a payroll deduction and a reduced radio and television set price list that was reporting improved sales. Significant savings resulted from the sale of the Marion, Indiana, manufacturing plant to RCA. The plant was sold for the "book value," of $485,000 [$3,445,310].[63] The bad news was that the shortage in cash meant that very little product was going out the doors, and distributors who had ordered were increasingly unhappy.[64] Less than a week later Jackson concluded, "May I say . . . but for our having disposed of these unneeded assets and utilized the proceeds as cash working capital, we would have been out of business with the company being forced into liquidation."[65]

FARNSWORTH HOLDS BUSINESS TOGETHER

Jackson credits Nicholas and Farnsworth with holding Farnsworth Television together and making possible its sale to ITT. In a letter to Everson, Jackson reported, "that now it can be told . . . that the U.S. Marshal was sitting on our doorstep" with the lien for past taxes.[66] However, Nicholas "did a marvelous job in negotiating the sale of the business . . . Pulling the rabbit right out of the hat when it appeared we had only a few days to live."[67] In the process, however, Nicholas had lost the support of most of his management team and the board of directors, with only Farnsworth and a few others supporting the sale.[68] The board of directors authorized the sale of the Farnsworth corporation, February 10, 1949, but the struggle was not yet over, and the sale not yet final—it had to be approved by the corporation's stockholders.[69] Philo Farnsworth played a vital role in the rallying of the final vote from the stockholders.

The vote of the Farnsworth corporation stockholders could not be taken for granted. Because of some of the differing reports from Jackson, some stockholders held out the hope that the company could survive. One stockholder from New York, Harry Hecht, claimed that the value of the assets "even after consideration of the value of patents of Farnsworth, and after writeoffs, the stock is worth many times" more than the ITT offer.[70] Robert W. Kenny, a stockholder from California, charged that the proxy material sent to the stockholders requesting the vote was "false and misleading as to the value of the [Farnsworth] stock."[71] Both filed suit in California and New York, respectively, to stop the sale. These stockholders mounted what Farnsworth called a bitter attack on the planned transaction.[72] Nicholas outlined the ITT offer, the corporate losses from 1946 to 1948, and informed them that without the sale the value of their holdings would be "a nominal amount, or even nothing."[73] The *New York Times* summarized the proposed sale as "Operation Rescue performed in peace times."[74] The stockholder meeting was scheduled and postponed several times as management struggled to convince stockholders to sell, and the opposition sought greater value for their stock.[75] Farnsworth wrote directly to the stockholders, urging them to vote for the sale. "We are in serious danger of losing our last chance to salvage anything for ourselves and stockholders," he wrote. The declaration of bankruptcy had already been approved by the board of directors, and, he continued, "it is important to note that management could find no other offer at this time." Even the stockholders' special committee had been unable to offer an alternative. Farnsworth stated his recommendation as follows, "I am voting in favor of the IT&T plan . . . enclosed [is] another form of proxy and a return envelope for your use."[76]

It was Vice President Philo Farnsworth who conducted the stockholders' meeting and on May 4 announced the sale had been approved.[77] The unofficial proxy votes were more than enough to carry the majority.[78] The official announcement came the next day. The agreed resolutions called for

1. Formation of a separate corporation, the Capehart-Farnsworth Corporation and assignment to it of properties, assets, and businesses of the Farnsworth corporation.

2. Transfer of Capehart-Farnsworth shares to ITT, in exchange for approximately 140,048 shares of ITT.
3. Change the name of the present Farnsworth corporation to F.A.R. Liquidating Corporation.[79]

The sale basically gave each of the Farnsworth corporate stockholders one share of ITT stock for every twelve Farnsworth corporation stocks (see Appendix C).

FARNSWORTH TELEVISION AND RADIO SOLD

During its existence the Farnsworth Television and Radio Corporation had not paid its investors a dividend, but good money was made in buying and selling its stock. By 1949 the wartime leadership of the company had bogged it down in manufacturing deficits and overextended the debt. As a result, it was undercapitalized and unable to meet the costs of the transition to peacetime manufacturing. During its last three years, with the corporation's fiscal years ending April 30, from 1946 through January 31, 1949 it lost $6,174,231 [$44,411,200].[80] According to *Newsweek,* "the Farnsworth Corporation [management], having muffed the best commercial chances in the industry, was on the financial rocks."[81] During the postwar years when the television industry was showing explosive growth potential, the Farnsworth corporation was weighed down with financial management problems and its war debt. In his history of ITT, Robert Sobel later commented that just before ITT purchased the Farnsworth corporation it was "woefully short on managers capable of leading the way in consumer products."[82]

Reflecting upon the loss, Robert Rexroad, ITT public affairs director, noted that although the Farnsworth corporation television sets were considered the "Cadillacs of the industry," the company simply, "never had sufficient financial backing," which was the reason for its downfall. He described the company as, "in dire straights by the time ITT bought it . . . [but] hindsight tells you that as popular as television turned out to be, he [the Farnsworth corporation] probably could have made a go of it, if he could have hung on awhile."[83]

In spite of the corporate and personal struggles, Philo Farnsworth himself had contributed to the war effort in terms of scientific military applications for television and "boxes for bullets." From 1938 to 1949, he had developed and filed for another eighteen patents (see Appendix A). However, only three years after the formation of the company in 1938, the war had derailed his dream for consumer television. Despite an aggressive growth program and the corporation's launch of television set manufacturing, he was simply too late.

8

Farnsworth Television—The Final Decades

1949–1971

Chronology

Farnsworth

1949 — The Farnsworth Television and Radio Corporation becomes Capehart-Farnsworth, a wholly owned subsidiary of ITT. Philo T. Farnsworth is appointed vice president and director of research. He's the only management officer carried from the old organization.

August 1950 — Capehart-Farnsworth television set orders exceed $3 million.

September 1950 — Farnsworth describes a new memory tube and its applications for military and industrial work.

1952 — Price reductions in Capehart-Farnsworth television sets are announced to make them more competitive in the mass market.

June 1953 — Farnsworth's 3-D television tube adds depth to the picture. It is promoted as advantageous for handling radioactive materials.

• Farnsworth describes his research as Buck Rogers projects.

1954 — Capehart-Farnsworth is divided into two entities. Capehart focuses on manufacturing and Farnsworth on research.

Electronic Media

1950 — FCC approves CBS color system.

1951 — Cold war leads to blacklisting. Manufacturing of color stopped due to Korean War.

1952 — FCC issues *Sixth Report and Order* ending freeze on station licenses and allocation of frequencies established.

1953 — FCC approves RCA standards for color television.

Farnsworth	Electronic Media
March 1954 — Farnsworth is hospitalized for perforated ulcer.	
August 1954 — Farnsworth Electronics organized for research and development of industrial television and defense applications.	
	1955 — Popular evening radio programs disappearing rapidly as television evolves. • Commercial television begins in England.
May 1956 — Capehart manufacturing interests are sold to the Ben Gross Corporation.	1956 — Ampex develops first monochrome videotape recorder. • Cable television emerges and FCC decides to regulate.
July 1957 — Farnsworth appears as a guest on the Garry Moore show, *I've Got a Secret.* The panel fails to identify him.	
	1960 — FCC issues statement of programming policy.
January 1961 — Outlook for fusion energy promising.	1961 — FCC approves stereo broadcasting on FM. • Alan Shepard, first man in space produces television coverage.
	1962 — First satellite launched for AT&T and television signal relay.
1965 — Farnsworth suffers a seizure and collapses while attending ITT convention.	
	1966 — Television coverage of Vietnam War
1967 — Farnsworth breaks ties with ITT and returns to Maine.	1967 — Carnegie Report helps to establish public radio and television. • *Public Broadcasting Act* passes Congress.
December 1968 — Philo T. Farnsworth & Associates is organized.	
	1969 — Man on the moon television coverage provided for worldwide audience.
March 11, 1971 — Farnsworth dies at age sixty-four.	

≈

PHILO T. FARNSWORTH HAD COME A LONG WAY SINCE THE CROCKER BANK'S RESEARCH organization in 1926. The companies bearing his name had been organized and reorganized four times, culminating in the foundation of the Farnsworth Television and Radio Corporation in Fort Wayne (see organization chart, p. 160). Farnsworth's personal achievements in television were capped at the inception of these Fort Wayne manufacturing, distribution, and research facilities, and he was one of the key leaders in the sale of Farnsworth Television and Radio Corporation to ITT.

FARNSWORTH AND CAPEHART: DIVISIONS OF ITT

The International Telephone and Telegraph Corporation brought the merits of three national companies together: Farnsworth, Capehart, and ITT. Farnsworth's assets were in the name, which was still valuable and became the property of ITT, along with existing patents and manufacturing plants. ITT felt it could give Farnsworth financial backing and make it profitable. The chief asset of Capehart also was its name—a name owned by Farnsworth. The assets of ITT were its international operations. The new organization formed from this acquisition was Capehart-Farnsworth, a wholly owned entity of ITT.

The purchase of the Farnsworth Television and Radio Corporation was but one small part of ITT's postwar expansion. The Farnsworth company was thought to be complementary to several other ITT operations: Federal Telephone and Radio, Federal Telecommunications, Kellogg Switchboard and Supply, and the Coolerator Company. Bringing these companies together was a part of ITT management's nationalization strategy. It was supposed to "achieve greater efficiency and infuse IT&T's domestic nonmilitary operations."[1] Kellogg, the money maker at the time, was expected to provide the leadership within the group. ITT felt Farnsworth would continue his research and Capehart would continue to manufacture. *Newsweek* reported the 1949 sale of the Farnsworth corporation, "look[ed] promising enough so that IT&T stock gained half a point."[2]

ITT MANAGEMENT SHUFFLES: FARNSWORTH IS THE CONSTANT

In order to understand some of the challenges of the Farnsworth organizations within ITT, it is important to view them within the historical context of ITT's struggles. Between 1949 and 1967, ITT and Farnsworth subsidiaries underwent eight management changes, each bringing new management philosophy, new improvements, new directions, and frustration (see Appendix F for ITT-Farnsworth management history). The only constant was Farnsworth, vice president and director of research and technical consultant to the ITT general operations. Pem Farnsworth reported the men at the plant used to say, that "presidents come and presidents go, but Farnsworth goes on forever."[3]

Farnsworth was one of only two company officers to carry into ITT. Nicholas was hired as Stone's assistant (Ellery E. Stone was the first president of the

Farnsworth Corporation Evolution: 1926–1968

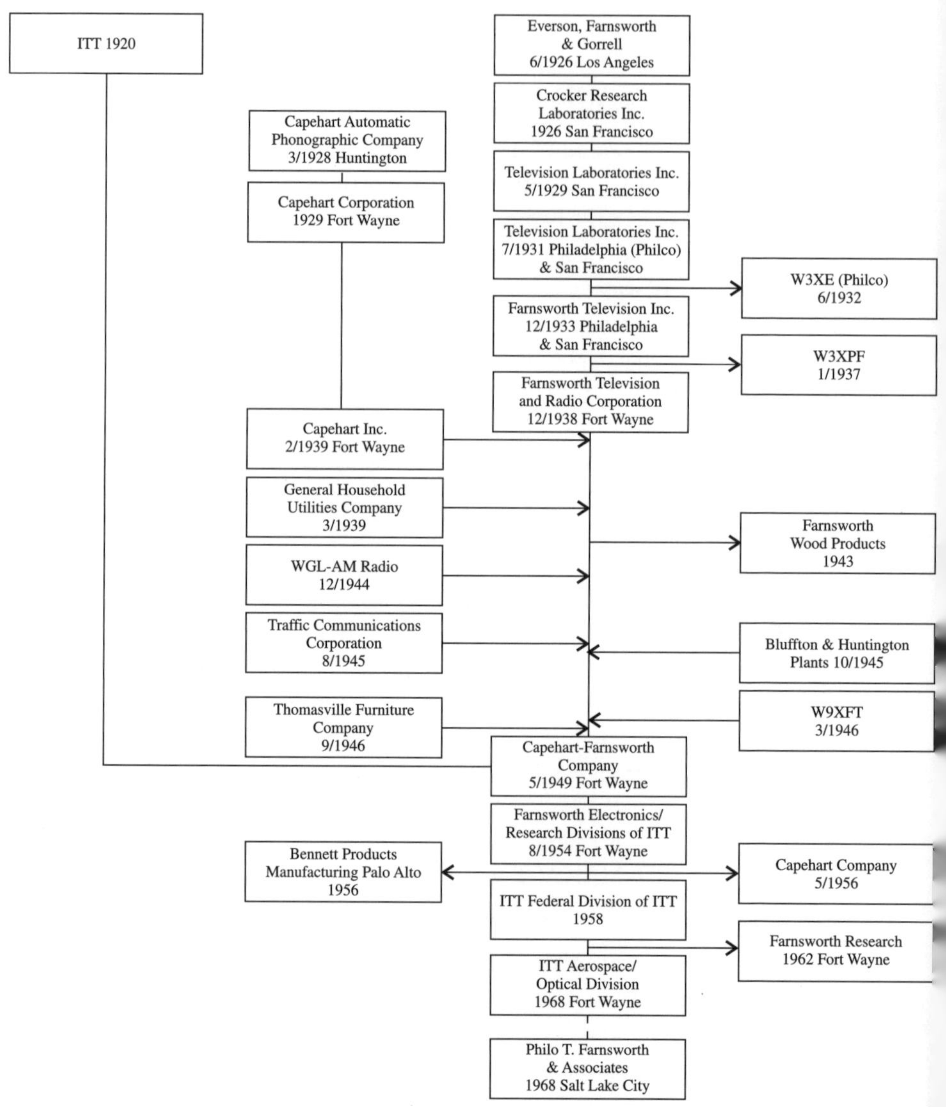

Adapted from ITT chart: ITT Capehart & Farnsworth Chronology File.

Capehart-Farnsworth division of ITT) during a brief transition period and worked for a short time at the New York offices, but died in 1953.[4] Everson's name appears within the papers of ITT, but merely as a member of the management advisory board and a consultant working to recruit engineers.[5]

At the launching of the Capehart-Farnsworth Corporation, Philo declared that the new ITT subsidiary would not only be building upon an established production record, but that production would be "increased particularly in the field of industrial television as well as in the production of commercial television receivers."[6] Industrial television and "fusion" would be the center of his research for the next two decades. Manufacturing was a Capehart corporate responsibility; research was a Farnsworth responsibility. In essence Capehart and Farnsworth were two entities under one ITT division.

CAPEHART-FARNSWORTH MANUFACTURING

The Farnsworth Television and Radio Corporation became Capehart-Farnsworth in 1949, one of five branches of ITT.[7] ITT assumed the debt obligations, as well as the manufacturing and research operations of the former Farnsworth Television and Radio Corporation.[8]

Farnsworth's Capehart model TV, one of the final sets made in the Fort Wayne plant, 1948–1949. Courtesy Elma G. Farnsworth.

Even with the financial backing of ITT, Capehart-Farnsworth television sets were never able to capture a significant share of the television market. They were competing against the giants—RCA, General Electric and Westinghouse, who were winning the battle for the television market.[9] Unfortunately for both ITT and the Farnsworth company, the other ITT businesses were losing the battle even more rapidly. Sluggish sales presented a difficult situation for Behn (ITT's founder), since the companies he'd purchased for manufacturing were doing poorly. As a result Capehart-Farnsworth was under scrutiny. Reflecting on the history of high-tech in Fort Wayne, *News-Sentinel* reporter Kevin Leininger concluded that ITT decided to get out of the business of manufacturing television, when "it could make more money by filling government Cold War defense contracts than making TV sets."[10] Anthony Sampson put it bluntly: "The Capehart-Farnsworth manufacturing operation, along with other acquisitions that had looked so promising in 1949, were disastrous."[11]

In 1954 the Capehart-Farnsworth Division of ITT split.[12] Philo Farnsworth continued his research, but Capehart was sold. Harrison wrote to Everson explaining that the sale was for the purpose of separating research and development from the consumer manufacturing product sales.[13] Two years later Capehart was sold again to the Ben Gross Corporation. The sale was officially announced May 7, 1956, and included all of the Capehart assets relative to the brand name and trademarks as well as one plant in Flora, Indiana. However, the Fort Wayne facilities were retained by ITT and expanded to meet the new research organization—Farnsworth Electronics.[14] This operation would become the foundation for today's Aerospace/Optical Division of ITT.

FARNSWORTH ELECTRONICS AND ITT FEDERAL

The official announcement of the formation of Farnsworth Electronics came August 5, 1954. Its responsibilities were related to industrial television, defense electronics, and atomic energy. The Farnsworth Electronics research enterprise evolved through several stages of organization and reorganization between 1949 and 1968, before Farnsworth broke with the ITT umbrella. What began as Capehart-Farnsworth (1949 to 1954) would be the foundation for Farnsworth Electronics (1954 to 1958), then ITT Federal (1958 to 1967).[15] Then Philo left ITT and moved to Salt Lake City, where he established Farnsworth & Associates (1968 to 1971). Farnsworth Electronics/ITT Federal continued in Fort Wayne and eventually became ITT Aerospace Optical (1968 to present).

Farnsworth personally had little to do with the early manufacturing operations of the Capehart television sets other than that they used his patents. His responsibilities were focused on management, research, and development.[16]

His individual contract stipulated that he was to devote his entire time and efforts toward research. His salary was $20,000 per year [$127,286], and the corporation was the beneficiary of all of his patents.[17] The research projects related to industrial television, military electronics, and national defense contracts, but as time progressed they focused entirely upon fusion.[18]

Everson: What Might Have Been

At the formation of Farnsworth Electronics, Everson was on retainer as a consultant working to support Farnsworth's personal research, but he was eliminated from the management advisory board. Writing Farnsworth, Everson contemplated what might have been: "You, Jess, and I had a long association; though we didn't always see eye-to-eye we did accomplish our purpose. I often wonder what might have happened had I been permitted to have a more active interest in the Fort Wayne operations."[19] In December 1954, H. L. Hull, president of Farnsworth Electronics sought to recognize Everson, presenting him with his twenty-five-year pin, "not only as a member of the Farnsworth family, but really the godfather of the whole organization."[20]

Everson's role as consultant was primarily a recruiting one. In 1955 he was touring universities throughout the nation, hiring engineers for Farnsworth Electronics.[21] We learn a great deal about Farnsworth's style in the lab from the directions Hull gave Everson in his search for people to hire as Farnsworth's assistants. Hull wanted "a strong applied physicist, preferably with experience in electron optics." "This man," Hull continued, "should be able to understand Phil, but in no case able to out-invent him. It would be desirable if he could lag behind and be able to finish a project while Phil goes ahead."[22] The memo clearly reflects the value of Farnsworth to ITT as a catalyst and prolific inventor, a man of ideas. He was forever refining the experiment. Whatever he was working on could always be made better.

Another Setback in Health

Farnsworth's health suffered another setback in 1954, when he was hospitalized with a perforated ulcer. Pem remembers that he was transported to the hospital alone, and by the time she arrived, Dr. Justin Arata "calmly informed me that he had just removed two-thirds of Phil's stomach!"[23] The recovery process was difficult, and again Philo was advised to take a vacation and get away from work. So he took a short break, during which H. H. Butner, vice president of ITT, reported that the delay was a bit of a setback that affected the development of Farnsworth's version of the color tube.[24] However, in a matter of months Philo was back at work.

FARNSWORTH INDUSTRIAL AND DEFENSE RESEARCH

Industrial and defense contracts were the mainstay of Farnsworth Electronics' work. Closed-circuit security and surveillance, submarine communications, memory tubes for color, and 3-D television were Philo's "Buck Rogers" projects during this era of the Cold War.

Industrial Surveillance

Industrial video was created for surveillance and handling hazardous materials and was targeted for banks, warehouses, racetracks, and newspaper offices as well as to a "wide variety of other national industries, political meetings and social activities."[25] The venture was an ambitious one in partnership with General Electric—Farnsworth produced basically closed-circuit monitoring equipment. In banks they would support security, and in public meetings they could provide a public record.

Cold War Defense Research

Farnsworth's personal energies were now primarily dedicated to producing electronic equipment for the armed services. His former patent lawyer, Donald K. Lippincott (now the patent lawyer for the army), was helpful in facilitating defense contracts. A $10 million contract [$64,603,800] awarded to the company from the Army Signal Corps "to produce communications equipment" and a visit to Puerto Rico to view Farnsworth's work on submarine detection devices are indicative of the Farnsworth defense focus.[26]

Memory Tube Increases Definition

Farnsworth hailed the memory tube as "revolutionizing television reception . . . expected to reduce manufacturing costs . . . make possible three-dimension pictures as well as simplify the projection of color . . . no matter which of the three different systems of color transmission is used."[27] Addressing the San Francisco press meeting just prior to the meeting of the Electrical Club, Farnsworth talked about the RCA versus CBS debates regarding color television standards under consideration by the Federal Communications Commission and credited the University of California-Berkeley scientist Ernest O. Lawrence for his monumental work on color.[28] His new memory tube, however, was to "absolutely, eliminate the flicker in television, increase the intensity of the images by 3,000 to 5,000 times over present tubes . . . and would have important applications in military and industrial field[s]."[29] When questioned by reporters, he refused to comment further on the military applications. America was in the middle of the Cold War.

3-D Television

By 1953 Farnsworth had a closed-circuit "three dimensional industrial television . . . Unlike conventional television, . . . Farnsworth 3-D television adds the all important depth dimension, which makes it possible for the operators to undertake the most delicate operations . . . a vital part in handling radio-active substances."[30] Describing 3-D television at a banquet in the Hotel Utah (Salt Lake City), he said he was "doing more work now on Buck Rogers gadgets than on television."[31] Farnsworth had left commercial television behind as both he and the company found more promise in military contracts. They had a diversified list of specializations: missile electronics, infrared, countermeasures, radar, electromagnetic theory, optics, solid-state and applied physics, and special-purpose tubes.[32]

I've Got a Secret

Farnsworth's commercial television research had long since ceased, but his Horatio Alger story continued to run in the media. On July 3, 1957, Garry Moore's I've Got a Secret focused on Farnsworth's early work in television. "Dr. X," appeared before the panel of experts that included: Bill Cullen, Faye Emerson, Jayne Meadows, and Henry Morgan.[33] Preparations for the program were not unlike those today. When Farnsworth arrived at the studio for rehearsal, he was informed that "if it appears we are ignoring you at times it is only because we are busy with other segments of the show. We will get to you shortly." Farnsworth signed the required release forms, was shown how to enter and exit, then worked with stand-ins.[34] On the show, the panel was unable to identify the mystery guest as the inventor of television. It was all in good fun and "Dr. X" received a carton of cigarettes as his prize and some inventor fan mail asking for his advice.

Back in Fort Wayne, more serious events were unfolding—another change in ITT management.

FARNSWORTH AND FUSION RESEARCH

In the mid-1930s when Farnsworth was working on his multipactor tube, he described a "phenomenon which was very puzzling: a minute, bright starlike glow in the center of the multipactor tube."[35] The phenomenon was observed a second time during World War II experiments while Farnsworth was working on "developing a Klystron-like vacuum tube."[36] Robert L. Hirsch, a later scientific colleague, described the "localized glow [as] at the center of a spherically symmetric high vacuum multipactor tube." Hirsch footnoted it as a "sustained, high-frequency, secondary-emission discharge."[37]

When Farnsworth first noticed this reaction, he was preoccupied with television research and unable to explain the energy being produced. However as his interests in commercial television abated and industrial and defense research progressed, it was an experiment he remembered. Two decades later it was this experiment that provided the foundation for reproduction of fusion, a new low-cost energy source.[38]

Farnsworth's approach to this energy source was contrary to the mainstream nuclear energy research of the time. His investigation into fusion was publicized as an electronic process, representing an "entirely new approach to fusion experiment[s]" that would result in a new "low cost nuclear fusion process."[39] His work met with skepticism from the beginning, but he was used to criticism and felt it was no different than that he had heard from the conventional scientists when he first began developing electronic television.

Farnsworth's proposals were privately funded by ITT in contrast with the government-funded Atomic Energy Commission, which had spent more than $28 million in 1957 and $32 million in 1960 on atomic energy experimentation.[40] The prevailing attitude favored what the *New York Times* erroneously referred to as fission.[41] This means splitting the atomic nucleus, which is the atomic bomb reaction or, in controlled situations as we have today, is a nuclear energy reaction producing electricity. But this type of energy was not only difficult to contain, it required a lot of heat and was costly to produce. Farnsworth contended that these limitations of the nuclear power system would not do the job over time. Nevertheless, it was the scientific direction of the day.

The Atomic Energy Commission acknowledged that they had been aware of Farnsworth's experimentation since the mid-1950s, but that it did not have enough information to evaluate the probability of success. The *New York Times* report sounded anything but promising. It noted studies from other scientists who found Farnsworth's methods unpromising, as well as "subsequent papers published by scientists refuting his [Farnsworth's] conclusions." It noted that the Farnsworth fusion experiment was being conducted without government funds or the support of the Atomic Energy Commission.[42]

Farnsworth's fusion work was entirely underwritten with a modest program from ITT.[43] Farnsworth described his fusion as an inexpensive energy source providing large amounts of power in small packages. However unpromising Farnsworth's experiments seemed to the scientific critics, the ITT stockholders were supportive. Rumors of fusion development resulted in ITT stock being extremely strong. ITT "wound up 1960 as the sixteenth most active stock traded on the New York Stock Exchange, closing the year with a gain of 9½ points at 48."[44] Farnsworth's fusion experiments initially drew enough attention that ITT considered moving the labs to New York. However, Philo was able to negotiate a new contract and the Farnsworth Research Corporation was established.[45]

FARNSWORTH RESEARCH CORPORATION: FUSION

The Farnsworth Research Corporation was still a wholly owned subsidiary, with offices and the lab in Fort Wayne at the same location. Operationally there was little that actually happened with this reorganization, but it did place Philo in a position of extended strength. His salary jumped from the earlier negotiated level of $20,000 to $50,000 annually [$289,189].[46] The new five-year contract included substantial benefits, retirement, and ITT stock-purchase options. It also continued assigning all of Farnsworth's patents to the company and restricted Farnsworth from engaging in any "business competitive with any business of Farnsworth Research or of International Telephone and Telegraph" for a period of three years following any termination of the contract.[47] In his research notes, Farnsworth records that the policy of the new company was "to make few if any model changes [in the tubes being manufactured and] concentrate development of product on improvement of reliability so that each sale may be guaranteed for life."[48] The sale of tubes for a variety of industrial and military purposes had become profitable for ITT.

Farnsworth was optimistic about the future of his fusion experiments. "Today [March 10, 1961] the latest model tube . . . was operated at the highest radiation count yet obtained."[49] Following initial successes, his descriptions take an almost prophetic humanitarian tone. The fusion unit, as he called it, was going to help "provide food for all the undernourished people of the Earth." Small units would be capable of providing "power for an entire community." Engineers from all over the world would be trained to operate the units so that the benefits would be "taken directly to *the people*" (emphasis in the original). In spacecraft the ratio of fuel to the payload would be reversed and thus capacities increased. Asteroids passing the earth could be towed by fusion-powered spacecraft. Fusion units would be used for reclaiming the deserts and building floating cities. Pollution would be a thing of the past, and tropical storms would be diverted away from populated areas. Just as was the case with television, "there would be countless industries . . . spin-offs . . . with fusion." Farnsworth concluded, "We just need to plan ahead to make the transition from a low energy culture to a high energy culture; to make it as painless as possible."[50]

Farnsworth was upbeat. His notes reflect optimism and a continual flow of ideas. In a few of the rare personal remarks appearing in his research journals at this time, he records man's landing on the moon, with no comment; a suggestion that if government wanted to provide for the aging, the best way to it was to "guarantee that their dollar shall [be] worth exactly what it was when they set up provisions for their old age;" and, a personal reminder to go home, "clean the garage and fix the ceiling."[51]

The early years at ITT were comfortable for Farnsworth. It was at ITT where he felt able to weather the storms of industry.[52] However, as time passed, ITT pressed to see a return on its fusion investments. Farnsworth's work was being underwritten without government or Atomic Energy Commission funding and ITT was growing impatient. So ITT put Farnsworth in a position of having to prove the operability of his research idea before giving him additional money for research, and thus did not pull back completely.[53] Because of pressure from the management, disappointing experiments, and friction with ITT, his health worsened.[54]

FUSION: A TELEVISION RERUN

The ITT patent portfolio was growing as a result of Philo's work, but so was ITT's impatience. While dressing for an ITT executives convention, Farnsworth suffered a seizure and fell unconscious.[55] He recovered and, although told to rest, returned to work shortly after the incident with increased personal determination. However ITT was withdrawing from the fusion project and Philo was withdrawing from ITT. The break between them was openly evidenced in a 1965 in-house newspaper article.

> The company [ITT] has been transformed from an international communications utility . . . to a manufacturer. This transformation was only possible as a result of the tremendous job of the original management.
>
> But several mistakes have been made, one being the acquisition of the Capehart and Farnsworth radio and electronic concerns. So there were differences in the board and the management which resulted in the decision to diversify into the fastest growing field, service.[56]

It is evident that the vision Behn saw, when ITT first purchased Farnsworth Television and Radio, had changed substantially under succeeding ITT management teams (see Appendix F). Then, too, there was the fact that fusion was a costly project receiving no government support nor public sponsorship. ITT was in fact competing against the millions of dollars that were being invested in the scientific community for atomic energy. In contrast, ITT's Farnsworth fusion project was a low-budget experiment with high hopes catalyzed from his vision. Farnsworth had been successful in creating fusion, but the experimental reaction had not been sustained to the point where it could produce unlimited energy resources.

Farnsworth felt he was making progress, but others were skeptical. According to his family, "what he [Phil] needed was about ten years rest, then he could have been a new man, but he didn't get it. They took him out of ITT on a stretcher up to Maine for him to recuperate . . . he didn't give up, that's the problem."[57] In May 1967 Farnsworth notified ITT's president that he was taking time off and had left "to recharge my human engines."[58] Resting and recuperating in Maine, Philo made plans to establish a new enterprise—Philo T. Farnsworth Associates, Inc.; at the same time ITT was preparing for his retirement and another reorganization.[59]

ITT was planning to end their agreement with Farnsworth. The personal contract, which Farnsworth had negotiated in the early 1960s, had a health clause. If, for any reason, Farnsworth were unable to perform his work, "for six consecutive months by reason of illness or other physical incapacity," ITT had the right to terminate the contract.[60] Albert E. Cookson, ITT vice president and technical director, sent Farnsworth the letter that would terminate employment, "due to your illness or physical incapacity."[61] Pem Farnsworth reports that she did not show the letter to her husband. Instead, she called Cookson, who assured her that there was "no intention of leaving Phil high and dry." He suggested they let the matter stand for thirty days, "at which time the case would be re-evaluated and a workable arrangement made according to Phil's health and wishes."[62] He would be on full salary until the matter was resolved. It appeared that ITT was willing to work with Farnsworth, wanted to retain him, but were also contractually and legally preparing the way for either eventuality. There is no indication in the records that Farnsworth ever saw the Cookson letter. However, by December 4, 1967, he was engaging in benefit and retirement negotiations and took a medical retirement from ITT early the next year.[63]

PHILO T. FARNSWORTH & ASSOCIATES

Farnsworth traveled to Florida, crisscrossed the country making a documentary on his life with KSL television, and traveled to Brigham Young University—where he was awarded his second honorary doctorate.[64] During this trip back to his roots, Farnsworth decided he would return to Utah.

After his travels, his health worsened, "I figure I have somewhere between three and five years to live . . . Within that time I want to give the world three things." They were fusion, a company organized to complete fusion, and other experimental contracts.[65] The mission statement of Farnsworth's new corporation involved the development of "some unique theories which may produce solutions to world problems."[66]

Financing Falls Through

Farnsworth moved to Salt Lake City because he felt it was home, even though he had not lived there for decades. From a business perspective he reasoned that

Salt Lake City could provide the labor market and the technical and business skills necessary to get the business started. Salt Lake City was also centrally located to the other business centers of the West—Los Angeles, San Francisco, Phoenix, and Denver. Financing for the business was to come from Midwestern Securities Corporation. The agreement outlined the sale of 5 million shares for long-term stabilized funding. William Sahley, president of Midwestern, promised $1.5 million in underwriting with an advance of $200,000 for interim financing [$7,379,310 and $983,908 respectively].[67] Philo T. Farnsworth & Associates was formed December 12, 1968,[68] its basis the continuing work on fusion. Farnsworth recruited a group of eight engineers from ITT who had worked for him in Fort Wayne and brought them to Salt Lake City.[69] Philo T. Farnsworth & Associates was located in a suburb of Salt Lake City (Draper, Utah). It was housed in an 8,000-square-foot manufacturing warehouse.

Unfortunately, financing did not come as promised, so Farnsworth took all of his personal assets, including his ITT stock and his retirement investments, to guarantee loans for the business. This personal investment was reported at more than $94,000 [$462,436].[70] When his money was all but used up, he placed a second mortgage on his home.

Midwestern Securities assured that support was forthcoming, but finances were continually postponed and plans eventually fell through.[71] It was too late. By 1970 Midwestern Securities had defaulted and Farnsworth was writing creditors to ask for understanding and patience.[72]

Despite the financial picture, there were glimmers of hope for the organization. In December 1969, while still working to get underwriting for the company, a status report records $61,700 in contracts awarded, and future estimates for corporate growth at more than $1 million "within 18 months, and two and one-half million within thirty-six months."[73] However, forecasts were overly optimistic from the start, and sales contracts were not sufficient to cover the investment and operations.

ITT Antagonism

Financing wasn't the only challenge faced by Farnsworth's new venture. Less than a month after its organization, ITT responded with vengeance. Farnsworth had written to Geneen just days after he organized in Utah, offering rights to "three new inventions of mine [which] should be patented by IT&T."[74] A response from Jack H. Vollbrecht, ITT vice president, acknowledged Farnsworth's new business and then accused Philo of a breach of his ITT contract. Farnsworth had hired ITT personnel, out of Fort Wayne, who were "under legal obligation not to disclose or use any of ITT's proprietary information" and "you [Farnsworth] are under legal obligation not to disclose." "Your company," the letter concludes, "and your proposed activities appear to breach

≈

Technical Progress to Date: 1969

Patents. Between 1950 and 1969, Farnsworth filed for fourteen patents. As tube manufacturing had become a profitable venture for ITT, much of this time was spent in research and testing various tubes — photo emission devices, image converter tubes, multiplier photo tubes, image dissector tubes, and storage tubes.[a] These were used in industrial television, surveillance, and defense applications. His most important patents of the time related to fusion

Notes of PHILO T. FARNSWORTH Page No. 1

RECORDED BY ME 10-20-55 (Date) Philo T. Farnsworth (Signature)

Nuclear Fusion Process

I propose to accomplish nuclear fusion for the purpose of energy liberation by direct nucleon scattering in a process which will be described in some detail. Broadly stated the process consists of the creation of a centrally directed electric field in which positively charged nuclear particles can be trapped and forced to oscillate through this central field until inelastic scattering occurs.

To achieve the creation of the required central field, an electron tube structure (see Fig. 1) will be used. This tube comprises essentially a spherical cathode 1, inside of which is positioned an anode 2 concentric with the cathode. This anode 2 is made from perforated metal (with round holes) of suitable mesh size and about 30% to 40% of the total area being hole area. Within the anode 2 is another anode 3 which is also spherical and concentric with cathode and anode 2. Anode 3 is to be made from a highly refractory material such as tungsten in the form of an open mesh or the equivalent.

The cathode emission is to be obtained by photo emission produced by very intense and very short ultraviolet radiation which is emitted at the center of the spheres as a result of the electron bombardment of gas ~~mole~~ atoms and by nuclear processes which occur there. This will be described later on.

Cathode 1 may be fabricated from such metals as nickel, copper, stainless steel etc. The inner surface of the cathode will be plated (or evaporated) with a coating of photoemissive material such as zinc.

Explained to Me October 20, 1955 (Date) Elma G. Farnsworth (Witness)

Explained to Me Nov 17 1955 (Date) [illegible] (Witness)

Farnsworth's work on nuclear fusion began early. Here some of his first notes reflect his earlier fusion process and theory.

Technical Progress to Date: 1969 (continued)

energy. These were Electric Discharge Device for producing interaction between nuclei (no. 2,941,100), Electron Gun in the form of a multipactor (no. 3,201,640), the Ion Transport Vacuum Pump (no. 3,181,028), Microwave Amplifier utilizing multipaction to produce periodically bunched electrons (no. 3,312,857), and his Method and Apparatus for producing nuclear-fusion reactions (no. 3,386,883). See Appendix A.

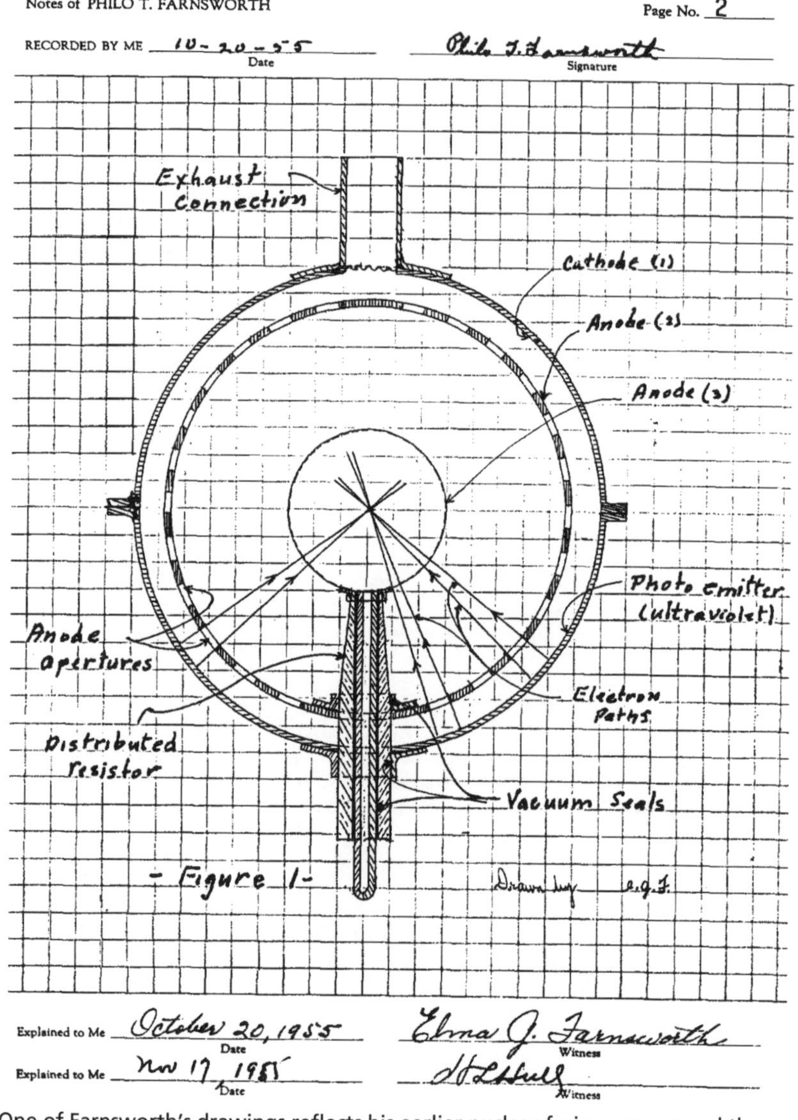

One of Farnsworth's drawings reflects his earlier nuclear fusion process and theory.

Technical Progress to Date: 1969 (continued)

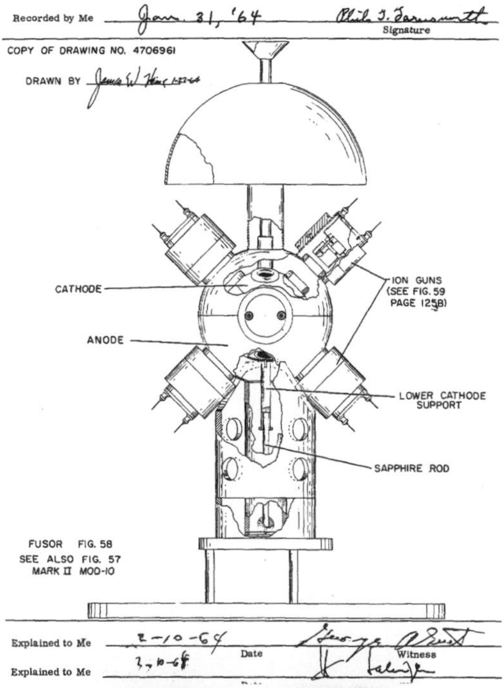

Recorded by Me
Signature
COPY OF DRAWING NO. 4706961
DRAWN BY
CATHODE
ANODE
ION GUNS (SEE FIG. 59 PAGE 125B)
LOWER CATHODE SUPPORT
SAPPHIRE ROD
FUSOR FIG. 58
SEE ALSO FIG. 57
MARK II MOD-10
Explained to Me
Date
Witness
Explained to Me

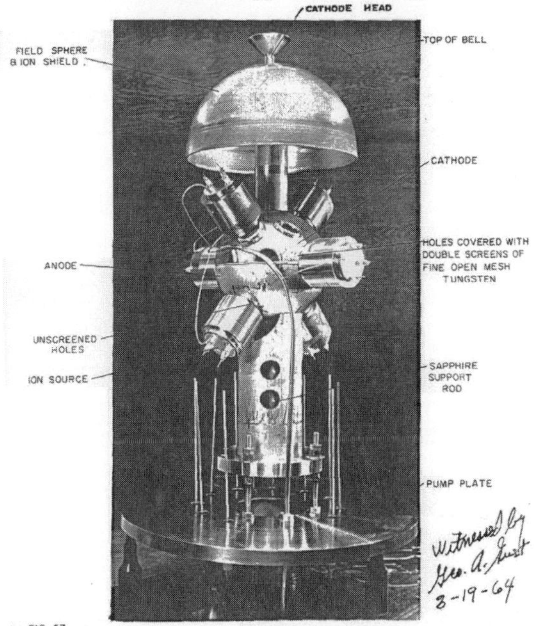

CATHODE HEAD
FIELD SPHERE & ION SHIELD
TOP OF BELL
CATHODE
HOLES COVERED WITH DOUBLE SCREENS OF FINE OPEN MESH TUNGSTEN
ANODE
UNSCREENED HOLES
ION SOURCE
SAPPHIRE SUPPORT ROD
PUMP PLATE
FIG 57

Test versions of the fusion equipment and Mark II are sketched and photographed from Research Notes.

Comments. Farnsworth's fusion experiments centered around what were referred to as Mark I, II, and III, the names given to the fusion generating equipment under experimentation.[b] Fusion was a low-cost energy source that Farnsworth believed would revolutionize the world. It would be a personal power source ... small units powering communities ... engineering applications for tunneling and metallurgy ... powering space exploration and scavenging ... salt water evaporation ... weather control ... and protective screens. All were possible with fusion energy for practical operation.

a. See Research Notes, Farnsworth Papers, Box 44, File 5.

b. See Research Notes and Journals, Boxes 37–38, 41–42, 44–47.

your obligations" with ITT and "[w]e want you to know that we will not tolerate any violation of our . . . agreement . . . I'm sure you do not wish any more than we to get into legal entanglements."[75] It was an unveiled threat.

Mixed signals were received from ITT. On one hand, the formal correspondence from ITT New York management and legal counsel was threatening. On the other, the Fort Wayne management, workers and Geneen seemed apologetic. Henri Busignies, ITT vice president, called Farnsworth within days apologizing for the "rude letter recently sent from IT&T."[76] The conversation appeared to be one of cooperation. Busignies apologized, Farnsworth explained his hiring of people, and they both talked about working out patents and the suggested ITT financing. Farnsworth was asked to put the proposal in another letter to Harold Geneen.[77]

In his communiqué to Geneen, Philo basically ignored the threats as nonissues resolved in his conversation with Busignies. He pleaded for the release of his name and expressed the desire to come to a "workable arrangement regarding existing patents and [his] new ideas."[78] He asked for the rights to use his own name in the formation of his business. "I feel it only fitting . . . that I be able to do this under my own name, since I had built this name up to its peak before ITT came into the picture." Expressing that he felt his name had been "played down . . . dragged through the mud . . . and now lapsed as a trademark," he wanted it released for his use in the Utah organization.[79] It was Farnsworth's hope that an amicable relationship could be established. Again the letter received a mixed response. Responding for Geneen, ITT's general counsel informed Farnsworth that ITT would not release the trademark "Farnsworth"—it was in fact ITT property—but he approved the title, Philo T. Farnsworth & Associates, provided such corporation "does not engage in any activity competitive to ITT."[80] The most important item in the response was the noncompetitive clause. Farnsworth was free to establish another business; ITT officials expressed the willingness to establish workable relations regarding the use and licensing of future patents, but the noncompetitive clause was a significant issue with ITT.

However, Philo T. Farnsworth & Associates was organized to continue work on fusion as an inexpensive energy source. It was always at the forefront of Farnsworth's plans. Philo wrote to the ITT patent attorney in June 1969, calling the attempts at ITT to produce fusion as "academic and impractical."[81] He was working on new math concepts he felt the group at Fort Wayne had failed to grasp. The letter reveals his own research as "a program in the concept stage which I believe will insure that the 'Fusor' will work," and requests ITT sell him the rights to a patent so that he could pursue the project. He offered cash and a royalty on the invention in exchange for the rights. At first ITT's response was a friendly one: "generally speaking, ITT management is agreeable to working out an equitable arrangement with you, but I feel . . . we must know the full extent of your needs."[82]

The proposed spirit of friendly cooperation was to end abruptly. Farnsworth's requests were seen as being in direct competition with ITT research and, as a result, in direct violation of his retirement agreements. In a final act ITT cut off Farnsworth's long-term disability benefits "because of your activities in the Philo T. Farnsworth Associates Corporation."[83] It was a complete severance.

THE END COMES QUICKLY

Not only were finances and ITT frustrating his work, Farnsworth was not well. He had moved back to Utah, "where it is our intention to be totally active in our Church," and where he hoped to continue his work on fusion. The work was not to be, however. He had "little energy . . . at present this is about one hour per day of effective work," and it was not enough.[84] Ironically, instead of working to regain his health, Farnsworth's acknowledging his deteriorating health only increased his desire to complete his work. Dr. Kenneth E. Dore described Farnsworth's promise and desperation. Farnsworth was portrayed as a man who insisted on pushing himself, one who needed to be on medical retirement, thus allowing "him to assume a work load more in keeping with his age." A visit with Dore in August 1969 prompted him to depict Farnsworth as a man "in full control of senses, acutely aware of surroundings, eating well . . . but not out of the woods . . . He is not in good health. He is on the verge of good health, but is also on the verge of breakdown and return" to problems of the past.[85] Writing personally to Pem and Phil, Dore pleaded with Pem to convince "Phil to slow down and be kind to himself *first* (emphasis in original), then he can and will be more able to help mankind later."[86]

But Farnsworth did not listen. His health continued to deteriorate, and early in 1971 he caught pneumonia. He died March 11, 1971. He was sixty-four.[87]

9
The Farnsworth Legacies

PHILO TAYLOR FARNSWORTH BELIEVED THAT HIS INVENTIONS WERE BENEFICIAL FOR mankind, and he worked throughout his life to serve humanity. Understanding his work and his total dedication to it helps us undertand his life, his contributions, and his character.

Farnsworth had little formal education, but he was an educated man. His two honorary doctorates speak to his lifetime achievements.[1] About education he said, "If you are truly progressing you will come to realize the amount of knowledge you *don't* (emphasis in original) have will increase directly in proportion to the amount of new knowledge you acquire. Recognition of this will keep you open minded and humble—two essentials of the great scientist."[2] Farnsworth will be known as an independent and charismatic inventor who dedicated his life to his dreams.

Farnsworth was a successful innovator. Philo, Pem, and Leslie Gorrell drafted the earliest business prospectuses, which Everson pitched to investors. His first business records include plans for a chain of stations, broadcast centers, and commercial manufacturing. It was under Farnsworth's singular leadership that the corporation, much to the consternation of one San Francisco executive, moved to the East Coast and then away from Philco Radio and Television to establish his Philadelphia laboratories. In 1938 at the pinnacle of Farnsworth's career, he, George Everson, and Hugh Knowlton put together the Farnsworth Television and Radio Corporation. In 1948 he rescued the corporation from bankruptcy, a position others had created by overextending debt. It was Farnsworth who rallied the stockholders for the successful sale to ITT. Farnsworth's work, patent portfolio, and name were so valuable that he was one of only a few from corporate management who moved to ITT. Today, ITT Aerospace/Optical, Fort Wayne, still stands with the foundation established by Farnsworth.[3]

Farnsworth was a successful inventor. Despite the constant hurdles he experienced with each stage of his corporate career, today there are more than 130 television patents filed under his name.[4] His strong, independent character as well as his tendency to be a scientific workaholic were the primary catalysts motivating his career. He was youthfully stubborn, a "man of iron will."[5] Farnsworth's self-confidence and humanitarian spirit were key factors in his success. Each time he was challenged, he returned to work with renewed enthusiasm and new ideas.

WHO WAS FIRST?

In discussing Farnsworth's contributions to electronic media, the question "who was first?" cannot be ignored. There are many in electronic media research who have called themselves "the father of . . ." and staked their claims to being first. Lee de Forest called himself the father of radio. Edwin Armstrong is without challenge the father of FM radio. David Sarnoff was declared in RCA promotional materials as the father of American television and RCA promoted a string of "RCA/NBC Firsts in Television."[6] Many have called Zworykin the father of television, but his most knowledgeable biographer, Albert Abramson, stops short of that declaration in describing him as the *Pioneer of Television.*[7] "Firsts and Fathers" have always fascinated the historian and the professional broadcast industry. For the historian, the drive to discover first is a natural curiosity. For the broadcaster, first has a promotional advantage within an increasingly marketplace-driven world. But defining first is not as easy as it sounds. First at what? First in theoretical development? First in technological development? First in private or public demonstration? Farnsworth was the first to have an all-electric television system (1929). Farnsworth was first to publicly demonstrate an all-electronic television system (1934). However, the history of television from an RCA perspective ignored growing evidence giving Farnsworth the credit where credit is due. The credits in the technology of electronic television go to both Farnsworth and Zworykin (see the chronology in Appendix B to help understand the technological chronology).[8]

Farnsworth would have cared little for the argument of who was first. He was willing to share the credits with scientists of his laboratory as well as scientists in England and Germany who contributed significantly to the history of television; and Farnsworth was comfortable in sharing credit with Zworykin. An RCA historian and media pioneer in her own right, M. Phyllis Smith summed up best and perhaps most accurately for the nonscientific reader: "I can accept that Farnsworth was first in system and experimental development" for a while during the early years, but she continues, "it was RCA that first developed the viable commercial operations,"[9] after it had settled its law suit with Farnsworth and thus combined their patent rights.

FARNSWORTH'S CONTRIBUTIONS TO ELECTRONIC TELEVISION

Farnsworth pioneered development of the electronic television system for almost fifteen years before his experimental work began to shift to differing applications for the television systems he'd developed. He is credited with more than 130 different U.S. and 100 foreign patents. Farnsworth's Television System, Television Receiving System, and Television Method are perhaps the most important overall contributions to commercial television (see Appendix A).

In September 1927, Farnsworth transmitted a line photo. The following year he conducted a demonstration for a small group of financial backers and transmitted the "$" sign to all of his investors. The first all-electrical television system was demonstrated in the laboratory, July 2, 1929, Farnsworth's most important event in the history of television. On that day, "for the first time in television history an all-electric television system was operating. There were absolutely no moving parts in the system, no spinning Nipkow discs, no mirror drums, tuning forks or vibrating reeds of any kind." This was an accomplishment of Farnsworth's that has never been fully appreciated.[10]

Use of Basic Farnsworth Patents in Modern Television Receivers

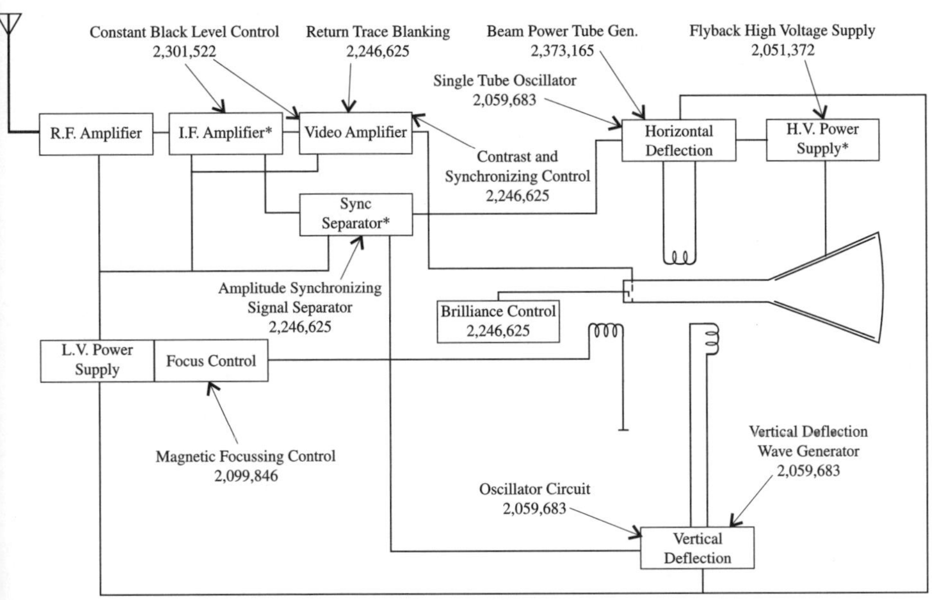

Note: The asterisks denote several of Farnsworth's most important contributions.
Source: "Use of Farnsworth Patents in Modern Television Receivers" (Fort Wayne, Indiana: Farnsworth Television and Radio Corporation, circa 1948, pp. 6–7).

Farnsworth's work is also still evident in our commercial television receivers (see chart; those patents asterisked are Farnsworth's most significant and lasting contribution to our television receivers).[11] Modern engineers have developed alternative methods for producing the same results, but Farnsworth was the pioneer accredited with the basic patents.

Another of Farnsworth's major triumphs still in use is his "Scanning and Synchronizing System." This provides the high voltage necessary for picture tubes.[12]

The next most important patent, the "Image Dissector," used a low-velocity scanning beam for the first time. This device was used by RCA as the basis for their later image orthicon tubes; RCA was astonished to find that Farnsworth had the prior patent.[13]

Most of the attention in Farnsworth's life has been given to his work in television, but substantial contributions were made in other areas such as industrial, defense, and government television. In chronicling Farnsworth's contributions, Jack Williams noted that his defense vidisector, one of the image dissector television tubes, did not make it into commercial television because it lacked significant image storage capacity. However, "what it lacked in storage it made up for in high resolution—more than 2,000 lines."[14] As a result it was used during World War II in the first sniperscope. The utiliscope was another defense application of the dissector in missile guidance and radar systems. According to Williams peacetime applications included the vidisector's use in astronomy and telescopic imagery. "The first all electronic star tracker [patented by Dr. John Clark] used the [Farnsworth] image dissector." The star trackers were used in the 1960s for navigating spacecraft. In the 1970s the print media used the image dissector tube for linotype sensing and font access in the newly developed electronic newspapers. And, Williams said the image dissector was a critical component measuring "alignment aboard the space shuttle." Bright radar was a concept emanating from Farnsworth's work on the iatron tube. This provided radar screens with brightness many times greater than television receivers. Many of the tubes created at Farnsworth Electronics, ITT Laboratories, ITT Federal, ITT Industrial Laboratories, and ITT Aerospace/Optical Division had their roots in the work of Philo T. Farnsworth.

FARNSWORTH AND HIS FAITH

Much of the mystique encircling Philo Farnsworth emanates from the folklore and stories surrounding his youthful genius and his Utah heritage. Farnsworth was a lifetime member of the Church of Jesus Christ of Latter-day Saints.[15]

Farnsworth had a profound impact on his Church and the state of Utah. Throughout the years, church leaders have evoked the image of Farnsworth as a scientist working under the influence of the Lord. Speaking before the worldwide church conference in 1969, church president David O. McKay focused on the existence of God, and he used Farnsworth as one of the "many scientists today, honorable, honest men, who are giving their all to help their fellow beings testify that there is a God." McKay commented that he'd had the opportunity of visiting with Farnsworth recently, "one of our own eminent scientists . . . who testified to me that he knows that he was directed by a higher source in gaining his scientific knowledge, and that he knows that God lives."[16] M. Russell Ballard wrote: "The wonder of television causes me to believe that Philo T. Farnsworth . . . must surely have been inspired of the Lord to develop this remarkable medium of communication . . . As you know, Brother Farnsworth was a member of the Church. Applying his scientific skills, he brought to the world this marvelous invention, which I believe is to be used for the primary purpose of furthering the work of the Lord."[17]

Although Farnsworth was not always active in his church, he was never far from it. He stopped attending church services at age seventeen, after his father died, and returned to church only after his move back to Utah in 1967.[18] Despite this formal religious inactivity, it would be incorrect to say that Farnsworth was not a man of high spiritual and humanitarian values. He even wrote about the nature of God and philosophized about the question "What is life?" His reflections tell us a little about his depth. "Life is a sentience," he writes, meaning life is full of feeling and perceiving and having the capacity for growth through the experiences of one's senses. This "sentience takes disorganization and organizes it . . . When you look about you, all the flora and fauna . . . both varieties are a part of such ecology and form the overall sentience. You are a part of that God. In a larger sense . . . God is not a term, but a sentient reality."[19]

In a KSL-TV, Salt Lake City documentary produced by Ted Capener and Bruce Christensen, Farnsworth was asked about Zworykin's contributions to television, and he responded, "I have no doubt that God could inspire two scientists at the same time and in different places with similar ideas." Interviewed at his home, a year before his death, he declared, "I am a deeply religious man, I know that God exists. I know that I have never invented anything. I have been a medium by which these things were given to the culture as fast as culture could earn them. I give the credit to God."[20]

Within Utah and the Church, the legacy of Farnsworth denotes a man of science, an inventor fighting against the odds, and a modern-day Horatio Alger.[21] In 1953 he was cited for his achievements by Brigham Young University, fifteen years before they bestowed upon him an honorary doctorate. He was honored by the Utah Broadcast Association and the Utah Cultural Society (1953). In 1969 a nearby mountain used for radio and television station transmission was named Farnsworth Peak. The Salt Lake Inventors Council and the

Intermountain Electrical Association bestowed honorary recognition upon him in 1970. His posthumous awards continued through to 1990. Most notably, he was voted to become the subject of the second Utah figure for the National Statuary Hall in the U.S. Capitol, Washington, D.C., a statue dedicated in 1990.

ELMA "PEM" GARDNER FARNSWORTH: WIFE AND PARTNER

The legacies of Philo Farnsworth are incomplete without a mention of his wife.[22] George Everson noted that "no small part of [Phil] Farnsworth's success is due to his charming and beautiful wife."[23] Carol McNalley, a contemporary journalist writing about television in Fort Wayne, Indiana, described Pem Farnsworth's role as mother and housekeeper and noted, "As a matter of fact she even helped make the first tubes for the small company."[24]

Pem devoted her life "exclusively to her home and the furtherance of his [her husband's] career."[25] In the earliest years, she worked in her husband's laboratories in their homes and at corporate headquarters. She was always his confidential secretary. After his death she crusaded to ensure his credit in the annals of television history. According to Farnsworth, "My wife and I started this TV," and "You can't write about me, without writing about us."[26]

Elma Farnsworth worked by her husband's side from the beginning. Their first laboratory was in the dining room of their Hollywood house; they worked there for only a short time before moving to San Francisco. "I just grew up with the [television] project . . . doing everything," Pem recalled.[27]

One of Pem's roles was to maintain the records. If she was not working in the lab during the day, Farnsworth would bring home the notes and drawings he wanted in his journal.[28] The early graphic figures she drew illustrated the general systems as well as electronic schematics for specific elements within the system.[29] These drawings were eventually incorporated into the briefs illustrating the Farnsworth television.[30]

According to the personnel listing from the Farnsworth Laboratories in San Francisco, Pem Farnsworth was one of the first technicians. As a member of the staff, her lab responsibilities included spot–welding the tube elements as they were assembled. She was taught how to use the precision tools needed to construct the elements of the first tubes.[31] Her salary was ten dollars per month.[32]

As the work on television progressed and the family grew, Pem Farnsworth divided her time between working with her husband and caring for their children.[33] But life was not easy for the family.[34] Nevertheless, the laboratory and her husband's work were never far from the center of her own activities. "He went to great lengths to make me a part of everything he did."[35]

Elma G. "Pem" Farnsworth, circa 1945. Courtesy Elma G. Farnsworth.

Beyond television and Farnsworth's experiments, the greatest of Pem's contributions was that of nursing Farnsworth. "My one ambition," she said, "was to get Phil really on his feet. My whole time has been spent to that end and I intend it shall be until the job is done."[36]

After Philo's death, Pem's work for her husband continued. She felt RCA had stolen recognition from Farnsworth in the development of television and began to promote the credit for his television work.[37] The confrontation with RCA, she says, was truly a David and Goliath situation. Even "today RCA claims this tube" [the image orthicon, a television camera tube], but according to Pem, "all it really invented was the name."[38]

Pem's struggle for her husband's recognition did not end with RCA—she believed that placing her husband's contributions to society in proper perspective remained her most important responsibility. Her interviews with the popular press have produced numerous articles discussing the Farnsworth television system. Each lauds Farnsworth's genius and reinforces the charges that RCA was heavy-handed in its dealings with others in trying to capture the public relations battle for television entrepreneurship.[39] The result of her campaign has been that the scholarly and textbook portrayal of both Farnsworth and Zworykin's [RCA's] contributions to the pioneering of television has been balanced. Several portrayals of Farnsworth are rather flattering and whereas earlier texts had ignored Farnsworth, the narrative today credits both inventors.[40] It was Pem Farnsworth's work, along with other supporters, that led to the Farnsworth commemorative U.S. postage stamp. The twenty-cent stamp was issued in 1983.[41] A historical marker was also affixed in 1981 to the San Francisco building where the first Farnsworth television image was projected.[42] In 1977 she led in the fiftieth anniversary re-creation of television's early history. The celebration included historic displays and appearances of others who had worked with Farnsworth in 1927.[43] Philo was inducted posthumously into the California Inventors Hall of Fame, the Utah Broadcasters Hall of Fame, and most notably, the National Inventors Hall of Fame.[44]

Farnsworth's professional work, a part of her life and his legacies, might all have been forgotten if not for her.

PHILO FARNSWORTH'S FUTURE

Everson lamented on what might have been: What if Farnsworth and Everson had been allowed greater management participation in the Farnsworth Television and Radio Corporation during World War II? In Farnsworth's writings, however, there is no looking back—only an eye toward the future. He could get depressed and withdrawn, but his will to create was the overriding force within his life. With his "astonishing intellect, unwavering tenacity, and sheer

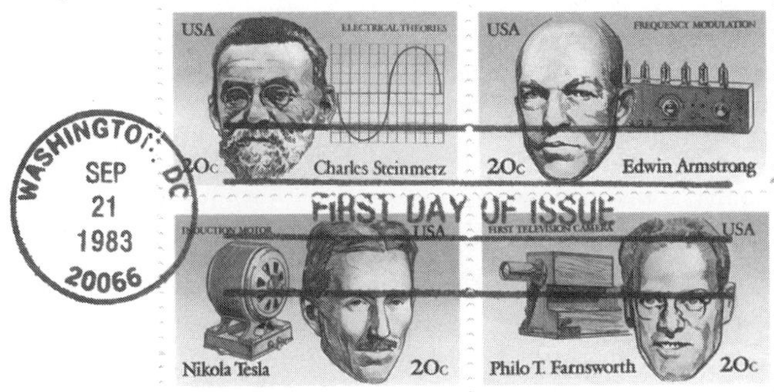

The U.S. Patent and Trademark Office houses the National Inventors Hall of Fame, which was initiated in 1973 with the induction of Thomas Alva Edison. Three of the men depicted on this block of four stamps have been inducted into the Hall – Tesla (1975), Steinmetz (1977) and Armstrong (1980). It is anticipated that the fourth person featured on the stamps, Philo T. Farnsworth, also will be so honored in the near future.

The technological contributions of these four American Inventors to the field of electroscience cannot be completely captured in the brief summaries written here. These commemorative stamps, however, will carry their names into millions of homes across the country and, indeed, the world, focusing attention on their noteworthy accomplishments.

- Edwin Howard Armstrong's crowning achievement was the invention of wideband frequency modulation in 1933, now commonly known as FM radio. And, many of his other inventions as an electrical engineer were so important that even today every radio and television makes use of one or more of his developments.
- Philo Taylor Farnsworth, with more than 300 inventions in television and related fields to his credit, is most famous for the first television transmission made in 1927, using only electronic equipment as opposed to the mechanical apparatus used in earlier experiments. For this, he has been called by many "the father of modern television."
- Charles Proteus Steinmetz pioneered research on the theories of alternating current and high-voltage power.
- Nikola Tesla had more than 700 inventions to his credit, with one of the most notable being the induction motor.

The block of four stamps was designed by Dennis Lyall of Norwalk, Connecticut, who also designed the Joseph Priestley commemorative and the Thomas H. Gallaudet Great Americans Series stamp, both issued earlier this year.

Program from first day of issue, American Inventors Stamps, Patent and Trademark Office, Washington, D.C., September 21, 1983.

determination," he was always inventing. "I get a great deal of satisfaction," he said, "in having seen many of my early flights of imagination come true."[45]

In 1951 Farnsworth predicted telephone-television and was ridiculed. An editorial in the *Deseret News* suggested that "in as much as telephones have a notorious tendency to ring while the callee is in the bathtub, . . . if P. T. is right, some new protective appliances will be necessary . . . A rubber arm and a loudspeaker to enable one to answer from a telephone instrument in the next room . . . a dark closet . . . a protective shield, with armholes."[46] Humorous as this sounded in 1951, telephone-television is approaching reality.

Dean Rhoads recalled Farnsworth speaking before the Fort Wayne Rotary Club about defense and Farnsworth's vision of a fusion-powered electronic fence circling the nation that could see planes, missiles, and such as they entered and departed our nation's airspace. Farnsworth was constantly addressing the future. "What will television be like in the future?" was a popular question. His answer was, "What do you want television in the future to be like?" Farnsworth believed "if you can imagine something, sooner or late we may be able to achieve it; and conversely, unless we can at least imagine it there can be no hope of it becoming a reality. Well then, what do we want?"[47]

In the 1950s, his vision of the future of television included color, high definition, three-dimensional pictures, and international broadcasting. Color, according to Farnsworth, was the natural progression of the industry, but it could not be achieved at the sacrifice of picture definition and image clarity. High definition meant improved picture quality and larger pictures, perhaps using external screens "over a fireplace."[48] Three dimension would provide pictures that would equal "more than 1,000 words. No, the ratio is far greater when we consider that a picture may be understood by any intelligent individual without reference to the spoken word."[49] Farnsworth's predictions of "Television and the International Language" and "Television as a means for better understanding . . . a common spoken language" are most intriguing forecasts for the 1950s. How could such a feat be accomplished? Farnsworth's answer was "centrifugal earth satellites revolving about the earth at distances of a few hundred miles. Admittedly fantastic," Farnsworth philosophizes, "but is it more fantastic than television itself was in say, 1925?"[50] We smile as we read these predictions. We have color, satellite, geostationary satellite distribution, and even high definition. Farnsworth's visions have come to pass—but not all of them. His vision for television and the family has only partially been fulfilled. "Television and the American home," Farnsworth predicted would "pull the family together."[51] It would change the architectural space of the household in order to accommodate "home theatre. Television will play an important part in halting the current trend toward the break up of the family unit." He saw leaders of the television industry as programming for the family. Educational public-service programs provided opportunities for learning, thus skilled jobs for men and women. Political telecasts were to arouse civic concern and interest. "In addition to [television as] a center of common family interest . . . [it will become] the actual physical center piece in small and medium sized homes . . . The magnetic appeal of television will tend to pull the family together."[52] His predictions about the architecture of the home surrounding the home theater have certainly been fulfilled and are being constantly refined. But few behaviorial scientists would say that television has pulled the family together.

Although we do not see his predictions fulfilled for television and the family, we do see the answer to his own question, "what would you like it to be," and, as a result, learn a lot about the man with a vision.

EPITAPH

Between 1927 and 1937 Farnsworth had grown out of obscurity to the point where his labs, the experimental TV stations, and his patent portfolio were used as the foundation for a major national television manufacturing corporation. These were the pinnacles of his television career. Farnsworth disagreed with the idea that television was his most important work; he placed "fusion" as his most significant contribution.

His fusion theory created lower-powered inexpensive energy sources, which he saw as revolutionizing the world. Fusion was intended as an energy source assisting in food production. Small units were seen as capable of providing power for whole communities. A military defense unit could see an approaching threat. Salt water could be made into pure drinking water using fusion in an inexpensive evaporation process. Farnsworth envisioned spacecraft and oceanographic exploration.

Scientists are still looking to that vision. Critical of using the technology of the 1960s, they are calling for a new power source. "Instead of burning fuel as rockets do now, these new space ships could use nuclear fusion,"[53] NASA engineer Homer Hickam, Jr. declared. Farnsworth may not have lived to see his vision of fusion become a reality, but it is still very much alive. Despite Philo's struggles, he never lost sight of his goals. His work and motivation were always directed toward his fellow man. He wrote his own epitaph, which reads, "He loved his fellow man."[54]

Appendix A
U.S. Patents Issued to Philo T. Farnsworth

THE FOLLOWING WAS COMPILED FROM VARIOUS LISTS AND PATENTS FOUND AT THE FORT Wayne–Allen County Museum, the University of Utah Archives, and the Arizona State University Library Special Collections; from lists published surrounding the *Acceptance and Dedication of the Statue of Philo T. Farnsworth, Presented by the State of Utah, Proceedings in the Rotunda of the United States Capitol, May 2, 1990* (Washington, D.C.: Government Printing Office, 1991); and from George Shiers, *Early Television.*

	Filing Date	Title	Patent No.	Issue Date
1.	01/07/27	Electric Oscillator System	1,758,359	05/13/30
2.	01/07/27	Television System	1,773,980	08/26/30
3.	01/07/27	Television Receiving System	1,773,981	08/26/30
4.	01/07/27	Light Valve (split and refiled 11/07/27)	1,806,935	05/26/31
5.	01/09/28	Photoelectric Apparatus	1,970,036	08/14/34
6.	01/09/28	Television Method	2,168,768	08/08/39
7.	04/17/28	Electrical Discharge Apparatus	1,986,330	01/01/35
8.	04/25/28	Synchronizing System	1,844,949	02/16/32
9.	11/26/28	Method and Apparatus for Television	2,037,711	04/21/36
10.	03/11/29	Admittance Neutralization Amplifier	1,986,331	01/01/35
11.	03/03/30	Electron Multiplier	1,969,399	08/07/34
12.	05/05/30	Slope Wave Generator (with H. Lubcke)	2,059,219	11/03/36
13.	05/05/30	Television Scanning and Synchronizing System	2,246,625	06/24/41
14.	06/14/30	Electron Image Amplifier	2,085,742	07/06/37
15.	06/14/30	Thermionic Oscillograph	2,099,846	11/23/37
16.	07/07/30	Dissector Target	1,941,344	12/26/33
17.	12/04/30	System of Pulse Transmission	2,026,379	12/31/35
18.	07/14/31	Scanning and Synchronizing System	2,051,372	08/18/36

	Filing Date	Title	Patent No.	Issue Date
19.	07/14/31	Projection Oscillight	2,140,284	12/13/38
20.	07/22/31	Thermionic Vacuum Tube	1,975,143	10/02/34
21.	04/14/32	Television Method	2,168,768	03/08/39
22.	05/31/32	Luminescent Screen (with B.C. Gardner)	2,098,000	11/02/37
23.	02/08/33	Luminescent Screen and Method of Use	2,104,253	01/04/38
24.	04/03/33	Scanning Oscillator	2,059,683	11/03/36
25.	04/26/33	Image Dissector	2,087,683	07/20/37
26.	04/26/33	Image Dissector (reissued)	Re 21,504	07/09/40
27.	10/07/33	Electron Multiplying Device	2,071,515	02/23/37
28.	07/05/34	Oscillation Generator	2,071,516	02/23/37
29.	11/05/34	Scanning Means and Method	2,280,572	04/21/42
30.	11/05/34	Method of Manufacturing Cathode Ray Tube Targets	2,286,478	06/16/42
31.	11/06/34	Projection Apparatus	2,091,705	08/31/37
32.	11/06/34	Projection Means	2,143,145	01/10/39
33.	02/06/35	Image Projector	2,233,887	03/04/41
34.	03/09/35	Incandescent Light Source	2,089,054	08/03/37
35.	03/12/35	Means of Electron Multiplication	2,143,262	01/10/39
36.	03/12/35	Cathode Ray Tube	2,149,045	02/28/39
37.	03/12/35	Oscillator (divided 4/26/37)	2,174,488	09/26/39
38.	04/26/35	Amplifier	2,221,473	11/12/40
39.	05/07/35	Incandescent Light Source (with H. Bamford)	2,066,070	12/29/36
40.	05/07/35	Multipactor Phase Control	2,071,517	02/23/37
41.	05/07/35	Means for Producing Incandescent Images (with H. Bamford)	2,155,478	04/25/39
42.	07/01/35	Electron Image Amplifier	2,292,437	08/11/42
43.	07/06/35	Charge Storage Dissector	2,140,695	12/20/38
44.	07/06/35	Charge Storage Dissector Tube	2,141,836	12/27/38
45.	07/06/35	Means and Method of Image Analysis	2,216,264	10/01/40
46.	07/06/35	Cathode Ray Amplifier	2,228,388	01/14/41
47.	07/06/35	Charge Storage Amplifier	2,233,888	03/04/41
48.	07/15/35	Image Receiving Tube	2,118,186	05/24/38
49.	08/10/35	Cathode Ray Amplifying Tube	2,251,124	07/29/41
50.	09/07/35	Image Analysis Tube	2,100,841	11/30/37
51.	09/14/35	Charge Storage Tube	2,100,842	11/30/37
52.	12/31/35	Dissector Tube	2,153,918	04/11/39
53.	12/31/35	Dissector Tube	2,235,477	03/18/41

	Filing Date	Title	Patent No.	Issue Date
54.	01/27/36	Multiplier Oscillator	2,137,528	11/22/38
55.	02/10/36	Scanning Current Generator	2,214,077	09/10/40
56.	02/11/36	Multipactor	2,135,615	11/08/33
57.	02/24/36	Multipactor Oscillator and Amplifier	2,091,439	08/31/37
58.	02/24/36	Radiation Frequency Converter (with D. K. Lippincott)	2,107,782	02/08/38
59.	03/09/36	Incandescent Light Source	2,089,054	08/03/37
60.	03/09/36	Absorption Oscillator	2,159,521	05/23/39
61.	03/24/36	Secondary Emission Electrode	2,139,813	12/13/38
62.	05/06/36	Luminescent Screen (with B. C. Gardner)	2,089,000	11/02/37
63.	05/16/36	Means and Method of Controlling Electron Multipliers	2,140,832	12/20/38
64.	05/16/36	Means and Method of Controlling Electron Multiplication	2,204,479	06/11/40
65.	05/18/36	Electron Multiplier (reissued)	Re 20,759	06/14/38
66.	05/18/36	Electron Multiplier	2,260,613	10/28/41
67.	06/01/36	Multi-stage Multipactor	2,141,837	12/27/38
68.	06/01/36	Cathode Ray Tube	2,158,279	05/16/39
69.	07/11/36	Image Source	2,213,070	08/30/38
70.	07/11/36	Means and Method for Transmitting Synchronizing Pulses in Television	2,155,479	04/25/39
71.	07/18/36	Concentric Multiplier	2,147,934	02/21/39
72.	08/18/36	Means and Method of Operating Electron Multipliers	2,128,580	08/30/38
73.	08/18/36	Image Dissector	2,216,265	10/01/40
74.	10/31/36	Repeater (with R. L. Snyder)	2,143,146	01/10/39
75.	11/02/36	High Power Projection Oscillograph (with F. Somers)	2,109,289	02/22/38
76.	11/02/36	Beam Scanning Dissector	2,124,057	07/19/38
77.	11/02/36	Cathode Ray Tube	2,139,814	12/13/38
78.	11/04/36	Cold Cathode Electron Discharge Tube	2,184,910	12/26/39
79.	11/04/36	Cold Cathode Electron Discharge Tube	2,263,032	11/18/41
80.	11/09/36	Electron Multiplier (with R. L. Snyder)	2,179,996	11/14/39
81.	03/22/37	Multiplier Coupling System	2,140,285	12/13/38
82.	03/22/37	Split Cathode Multiplier Tube	2,141,838	12/27/38
83.	03/22/37	Self-energized Alternating Current Multiplier	2,174,487	09/26/39
84.	03/22/37	Method of Operating Electron Multipliers	2,180,279	11/14/39
85.	03/22/37	Diode Oscillator Tube Construction	2,189,358	02/06/40

	Filing Date	Title	Patent No.	Issue Date
86.	03/22/37	Two-stage Oscillograph	2,216,266	10/01/40
87.	03/22/37	Split Cathode Multiplier	2,217,860	10/15/40
88.	03/22/37	X-ray Projection Device	2,221,374	11/12/40
89.	03/26/37	Detector	2,156,807	05/02/39
90.	04/26/37	Two-stage Electron Multiplier	2,161,620	06/06/39
91.	09/20/37	Means for Producing an Incandescent Image (with B. C. Gardner)	2,179,086	11/07/39
92.	01/05/38	Electronic Amplifier	2,239,149	04/22/41
93.	02/21/38	Radio Frequency Multipactor Amplifier	2,172,152	09/05/39
94.	03/12/38	Dissector Tube (original date 12/31/35)	2,235,477	03/18/41
95.	06/13/38	Shielded Anode Electron Multiplier (with R. Snyder)	2,203,048	06/04/40
96.	06/13/38	Image Projector (original date 02/06/35)	2,233,887	03/04/41
97.	09/10/38	Image Analyzing System	2,254,140	08/26/41
98.	12/31/38	Dissector Tube	2,153,918	04/11/39
99.	04/05/39	Image Amplifier	2,257,942	10/07/41
100.	04/24/39	High Efficiency Amplifier	2,223,001	11/26/40
101.	07/05/39	Electron Image Amplifier (reissued)	Re 22,009	01/20/42
102.	12/29/39	Image Dissector (reissued)	Re 21,504	07/09/40
103.		Electronic Amplifier (reissued)	Re 21,818	06/03/41
104.	02/15/40	Electric Recording and Reproducing System	2,304,633	12/08/42
105.	02/23/40	Apparatus for Method of Electron Discharge Control	2,274,194	02/24/42
106.	03/05/40	Rectifier	2,287,607	06/23/42
107.	03/11/40	Dissector Tube	2,264,630	12/02/41
108.	04/03/40	Electron Control Device	2,286,076	06/09/42
109.	07/25/40	Electron Control Device	2,311,981	02/23/43
110.	09/07/40	Image Dissector	2,292,111	08/04/42
111.	09/07/40	Television Projection System	2,315,113	03/30/43
112.	10/09/40	Cathode Ray Signal Reproducing Tube	2,301,388	11/10/42
113.	12/27/40	Method of Manufacturing Cathode Ray Tube Targets	2,286,478	06/16/42
114.	05/22/41	Deflecting System	2,297,949	10/06/42
115.	07/05/41	Image Amplifier	2,291,577	07/28/42
116.	06/20/42	Image Reproducing Device	2,355,212	08/08/44
117.	07/29/50	Television Image Analyzing Tube	2,641,723	06/09/53
118.	11/25/50	Cathode Ray Tube and System	2,754,449	07/10/53
119.	05/07/52	Light Translating Device	2,992,346	07/11/61

	Filing Date	Title	Patent No.	Issue Date
120.	03/03/54	Radio Translating Device	2,992,358	07/11/61
121.	05/18/54	Color Television Apparatus	2,921,228	01/12/60
122.	03/06/57	Cathode Ray Tube	2,941,100	06/14/60
123.	01/11/62	Electric Discharge Device for Producing Interaction between Nuclei	3,258,402	06/28/66
124.	03/07/62	Electron Gun in the Form of a Multipactor	3,201,640	08/17/63
125.	03/29/62	Ion Transport Vacuum Pump	3,181,028	04/27/65
126.	04/19/63	Microwave Amplifier Utilizing Multipaction to Produce Periodically Bunched Electrons	3,312,857	04/04/67
127.	06/09/64	Process and Apparatus for Drying and Treating Lumber (vacuum process)	3,283,412	11/08/66
128.	05/13/66	Method and Apparatus for Producing Nuclear-Fusion Reactions	3,386,883	06/04/68
129.	04/01/69	Lumber Drying (vacuum method)	3,574,949	04/13/71
130.		Ion Transport Pump	3,240,421	03/15/66

Appendix B
The Chronology of "Firsts"

Farnsworth	**Zworykin**	**Comments**
• 1922 — Farnsworth draws his schematic for electronic television for his high school teacher Justin Tolman (see chapter 1, "High School with an Inspirational Teacher."	• 1922 — Zworykin as young Ph.D. goes to work for Westinghouse.	• These Farnsworth drawings, later produced by Tolman, were pivotal in the patent interference case between Zworykin and Farnsworth.
	• October 1923 — Zworykin demonstrates his system to Westinghouse executives, who were less than enthusiastic. The picture results were erratic and the executives walked out on the demonstration. It produced no press, only disappointment (Abramson, *Zworykin*, p. 50–52; Shiers, p. 66).	• Some independent sources have questioned the testimony regarding this demonstration, recalling the experiment only after Farnsworth had filed for the patent.

Farnsworth	Zworykin	Comments
	• December 29, 1923 — Zworykin, working for Westinghouse, files a patent for his system of television.	• There was no immediate action taken either at the patent office or on Zworykin's part to reduce the patent to practice. There was no rush and no competition at the time. Zworykin continued to file amendments to the application that also prolonged consideration (Abramson, *Zworykin*, pp. 44–46).
	• 1924 — Zworykin works on interactive two-way telephone circuits with sight and sound (Shiers, p. 66).	
	• 1925 — Zworykin working with mosaic screen for electronic color system (Shiers, p. 84).	
• September 7, 1927 — Farnsworth demonstrates his first all "electrical television system." He filed for the patent (January 1927) that was granted August 26, 1930. The 1927 demonstration produced a one-dimensional single-line picture (see chapter 2, "Farnsworth Goes Public," and "Demonstrations for Potential Investors." • October 1927 — Farnsworth works on electro-optical receiver (Shiers, p. 113). • December 1927 — article on high-definition images.	• May–September 1927 — Zworykin working on opto-mechanical system (Shiers, p. 111).	• All would agree Zworykin's picture tube was a major development in making for electronic television possible.

Farnsworth	Zworykin	Comments
	• March 1929 — film system with a picture tube. • August 1929 — picture tube was created and demonstrated to Goldsmith (Abramson, *Zworykin*, p. 80).	
• April 1930 — experimental picture tube (Shiers, p. 214). • June 1930 — improved image dissector. • August 26, 1930 — Farnsworth was granted a patent for the electronic television system. The patent application was originally filed January 7, 1927. A second patent issued that same day described the receiving tube (see chapter 2, "Optimism Amidst the Depression"; Shiers, pp. 111, 137). • December 1930 — Farnsworth has 300-line system (Shiers, p. 215).	• May 1930 — improved photoelectric mosaic (Shiers, p. 214).	
	• 1932 — Zworykin was a poor witness in this case. Actually there was only one point in contention in this suit—it all hinged on Farnsworth's claim #15, the forming of an electrical image. Farnsworth won the claim and the rest of the patent was still valid (Abramson, *Zworykin*, pp. 119–20).	• The television rights granted in this decision were broad and meant that RCA had to negotiate with Farnsworth for use of his patents (see chapter 4, "RCA vs. Farnsworth").

Farnsworth	Zworykin	Comments
	• June 1933 — Zworykin lecturing on 240-line system.	• Some have been critical of the first patent as not including the receiving tube, but for some reason this was included as a second patent application, filed and granted the same day. In actuality there were four patents filed January 7, 1927; and another five filed in 1928. Other elements such as the "sawtooth" came later (see Appendix A).
• March 6, 1936 — patent interference case ruled in favor of Farnsworth (see chapter 4, "RCA vs. Farnsworth.").		• There were other patents and patent struggles with RCA and Farnsworth competitors, but Farnsworth won the all-important patent battle in the interference case. The battle alone had cost him dearly in terms of finances, which were diverted from experimentation to litigation; and, in the time it took to file, grant, defend and adjudicate the patent. By the time it was all over RCA had taken over the role as leader.

Appendix C
Farnsworth Television and Radio Corporation Transactions on the New York Stock Exchange

New York Times Dates	Year	Range	High to Low	Comment
October 30, 1943	1943	10 to 9	10 to 9	Began trading 10/43
January 28, 1944	1943–44	14 to 8	13 to 12½	
May 30, 1944	1944	14 to 9	12 to 12	
September 29, 1944	1944	14 to 9	14 to 13	
January 31, 1945	1944–45	16 to 9	15½ to 15	
May 30, 1945	1945	16 to 12	15 to 15	
September 28, 1945	1945	16 to 12	16 to 13½	
January 31, 1946	1945–46	20½ to 12	19½ to 19	
May 30, 1946	1946	19 to 14½	15 to 15	
September 27, 1946	1946	19 to 8	9 to 9½	
January 31, 1947	1946–47	19 to 7	8 ½ to 8	
May 30, 1947	1947	9 to 4	5 to 5½	
September 30, 1947	1947	9 to 4	6 to 6	
January 29, 1948	1947–48	9 to 4	7 to 7	
May 29, 1948	1948	9½ to 5	9 to 8	
September 30, 1948	1948	11 to 5	6½ to 6	
January 29, 1949	1948–49	11 to 4	4 to 4	(Closed @ 4)

International Telephone & Telegraph Corporation Stock at Time of Farnsworth Purchase

January 29, 1949	1948–49	16½ to 8	10 to 10	

Appendix D
Farnsworth Wood Products

FARNSWORTH WOOD PRODUCTS WAS AN ENTERPRISE OF THREE BROTHERS: PHIL, CARL, and Lincoln. Farnsworth purchased 3,000 acres of forestland to set up the lumbermill. Their venture into "boxes for bullets" came about as a result of Farnsworth's concern for the forest surrounding his property. A neighbor was considering clear-cutting some timber next to Farnsworth's property and using the lumber for manufacturing ammunition boxes. Not wanting his view devastated, Farnsworth purchased the acreage and the neighbor's Fryeburg Box Shop and established Farnsworth Wood Products. Instead of clear-cutting, trees were selectively cut, and the lumber was used to manufacture boxes for the war effort. It was a homespun business: Farnsworth was president, brothers Carl and Lincoln were vice presidents, and Pem was the treasurer.

It took several years to build a sawmill, shop, and supporting structures. Carl and Lincoln were the primary brothers in the enterprise and "assumed full responsibility for management."[1] By the end of the war, the two brothers were manufacturing prefabricated homes and airplane hangars.[2] However, business struggled when war contracts expired. Then tragedy struck. Returning from a business trip, the two brothers were in an airplane accident on September 8, 1946. Lincoln was not hurt seriously, but Carl was killed.[3] Lincoln recovered and worked to keep the lumber business afloat, but after the war it eventually failed.

Appendix E
A History of Farnsworth Television and Radio Corporation
1942-1948

THE FORT WAYNE CORPORATION: WARTIME BUSINESS

The key Farnsworth Television and Radio Corporation wartime management people under E. A. Nicholas were Edwin M. Martin, vice president, secretary, and counsel; Ernest H. Vogal, vice president–sales; J. P. Rogers, vice president, treasurer; and B. Ray Cummings, vice president–engineering.[1] These decision-makers took Farnsworth's experimentation from the laboratory into commercial production manufacturing military electronics, and then worked to make the transition from wartime production back to the commercial-consumer production of television and radio receivers.[2]

Early in 1942 the Farnsworth plants in Marion and Fort Wayne were converted from consumer production to military production in order to meet military contracts.[3] The conversions were massive. The Fort Wayne plant sat on twenty-one acres and was a two-story, brick complex comprising 125,000 square feet; the Marion plant was on fifty-four acres and had 175,000 square feet. Both were equipped with assembly-line machinery that had to be retooled from consumer to military needs. The Navy's contracts were the impetus behind the construction of an additional plant in Fort Wayne. In addition, two plants in Bluffton and Huntington, Indiana, added 80,000 square feet—all for manufacturing war materials.[4]

MILITARY CONTRACTS

One of the first contracts, dating from 1941, was with the Civil Aeronautics Administration and the Signal Corps. It was to produce an electronic direction-finding radar device used in airport nighttime landings—particularly on the West Coast, where airports were often darkened in fear of an enemy attack.[5]

In 1942 the Farnsworth corporation began work on radar jamming and electronic communications. The Farnsworth corporate research engineer working and testing the "radar jammer" was Robert Sanders. The first test of

Sanders's work was to jam the communications of an army technical exercise. The ground maneuver, to be completed within an hour and a half, required a large number of army personnel and more than a thousand radio receivers and transmitters. As the exercise began, Sanders and the officers boarded a B-18 to jam all communications so that the men on the ground could not complete the exercise within the allotted time. The test was a success. The climax of this research according to the local press was that the "radar-jamming equipment developed by Farnsworth Television and Radio" was credited as "largely instrumental in the successful storming of the Normandy Coast on D-Day by the Allied military forces and in establishing a secure beachhead in the following crucial days."[6]

The bulk of the Farnsworth company manufacturing lines created radio transmitters and receivers. These varied in size and application depending upon military dictates. Materials for ships, tanks, and aircraft were all different. Describing a battleship transmitter, the Fort Wayne *News-Sentinel* indicated "that it towered above the heads of the workmen, weighed many hundreds of pounds, and incorporated enough wire to build scores of phonograph radios."[7] The newspaper heralded the Farnsworth corporation as the "eyes and ears of U.S. fighting craft."[8]

THE BUSINESS OF WAR

The military needs produced good business. At the April 1942 Farnsworth corporation stockholders meeting, management announced the company was 100 percent into wartime manufacturing.[9] Company morale was high and employees were called upon not only to produce more, but to buy war bonds and personally contribute financially to the war efforts.

In 1943 employees were asked to step up production by 40 percent. "Electronic equipment requirements in the war program are mounting steadily, and the electronics industry faces a fresh challenge in the form of higher production schedules."[10] In that same year, Farnsworth employees were honored by receiving one of the many official presentations of the Army Navy Production Award to the "men and women of Farnsworth . . . for high achievements in the production of War Equipment." It was a "big day for Marion [Plant] employees" as national acknowledgment for their work.[11] The company's newsletter, the *Farnsworth Employees Victory Record,* portrayed a picture of dedicated employees and promoted the war effort. It was an effective in-house communications tool and was often combined with national advertising efforts to promote television in the postwar era.

POSTWAR FOUNDATIONS

The postwar outlook for the company was optimistically described by Nicholas as "in the immediate future all the company's efforts . . . must necessarily remain subordinate to its war production, [however] substantial benefits can be expected to flow to the radio industry, especially in the fields of television and radio broadcasting, from the scientific progress which has been made during the war." He told the stockholders that the Farnsworth corporation's "active electronic research and engineering program during the war period assures it of a prominent place in the radio and electronic industry after the war."[12] The Farnsworth corporation planned aggressively for the transition to a peacetime economy.

The company newsletter, in addition to selling war bonds and esprit de corp, regularly published information about the coming Fort Wayne national television center, and duplicated the company's national advertising campaigns. The purpose of placing the advertisements in the *Victory Record* was to let "employees know what is being done to build jobs for them."[13] The Farnsworth corporation's management was planning for the future.

Farnsworth Television Advertising

The corporation embarked on an aggressive advertising campaign immediately upon its organization in 1939. The next year its national advertising budget—which included radio, magazine, newspaper, and billboard advertisements—doubled.[14] Following the war, the annual advertising budget grew to $623,000, a substantial amount for the time.[15] The general public could not buy Farnsworth products during the war, but advertising continued to build the image for postwar markets.

Magazine ads were generally full page, artistic interpretations of classical themes along with a sales narrative. These advertisements connected the old Capehart name to the new Capehart division, a part of the Farnsworth Television and Radio Corporation.

The artwork of the advertisements was marketed by the corporation as collectible, and readers were invited to contact their local Capehart-Farnsworth dealer for a portfolio. The full page four-color advertisements and similar ones carried the same themes and appeared throughout the war in *Life, Time, The New Yorker, Newsweek, Business Week, U.S.News & World Report, The Atlantic, Colliers,* and the *Saturday Evening Post:*

> This war work is teaching us how to make better peacetime products. Finer Phonograph-Radios will come after the war from Farnsworth. Then television equipment for telecasting studios, and for scores of industrial and commercial applications . . . and finally, Farnsworth television receiving sets to let you see as well as hear, *in your*

own home, sports and entertainment, historical and news events *while they are taking place.*[16]

The Farnsworth Broadcast Center

In 1944 Nicholas announced that the corporation was planning a broadcast center with TV and AM/FM radio stations. The company had just purchased station WGL-AM, Fort Wayne, for $235,000 cash.[17] The acquisition was, of course, pending approval of the FCC, which was given in the fall. The radio station was licensed to the Farnsworth Television and Radio Corporation, December 28, 1944. According to Nicholas, WGL-AM was to be the centerpiece of the new corporate broadcast division.[18] The Farnsworth corporation would continue operating WGL-AM as a commercial station, but it would also provide the foundation for the corporation's move back into television and hoped to be the beginning of a network of stations. Speaking before the New York Press Club Farnsworth's B. Ray Cummings, vice president of engineering, reminded the audience that Farnsworth was essentially a television company.[19] By September 1944, the Farnsworth corporation had already applied for an experimental television station license, although such licenses were still not being granted by the FCC.[20]

In January 1945, Frank V. Webb, a former sales manager for Westinghouse's Pittsburgh station KDKA, was appointed general manager of the new corporate broadcasting division. His responsibilities included the management of WGL-AM and planning for the development of the division that was to include commercial television.[21] Experimentation continued in the laboratory and while the station and the lab were separate entities, WGL-AM provided the "actual operating conditions essential to test . . . production."[22]

The Farnsworth corporation commenced immediately to improve the station. Applications were made with the FCC for increased power, a change in the frequency assignment, and new studio facilities. It would take several years to work through the regulatory bureaucracy and acquire approval for these changes, but they were granted with a little help from the new Senator from Indiana, Homer E. Capehart.[23] The increase in power was to one kilowatt and the frequency was changed to 1250 kilohertz.[24] The results were improved coverage of the Fort Wayne region with both day and night transmissions.[25] The station was on the air eighteen hours per day with a reported 76 percent commercially sponsored programming and 24 percent carried no advertising.[26]

At end of the war WGL-AM was being promoted as the "Radio Center Round[ing] Out [the] Full [Farnsworth] Experience."[27] A request filed before the Securities and Exchange Commission asked for an additional 219,571 shares of common stock to be sold on the market to finance the new facilities.[28] FCC applications for the addition of an FM radio station and another

Farnsworth experimental-television station were in the works, but the FCC still wasn't granting licenses.

The corporation's failure to act on earlier construction permits had aggravated the FCC. A 1945 letter from the Secretary of the FCC, T. J. Slowie, chastised the corporation for letting the experimental station licenses expire. Slowie concluded with an unveiled threat of cancellation, "unless you intend to diligently prosecute the erection of your station . . . within the next few months, it may be proper to withhold further consideration of your application."[29]

Finally, in May 1946 the FCC granted the application for the experimental television station, W9XFT, and hearings were set on a new FM station license request for June 1946.[30] A year and a half later, the Fort Wayne *News-Sentinel* heralded the corporation as becoming "one of the potential television centers of the world." W9XFT went on the air and began broadcasting live shows in their experimental theater.[31] WGL-AM, the experimental-television station, was the beginning of a planned AM-TV-FM combination. According to Nicholas, it was the fourth dimension to the corporation's postwar activities. In addition to manufacturing television sets for homes and transmitters, traffic control systems, phonographs, tubes, and studio gear for industries, Farnsworth was entering the field of commercial television and program experimentation.[32]

THE CORPORATION: WARTIME PROFITS AND LOSSES

In a corporate report filed with the Securities and Exchange Commission, February 12, 1946, the Farnsworth Television and Radio Corporation listed a gross income of $119,091,227 from 1940 to 1945.[33]

The early figures reflect a growing company, but it was clearly one dependent upon manufacturing military communications apparatus. The net figures were a bit more revealing as they take into account expansion, expense, and debt.[34] From early 1939 to 1941, the losses presumably reflected startup, retooling, and factory purchase costs. But they were declining while the demand for wartime manufacturing was growing. The sales were up almost $3 million from 1940, and orders on file had increased to almost $7 million.[35] The year 1942 was an optimistic one for the Farnsworth corporate leadership. The *New York Times* headlined the achievements: "Television and Radio Concern Operations Doubled Those Reported in 1941." The emphasis here was on its having doubled its income from the previous year. Translated, that first profit meant a stockholder's dividend was worth $0.46 per share.[36] However, stockholders did not receive a dividend because the profits were contracted for payments on the corporation's credit line, extending the limit to $5 million. The corporation had almost a $1.5 million debt on this line of credit, but a credit extension was seen as a means of producing the cash necessary to meet growing production demands. The contract agreements between the New York Bankers Trust Company also forbade the corporation from paying its stockholders until the debt was retired, a debt that would become due at the end of the war production contracts.[37] Still, profits were rising and optimism was running high. Six months into 1943, the value to the stockholders was equivalent to $.84 per share.[38]

In an effort to raise money, the Farnsworth management received permission from the Securities and Exchange Commission to place the company's stock on the New York exchange: It began trading later in October 1943.[39] This

Corporate Profit and Loss Reports

Dates	SEC Reported Gross Income[a]	*New York Times* Reports Net Profit(Loss)[b]
December 13, 1938 to April 30, 1939	—	$(250,000)[c]
Year to April 30, 1940	$ 2,964,920	(749,741)[d]
Year to April 30, 1941	5,165,905	(181,858)[e]
Year to April 30, 1942	10,433,119	642,237[f]
Year to April 30, 1943	19,204,377	1,170,005[g]
Year to April 30, 1944	30,946,603	1,137,112[h]
Year to April 30, 1945	33,920,948	953,385[i]
Seven Months Ended November 30, 1945	16,455,405	—
Year to April 30, 1946	—	476,190[j]

a. Gross income listed from "Sales, Royalties and License Fees," Farnsworth Television and Radio Corporation, Securities and Exchange 1946 Report, p. 5.

b. Note the Farnsworth corporation's reporting year was April to April. Net incomes reported from the *New York Times.* Corporate annual reports were not consistently retained in Farnsworth's papers, so *New York Times* figures are used and where possible, primary sources are cited.

c. "Farnsworth Television and Radio Corporation," *New York Times,* February 9, 1940, 31: 4.

d. "Farnsworth Television and Radio Corporation," *New York Times,* September 12, 1940, 37: 4. (There is a difference here from what was reported as a loss on February 9. In this report, Nicholas reports the loss in the February 9 report at $80,851. This is likely the figure for only the nonrecurring items. See both reports for comparison.)

e. "Farnsworth Television and Radio Corporation," *New York Times,* August 16, 1941, 23: 4. (There are two separate "loss" figures used in this report: $194,322 and $181,858. We have reported the latter in this writing because it was confirmed in a later report. See "Farnsworth Television and Radio," *New York Times,* August 21, 1941, 21: 5.)

f. "Farnsworth Net $642,237 in Year," *New York Times,* July 13, 1942, 23: 5.

g. "Farnsworth's Net Rises to $1,170,005," *New York Times,* July 8, 1943, 29: 1.

h. "Farnsworth Television and Radio Reports 1943–44 a Record Year," *New York Times,* July 21, 1944, 24: 5, and 27: 1.

i. "Farnsworth Television and Radio Corporation," *New York Times,* July 27, 1945, 26: 5.

j. "Farnsworth Television and Radio Corporation," *New York Times,* July 25, 1946, 31: 2.

meant that Farnsworth stock could now be bought and sold on the open market. The stock was traded in New York, San Francisco, and Los Angeles at first, and a few months later, the Philadelphia Stock Exchange made application to trade Farnsworth stock.[40] Transactions reported on the New York Stock Exchange listed Farnsworth Television and Radio stock ranging from 10 to 9.[41] (See Appendix G.) This listing had two benefits: First it brought in extra financial support for the corporation, and second, it allowed existing stockholders who had not received any dividends a chance to sell their shares on the open market. The public sale of Farnsworth company stock on the stock exchange also meant the corporation's financial status would now be under increased scrutiny.[42]

Earnings dipped "sharply" in the next six months to December 15, 1943, down more than $240,000 from the previous year's same reporting period.[43] Nicholas was quick to respond to the decline, noting that there were price reductions that had forced the company to pay a refund on government contracts, and this, in conjunction with the changing tax situation, had created the decline. Unfortunately, the refund to the government appears to be for "the company's unfilled orders."[44]

Not long after the stock went public and net profits declined, Nicholas sold most of his 5,000 shares, retaining only 500.[45] This was obviously the majority of the stock he had received as part of his initial agreement to serve as president. The New York Stock Exchange listed Farnsworth stock values at 12¼.[46]

In January 1944, stock was more positive at $.48 per share—up $.08 per share from the same period in 1943.[47] In the annual report to the stockholders, Nicholas reported that income from "sales, royalties, and license fees . . . was the largest on record."[48] At a board of directors meeting in November 1944, the corporate debt ceiling was increased again—up to $12 million.[49]

Earnings for 1945 dipped slightly, with the dividend valued at $.67 per share.[50] Just weeks earlier on April 8, 1945, victory had been declared in the war in Europe. Four months later, victory would be declared over Japan on August 14, 1945. The result was an end to military contracts and bank loans coming due.

THE DIFFICULT POSTWAR TRANSITION

This was a critical phase in the Farnsworth corporate history. The end of the war was financially devastating to many companies. However, the corporation expanded, reorganized, and went deeper into debt. By early 1946, net profit dipped substantially to $476,190, with earnings reported down $.29 per share. It should have been worrisome that these calculated earnings included more than a $2.5 million base of new financing.[51]

The most significant manufacturing challenge in the transition to a commercial economy was a shortage of cabinets and technical components. The drastically curtailed production of radio receivers was created by a shortage of cabinet furniture, which was caused by the unprecedented demand for furniture and lumber for new home construction. Explaining this difficulty, Nicholas informed the Farnsworth corporate management that "RCA, GE, Philco, and Zenith had purchased outright ongoing furniture and cabinet factories. This has [also] naturally resulted in a further curtailment of sources of cabinet supply to others. The cabinet shortage has thus become more and more critical."[52] Nicholas's answer to the cabinet shortage was yet another expansion—the purchase of the Thomasville Furniture Company.[53] The Farnsworth corporation was also having trouble obtaining radio and TV parts from suppliers. The result was a delay of "at least several months in making deliveries."[54] The shortages dictated a direct call for cutback action.

Nicholas announced, that with continued shortages:

> which threaten to continue some time, particularly with respect to end product manufacturers such as our company, together with a few of our operations, clearly discloses that we are confronted with a critical situation that calls for quick and drastic action . . . There are no indications that the overall material problems will be cleared up for many months ahead. Consequently material and component part shortages will continue to be our day-to-day problem in production . . . Analyzing our net accomplishment as reflected by operating figures for the past four months, it becomes clearly evident that we have not been as effective as others in our industry. It would appear that we have become cumbersome and unwieldy in some of our operations, and have lost much of our flexibility in a business where speed, drive, and cost consciousness are fundamental requirements. We must correct these conditions immediately.[55]

The quick and drastic actions proposed were cutbacks, consolidation, and reorganization.[56] Nicholas asked his management for a 10 percent reduction in overall expenses (including the elimination of employees), a 35 percent cut in advertising, and a study of all costs in order to reduce expenditures.[57] Farnsworth Television and Radio operations were to be consolidated at Fort Wayne. In yet another reorganization plan, Nicholas called for a corporation restructuring in accordance with divisional activities, with divisional heads on a fixed budget and charged with responsibility for divisional profits and losses. "There is an indication that we may have carried over from our war activity an organization structure which is not essential for civilian production, and which is injecting factors into our costs which before the war were not standard in radio industry practice." Nicholas urged his management to "uncover them now and take steps to eliminate them."[58] He specifically directed the television receiver design be centralized under a single division manager and indicated that the plans for the broadcast center were now in question. The financial picture of the broadcast center seemed to support either option as WGL-AM was operating at a reported net loss.[59]

Under the new organization, research activities were also to pay for themselves through royalties. In order to accomplish this, a new subsidiary would be formed. The Farnsworth Research Corporation was a division of the Farnsworth Television and Radio Corporation and would soon be headed once again by Farnsworth. He was to conduct all "research and patent activities of the parent company."[60]

Moving into the 1947 reporting year (to April 30) the outlook weakened even further. Six months into the year the corporation reported a net loss of $259,075.[61] In the December 1946 financial report for WGL, overall corporate losses were indicated at $722,738.[62] Not only was the Farnsworth corporation now operating at a loss, but the war debts were looming at the bank.

THE FIGHT TO STAY ALIVE

From 1947 to 1949 the Farnsworth corporation fought to stay alive. Even budget cuts were not enough. On October 8, 1947, the board of directors announced that the company had $3 million in unpaid war debts that were due October 30, 1947.[63] The board immediately declared for the liquidation of assets not just to pay the debt, but also to remove obsolete items from the company inventory. The obsolete items were component parts and unfinished products, most likely from military inventories. The board also decided the corporate departments that were ancillary to the "principal operation of manufacturing and distributing high-grade radio and television sets would be liquidated."[64] The minutes of the board meeting make no specific mention of which assets would be sold, but all the plants outside of Fort Wayne were eventually sold.

The board's decisions created a flurry of activity. At a special meeting on October 17, it was revealed that ITT wanted to purchase some Farnsworth stock.[65] Just five days later the Farnsworth corporation was negotiating with RCA to use the Farnsworth Research Corporation's patents "in perpetuity . . . in consideration of the payment of $2,500,000 cash."[66] General Electric was also a party to these discussions and offered $400,000 for the same rights.[67] These patent sales proposals were not acted upon, but one year later RCA did purchase the Marion manufacturing plant from the corporation. It would become RCA's center for television tube production.[68]

PROGRESSIVE GROWTH

The picture for Farnsworth television was not all bleak. In fact, the contrast between the financial realities and the aggressive growth program was startling. In addition to the promotions, improvements, and plans surrounding the WGL Broadcast Center, industrial work was expanding.

In November 1946, the Farnsworth corporation demonstrated a new railroad radio communication system — a two-way radio test in conjunction with the Texas and Pacific Railway. The *Dallas Morning News* described it as the use of "radio communications in switching railroad cars."[69] Three months later, the largest demonstration of its kind was conducted in the railroad radio field.[70] This was sponsored by the Ford Motor Company, the Irontron Railroad Company, and the Farnsworth corporation. Over several days 150 executives and engineers witnessed the use of FM radio transmissions "in maintaining train-to-train, train-to-fixed station, and intra-train communications."[71] In January 1947, the corporation unveiled a new product for industrial monitoring. Called the Farnsworth utiliscope, it was somewhat like today's security cameras but it was used to monitor utility and power plant operations. The utiliscope, tested for nine months at the New York Hell Gate Station Power Plant, was distributed through the Diamond Power Specialty Corporation, a partner with Farnsworth in the scope's development.[72]

Corporate growth included more than demonstrations and new products. There were new facilities for research and television manufacturing. Meeting the need for facilities, in March 1947 the corporation announced that the Fort Wayne plant had expanded again accommodating research and engineering functions.[73]

In May 1947, a live television demonstration was conducted for members of the International Harvester Foremen's Club. The demonstration attracted several hundred members of the International Harvester Corporation, who were gathered at the Farnsworth corporate headquarters, where at the "flip of a switch ... the foremen saw their bosses and heard the short message ..." and had a panoramic view of Fort Wayne taken from a camera placed just outside of Farnsworth headquarters.[74] These experiments marked the Farnsworth corporation's postwar expansions beyond commercial television and into industrial nonbroadcast video functions.[75]

Postwar Farnsworth Receivers

The highlight of hope during this critical period was the manufacture of the television receiver. The postwar Farnsworth television receiver was introduced to the officers of the J. N. Ceazan Company in San Francisco, August 26, 1947, and to the D. W. May Corporation in New York, September 2, 1947. The

California meeting featured the compact model television set with D. A. McMullen, sales manager for the Ceazan Company, and Eustace Vynne, the Farnsworth corporation's western regional sales manager, in charge of the dealers meeting.[76] The New York May Company dealer meeting was a four-day affair introducing television and various Farnsworth products to approximately 150 dealers. These dealers represented only one-quarter of the almost 600 May distribution dealers scattered throughout the New York and New Jersey areas, but those in attendance were excited. They were each provided with a "dealer sampling" set — a table model television, with a ten-inch tube that retailed for $349.50.[77] According to J. S. Hammer, the May Company general sales manager, following the dealers' sampling period, "deliveries to retailers will be immediate and sufficient to fill demand in the May area."[78] The price was to be $25 to $50 lower than rival models. The additional 1948 models included two television console sets, both featuring ten-inch screens. There were a number of AM-FM consoles, AM-FM record changers, and combination sets. In addition the Farnsworth table model radio was available for immediate delivery.[79] Hammer estimated the television and radio set orders from the meeting totaled $250,000.[80] The choice of the Farnsworth corporation to emphasize sales in New York and the Northeastern states using the May Company was directed by the knowledge that this was where most of the stations were at the time.[81]

Nicholas launched the new 1949 model line at a meeting of his own Farnsworth dealers in August 1948 in New York at the Hotel Pierre. Four new models featured a twelve-inch screen and varied in price depending upon the furniture and the combination of AM-FM–TV–record changer desired. The models were the Farnsworth and the Capehart.[82] Nicholas used this platform to announce price increases due to "higher production costs ... the shortage of glass blanks for cathode ray receiving tubes ... [and] tube production," which "keep production behind demand and substantially increased unit costs of end-products."[83] In the last two paragraphs of the *New York Times* article announcing the new 1949 line of Farnsworth television receivers, it was noted that the Sightmaster's Corporation exhibited a new set in its line where the screen could be coupled as a decorative mirror when the set was not in use. The Transvision Company also unveiled a television kit for the public, whereby those desiring to receive the television signal could assemble their own set. Other manufacturers were also on the bandwagon — DuMont, RCA, Philco, Motorola, and Zenith were already leaders in the market, and many others would soon follow.[84]

POSTWAR INDUSTRY IN TRANSITION

From 1946 through 1949, public ownership of television sets grew from 8,000 to 940,000 households, respectively.[85] There was still only a handful of stations, most in the Northeast, but audience awareness was definitely increasing. Consumers were excited about this new piece of entertainment furniture and wanted to make it a part of their homes. The FCC also proposed licensing more commercial television stations in each market and, although prior to September 1948 only twenty-nine stations were on the air, an additional eighty construction permits were authorized; 294 applications were pending, but things were moving too fast.[86]

Finally realizing that the current television frequency allocation system was insufficient for the rapid postwar growth, and taking note of other pressing television issues (such as station channels, use of the UHF band, and color television standards), the FCC ordered a freeze on television station licenses on September 20, 1948, halting further expansion of stations while the Commission studied television allocations. This shutdown of potential competition was a brief boon to the existing stations but frustrating to those who anxiously awaited FCC decisions before they could go on the air.

Of the major broadcast corporations, CBS gained the most from the hiatus. It gave them time to catch up with RCA. This time the major players were RCA and CBS and the issue was color television standards. RCA already had black-and-white sets on the market, and standards for them approved. RCA was only embarking on color research and developing color television standards. CBS had a mechanical color reproduction system. However, because of the incompatibility of CBS color with NTSC's monochrome sets already on the market, CBS reasoned that its color would be precluded. CBS's strategy was to push the FCC for rapid approval of its color system, thus preempting RCA's sale of receivers. In this second battle over television standards, CBS played the underdog, as RCA already had support of the manufacturers and its public relations and manufacturing machinery was in place.

After considerable debate and extended hearings, the FCC approved CBS's color system (October 1950), then rescinded its order approving the RCA color system (December 1953). Although CBS standards were not adopted, it did gain the time it needed to be competitive with RCA once standards were announced.

The freeze lasted for four years, until 1952. The FCC's April 1952 *Sixth Report and Order* established the foundation of today's system. Spectrum allocation for commercial and educational broadcasting, VHF (very high frequency) and UHF (ultra high frequency) channels were allocated. The FCC created a table of assignments for cities and towns throughout the nation. During the freeze the number of home receivers grew from 172,000 to 15,300,000.[87] By 1952 there were 108 commercial stations on the air, double that of two years earlier.[88]

The Farnsworth corporation was fading from the commercial television picture. The cancellation of military contracts and heavy war debts were inhibiting the transition to peacetime manufacturing. The corporation was sold.

Appendix F
ITT-Farnsworth Management History

THE FOUNDER AND PRESIDENT OF ITT WAS COLONEL SOSTHENES BEHN. BY THE TIME ITT purchased the Farnsworth company, ITT was a multinational conglomerate. Behn served as president of ITT from its inception in 1920 to 1947 and then as chairman of the board until 1956. He had expected that "Farnsworth Television and Radio would become the centerpiece for ITT's consumer-products division."[1] Robert Sobel described the acquisition as a positive one. "That company [Farnsworth] had a fine and respected name, but a weak product line and poor prospects. Its founder and leader, Phil Farnsworth, was a talented scientist who held several of the most important patents for television."[2]

The president of ITT, at the time of the Farnsworth purchase, was William H. Harrison, a former AT&T executive lured to ITT in 1947. He was described as the opposite of Behn, meaning that while Behn appreciated Harrison's executive and domestic experience, he described him as an administrator lacking in "manufacturing experience."[3] This weakness did not help Behn's manufacturing acquisitions, including Farnsworth. Both Behn and Harrison left ITT in 1956 and, according to Anthony Sampson, left a vacuum in ITT leadership.[4] Into this vacuum came a caretaker president, Edmund Leavey, who served only two years before being replaced by Harold S. Geneen, who would build ITT into a massive conglomerate in the 1960s.[5]

Working under all of these ITT corporate personalities, the first president of the new Capehart-Farnsworth television division was Ellery Stone, an eighteen-year veteran of ITT.[6] At the time of his election to president of Capehart-Farnsworth, he had served as a vice president of ITT as well as president of two other ITT operations: Federal Telephone and Radio and the International Standard Corporation. However, Stone was a short-timer. His successor, Fred W. Wilson, was brought to ITT with twelve years of experience at RCA. It was Wilson who first directed the Capehart manufacturing operations under ITT President Harrison.

In 1954 Wilson was replaced by Harvard L. Hull, who served just two years.[7] Hull had a Ph.D. from Columbia University and was known as the "father of the hot lab"—a title he acquired for work he conducted in relation to the separation of radioactive materials. During World War II, Hull had worked on the Manhattan project, which led to the development of the atomic bomb. He was a vice president at Capehart-Farnsworth from 1949 to 1953 and president of Farnsworth Electronics from 1954 to 1956.[8] In 1957 Hull's replacement was Lawrence G. Haggerty,[9] who had served at Capehart-Farnsworth since 1950 as director of operations and vice president from 1952. His experience prior to Farnsworth was at the Indianapolis Division of RCA.[10]

Appendix G
ITT Capehart-Farnsworth History

At the outset of the ITT Capehart-Farnsworth manufacturing operations the forecasts were bright. Just a year after the ITT takeover, C. R. Ward, the Capehart sales and marketing manager, disclosed the first postwar ITT Capehart consumer electronics lines. A warehouse in Fort Wayne accommodated distribution, and the new "Capehart deluxe model: the Concert Grand television-phonograph-radio combination console with a 16-inch picture tube, was announced."[1] The *New York Times* reported that by August 1950, orders had "exceeded $3,000,000." These reports were optimistic and, by December 1950, Capehart-Farnsworth was paying dividends to ITT.[2] Two 16-mm training films, "It's Murder" and "The Sale after the Sale," were produced for the company by the J. M. Mathes agency of New York.[3] These were intended as sales support tools for training local dealers and repair technicians. In June 1951, Capehart exhibited one of the first televisions in Japan at Tokyo's National Trade Show.[4]

The news seemed all good, however, the ITT Capehart management was making the same mistake Homer E. Capehart himself had made during the Depression and that Edwin A. Nicholas had made with the Capehart-Farnsworth models prior to and following World War II—the luxury models and high prices were beyond the average consumer's expendable income.

The new 1950 Capehart line, although publicly declared to be seeking a larger market, did not compete. Nevertheless, Capehart advertising continued to emphasize the famous high-end cabinet designs and even headlined some articles with Farnsworth's youthful television research success stories.[5] Although competitive with the expensive sets, Capehart was not priced to sell aggressively against the mass-market brands. By 1952 price reductions were announced at the company's dealer meetings. The prices came down by twenty to forty dollars, but still listed for $229.95—simply too high for the mass market.[6] Minutes of the January 1954 management advisory meeting reflect concerns reminiscent of the former Farnsworth corporation postwar demise. There were issues concerning the "volume of unfilled orders," future sales prospects, "plans for reducing costs," and "plans for reentering the business of industrial television equipment sales."[7] Just three months later, at another advisory meeting, discussion focused on possible negotiations with RCA for sublicensing rights under the unexpired Farnsworth television patents.[8]

Appendix H
Farnsworth Electronics History

AT THE SAME TIME CAPEHART MANUFACTURING WAS BEING SOLD, FARNSWORTH Electronics purchased the Bennett Products Manufacturing Company of Palo Alto, California. The Bennett company, like others purchased by ITT, had been having "management difficulties and was available."[1] This acquisition added to ITT's ability to produce component parts for its military contracts and established a Pacific Division sales headquarters.[2] The name of the Bennett company was changed to Farnsworth Electronic Company–Pacific Division.[3]

Farnsworth Electronics would grow significantly over the next few years. In November 1956, L. G. Haggerty was appointed the new president of Farnsworth Electronics when Hull resigned to become president of the Lipton Industries.[4] By 1957 there were approximately 2,500 people employed and "in excess of half-million square feet of floor space . . . modernized and expanded laboratories alone occupied approximately two-hundred and forty thousand square feet."[5]

In July 1957 ITT president Edmond H. Leavey visited Fort Wayne to dedicate a fourth Farnsworth plant, a $3-million facility. A telegram from then-President Dwight D. Eisenhower congratulated the Farnsworth company for its advancement and important contributions to "the future security of our nation and on furthering the cause of world peace."[6] The company celebrated with an open house at the new facilities where, with clearance, Farnsworth company employee families, ITT dignitaries, and the press were guided through controlled settings to see the elements of the "secret government work involving national defense," being conducted at the plant.[7]

The new plant was made possible by another government contract. This one, via the Boeing Corporation, was for an "interceptor missile."[8] The Boeing Bomarc missile contract amounted to more than $12 million for the Farnsworth organization, which had 170 engineers active on this single project.[9]

Leavey was the shortest-term administrator and considered to be the caretaker president at ITT, but he was there long enough to dedicate the new plant and reorganize Farnsworth.[10] It was Leavey's idea to consolidate the research and development work at ITT by forming a new division called ITT Laboratories—the result was the formation of ITT Federal. The move involved: Federal Telephone and Radio and Farnsworth Electronics.[11] The move was meant to promote efficiency and cost-cutting, but the impact on the Farnsworth corporation, according to Haggerty, was thought to be gradual and of a minor consequence.[12]

Even under Leavey (ITT president) and Haggerty (Farnsworth president), the company continued to grow. In March 1957 ITT purchased a large piece of industrial property owned by the federal government. Referred to as the Camp Scott purchase, it reflected ITT's expansions.[13] A special edition of the company newsletter, *Farnsworth News,* July 11, 1957, announced plans for a fourth plant at the Camp Scott site. The three plants then in existence totaled more than 420,000 square feet of floor space, and employed approximately 2,500 people, "including a technical staff of over 450 engineers, physicists and mathematicians, augmented by 650 technical assistants."[14] Most important, Leavey reported that 1956 marked the first year, "every major unit of the IT&T System operate[d] . . . at a profit."[15] Farnsworth Electronics was "one of the fastest growing units of the IT&T system."[16]

≈

Notes

PREFACE

1. See the exchanges in *Broadcasting* magazine: David Rapaport, "History Lesson," *Broadcasting* 122:2 (January 13, 1992): 108; Albert Abramson letter in "Open Mike," *Broadcasting* 122:6 (February 3, 1992): 46–47; and David Rapaport, *"Farnsworth v. Zworykin,* Cont." *Broadcasting,* 122:8 (February 17, 1992): 53.

2. The history of Philco is told by Ron Ramirez and Michael Prosise, *Philco Radio: 1928–1942* (West Chester, Penn.: Schiffer Publishing, 1993).

3. The notebooks are in the Curator's Collection, Electrical Collections, Division of Information and Technology, Society, National Museum of American History, Washington, D.C.; hereafter referred to as National Museum of American History.

4. T. Ropp, "Philo Farnsworth: Forgotten Father of Television," *Media History Digest* 5:2 (Summer 1985): 42–58. See also Stephen F. Hofer, "Philo Farnsworth: Television's Pioneer," *Journal of Broadcasting* 23:2 (1979): 153.

5. George Everson, unpublished autobiography, Arizona State University Library Special Collections, Box 4, File 1, p. 33. Hereafter referred to as the Farnsworth-Everson Papers.

6. Kenneth Kistler, "The Lab Left Holds Distinction," *Sunday Magazine,* unidentified newspaper clipping file, File 2. Arizona State University Library Special Collections, materials donated by Gene Meeks. Hereafter referred to as the Farnsworth-Meeks Papers.

7. See Hofer, "Television's Pioneer," pp. 153–165.

8. Hofer, "Television's Pioneer," p. 164.

9. Kenneth Bilby, *The General: David Sarnoff and the Rise of the Communications Industry* (New York: Harper & Row, 1986), p. 128. See also, David Sarnoff's statement on Farnsworth, "Development of Television" Hearings before the U.S. Senate Committee on Interstate Commerce, U.S. Senate, 76th Congress, 3rd Session, April 10–11, 1940, p. 47 on Senate Resolution 251.

10. George Eckhardt, *Electronic Television* (Chicago: Goodheart Willcox, 1936; reprinted, New York: Arno Press, 1974), p. iii. See pp. 10–17 for a description of the Farnsworth electronic system, pp. 26–33 for the Farnsworth camera, and pp. 97–111 for the Farnsworth receiving system.

11. Albert Abramson, *The History of Television: 1880–1941* (Jefferson, N.C.: McFarland & Company, 1987).

12. Albert Abramson, *Zworykin: Pioneer of Television* (Chicago: University of Illinois Press, 1995), pp. 1–5. Abramson notes that the title was also given to Sarnoff in 1944. See p. 176.

13. R. W. Burns, *Television: An International History of the Formative Years* (London: IEE/Science Museum "History of Technology Series 22," 1997).

14. George Everson, *The Story of Television: The Life of Philo T. Farnsworth* (New York: W. W. Norton, 1949; reprint, New York: Arno Press, 1974).

15. Elma G. Farnsworth, *Distant Vision: Romance and Discovery on an Invisible Frontier* (Salt Lake City: Pemberly-Kent Publishers, 1989). Written by Farnsworth's wife, this is a biography, a love story, and an autobiography. See also www.songs.com/philo/.

16. Robert Cremer, "A Tinkerer Who Became the Father of Video," *San Francisco Examiner and Chronicle,* Sunday Television Report, 17 January 1978.

17. Mark Warbis, "TV Inventor Finally Getting Public's Respect," *Electronic Media* (19 June 1989), p. 55.

18. Frank Lovece, "Zworykin vs. Farnsworth," *Video* IX (September 1985), pp. 96–98, 135–38.

19. Frank Lovece, "Is It TV's 50th Birthday or Not?" *Channels* (June 1989), p. 9. The arguments of Lovece are somewhat reinforced in *Empire of the Air.* Although this is a radio history, it discusses the charge that Sarnoff and RCA were heavy-handed in their dealings with others. See Tom Lewis, *Empire of the Air* (New York: Harper-Collins, 1991).

20. Christopher H. Sterling and John M. Kittross, *Stay Tuned: A Concise History of American Broadcasting,* 2nd ed. (Belmont Calif.: Wadsworth, 1990), p. 551.

CHAPTER 1

1. Neil Postman, "Electrical Engineer: Philo Farnsworth," *Time 100,* Special issue, 153:12 (29 March 1999): 92–94.

2. Sydney W. Head, *Broadcasting in America,* 3rd ed. (Boston: Houghton Mifflin Company, 1976), p. 155.

3. Erik Barnouw, *Tube of Plenty: The Evolution of American Television,* 3rd ed. (New York: Oxford University Press, 1990), pp. 77–78.

4. R. Glen Nye, *Farnsworth Memorial II,* 2nd ed. N.C.: Family Publication, Library of Congress, No. 74-81077, n.d., p. 561. For additional family history, see the collection of papers compiled for the family by Laura Farnsworth Player, Arizona State University Library Special Collections, p. 17; hereafter referred to as the Player Papers. Also Farnsworth, *Distant Vision;* Barnouw's *Tube of Plenty,* p. 77, and *The Golden Web: A History of Broadcasting in the United States, 1933–1953* (New York: Oxford University Press, 1968), p. 39, provide a brief biography. See also Mitchell Wilson, "The Strange Birth of Television," *Reader's Digest* 62 (370): 19–22; Dennis May, "Philo T. Farnsworth: The Father of Television," *BYU Today* 43:3 (May 1989): 33–35; Hofer, "Television's Pioneer," pp. 154–56, and "Quiet Contributor," p. 10. The Church of Jesus Christ of Latter-day Saints, Historical Department, Church Archives, Ancestral File, 1993, Family Group Records AFN:6B4X-K3 has a complete pedigree chart of Philo T. Farnsworth. Care must be taken in depending on these ancestral files because

they are often full of errors. An extensive history also appears on the Internet. See Paul Schatzkin, "The Farnsworth Chronicles," http://www.songs.com/philo/.

5. Player Papers, p. 13.

6. For an objective history, see Leonard J. Arrington and Davis Bitton, *The Mormon Experience: A History of the Latter-day Saints,* 2nd ed. (Urbana: University of Illinois Press, 1992). The U.S. flag was first raised over Salt Lake City in October 1847. In 1861 the telegraph brought eastern and western settlements closer together. The transcontinental railroad came together at Promontory, Utah, in 1869. Statehood was achieved in 1896.

7. T. R. Carskadon, "Phil, the Inventor," *Collier's* (3 October 1936) p. 28.

8. See Nye, *Farnsworth Memorial II,* pp.560–61: Philo Taylor Farnsworth Sr., and Lewis Edwin Farnsworth. The wives' names were Margaret Yates, Margaret Adams, Agnes Ann Patterson, and Mary Priscilla Griffith. He was a polygamist, and at this time it was not yet outlawed by the government or the Church.

9. The sego, or sego lily, is a variety of perennial herbs whose bulb is edible. The plant was wild, plentiful, and commonly eaten by Utah settlers during difficult times. The blossom of the sego is the state flower of Utah.

10. They began in Indian Creek, Utah, and moved to Parowan, Mountain Home, Altonah, Filmore, Washington (in southern Utah), and Rigby (Idaho) before ending up in Provo.

11. See T. Earl Pardon, *The Sons of Brigham* (Provo, Utah: Brigham Young University Alumni Association, 1969), p. 318. Philo's brothers were born in Parowan, Utah (Carl), and in Mountain Home, Utah (Lincoln).

12. Autobiographical statement dictated by Philo T. Farnsworth to his wife Elma G. Farnsworth, undated, Arizona State University Library Special Collections, Godfrey Papers, Box 8, File 2; hereafter referred to as Godfrey Papers.

13. Philo turned twelve on August 19. Edwin C. Hill, a commentator for the *Deseret News,* reported that Philo's wagon was full of "coils of wire, tubes and curious dials and switches of his own devising mystifying to his family." This seems unlikely as most later accounts indicated Philo's real interest in electronics began in Idaho, fostered by his finding books and magazines on the subject in the attic of his new home. See Edwin C. Hill, "Philo T. Farnsworth's Story Told by Commentator," *Deseret News,* 1 November 1939, p. 3.

14. Player Papers, pp. 18–19.

15. The ranch owned by Albert was used to raise racehorses. There are differing reports as to the ownership of the ranch. The autobiography of Vernal T. Sorensen indicated that the ranch was owned by a "Mr. Hill and Associates" and that Philo's father was hired as manager of the ranch. See the *Autobiography of Vernal R. Sorensen,* p. 9. Jefferson County Historical Society and Farnsworth TV Pioneer Museum, Rigby, Idaho, General Files; hereafter referred to as Jefferson County Historical Society.

16. Player Papers, p. 73.

17. Patricia Lyn Scott, *The Hub of Eastern Idaho: A History of Rigby, Idaho, 1885–1986* (Rigby, Idaho: City of Rigby, 1976), p. 95. The Farnsworth family experiences during these years are not detailed within this history. They were in Idaho only a few short years. However, the detail of the farming experiences reflects the challenges the Farnsworth family faced while they were there.

18. Paul Schatzkin and Bob Kiger, "Philo T. Farnsworth: Inventor of Electronic Television," *Televisions* 5:1 (1977): 6.

19. The magazines in the attic apparently had been left there by the former owner. At this writing, which titles or why they were left is unknown. It is assumed that they were some of the popular science magazines of the time.

20. Hill, p. 3.

21. "Banker Backed," *Time* (20 February 1939) p. 62. See also Leonard J. Arrington, "Philo T. Farnsworth, Inventor of Television," published in *Acceptance and Dedication of the Statue of Philo T. Farnsworth, Presented by the State of Utah, Proceedings in the Rotunda of the United States Capitol, May 2, 1990* (Washington, D.C.: Government Printing Office, 1991), p. 34.

22. See J. L. Blair, "Television, or Seeing by Wireless," *Discovery* 6:142 (April 1925): 143. See also numerous articles published by C. F. Jenkins in *Transactions of the SMPE,* 1922–25. Also C. A. Herndon, "Motion Pictures by Ether Waves," *Popular Radio* 8:107 (August 1925): 113. W. B. Arvin, "See with Your Radio," *Radio News* 7:278 (September 1925): 384–87. Stories like these were not only a catalyst for the young inventor but provided him information on earlier experiments and experimenters.

23. Player Papers, p. 19.

24. *Autobiography of Vernal T. Sorensen,* n.d., p. 10. Jefferson County Historical Society.

25. Ibid.

26. Philo T. Farnsworth, "Notes on Biography for Rigby," n.d., Godfrey Papers, Box 8, File 2, p. 1.

27. Player Papers, p. 19. See "Big Dream Small Screen: The Story Behind Television," Windfall Films, 1997.

28. There are differing reports as to this contest. In "Quiet Contributor," p. 14, Hofer reports the contest was for a "theft-proof lock for automobiles." Everson agrees, see *Story of Television,* p. 17. According to his sister Laura, it was a bicycle safety switch. See Thomas Ropp, "The Real Father of Television," *Arizona Republic Magazine* (6 May 1984), p. 5. In the majority of the reports it is referred to as a "thief proof ignition switch," actually a car lock. The more important point is that it exemplified a young mind at work.

29. Everson, *Story of Television,* p. 17.

30. Ropp, "Real Father," pp. 4–5.

31. Ibid., p. 5.

32. Schatzkin and Kiger, "Philo T. Farnsworth," p. 6. See also Ropp, "Real Father," p. 5.

33. May, "Father of Television," p. 34.

34. Everson, *Story of Television,* p. 26.

35. Justin Tolman, "The Cradle of Television," University of Utah Marriott Libary, Farnsworth Papers, Box 3, File 2, p. 1; hereafter referred to as the Farnsworth Papers. This is an article apparently written circa 1940 for a University of Utah science and mathematics publication, but this author could not locate the published article.

36. Tolman "The Cradle of Television,", p. 2.

37. Player Papers, p. 20. Compare with Tolman, "The Cradle of Television," pp. 1–2. Although Tolman here states some of the drawings were on "scraps of paper," these

documents could not be located at this writing. It is presumed this figure (see p. 13) is a reproduction.

38. Tolman, "The Cradle of Television," p. 3.

39. Arrington, Statue Dedication, p. 35.

40. Ropp, "Real Father," p. 5.

41. Arrington, Statue Dedication, p. 35.

42. The National Radio Institute (NRI) was founded in 1914 for instruction in "wireless radio." It was a home-study program founded by James E. Smith, a high school teacher. At this writing, NRI is owned by the McGraw-Hill Companies and over the years was a "leader in distance education" (see http://www.mcgraw-hill.com/index.html).

43. Tolman, "The Cradle of Television," pp. 3–4.

44. Correspondence from Carol Quist to Donald G. Godfrey dated spring 1995. Quist is one of Tolman's former students. See Godfrey Papers.

45. Player Papers, p. 74.

46. "Education," a résumé written in Farnsworth's personal handwriting provides a brief educational summary. Rigby High School 1921–1923, BYU High School (a high school program run by the University) and Brigham Young University. Godfrey Papers, Box 13, File 9.

47. Everson, *Story of Television,* p. 170. It is unclear where Everson acquired this impression. It seems a bit odd that Farnsworth would be "given the run of the University research lab" by professors who were unimpressed. The statement likely reflects Farnsworth's exuberance for learning.

48. Player Papers, p. 22. Crawford went on to head the Utah State Geology Department.

49. Certificate no. 102, issued January 4, 1924 to Philo T. Farnsworth, certified that he had passed the requirements to be recognized "as a Junior Radio-Trician." Certificate No 638, issued March 3, 1925 to Philo T. Farnsworth, certified that he had "satisfactorily completed our prescribed course of study and had been granted our diploma as a 'Certified Radio-Trician.' He had a thorough knowledge of the laws, principles, and practices of Radiotelegraphy and Radiotelephone and the regulation speed in code transmission and reception." Farnsworth Papers, Box 2, File 1. Copies in Godfrey Papers, Box 13, File 9.

50. See Farnsworth Papers, Box 1, File 5–6 for student notebooks listing BYU activities. Pem Farnsworth indicates one party Farnsworth sponsored was at a time he was working for Bates Furniture, in Provo, installing radios and antenna. He borrowed a set from the store and brought in signals from Denver, Los Angeles and Cincinnati. It was a private party for Farnsworth and his friends

51. "Utah Youth Astounding World with Radio-Television Inventions," *Deseret News,* 5 March 1936. In Journal History of the Church, CR100/136. Reel no. 176, 5 March 1936, p. 4. The Journal History of the Church is a newspaper clipping file service maintained by the Church of Jesus Christ of Latter-day Saints, Church Library, Salt Lake City, Utah; hereafter referred to as Journal History.

52. The affluent V. K. Zworykin family is in direct contrast with the Farnsworths. Zworykin, the youngest of seven children, was born July 30, 1889 in Muron, Russia. He was raised in the three-story stone mansion that had belonged to his family for several

generations. Like Farnsworth, Zworykin had a thirst for learning and it came easily to him. These were turbulent years in Russia and in Europe as World War I approached. In August 1919 Zworykin arrived in New York and, in 1920, took a job with Westinghouse. In 1923 he filed for a patent on his television system, patent no. 2,141,059 filed on December 29, 1923, and issued on December 20, 1938. See Abramson, *Zworykin,* pp. 42 and 49–51. See also Joseph J. Binns, "Vladimir Kosma Zworykin," *Those Inventive Americans* (Washington, D.C.: National Geographic Society, 1971), pp. 188–92.

53. Player, pp. 22, 74.

54. Ropp, "Real Father," p. 6.

55. Autobiographical notes dictated from Philo T. Farnsworth to Elma G. Farnsworth, Godfrey Papers, Box 8, File 2, p. 3.

56. Hofer, "Quiet Contributor," p. 25.

57. Farnsworth, *Distant Vision,* p. 42.

58. Lincoln Farnsworth oral history interview (audio tape). Godfrey Papers. See Farnsworth, *Distant Vision,* p. 37. Also Agnes and Claude Lindsay and Laura Player, oral history interview by Timothy Larson, February 14, 1985, Farnsworth Papers, pp. 31–32.

59. The U.S. Senators from Utah at the time would have been Senator Reed Smoot (R) and Senator William Henry King (D). This author could find no mention of the request. However the incident is mentioned in family writings. See note 5.

60. *Newsweek* indicated that Farnsworth was "goaded into individuality by his Mormon background." See "The Story of Farnsworth," *Newsweek* (28 March 1949), p. 56. However, it would seem from the evidence that Farnsworth's independent spirit was created from a number of differing experiences during his youth. While his theology would have encouraged the search for education and independence, the death of his father placed a sense of responsibility on Philo as the oldest son. He was now responsible for a family in financial and emotional crisis. In the Navy, the chaplain's advice implied the inventions and resulting royalties would not be Philo's but the Navy's, so Philo left. During his earlier years, his father had expressed concern that people would steal his son's ideas; and Tolman, his high school teacher, had also told him to "stay mum." Circumstances and influential people surrounding Philo seemed to have as much to do with developing his independence as did his theology.

61. His university mentors were Dr. Carl Eyring and Dr. Milton C. Marshal.

CHAPTER 2

1. In 1926 there were only 556 AM radio stations on the air in the United States with 16 percent radio receiver household penetration. By 1927 that number had grown to 681. Most stations were programmed only in the evenings with general music and concerts; see Sterling and Kittross, *Stay Tuned,* Appendix C.

2. Schatzkin and Kiger, "Philo T. Farnsworth," p. 6.

3. Little is known of Leslie Ewing Gorrell other than brief descriptions provided by Everson. They were both fund-raisers. See Everson, *Story of Television,* p. 45. According to the Stanford University records, Gorrell was a mining graduate of Stanford University, 1924. He died February 18, 1956.

4. "Philo T. Farnsworth: Inventor of Electronic Television," booklet prepared for editors and writers by Farnsworth Television and Radio Corporation, Fort Wayne, Indiana, October 1939, ITT Aerospace/Communications Division Library Papers, Fort Wayne, Indiana, pp. 3–5; hereafter referred to as ITT Library Papers. Note this booklet's publication predates Everson's *Story of Television,* yet it contains many of the same dramatic quotes. The theme of Farnsworth's youthful genius carried through this and earlier popular-press publications appears to emanate from the public relations activities of Everson and the corporation.

5. See "Life Story," in Stenographer's Notebook–5, titled, "Requisitions, Materials and Work." Godfrey Papers, Box 9, File 8.

6. Everson, *Story of Television,* p. 37.

7. Letter from Elma G. Farnsworth to Donald G. Godfrey, February 13, 1996, Godfrey Papers. Farnsworth, *Distant Vision,* p. 6.

8. George Everson, interview with Elma G. Farnsworth, March 2, 1977. Audiotape interview in the personal possession of Pem Farnsworth. This author's notes of this and other interviews conducted by Elma G. Farnsworth are with the Godfrey Papers.

9. Farnsworth, *Distant Vision,* p. 6.

10. Everson, *Story of Television,* p. 38.

11. For reports on these early meetings, see Everson, *Story of Television,* p. 45; Farnsworth, *Distant Vision,* pp. 8–9; and the Player Papers, pp. 23–25. See also "Inventor of Electronic Television," ITT Library Papers.

12. Everson, *Story of Television,* p. 40.

13. Ibid.

14. Ibid., p. 41.

15. Ibid., p. 44.

16. In order to compare dollar values throughout the manuscript, two consumer price tables were consulted: the Bureau of Labor Statistics, Consumer Price Indexes Inflation Calculator from http://stats.bls.gov/cpihome.htm; and the Consumer Price Index Inflation Calculator from the National Aeronautics and Space Administration, http://www.jsc.nasa.gov/bu2/inflateCPI.html. These sites provided value comparisons for the years 1913 through 2000. As the dollar values appear throughout the manuscript, the Farnsworth period value appears first, followed by the year 2000 dollar value in brackets.

17. Everson, *Story of Television,* p. 45. Reports differ as to the exact amount of money Everson first provided. *The Inventor of Electronic Television,* ITT Library Papers, p. 12, records the amount as $8,000.

18. The partnership agreement is discussed in a letter from attorneys Lyon and Lyon to Roy Bishop, September 14, 1926, Farnsworth–Everson Papers, Box 1, File 3. At this writing the actual agreement has not been located.

19. Farnsworth, *Distant Vision,* p. 9.

20. Elma Gardner Farnsworth, unpublished oral history interview conducted by Alf Pratte, Brigham Young University, September 10 and November 7, 1987, Farnsworth–Everson Papers. See also *Inventor of Electronic Television,* ITT Library Papers, p. 9.

21. Several publications indicated they were married by a church bishop. This originates with Everson. They were actually married by their stake president. A bishop in the church's terminology is the lay minister who presides over a local geographically defined

congregation, each congregation consisting of sixty to eighty families. These local congregations are called wards. A stake president is a regional authority presiding over six to eight wards.

22. Farnsworth, *Distant Vision,* pp. 12–13, 17–22.

23. May, "Father of Television," p. 35.

24. *Inventor of Electronic Television,* ITT Library Papers, p. 9.

25. Ibid., p. 10.

26. Farnsworth's research journals are housed at the University of Utah Marriott Library, Farnsworth Papers. A copy of the 1929 journal is at the Arizona State University Library, Farnsworth–Everson Papers. Two of his original diaries for 1928 and 1929 are in the National Museum of American History. Several journals, a newspaper-clipping scrapbook, and research notes were lost in a 1947 fire in Maine. The existing log books contain a record of Farnsworth's work as well as the engineers working with him, filed as Daily Notes.

27. Farnsworth, *Distant Vision,* p. 53.

28. Farnsworth's first engineering journals were written in his own hand. The record of the work performed by others was often typed by his wife from the workers' notes or left in the handwriting of the individual as Farnsworth's career progressed.

29. *Inventor of Electronic Television,* ITT Library Papers, p. 11.

30. Everson, *Story of Television,* p. 55. Compare with *Inventor of Electronic Television,* ITT Library Papers, pp. 11–12.

31. Letter to Roy Bishop from Lyon and Lyon, September 14, 1926, Farnsworth–Everson Papers, Box 1, File 3.

32. See Sterling and Kittross, *Stay Tuned,* pp. 56–57.

33. The patent pooling occurred at the end of World War I. It placed the major corporations (RCA, General Electric, AT&T, and Westinghouse) in control of radio development. It comprised complex agreements in which each held important patent rights. RCA was the administrator of the pool agreements and it collected royalties. AT&T sold transmitters and had the rights to radiotelephone (wire and wireless communication for hire). GE and Westinghouse manufactured radios, which in turn were sold by RCA. See Sterling and Kittross, *Stay Tuned,* pp. 53–58.

34. For an explanation on the differences between mechanical and electronic television, see Abramson, *History of Television,* pp. 75–107.

35. Albert Abramson, "Pioneers of Television—Philo Taylor Farnsworth," *SMPTE Journal* 101:11 (November 1992): 770–71. Binns, "Vladimir Kosma Zworykin," pp. 188–92.

36. George Shiers, "Television 50 Years Ago," *Journal of Broadcasting* 19:4 (Fall 1975): 387–99. For a detailed history of these experiments, see J. L. Baird, "Television, or Seeing by Wireless," *Discovery* 6:142 (April 1925): 143.

37. Shiers, "Television 50 Years Ago," p. 390. See also C. F. Jenkins's autobiography, *The Boyhood of an Inventor* (Washington, D.C.: Jenkins Laboratories, 1931). Also numerous articles authored by C. F. Jenkins in *Transactions of the SMPE* 1922–1925. Abramson points out that Jenkins had conducted earlier private demonstrations for the press, the first in December 1923. See Abramson, *History of Television,* pp. 64–65.

38. "Far-Off Speakers Seen as Well as Heard Here in Test of Television," *New York Times,* 8 April 1927, p. 1.

39. See George Shiers, with May Shiers, *Bibliography of the History of Electronics* (Metuchen, N.J.: Scarecrow Press, 1972).

40. Letter to George Everson from J. B. McCargar, November 12, 1924, Godfrey Papers, Box 9, File 10. The letter praises Everson for his work in "raising funds for Californians, Inc." and expresses appreciation for the opportunity McCargar had to work with him.

41. Schatzkin and Kiger, "Philo T. Farnsworth," p. 8. See Everson, *Story of Television,* pp. 63–64.

42. David Warren Ryder, *Great Citizen: A Biography of William H. Crocker* (San Francisco: Historical Publications, 1962), p. 159.

43. Ibid., p. xiv and p. 139. Crocker's biographer describes him as a humanitarian interested in helping new ideas that he felt would "lead to discoveries by which the most elemental and powerful forces of nature could be directed to the use and benefit of man" (p. xiv). Crocker's philosophy no doubt was influential in the development of young Farnsworth's growth and his humanitarian approach to television and scientific discovery.

44. For a description of work conducted in this laboratory and similar scientific interests, see Ryder, *Great Citizen,* pp. 169–83.

45. Everson, *Story of Television,* p. 64.

46. Roy Bishop was William H. Crocker's longtime friend and business associate. He was particularly noted for a successful oil project the bank was almost ready to give up. Bishop later became president of Universal Oil and the Universal Consolidated Oil Company; see Ryder, *Great Citizen,* pp. 143–44.

47. At this writing, copies of these early reports have not been located.

48. Everson, *Story of Television,* p. 66.

49. Ibid., pp. 71–72. Reports of these stories differ slightly as to which events took place at which meeting. We have held to the Everson account as the primary source because he was present. See also, Farnsworth, *Distant Vision,* pp. 60–61.

50. Telegraph Hill has a telecommunications history. Some familiar names conducted experiments from the hill: Marconi, Herrold, and de Forest. At one time it was the site of station KFDB. See Bart Lee, "The Radio History of Telegraph Hill" *Journal of the California Historical Radio Society* 20:2 (August 1996): 12–13. Also David Myrick, *San Francisco's Telegraph Hill* (Berkeley: Howell-North Books, 1972).

51. Everson, *Story of Television,* pp. 74–75.

52. Philo T. Farnsworth, speech to Indiana College, circa 1960, Farnsworth–Everson Papers, transcribed audio recording, p. 2. See also Farnsworth, *Distant Vision,* p. 68, for a description of the first lab. The Green Street building is still in existence and, in recognition of the work accomplished there, a historical marker has been affixed to the corner. See Alace Yarish, "The Genius of Green Street Got the Damn Thing to Work," *San Francisco Sunday Examiner & Chronicle,* 4 September 1977, sec. A, p. 16.

53. Everson, *Story of Television,* p. 71.

54. Early Television Laboratory Personnel, Farnsworth Papers, Box 6, File 2. Everson later criticized this hiring as retarding progress. See Everson, *Story of Television,* p. 76; this same criticism was repeated by Hofer in his dissertation ("Quiet Contributor," pp. 37–39). These authors indicate the hiring was based on the idea that the three had a common religious background and would trust one another, they were afraid of the

"better-equipped technicians," and they liked to have family members around. This was a criticism not soon forgotten by Pem Farnsworth. According to her, the reason family members were on the payroll was to keep the costs down. She also indicated that the family made direct contributions to the television experiments. Cliff (Pem's brother) became an expert glass blower and manufactured the first tubes. Carl (Farnsworth's brother) operated a coil-winding machine to develop component parts for the system. It was true, according to Pem, that "Philo enjoyed having his family around him [but if having the family work] freed the engineer for more important work, why not?" See Elma G. Farnsworth, oral history interview, September 1987, p. 4. Also note that six college-trained engineers were among the twenty-four employees listed as early personnel. It seems to this author that these hiring practices had not so much to do with religion as they did the youthfulness of Farnsworth—he was just turning twenty—and the budget was only $25,000 for the first year. Even at this early stage of his career he had already explained and defended his system to several educated engineers of southern and northern California. There were engineers on the payroll, and he no doubt would have had access to the Crocker Laboratory engineers had he so chosen. However, hiring family had more to do with Farnsworth's youthful inexperience than religion or science. He felt electronic television was his idea, and his actions exhibited the spirit of an independent inventor who wanted to see his idea developed.

55. Farnsworth, speech at Indiana College, p. 3.

56. Two drawings initialed by Pem are found in the Farnsworth Daily Logs, Vol. II, August 27, 1927, p. 7, and June 7, 1928, p. 103. See also Donald G. Godfrey and Alf Pratte, "Elma 'Pem' Gardner Farnsworth: The Pioneering of Television," *Journalism History* 20:2 (Summer 1994): 74–79. See Farnsworth, *Distant Vision,* p. 81.

57. U.S. patent no. 1,773,980, P. T. Farnsworth of Berkeley, California, assignor, by Mesne Assignments to Television Laboratories, of San Francisco, California, a corporation of California, Television System, August 26, 1930. See the drawings and explanation in the Allen County Historical Society Library, Farnsworth Papers, Fort Wayne, Indiana; hereafter referred to as the Farnsworth–Allen County Papers. The drawing for this patent that appears in Abramson, *History of Television,* p. 98, is different. Abramson has used sheet number 3 from the patent application. He noted that while the entire patent system drawings covered four pages, it was sheet three, which "best represents the entire patent." Letter from Albert Abramson to Donald G. Godfrey, July 17, 1998.

58. U.S. patent no. 1,773,980, August 26, 1930, "Digest of Farnsworth's Patents," Farnsworth–Allen County Papers, p. 1. Each patent is reproduced here and the apparatus/method claims are summarized. Elma G. Farnsworth reports that years later the RCA patent attorney complained that the patent office had no right allowing such broad claims. She of course reminded him that "had Phil not been the first in his field, they would have been unable to do so"; see Farnsworth, *Distant Vision,* p. 82. The first image-scanning apparatus was actually patented in 1925 by Max Dieckman and Rudolf Hell in Germany. Camera tubes of this nature were later called "image dissectors." The design was patented, but a working tube was not constructed at this time; see Abramson, *History of Television,* pp. 74–75.

59. U.S. patent no. 1,806,935 Light Valve (issued May 26, 1931); no. 1,758,359 Electronic Oscillator System (issued May 13, 1930); no. 1,773,981 Television Receiving System (issued August 26, 1930). See "U.S. Patents Issued to Philo T.

Farnsworth," Farnsworth–Everson Papers. Issue dates are taken from Book 9, "Digest of Farnsworth Patents," Farnsworth–Allen County Papers. Lists of Farnsworth's patents have been published in numerous locations, and some differ slightly. See Farnsworth, *Distant Vision,* Appendix. Also *Acceptance and Dedication,* Appendix I. The most complete listing and description of the patents come from the Farnsworth–Allen County Papers. See also Appendix A.

60. U.S. patent no. 1,773,980, sheet 1. Farnsworth–Allen County Papers.

61. There is a set of letters written by Farnsworth while he was away from home at this time. He had gone to Los Angeles to facilitate filing the patents and work out papers for the change to San Francisco offices. The letters are from Philo to Pem, dated December 8, 11, 12, and 13, 1926 (see Godfrey Papers). Portions are cited here in footnote form because this is one of the few recorded moments that Farnsworth expressed his inner feelings. On December 8, 1926: "Don't get frightened if the house squeeks [sic] or the doors slam—just remember it's what it is." On December 11, 1926: "Would you like another letter tonite [sic]? I feel in the mood tonite to tell you I love you and hope you will take this letter to mean just that. You know dear when I'm home I'm too close to fully appreciate you—I just take my good fortune for granted then, but when I'm away from you I realize how much a part of my life you really are. It's like being on the steps of a beautiful building. I realize my surroundings are beautiful, but am too close to really see them. I should surely love to be home tonight to be close to you—to hold you on my arm—to feel you warmly against me. I'm afraid you may be ill even while I'm writing this, but if you're not ill in spirit, I guess you can stand it. And dear, I'll be home as soon as I can." On December 13, 1926: "Just my little note tonight to let you know how everything is. I came pretty near having to stay here another week, but I believe that I will be able to leave now in a day or two as soon as we get the claims drawn . . . We're anxious to get it right to the patent office. I'll come soon, but dear you mustn't expect me before Thurs. or Friday morning at best."

62. U.S. patent no. 1,773,981, Farnsworth–Allen County Papers, sheet 1.

63. Everson, *Story of Television,* p. 85. See also Hofer, "Quiet Contributor," p. 40.

64. Everson, *Story of Television,* p. 90–91. See also Kent Farnsworth oral history interview with Anthony Whittaker, November 1989, Farnsworth–Meeks Papers.

65. Farnsworth, Daily Logs, National Museum of American History, September 7 and 8, 1927, pp. 11–12.

66. Letter to George Everson from Philo T. Farnsworth, February 13, 1927, Godfrey Papers, Box 9, File 10.

67. The dollar sign and glass mounting are today a part of the Farnsworth Papers at the University of Utah. For discussion concerning the line experiments, see Farnsworth, Daily Logs, Vol. II, September 7, 1927, p. 12. The journal for 1928–29 is located in the National Museum of American History; hereafter referred to as Farnsworth, Daily Logs, National Museum of American History. For a description of the "radio news" line experiments see Farnsworth, Daily Logs, National Museum of American History, August 20–25, 1928.

68. Ibid., September 19–24, 1927, pp. 14–15; May 7–12, 1928, pp. 96–97; June 8 to 23, 1928; and, July 23 to 28, 1928, pp. 114–115.

69. See Farnsworth, Daily Logs, National Museum of American History, Vol. II, October 19, 1929, p. 45. Philo T. Farnsworth and Harry Lubcke, "The Transmission of

Television Images," *California Engineer* 8:5 (1930): 12–33. For Pem's personal description of this first experiment and the excitement of the day, see Farnsworth, *Distant Vision,* pp. 90–91.

70. Correspondence from Philo T. Farnsworth to George Everson, February 27, 1927, Farnsworth Papers, Box 2, File 1. See also Everson, *Story of Television,* p. 93.

71. Farnsworth, Daily Logs, National Museum of American History, January 23, 1928, pp. 59–60.

72. "The History of Farnsworth," ITT Library Papers, p. 14.

73. "Obit of George Everson," Godfrey Papers, Box 9, File 10.

74. Abramson, *History of Television,* p. 155.

75. Tobe Rutherford interview with Elma G. Farnsworth, circa 1974, recording in the personal possession of Elma G. Farnsworth. This author's notes on this interview are filed in the Godfrey Papers.

76. *Inventor of Television,* ITT Library Papers, p. 13.

77. Harry R. Lubcke, oral history interview with Steven C. Runyon, September 21, 1974, p. 4. Transcribed audio recording from the personal files of Steven C. Runyon, Department of Radio-Television, University of San Francisco. Lubcke later became a well-known engineer who worked for the Don Lee television system out of Los Angeles.

78. Early Television Laboratory Personnel, Farnsworth Papers, Box 6, File 2. The exact number employed at any one time seems to be in question. This list appears to have been compiled some years later, circa 1933. Hofer reports there were twelve working in the lab; see Hofer, "Quiet Contributor," p. 58. However, the people listed by Hofer have different hiring dates recorded on the personnel record: Albert B. Mann [not listed, was appointed by investors to pay the late bills], B. Cliff Gardner [1926], Arch Brolly [1930], Herbert Metcalf [not listed], Harry Lubcke [1928], Robert Rutherford [1928], Harry J. Lyman [1928], Romely Rutherford [1930], Russell Varian [1930], Philip Tait [1930], and Doris Hagerty [1929]. Nathan C. Clark is also reported to be among those early employees but is not on either this or Hofer's list. The confusion results from the fact that McCargar would fire engineers that Farnsworth would then rehire; see oral history interview of Nathan C. Clark, Sierra Club leader, outdoorsman, and engineer, conducted by Richard Searle, Sierra Club History Committee, San Francisco, California, 1977, p. 26.

79. Everson, *Story of Television,* p. 79.

80. Farnsworth, Daily Logs, National Museum of American History, Vol. II, December 27, 1928, p. 44..

81. Everson, *Story of Television,* pp. 114–15. Prior to Farnsworth's forming an independent company, Bishop was the trusted Crocker Bank consultant on the investment.

82. Ibid. Telegraph Hill is one of San Francisco's high points.

83. Ibid., p. 180.

84. Farnsworth, Daily Logs, National Museum of American History, Vol. II, August 24, 1927, p. 4.

85. Hofer indicated this meeting took place March 28; see Hofer, "Quiet Contributor," p. 62. This is in error. The meeting took place March 1; see Farnsworth, Daily Notes, National Museum of American History, Vol. II, March 1, 1928, pp. 72–73. Little is known of Leonard F. Fuller and James A. Cranston. Abramson indicates the meeting of the two with Farnsworth was brought about as a result of communication

between Roy Bishop and C. E. Tullar of the General Electric patent department. Bishop was trying to sell GE on the Farnsworth television system. Fuller and Cranston were there to inspect the system. As a result of the meeting, GE indicated that they would be taking Farnsworth on staff as an engineer, realizing that "whatever he invents while in our employ comes to us under the regular engineering contract"; see Abramson, *History of Television,* pp. 115–16 and footnote 22. Douglas notes that Fuller worked for the Collin B. Kennedy Company circa 1922 and was vice president, chief engineer at the R. E. Thompson Manufacturing Company; see Alan Douglas, *Radio Manufacturers of the 1920s,* 3 vols. (Vestal, N.Y.: Vestal Press, 1991; reprint, Chandler, Ariz.: Sonoran Publishing, 1995), vol. 2, pp. 90–91; vol. 3, p. 175.

86. Farnsworth, Daily Logs, National Museum of American History, Vol. II, March 1, 1928, p. 73.

87. "Television of New Kind in S.F. Test," unidentified newspaper clipping, Godfrey Papers, Box 12, File 4.

88. Farnsworth, Daily Logs, National Museum of American History, Vol. II, January 10, 1928, p. 53; also pp. 59, 64, and 69.

89. Barnouw, *Tube of Plenty,* p. 78. See also "The History of Farnsworth," ITT Library Papers, p. 14. See also Tobe Rutherford interview with Elma G. Farnsworth, circa 1974, Notes in Godfrey Papers.

90. Farnsworth, National Museum of American History, Daily Logs, Vol. II, pp. 54, 115, and 122.

91. Farnsworth, Daily Notes, National Museum of American History, December 31, 1928. See Farnsworth, *Distant Vision,* p. 112, for a description of the fire. It is interesting to note that although the fire broke out October 28, it is not reported in the journal until December 31.

92. "The History of Farnsworth," ITT Library Papers, p. 14.

93. "S.F. Man's Invention to Revolutionize Television," San Francisco *Chronicle,* 3 September 1928, Section 2, p. 11.

94. "True Electrical Scanning Radio Television Step," *Christian Science Monitor,* 27 September 1928, newspaper clipping, Godfrey Papers, Box 12, File 4.

95. Farnsworth, Daily Notes, National Museum of American History, Vol. II, October 1, 1928, p. 125. Philo's journals carry significant detail regarding his work. It helps to be an engineer to understand the experiments, but there are bits of business and history information scattered within the entries.

96. This attitude is in complete contrast to RCA and its chief David Sarnoff. RCA had a constant public relations campaign under way, as well as an established business operation based on radio broadcasting, station and network ownership, and manufacturing. Sarnoff was a businessman first, but had a constant interest in the lab.

97. Barnouw, *Tube of Plenty,* pp. 48–49; Sterling and Kittross, *Stay Tuned,* pp. 99–100; Abramson, *History of Television,* pp. 64–65; and David E. Fisher and Marshall Jon Fisher, *Tube: The Invention of Television* (Washington, D.C.: Counterpoint, 1996), pp. 89–90. The Jenkins program schedule was silent pictures broadcast Monday, Wednesday, and Friday at 8:00 p.m. Horace Newcomb (ed.), *Encyclopedia of Television* (Chicago: Fitzroy Dearborn Publishers, 1997), pp. 857–58.

98. McCargar had some conflict with the Crocker Bank authorities and resigned in May 1928. His banking reputation remained intact. He was the bank's vice president

for twenty-three years; see "J. B. McCargar Resigns from Crocker Bank," San Francisco *Chronicle,* 16 May 1928; "J. B. McCargar Quits Post in Crocker Bank," San Francisco *Examiner,* 18 May 1928; also "McCargar Resigns from Crocker First National," *Financial Trade,* 2 May 1928, Wells Fargo Bank historical services, scrapbook. For a description of McCargar's financial activities following his resignation, see "Last Rights for Jesse B. McCargar," San Francisco *Chronicle,* 8 April 1954, sec. C–1, p. 25.

99. Letter from George Everson to Roy Bishop, May 28, 1929, Farnsworth Papers, Box 1, File 3. This constituted the first formal incorporation and fund-raising effort beyond Everson and the Crocker Bank principals.

100. See partnership agreements and the needs for funding described in correspondence from Lyon and Lyon to Roy Bishop, September 14, 1926; Assignment and Agreement, March 1929; and a letter from Roy Bishop to George Everson, May 29, 1929, Farnsworth–Everson Papers, Box 1, File 3.

101. "Articles of Incorporation of Television Laboratories, Inc.," California State Archives, Secretary of State, Department of State Corporation Division, Sacramento, California, no. 133225, March 23, 1929.

102. Ibid., p. 1.

103. Ibid., pp. 1–2.

104. Ibid., pp. 2–4.

105. The first board of directors included Herman Phleger and Gregory A. Harrison from San Francisco, James J. Fitzgerald and K. L. Ferguson from Berkeley, and Robert G. Hooker Jr. from San Mateo; see "Articles of Incorporation," California State Archives, p. 8.

106. Everson, *Story of Television,* p. 180.

107. Farnsworth Television Journal, Weekly Record, weeks ending July 6 and July 13, 1929, handwritten bound journal, Vol. III, Farnsworth–Everson Papers, pp. 30–32.

108. The 1929 journal is peppered with such comments. See Farnsworth Television Journal, Weekly Record, Farnsworth–Everson Papers.

109. Farnsworth Television Journal, Weekly Record, March 23 and 30 and April 1–27, 1929, Farnsworth–Everson Papers.

110. The Farnsworths' first son was born September 23, 1929. He was named Philo Taylor Farnsworth III. See genealogical information in Chapter 1.

111. Player Papers, p. 27.

112. Letter from George Everson to James A. Lowsley, May 29, 1929, Godfrey Papers. The second page of this letter is missing, but the authorship is obviously Everson's (compared typewriter to other Everson correspondence). Lowsley held 100 shares in the Farnsworth corporation. See Television Laboratories Shares of stock sold by George Everson, January 29, 1931.

113. Stenographic notebook. Re: Recommendations of BCG [B. Clifford Gardner] for Fellow IRE (IEEE), Godfrey Papers, Box 9, File 8.

114. RCA's David Sarnoff was enthusiastic about Zworykin's ideas and estimate of $100,000 to develop a working television system. In 1929 RCA organized its own television research laboratory in Camden, New Jersey, at a plant RCA had just purchased from the Victor Talking Machine Company. Here Zworykin received the support he needed and the Zworykin system developed rapidly. See Andrew F. Inglis, *Behind the Tube: A History of Broadcasting Technology and Business* (Boston: Focal Press, 1990), pp.

169–72; also Abramson, *Zworykin,* pp. 86–87, and *History of Television,* pp. 141–48. This was an important move for Zworykin's work. He was happy to get away from Westinghouse. At the new RCA laboratory in Camden, Zworykin was in charge, and his work progressed rapidly. See also Vladimir K. Zworykin, "The Early Days: Some Recollections," reprinted in *American Broadcasting,* edited by Lawrence W. Lichty and Malachi C. Topping (New York: Hastings House, 1975) pp. 53–56. Original article was in *Television Quarterly* 1:4 (November 1962): 69–72.

115. Orrin E. Dunlap, Jr., *The Future of Television* (New York: Harper & Brothers, 1942; revised ed., 1947), p. 153. Farnsworth rejected the principles of mechanical television—he never experimented with it. His work was with electrical theory.

116. The New York City *Mirror,* 13 January 1930, shows Farnsworth with Albert Mann, a consulting engineer and investor, examining a transmitter. Journal History, CR100/137, reel no. 164, January 13, 1930, p. 3.

117. Farnsworth, *Distant Vision,* p. 110.

118. Abramson, *Zworykin,* p. 246, note 68. See also Barnouw, *Tube of Plenty,* pp. 67–73.

119. Abramson, *Zworykin,* pp. 86, 246, and his footnote. Zworykin moved from Westinghouse Electric to RCA in 1929, not so much because of the Depression, but due to the opportunity RCA presented. Zworykin would have his own lab and be free to work totally on electric television.

120. Barnouw, *Tube of Plenty,* p. 72.

121. See Abramson, *History of Television,* pp. 75, 97, and 291. See also "Listing of U.S. Patents," Farnsworth Papers, Box 6, File 2.

122. U.S. patent no. 1,758,359, Electric Oscillator System, granted May 13, 1930; patents no. 1,773,980 and no. 1,773,981, Television System and Television Receiving System, granted August 28, 1930; and patent no. 1,806,935, Light Valve, granted May 26, 1931. See digest of Farnsworth Patents, Farnsworth–Allen County Papers.

123. "Present Status of Television," 1929, Godfrey Papers, Box 8, File 3, p. 5. Paper author not listed; however, it is likely Farnsworth and Lubcke.

124. "Present Status of Television," pp. 5–6.

125. Letter from Dorothy Varian to Cliff Gardner, undated. Russell Varian letter excerpt, June 14, 1930, Godfrey Papers, Box 8, File 3, cited in p. 4. This letter copies excerpts from "Russell's letters while he was working with Farnsworth." Apparently Cliff Gardner and the Farnsworths were gathering information from the Varian Papers at the electronics museum, Los Altos Hills, California, June 14, 1977. The excerpts of the historical letters were dated and cited with the page reference; hereafter cited as Varian Correspondence.

126. See "Appendix: Application of Our Developments to Radio and Telephotography," Godfrey Papers, Box 8, File 3.

127. "S.F. Television Broadcasting Proposed," San Francisco *Call Bulletin,* unidentified clipping, 27 July 1931, San Francisco Archives, San Francisco Public Library, San Francisco History Room, Vertical Files–Farnsworth; hereafter referred to as San Francisco Public Library Vertical Files.

128. Farnsworth made his first appearance before the Federal Radio Commission (FRC) in Washington, D.C., on December 4, 1930. He was testifying as a television expert on the subject of bandwidth. At a conference meeting called by the FRC,

Farnsworth presented a paper and declared television was "immediately practical due to a revolutionary new tube." Farnsworth reported he had obtained a 300-line picture on a channel only six kilocycles wide." This was an important public appearance for Farnsworth, again generating publicity; special from *Monitor* bureau. "New Tube Makes Television Practical, Californian Tells Radio Commission," December 5, 1930, unmarked newspaper clipping from the Godfrey Papers, Box 12, File 5. Interestingly, in this same newspaper article, RCA was working to persuade the FRC to reject a CBS application for an experimental station claiming that the station would be carrying out duplicate experiments. This is another good example of the RCA competitive tactics. The license was granted but only after significant delay. See also "A Radio Idea from the West," *New York Times,* X (14 December 1930), p. 6: 14. Abramson indicates that this appearance created later problems for Farnsworth when he disclosed plans regarding bandwidth problems that later did not work. See Everson, *The Story of Television,* p. 125; also Abramson, "Pioneers of Television," p. 777. At this writing Farnsworth's FRC paper could not be located.

129. Varian Correspondence, July 9, 1930, cited in p. 4. Varian here indicates the screen was 12" x 14". Reports differ as to screen sizes, ranging from 2" x 3" to 12" x 14"; also "S.F. Television Broadcasting Proposed."

130. Robert H. Stern, "Television in the Thirties," *American Journal of Economics and Sociology* 23 (1964): 285–301.

131. Letter from Elma G. Farnsworth to George Everson, January 4, 1932, Farnsworth–Everson Papers, Box 1, File 2.

132. Everson, unpublished autobiography, p. 39.

133. Harry R. Lubcke, oral history interview with Steven C. Runyon, September 21, 1974, p. 4.

134. Varian Correspondence, September 30 and November 14, 1930, p. 6.

135. Letter to Jesse B. McCargar from George Everson, May 20, 1931, Farnsworth–Everson Papers, Box 1, File 2.

136. "Shares of Stock," Television Laboratories, Farnsworth–Everson Papers, Box 1, File 3.

137. Philo T. Farnsworth, speech to Indiana College, p. 4.

138. Correspondence from Jesse B. McCargar to George Everson, August 5, 1936, Farnsworth–Everson Papers, Box 1, File 3.

139. Everson, *Story of Television,* p. 125.

140. There is some debate as to the exact date of this visit. In Hofer, "Quiet Contributor," p. 69, the date is April 10. However, according to Abramson, *Zworykin,* p. 247, note 8, the date was April 16. See patent interference no. 64,027, brief in behalf of Philo T. Farnsworth, testimony of D. K. Lippincott (Farnsworth's patent attorney), p. 270.

141. Abramson, *Zworykin,* pp. 91 and 248, note 11. This reference cites Alexanderson as the recipient of this letter. Abramson corrects his error in correspondence from Albert Abramson to Donald G. Godfrey, July 17, 1998.

142. Everson, *Story of Television,* p. 125.

143. Farnsworth, *Distant Vision,* p. 130. A little radio history here may provide a more appropriate business view of these visits and the charges of deceit. It is unlikely that Everson and Farnsworth understood the detailed relationships created by the radio groups of the 1920s. In an effort to protect itself against a British monopoly in radio, the

American government supported the sale of Marconi's American interests to General Electric, which organized the Radio Corporation of America to manage those interests on October 17, 1919. In other words, what happened was that a British monopoly was exchanged, with governmental approval, for an American monopoly. Shortly thereafter, RCA formed alliances with Western Electric and its parent corporation AT&T; see Erik Barnouw, *A Tower of Babel: A History of Broadcasting in the United States to 1933* (New York: Oxford University Press, 1966), pp. 59–61. These relationships were rocky at best, but continued for some time; and the governmental attitude toward monopoly also changed. It was 1931 when GE and RCA were divorced; see Barnouw, *Tower of Babel,* pp. 252–53. In what RCA called their unification program, RCA purchased all of the engineering and manufacturing facilities of both GE and Westinghouse "used in the production of radio receiving sets, tubes, etc." It also centralized these efforts at the RCA plant in Camden, New Jersey; see "Unification Plan Is Announced by David Sarnoff," *The Wireless Age* XI (May 1930): 3–4, in Sarnoff Corporation Library. Zworykin was in transition between the two when he reported to Everson that he was from "Westinghouse *and* RCA"; see also Emil E. Bucher, "Radio and David Sarnoff," "Television and David Sarnoff," "Black and White Television," unpublished manuscript, Sarnoff Corporation Library, Princeton, N.J., n.d., part IV, p. 936; see also Sterling and Kittross, pp. 52–58, 66–68, 146–50.

144. See B. C. Gardner, April 16, 1930, Daily Notes: Television Laboratories, Vol. III, April to June 1930, Farnsworth Papers, Box 53, Book 1, p. 212. H. R. Lubcke, April 9–18, Daily Notes: Television Laboratories, Vol. III, April to June 1930, Farnsworth Papers, Box 53, Book 1, p. 92. Philo T. Farnsworth, April 10–18, Daily Notes: Television Laboratories, Vol. III, April to June 1930, pp. 39–41. DEH [Doris E. Haggerty], April 16, 1930, Daily Notes: Television Laboratories, Vol. III, April to June 1930. Farnsworth Papers, Box 53, Book 1. In the Daily Notes, each engineer filed a separate report, and they are all filed chronologically. Regarding visits and demonstrations, such are recorded only briefly throughout the notes. Such mentions as "gave another demonstration" today are common and that is most often the only explanation. The focus of these logs was almost entirely to record engineering tests and note progress.

145. Dorothy Varian, *The Inventor and the Pilot: Russell and Sigurd Varian* (Palo Alto, California: Pacific Books, 1983), pp. 136–38.

146. "Zworykin Visited," Elma G. Farnsworth handwritten notes, Godfrey Papers, Box 8, File 3, p. 3.

147. Ropp, "Real Father," p. 6.

148. Suzanne Bigelow, "Philo Farnsworth: Television's Frustrated Genius," *This People* 10:1 (Spring 1989): 27. Dennis May ("Philo T. Farnsworth") implies Zworykin "had been working . . . on the old mechanical television system." This is incorrect. Farnsworth and Zworykin were *both* promoters of electronic television—who was leading in this experimentation is the key question.

149. Everson, *Story of Television,* pp. 126–27. See also Farnsworth, *Distant Vision,* p. 130.

150. Letter to Philo T. Farnsworth from Albert B. Mann, April 17, 1930, Farnsworth Papers, Box 20, File 2. See Hofer, "Quiet Contributor," p. 70.

151. Everson, *Story of Television,* p. 128.

152. Abramson, *Zworykin,* p. 91.

153. "G. Harold Porter Is Elected Vice President of the Radio Corporation," *RCA News* XI (July 1930): 5, Sarnoff Corporation Library. Porter was head of RCA Pacific Coast activities. The fact that Porter worked out of San Francisco gives us some comprehension of RCA's extensive operations.

154. Farnsworth Television Journal, week ending May 10, 1930. The Daily Notes of Doris Haggerty indicate the visit of Crocker and Bishop was May 9. See DEH, May 9, 1930, Daily Notes; Television Laboratories Inc., Vol. III, April to June 1930, Farnsworth Papers, Box 53, Book 1, p. 223.

155. Albert Murray was head of the Advanced Development Division and Thomas Goldsborough was the RCA patent attorney; see Abramson, "Pioneer of Television," p. 776.

156. Arthur H. Halloran, "Scanning Without a Disc," *Radio News* 12 (May 1931): 998–99, 1,015.

157. Letter to Philo T. Farnsworth from George Everson, May 15, 1931, Farnsworth–Everson Papers, Box 1, File 3.

158. Ibid.

159. Ibid.

160. David Sarnoff became president of RCA on January 3, 1930. It appears Sarnoff's visit occurred during an engagement to speak in Hollywood; see Bucher, part XII, p. 54. While there is no specific mention of this visit in Sarnoff's records from 1931 to 1932, Sarnoff did report to the RCA stockholders, May 5, 1931, that "you may be sure . . . your corporation is in an exceptionally strong position in respect to this new art because of its resources and facilities and engineering development, and also because of its patent rights"; see "Proceedings of Annual Meeting of Stockholders," Radio Corporation of America, May 5, 1931, p. 7, Sarnoff Corporation Library, Addresses, Press Releases, Articles: David Sarnoff, Vol XIV, pp. 17–31.

161. Abramson says this visit was to Philadelphia where the two were negotiating with Philco; see Abramson, *Zworykin,* p. 91. Pem Farnsworth indicates they were in Washington testifying before Senator O'Mahoney's committee on radio monopoly. McCargar, although no longer with the Crocker Bank, remained an influential stockholder and would shortly become president of Farnsworth's enterprise.

162. Letter to Philo T. Farnsworth from George Everson, May 20, 1931, Farnsworth–Everson Papers, Box 1, File 3. This letter does say ITT, not AT&T. At the time AT&T was interested in TV and ITT had not shown public interest. However, as we shall see, Everson did have a contact with ITT through Hugh Knowlton; see also Farnsworth, *Distant Vision,* p. 131. Note again the different picture size reported.

163. Abramson dismisses this visit a little too casually indicating that "it was brought to RCA's and Sarnoff's attention that Farnsworth's television laboratories were again for sale." See Abramson, *Zworykin,* p. 104. This was an unusual visit for the president of RCA, as Abramson admits, motivated by his concern that Farnsworth might become a competitor.

164. Abramson, *Zworykin,* p. 105. See Farnsworth, *Distant Vision,* p. 131.

165. Letter from George Everson to Philo Farnsworth, May 15, 1931, Farnsworth–Everson Papers, Box 1, File 3.

CHAPTER 3

1. The challenges faced by Farnsworth in competition with the nation's leading electronic media are descriptively listed in the article by T. R. Carskadon, "Phil the Inventor," p. 28.

2. William E. Denk, "An Elusive Frame of Television History Preserved," *AWA Review* 4 (1989): 99–109.

3. Abramson, *Zworykin,* p. 104.

4. For an explanation of this strategy see John Paul Wolkoniwicz, "The Philco Corporation: Historical Review and Strategic Analysis, 1892–1961," unpublished masters thesis, Massachusetts Institute of Technology, June 1981, pp. 31–32. It is unclear how this Philco reorganization got them out from under the fees due RCA. No additional documentation could be located at this writing. However, the tension between the two companies is without question. See also Ramirez and Prosise, *Philco Radio,* p. 32.

5. Abramson, *Zworykin,* p. 104.

6. Michael Woal and Linda Kowall Woal, "Forgotten Pioneer: Philco's WPTZ," in Michael D. Murray and Donald G. Godfrey (eds.), *Television in America: Local Station History from Across the Nation* (Ames: Iowa State University Press, 1997), pp. 40–41.

7. Securities and Exchange Commission, Registration Statement for the Farnsworth Radio and Television Corporation, January 24, 1939, pp. 21–22. Farnsworth Papers, Box 7, File 5.

8. Users licensed for Farnsworth transmitter tubes paid usage fees. The equipment was not mass assembled at this time, but constructed and licensed for use by specific organizations.

9. McCargar's offices were in San Francisco, and he was still the president of Television Laboratories. When Farnsworth moved, a small contingent of three engineers was left behind, under the direction of Bart Molinary, and charged with maintaining television demonstration capability for purposes of publicity. He also worked on specific elements of the overall research program and maintained constant communication between the West and East Coast.

10. Carle H. Bennette, "Philo T. Farnsworth, Former B.Y.U. Student, Goes East to Build Production Model," Salt Lake City *Tribune,* 12 July 1931; Journal History, CR 100/137, reel no. 166, July 12, 1931, p. 6. Note again a different picture size reported. Also, it may seem odd to conduct one final experiment and then move everything to Philadelphia. However, everything was not dismantled. A small lab remained and there was constant communication between the two labs (Philadelphia and San Francisco) as work progressed.

11. Kenneth Gardner Farnsworth was born January 15, 1931. Kenneth was the couple's second son born just fifteen months after his older brother "Philo Jr."

12. See Everson, unpublished autobiography, p. 39.

13. F. M. Randlett, "Report on the Farnsworth Television System," Robert W. Hunt Company engineers, San Francisco, March 16, 1931. Farnsworth Papers, Box 1, File 3. At this writing no information is available on these people and the corporations they represented.

14. Farnsworth, *Distant Vision,* p. 140.

15. Paul Schatzkin, "Farnsworth: TV's Inventor: RCA Battles, Sarnoff, the Philco Years, and the Philadelphia Demonstration," part 2, *Televisions* 5:2 (1977): 19. This is the second in a four-part chronicle written by Schatzkin.

16. See Appendix A.

17. U.S. patent no. 2,168,768, Television Method, filed April 14, 1932 [granted August 8, 1939]; and patent no. 2,098,000, Luminescent Screen, filed May 31, 1932 [granted November 2, 1937]. See the list of patents in Farnsworth–Allen County Papers; also Appendix A.

18. Letter to George Everson from Antoini De Vally, June 23, 1932, Farnsworth Papers, Box 1 File 3. De Vally was a management consultant hired to evaluate Television Laboratories. His response to the evaluation, conducted while Farnsworth was at Philco, was that the corporation be restructured. Although Everson did not follow the exact recommendations in terms of Hollywood distribution, the reorganization later created Farnsworth Television Incorporated.

19. "Graphic Analysis of the Broadcast Structure." Chart accompanying a letter from Antoine De Vally to George Everson, July 9, 1932, Godfrey Papers, Box 16, File 3.

20. "Sarnoff Sees Television in Home by End of 1932," unidentified newspaper clipping, 14 June 1931; in Sarnoff Corporation Library, *David Sarnoff: A Newspaper History, 1917–1966.* Much of this system was already in place for RCA radio, and it would be a matter of transposing the new radio operation for television. The key was the development of an experimental station for distribution of television programming.

21. Letter from Philo T. Farnsworth to George Everson, May 26, 1932, in Daily Notes, Television Lab. Ltd., Farnsworth Papers, Box 55, Book 2, Vol. XI, pp. 134–36.

22. Ibid., pp. 134–35.

23. Ibid.

24. In fairness the early forecasts of both RCA and Farnsworth varied greatly. For RCA forecasts, see David Sarnoff's remarks before the "Proceedings of the Annual Meeting of Stockholders, Radio Corporation of America," May 5, 1931, and May 3, 1932, pp. 6–7, 71. Also, "Television for Public Far Off Says Sarnoff," Philadelphia *Eagle,* June 15, 1938. Unidentified newspaper clipping, in *David Sarnoff: A Newspaper History: 1917–1966.* Sarnoff Corporation Library.

25. Letter from Philo T. Farnsworth to George Everson, May 26, 1932, in Daily Notes, Television Lab. Ltd., Farnsworth Papers, Box 55, Book 2, Vol. XI, pp. 134–36.

26. "Application for Radio [sic] Construction Permit: Paragraph Setting Forth Qualifications of Philadelphia Storage Battery Company," Daily Notes: Television Lab. Ltd., Vol. VI, Farnsworth Papers, Box 54, Book 1. See also "Philadelphia to Look-in," *New York Times,* 20 December 1931, IX, 10:8.

27. "Outline of Experimental Work Accomplished at Station W3XE Since It Was First Licensed," a typewritten report from Philco to the Federal Radio Commission, circa 1933, National Archives, General Correspondence 1927–1946, Box 415, File 89-6, Philco Radio and Television Corporation; hereafter referred to as National Archives. See also Ramirez and Prosise, *Philco Radio,* p. 32. Woal and Woal, "Forgotten Pioneer: Philco's WPTZ," p. 41. According to Woal, this was the second station licensed in the United States. It was more likely the fourth: The second station was RCA, whose first station W2XBS began broadcasting experimentally on July 30, 1930, from the Empire

State Building, the third station was CBS's experimental station W2XAB that had opened in New York on July 21, 1931.

28. William N. Parker, "Early Philadelphia Television," unpublished paper, May 13, 1986, p. 7, W3XE file, Theater Collection, Free Library of Philadelphia, Philadelphia, Pennsylvania. Parker goes on to describe the studio operation as including a camera and a few lights (p. 1), and the problem of sound from the "intolerable rumble" from the manufacturing being overcome with the creation of a floating studio, by "Farnsworth's Chief Engineer, A. H. Brolly" (p. 7).

29. Schatzkin, part 2, p. 19.

30. See an analysis of the differing Mary Pickford films sampled in Philo T. Farnsworth, Daily Notes, Television Lab. Ltd., Vol. VI, pp. 257–60, Farnsworth Papers, Box 54, Book 1. "Steamboat Willie" is the classic 1928 Walt Disney animated cartoon, in which the character Mickey Mouse first appeared.

31. Parker, "Early Philadelphia Television," p. 6.

32. Ibid. Parker, in his history, notes that one of the later receivers was taken to the home of Mr. Grimditch for a W3XE shakedown. This would be the same Grimditch who was seeking to enforce dress codes for the Farnsworth engineers.

33. These reported hours have to be for the latter years of W3XE's operation, likely the mid-1940s. There were no hours reported for 1932, and the hours for 1933 through 1936 were as follows: 1933, 150; 1934, 70; 1935, 159; and 1936, 463. See "Outline of the Experimental Work Accomplished at Station W3XE Since It Was Licensed," National Archives, General Correspondence 1927–1946, Box 425, File 89-6, Philco Radio and Television Corporation. Note the significant dip in W3XE's programming hours after Farnsworth left in 1933. It was 1935 before Philco was back to the same hours.

34. Letter from Philo T. Farnsworth to his mother Serena Farnsworth, December 13, 1933. Contained in the Player Papers, p. 28.

35. See National Archives, General Correspondence 1927–1946, Box 415, File 89-6, Philco Radio and Television Corporation.

36. See Farnsworth, *Distant Vision,* p. 145 for some of the more personal and humorous complaints.

37. See Ramirez and Prosise, *Philco Radio,* p. 12. Ramirez and Prosise indicate that many competitors of the time felt RCA's A.C. tubes would simply outsell and consequently make it impossible for Philco to enter the radio market. However, Philco was aggressive in sales, manufacturing, advertising, and research.

38. Wolkonowicz, pp. 32–33.

39. Farnsworth, *Distant Vision,* p. 145. There was no further documentation of this threat available at this writing.

40. When RCA threatened to cancel the Philco license, Philco filed suit. In the meantime, however, it continued to pay royalties to RCA. By the time the suit was settled in 1939, Philco won, but it had to pay $750,000 in excess royalties; see Wolkonowicz, p. 32. Also William R. Maclaurin and R. Joyce Harmon, *Invention & Innovation in the Radio Industry* (New York: Macmillan, 1949; reprint, New York: Arno Press, 1971), p. 52.

41. Varian, *The Inventor and the Pilot,* pp. 144–49.

42. Farnsworth, *Distant Vision,* p. 143.

43. The grief this caused within this family is unmistakable, parallel in anguish to the death of Philo's father. Farnsworth promised his young son that he would find a cure for streptococcal infection and even worked with the doctors at Pennsylvania Medical College for experimental serums that were somewhat successful, until penicillin and streptomycin were later developed; see Farnsworth, *Distant Vision,* p. 144.

44. Letter from Elma G. Farnsworth to Philo T. Farnsworth, March 6, 1932, Godfrey Papers, Box 8, File 4.

45. At this point there is a reported gap in the log books. The gap in Farnsworth's Daily Notes is from February 22, 1932 to March 22, 1932. It does not really appear significant, since the notes and log-ins are full of such omissions. However, there is no mention here of his son's death or the conflicts that followed, only detailed technical notes. See Philo T. Farnsworth Daily Notes, Television Lab. Ltd., Vol. VI, August 31, 1931 through June 13, 1933. Note specifically pp. 27–29, Farnsworth Papers, Box 54, Book 1.

46. Schatzkin, part 2, p. 19.

47. Varian Correspondence, March 23, 1933, and June 27, 1933, p. 10.

48. Ibid., July 16, 1933, p. 10.

49. Ibid.

50. Abramson leaves the impression that the Farnsworth contract was terminated; see Abramson, "Pioneers of Television," p. 778. It seems just as likely, in view of all we know, that the separation was by mutual agreement. The Philco documents for the period ending September 30, 1933, indicate he left Philco; see National Archives, General Correspondence 1927–1946, Box 415, File 89-6, Philco Radio and Television Corporation.

51. Robert H. Stern, "Television in the Thirties," *American Journal of Economics and Sociology* 23 (1964): 285–301.

52. Hofer, "Quiet Contributor," p. 72.

53. There is no mention of the split with Philco in the Daily Notes, Television Lab. Ltd., Vol. XII, July 11, 1933 to December 31, 1935, Farnsworth Papers, Box 55, Book 3.

54. "Certificate of Authority," Pennsylvania State Archives, Department of State, Corporation Bureau, Harrisburg, Pennsylvania; hereafter referred to as Pennsylvania State Archives.

55. Ibid., paragraphs 2 and 5–8.

56. This is the name usually associated with Farnsworth's work immediately after his separation from Philco. In actuality the name remained "Television Laboratories Limited, Inc." in both California and Pennsylvania until 1935. On May 3, 1935, application was made with the State of Pennsylvania for the name change to "Farnsworth Television Incorporated." The state-required Amended Certificate of Authority to operate in Pennsylvania was granted July 1, 1935.

57. Oral history interview with Seymour "Skee" Turner conducted by Elma G. Farnsworth, fall 1977. See notes in Godfrey Papers.

58. Allen B. DuMont Papers at the Library of Congress and National Museum of American History, Archives Divisions, Box 126, Biographical File. As a side note here, eventually Tobe Rutherford, one of Farnsworth's original engineers, took a job with DuMont.

59. Schatzkin, part 2, p. 19. Abramson reports that one year later in 1934, Zworykin was working with 343 lines per frame. See Abramson, *Zworykin,* p. 136.

60. See Appendix A.

61. "Radio Picture Test Successful," *San Francisco Chronicle,* circa 1933. Newspaper clipping from Farnsworth-Everson Papers, Box 6, File 6.

62. John V. L. Hogan (1890–1960) is mentioned only briefly in the literature of television. He too was an inventor. Gleason L. Archer refers to Hogan's 1924 testimony on behalf of the Radio Group and notes that Hogan worked for de Forest in 1906 and 1907. See Gleason L. Archer, *Big Business and Radio* (New York: Arno Press, 1971), p. 158. Sterling and Kittross mention Hogan in reference to the invention of tuning and volume knobs for radio (Sterling and Kittross, *Stay Tuned,* p. 81). Hilliard and Keith note that Hogan experimented with facsimile transmission, calling it a "radio pen producer" (Robert L. Hilliard and Michael C. Keith, *The Broadcast Century: A Biography of American Broadcasting,* 2nd ed. [Boston: Focal Press, 1997], p. 74). He is identified by Abramson in connection with his participation in the *Electronics* survey and his input during the Radio Manufacturers Association's deliberations regarding television standards. See Abramson, *History of Television,* pp. 212, 262. Hogan is not mentioned by the other mainstream historians such as Barnouw, Dunlap, or Inglis.

63. "Television: A Survey of Present Day Systems," *Electronics* 7 (October 1934): 300–305.

64. Seymour Turner, oral history interview. See also "The Farnsworth Claim," *Tele Vision* 4:37 (March 1931): 40. This letter to the editor is reflective of the pressures to produce demonstrations. "Until Mr. Farnsworth gives a demonstration, his claims cannot be taken seriously."

65. "Tennis Stars Act in New Television," *New York Times,* 25 August 1934, 14: 4. See also Everson, *Story of Television,* pp. 142–45. Farnsworth's Daily Notes skip from August 7, 1934 to September 11, 1934. See Daily Notes, Television Lab. Ltd., Vol. XII, pp. 117–18. Farnsworth Papers, Box 55, Book 3.

66. "Television on 4-Foot Screen," *Philadelphia Record,* 25 August 1934, p. 3. "Scientists See Exhibition," *Philadelphia Inquirer,* 25 August 1924, pp. 3, 10. See *Philadelphia Record,* Photographic Archives, Pennsylvania Historical Society, Philadelphia Pennsylvania. The "4-foot" has reference to square feet as the screen was mounted in a six-foot cabinet so the audience could see, but was only a one-foot-square screen. "Home Television Due in 10 Years, Utahan Says: House Sets to Compete with Radio Predicted by Philo T. Farnsworth, Inventor," Salt Lake *Telegram,* 25 August 1934. In Journal History, CR100/137, reel no. 172, August 25, 1934, p. 16.

67. "Televising Football Maneuvers at Franklin Institute," photo caption, *Philadelphia Record,* Morgue Collection [Accession #V7:2272]. See the Pennsylvania Historical Society.

68. "Moon Makes Television Debut in Pose for Radio Snapshot," *Christian Science Monitor,* 25 August 1934. Newspaper clipping, Godfrey Papers, Box 12, File 4.

69. Schatzkin, part 2, p. 20. This idea was apparently so effective it was used by RCA again at their 1939 World's Fair exhibition.

70. "Tennis Stars Act in New Television," *New York Times,* 25 August 1934, p. 14: 4.

71. "Utah Lauded for Progress of Television," Salt Lake *Tribune,* 3 September 1934. Journal History, CR 100/137, reel no. 173, September 3, 1934, pp. 4–5.

72. Ibid.

73. Philo T. Farnsworth, Indiana College Speech.

74. C. William Duncan, "Television Is Near as Adjunct to Radio, Young Inventor Says," *Philadelphia – Evening Public Ledger,* 30 August 1934, p. 10. See the Philadelphia Free Library files.

75. Ibid., p. 10.

76. Philo Taylor Farnsworth, "Television by Electron Image Scanning," *Journal of the Franklin Institute* 218 (4) (October 1934): 411–44.

77. Duncan, "Television Is Near," p. 10.

78. "Farnsworth Presents a 'Cold' Radio Tube," *New York Times,* 23 September 1934, IX, 11: 3. See also "Invention Stirs Television Hopes," *Philadelphia – Evening Public Ledger,* 14 September 1934, p. 16. The *Ledger* indicates signals were transmitted between the laboratories in San Francisco, New York, Honolulu, and Manila, differing slightly from the *Times* report a week later. Neither source explains the workings of these tests and it is somewhat confusing; nevertheless, it was also an experiment that would not be ignored.

79. Ibid.

80. There is some question as to the exact date of this invitation and how it was actually extended. Abramson says the invitation came in June 1934, Turner says it was during the demonstrations at the Franklin Institute. Turner claims the invitation came via a call from a friend to him during the institute demonstrations, and Everson claims that Farnsworth was cabled in Philadelphia from a young man who had worked for Farnsworth and was at the time working for Baird. This could be the friend Turner mentioned as they would have worked together; see Abramson, *Zworykin,* p. 135; see also Seymour Turner, oral history interview; and Everson, *Story of Television,* p. 147.

81. For the best explanation of the history of mechanical television see, Abramson, *History of Television,* pp. 73–107. This is Chapter 6 of Abramson's book titled "The Mechanical Era Begins: 1924–1927."

82. Abramson, *History of Television,* pp. 207–08.

83. Unfortunately Farnsworth's Daily Notes skip from September 19, 1934 to December 1, 1934. The omission is understandable in that these records are technical in nature and detail little of such demonstrations. See Daily Notes, Television Lab. Ltd., Vol. XII, pp. 120–21, Farnsworth Papers, Box 55, Book 3.

84. A. H. Brolly, Daily Notes, Television Lab. Ltd., Vol. XV, pp. 328–29, Farnsworth Papers, Box 56, Book 2.

85. See Seymour Turner, oral history interview conducted by Elma G. Farnsworth. See notes in Godfrey Papers. Also Farnsworth, *Distant Vision,* p. 166.

86. Farnsworth, *Distant Vision,* p. 167. Mrs. Farnsworth was not present at these first demonstrations, but Mr. Farnsworth was constantly reporting to her for the lab books and other records she kept.

87. Seymour Turner, oral history interview conducted by Elma G. Farnsworth. See notes in Godfrey Papers.

88. A. H. Brolly, Daily Notes, Television Lab. Ltd., Vol. XV, p. 352, Farnsworth Papers, Box 56, Book 2. For other descriptions of the demonstration see Everson, *Story of Television,* pp. 146–51; "Philo T. Farnsworth, Inventor of Electronic Television," ITT Library Papers; and Farnsworth, *Distant Vision,* pp. 166–68. Paul Schatzkin, in

"Farnsworth: TV's Inventor: To England for Cash, On the Air in Philadelphia, Last Days of the Lab Gang," part 3, *Televisions* 5:3 (1977): 16, suggests this was the 300 lines per frame experiment.

89. A. H. Brolly, Daily Notes, Television Lab. Ltd., Vol. XV, p. 352, Farnsworth Papers, Box 56, Book 2.

90. Abramson, *Zworykin,* p. 136.

91. The British Television Advisory Committee was headed by Lord Selsdon (Sir William Mitchell-Thomson) with Sir Harry Greer representing Baird interests on the committee. While Farnsworth was conducting his experiments in Britain, Lord Selsdon sent a subcommittee to visit the laboratories of RCA, Philco, and Farnsworth. Although Abramson indicates that their report made no mention of Farnsworth (Abramson, *History of Television,* p. 212), this would have been understandable because another part of that committee was witnessing the Farnsworth demonstrations in London. The most significant demonstration of what Farnsworth had to offer was in London. As a result of the committee's study, the British Television Advisory Committee recommended that Baird and Marconi-EMI be given the opportunity to supply British system electronic components. Baird was included because of the arrangements it made with Farnsworth.

92. See A. H. Brolly, Daily Notes, Television Lab. Ltd., Vol. XV, pp. 328–29. Farnsworth Papers, Box 56, Book 2. See also "British Get Television: Empire Rights to American Invention Are Obtained," *New York Times* 21 (20 June 1935), p. 1.

93. "P. T. Farnsworth in Deal with Foreign Stations," San Francisco *Call Bulletin,* 20 June 1935, San Francisco Public Library Vertical Files.

94. Report "To the Stockholders of Farnsworth Television Incorporated," December 30, 1935, p. 2, Godfrey Papers, Box 9, File 1.

95. A. H. Brolly, Daily Notes, Television Lab. Ltd., Vol. XV, pp. 328–29, Farnsworth Papers, Box 56, Book 2. For a sketch of the engineering necessary to make the transition to the Farnsworth system, see pp. 329–53.

96. Records of the State of Pennsylvania at this time show J. B. McCargar, president; Philo T. Farnsworth, vice president; and George Everson, secretary. See Pennsylvania State Archives.

97. Schatzkin, part 3, p. 16.

CHAPTER 4

1. *Big Dream, Small Screen.* This popular film suggests RCA organized patent lawyers and finances to specifically fight Farnsworth. This is only partially correct and as presented it was somewhat misleading. The lawyers were already on board at RCA. They were not hired solely to fight the *Farnsworth v. Zworykin* interference case. Litigation was a part of the way RCA did business.

2. Barnouw, *Tube of Plenty,* p. 52.

3. Barnouw, *Tower of Babel,* pp. 117 and 161–62. See *Report of the Federal Trade Commission on the Radio Industry: In Response to House Resolution 548,* 67th Congress, 4th session (Washington, D.C.: Government Printing Office, 1924, reprint, New York: Arno Press, 1974).

4. Douglas, *Radio Manufacturers,* vol. 3, pp. 125–32. See also Maclaurin and Harmon, *Invention and Innovation,* Appendices.

5. Douglas, *Radio Manufacturers,* vol. 3, p. 129.

6. Lawrence Lessing, *Man of High Fidelity: Edwin Howard Armstrong* (Philadelphia: Lippincott, 1956), pp. 209–10.

7. Kenneth Bilby, *General: David Sarnoff,* pp. 198–200.

8. See Lessing, *Man of High Fidelity,* pp. 277–99; Barnouw, *Golden Web,* pp. 284–85; Bilby, *General: David Sarnoff,* pp. 199–200.

9. Bilby, *General: David Sarnoff,* p. 200.

10. Barnouw, *Golden Web,* p. 283.

11. Patent interference case no. 54922.

12. Abramson indicates that McCreary was with Associated Electric Laboratories in April 1924. See Abramson, *Zworykin,* p. 82. Hofer indicates that little is known of McCreary or his contributions to television beyond this suit. He does have patents registered to his name from the 1920s through the 1960s. See Hofer, "Quiet Contributor," p. 54.

13. See interference case no. 54,922, November 25, 1927. *Farnsworth v. Reynolds v. Case v. Sabbath v. McCreary v. Zworykin,* p. 1.

14. Patent interference case no. 64027. Final hearing, April 24, 1934. *Farnsworth v. Zworykin,* United States Patent Office, p. 1.

15. Farnsworth testified before the Federal Monopoly Committee that there had been more than twenty patent lawsuits filed against him since 1927. The Federal Monopoly Committee was called in 1938 to investigate the effect of the U.S. Patent and Trademark Office on the economic system of the nation. See "Patent Lawyers Are Assailed at Trust Inquiry," unidentified newspaper clipping, circa 1938, Godfrey Papers, Box 12, File 4.

16. Patent interference case no. 64027, p. 2. See Abramson, *Zworykin,* pp. 118–19. Also Hofer, "Quiet Contributor," p. 74.

17. Everson, *Story of Television,* p. 153.

18. Hofer, "Quiet Contributor," p. 76. Hofer cites the brief for appellant, *Farnsworth v. Zworykin,* pp. 7–65 passim.

19. Donald K. Lippincott, brief on behalf of Philo T. Farnsworth, in *Farnsworth v. Zworykin,* interference case no. 64027, p. 76.

20. Stephen L. Carr, "Remarks at the Acceptance and Dedication of the Statue of Philo T. Farnsworth," in *Acceptance and Dedication,* p. 12. At this writing, these notebooks could no longer be located.

21. Everson, *Story of Television,* p. 153.

22. Hofer, "Quiet Contributor," p. 76. Hofer cites the brief for appellant, *Farnsworth v. Zworykin,* pp. 41–56; and the brief for appellant, *Farnsworth v. Zworykin,* pp. 11–55 passim.

23. Patent interference case no. 64027, p. 2. The 1922 dates are in reference to the drawings Farnsworth made while in high school. The 1926 date is in reference to the first experiments that were documented and used to raise funds from the San Francisco bankers. The 1927 reference is to the Green Street laboratory's experiments.

24. Ibid, pp. 2–4.

25. Ibid., pp. 4, 10.

26. Ibid., p. 11.

27. Abramson, *Zworykin,* p. 119.

28. Interference case no. 64027, p. 33.

29. Abramson, *Zworykin,* p. 119.

30. Abramson indicates that this was Zworykin's camera tube.

31. Abramson, *Zworykin,* p. 120.

32. Patent interference case no. 64027, pp. 45–46.

33. "S.F. Inventor's Claims Win," unidentified newspaper clipping, July 26, 1935, San Francisco Public Library Vertical Files.

34. Patent interference case no. 64027. Appeal no. 15,552 (Washington, D.C.: U.S. Patent Office, Board of Appeals, January 31, 1936).

35. Tom McArthur and Peter Waddell, *The Secret Life of John Logie Baird* (London: Century Hutchinson, 1986), p. 176.

36. See Godfrey Papers for a copy of the agreement. Letters cited in Hofer, "Quiet Contributor," pp. 82–83; E. A. Nicholas to Radio Corporation of America, September 15, 1939, New York, N.Y., Godfrey Papers, Box 19, File 11; E. A. Nicholas to J. T. Buckley, October 13, 1939, Philadelphia, Penn.

37. "Patent Lawyers Are Assailed at Trust Inquiry," Godfrey Papers, Box 12, File 4.

CHAPTER 5

1. "Rules and Regulations—Visual Broadcasting," Federal Radio Commission, Washington, D.C., February 18, 1929. Hyde Papers, Box 13, File 2. See also Federal Communications Commission, "The Evolution of Television, 1927–1943," *Journal of Broadcasting* 4:3 (Summer 1960): 199–207. The journal editor prefaces these excerpts from the FCC Annual Reports by noting the bias they show toward RCA.

2. "Television: A Survey," p. 300.

3. Abramson, *History of Television,* p. 255.

4. Bucher, part XII, "Black and White Television," chapter VIII, p. 112.

5. This "catch-up" theory is clearly illustrated in the development of color television and the battles over color technology between RCA and CBS. See Sterling and Kittross, *Stay Tuned,* pp. 232–34.

6. Charles W. Hart and Jerome O'Neill, "Inventor of TV Worked in Hill Studio," *Chestnut Hill Local,* 27 August 1992, p. 23.

7. See Appendix A.

8. "Says Use of Television Waits on Public Demand," *Public Ledger—Philadelphia,* 15 February 1935, p. 10.

9. "Gain in Television Is Demonstrated," *New York Times,* 31 July 1935, 15: 4.

10. William C. Eddy was one of the engineers who worked on the station. He is doubling here as an arranger of programming. Eddy, prior to his work with Farnsworth, had been a naval officer and had some experience in arranging entertainment functions within the armed forces. He would later work for RCA and be instrumental in establishing WBKB, Chicago. See Jeff Kisseloff, *The Box: An Oral History of Television, 1920–1961* (New York: Penguin Books, 1995), pp. 80–92. William C. Eddy, *Television: The Eyes of Tomorrow* (New York: Prentice-Hall, 1945).

11. "Gain in Television Is Demonstrated," 15: 4. See also "Television: 10 Years to Go, Says RCA; 1, Insists Inventor," *Newsweek,* 10 August 1935, p. 24. See Arch Leonard

Madsen Papers, Manuscripts Division, Special Collections, University of Utah Marriott Library, Salt Lake City, Utah, Box 171, File 5; hereafter referred to as the Madsen Papers.

12. Abramson, *History of Television,* pp. 220–21. For a description of the 343-line experiments, see Frank J. Somers, Daily Notes, Farnsworth Television Inc., XXVII, pp. 39–40, Farnsworth Papers, Box 58, Book 2.

13. "Television: 10 Years to Go," *Newsweek,* 10 August 1935, p. 24, Madsen Papers.

14. Hart and O'Neill, "Inventor of Television," p. 23.

15. Letter "To the Stockholders of Farnsworth Television Incorporated," December 30, 1935, Godfrey Papers, Box 9, File 1, p. 1.

16. Daily Notes, Television Lab. Ltd., Vol. XII, Farnsworth Papers, Box 55, Book 3, pp. 228–29. At this writing there was no information as to the source or disposition of this bid.

17. This is a significant contrast to David Sarnoff at RCA. Sarnoff Library records reflect a constant public relations campaign everywhere Sarnoff appeared, consistently praising the leadership of RCA radio and television.

18. Everson, *Story of Television,* p. 165.

19. Ibid., p. 166.

20. "'Cold' Tube Yields More Radio Power," *New York Times,* 5 March 1936, 2: 1.

21. See Appendix A.

22. Everson, *Story of Television,* p. 166.

23. Ibid., p. 167.

24. "Bars Television Gains," Philadelphia Evening *Public Ledger,* 7 May 1936, p. 6.

25. Securities and Exchange Commission, Registration Statement, Farnsworth Television and Radio, January 24, 1939, Farnsworth Papers, Box 7, File 6, pp. 22–23. A copy of this registration statement and appended items can also be located in the Donald K. Lippincott Papers (Banc MSS 79/39C), Bancroft Library, University of California–Berkeley; hereafter referred to as the Lippincott Papers.

26. Ibid., pp. 23–24. For a draft copy of the supplemental agreement, see Godfrey Papers, Box 9, File 10. At this writing, no documentation could be found as to how this agreement with Germany came about.

27. "Famed Tube Recognized by Germans," San Francisco *Call Bulletin,* 26 April 1935, unidentified clipping, San Francisco Public Library Vertical Files.

28. Abramson, *History of Television,* p. 227.

29. Ibid., p. 230.

30. Schatzkin, part 3, p. 18.

31. Ibid., p. 18.

32. "Television News Shorts," *Radio-Craft* 8 (March 1937): 518. See also McArthur and Waddell, *Secret Life of John Logie Baird,* pp. 179–80; and Abramson, *History of Television,* p. 234.

33. Abramson, *History of Television,* p. 235.

34. Bucher, part XII, chapter VIII, p. 120.

35. Abramson, *History of Television,* pp. 224–25.

36. "Olympic Games to Be Televised," undated clipping, *Wall Street Journal,* 1936, Godfrey Papers, Box 12, File 4.

37. Abramson, *History of Television,* pp. 232–33.

38. The name Goerz appears with several different spellings in writings on Farnsworth—Georz, Goertz, and Goerz. The last is correct.

39. Seymour Turner, oral history interview. Notes on this interview are filed in Godfrey Papers.

40. Farnsworth was careful to hire people who could work together. The list of patents emanating from the laboratory includes many filed by engineers working for the lab. Farnsworth encouraged this type of independence but was also an engineer who was in charge of the lab. See Donald G. Godfrey interview with Robert Hirsch, August 1997; also Schatzkin, part 3, p. 17.

41. Television Laboratories Limited, Inc. was formed December 19, 1933, immediately after Farnsworth left Philco. Its name was changed to Farnsworth Television Incorporated, July 1, 1935. See Pennsylvania State Archives.

42. FCC docket no. 4047, p. 3.

43. Letter from Elma G. Farnsworth to her father, October 12, 1949, Godfrey Papers, Box 8, File 4.

44. Turner oral history interview. Notes on the interview are contained in the Godfrey Papers. A web page, http://comnetinc.com/tvphila.htm, indicates the funding for the station came from Farnsworth's licensing agreement with Baird. This is incorrect. The funds came from the San Francisco Turner family, and operational finances for the station came from the sale of Farnsworth stock.

45. Everson, *Story of Television,* p. 160.

46. Letter from Jesse McCargar to George Everson, November 5, 1936. Farnsworth Papers, Box 25, File 2. See also Godfrey Papers, Box 9, File 10.

47. Farnsworth, *Distant Vision,* p. 184.

48. Everson indicated that in addition to Sleeper an engineer named Molinari was also sent to Philadelphia. See Everson, *Story of Television,* p. 209. However, in checking the Farnsworth log books, there were no listings for any engineer with that name. Engineers reporting in the research journals at the time (between 1934 and 1939) and listed in order of the appearance of their reports were Harry R. Lubcke, Harry L. Lyman, A. H. Brolly, Russell H. Varian, B. C. Gardner, C. W. Cararhan, Robert C. Rutherford, Nathan C. Clark, F. C. Miramontes, Romely Rutherford, W. E. Gilbert, George Fernsler, Charles Stec, Frank J. Somers, R. L. Snyder, George E. Sleeper, Jr., W. E. Eddy, Fredrick W. Millspough, Philip Snell, Hans Salinger, and B. J. [sic] Herbert. The only mention in the correspondence of people sent was Pond and Sleeper.

49. Letter from Jesse B. McCargar to Russell G. Pond, November 5, 1936. Godfrey Papers, Box 9, File 10.

50. Letter from Jesse B. McCargar to George Everson, circa November 5, 1936 (letter undated). Godfrey Papers, Box 9, File 10.

51. Ibid.

52. Everson, *Story of Television,* p. 209

53. Ibid., p. 210.

54. See Farnsworth Research Journals, Vols. XIX–XXXIV, Farnsworth Papers, Boxes 57–59.

55. Quoted in Everson, *Story of Television,* pp. 210–11.

56. It was Everson's networking with Hugh Knowlton that would eventually lead Farnsworth into radio and television financing. Everson and McCargar also had another

invention they were underwriting called the Oigum engine. At this writing, little is known of these ventures other than simply their existence. See Letter from George Everson to Donald K. Lippincott, May 15, 1941, Lippincott Papers, Box 1.

57. Everson, *Story of Television,* pp. 209–10.

58. Ibid., p. 211.

59. Letter from Donald K. Lippincott to George Everson, February 2, 1937, Godfrey Papers, Box 16, File 3.

60. Ibid., pp. 1–2.

61. Handwritten note from Donald K. Lippincott to George Everson, not dated, circa February 2, 1937, Godfrey Papers, Box 16, File 3.

62. In the Matter of Farnsworth Television Incorporated of Pennsylvania, before the Federal Communications Commission, Washington, D.C., FCC docket no. 4074. National Archives, General Correspondence, 1927–1946, Box 359, File 89-6, Farnsworth Television & Radio Corporation from June 14, 1935 to December 31, 1946, pp. 1–2.

63. FCC docket no. 4074, p. 2. The phrase "public interest, convenience, and necessity" is a key regulatory phrase from the *Communications Act of 1934.*

64. Ibid., p. 1.

65. "'Flicker' Removed in New Television," *New York Times,* 21 August 1936, 13: 1.

66. Ibid.

67. Philo Farnsworth, FCC docket no. 4074, p. 2, para. 13. Hyde Papers, Box 9, File 8. This document contains the notes of Rosel H. Hyde taken at the hearing for the station.

68. Ibid., pp. 2–3, para. 13, 17, and 19.

69. Ibid.

70. Ibid., p. 1, para. 8. It is likely that this figure came from the oral testimony of one of the witnesses at the hearing. These witnesses included Philo T. Farnsworth, Donald K. Lippincott, and FCC engineer James P. Buchanan. All three were questioned by Farnsworth's attorney Henry Temin, the FCC attorney Tyler Berry, and FCC examiner Rosel H. Hyde. The notes Rosel H. Hyde took during the hearing reflect this same figure.

71. Ibid., p. 3.

72. Ibid., p. 1, para. 7.

73. Ibid., para. 9.

74. Ibid., p. 4, para. 31–32. The financial report does not appear within this docket information.

75. Ibid., p. 3.

76. Rosel H. Hyde served a long term as an FCC commissioner, 1946 to 1969; and chair from 1953 to 1954 and 1966 to 1969. Hyde and Farnsworth were both members of the Church of Jesus Christ of Latter-day Saints. At this writing there was no evidence that this commonality produced any advantage or disadvantage for Farnsworth. Despite Hyde's many years at the FCC and Farnsworth's frustration with regulators, there was no communication found between them. See register of Hyde Papers, "Index to General Correspondence."

77. "FCC Approves Television Station," *New York Times,* 31 October 1936, 24: 6.

78. FCC docket no. 4074, p. 4. See also "Television Station Licensed," *New York Times,* 2 December 1936, 34: 4. While work focused around the new station, 1936 was another year of significant patent filings, see Appendix A.

79. "New Television Station Planned for Philadelphia," *New York Times,* 13 December 1936, X, 14: 3.

80. For studio design and plans, see W. C. Eddy, Daily Notes, Television Lab. Ltd., Vol. XXV, Farnsworth Papers, Box 58, Book 1, pp. 11–12.

81. Everson, *Story of Television,* pp. 203–04.

82. Paul Schatzkin, "Farnsworth: TV's Inventor: Refinanced, Relocated and Bought Out, Sarnoff Pays," part 4, *Televisions* 5:4 (1978): 16.

83. There is evidence that Farnsworth Television Inc. was working on a switcher at this time, but none that would document this development as a "first." See F. J. Somers, Daily Notes, Farnsworth Television Inc., Vol. XXXVII, April 18, 1937, Farnsworth Papers, Box 58, Book 3. Also B. J. Herbert, Daily Notes, Farnsworth Television Inc., Vol. XLI, April 7, 1939, Farnsworth Papers, Box 60, Book 3.

84. Everson, *Story of Television,* p. 204.

85. Eddy, *Television,* p. 6. He recorded that there were three major studio lighting considerations: (1) the light "must be uniform and of such intensity that the general light alone will produce a good picture"; (2) the "eye-fatigue must be kept at a minimum"; and (3) "the burning effect or directed heat of the spots should be diminished." See also Eddy, p. 107. See Kisseloff, *The Box,* p. 81. Kisseloff credits Eddy as "virtually inventing television lighting."

86. Eddy, *Television,* p. 11.

87. FCC docket no. 4074, pp. 2, 5.

88. "Farnsworth Expects Experimental Television in Philadelphia, Area 5 x 7 Inches, After January," *Variety,* 9 December 1936, p. 36. In National Archives, General Correspondence, 1927–46, Box 359, File 89-6. It is assumed that the construction permit was modified to allow for the visual discrepancy recorded here, although no Farnsworth or FCC documents were located. See also, Report to the Stockholders of Farnsworth Television Incorporated, August 9, 1939, Godfrey Papers, Box 9, File 1, pp. 1–2. This report written by McCargar indicated the transmitter was 250 watts.

89. "Farnsworth Expects Experimental Television in Philadelphia," p. 36.

90. Kisseloff, *The Box,* p. 81. Farnsworth, *Distant Vision,* p. 172. See also Everson, *Story of Television,* p. 167.

91. Everson, *Story of Television,* p. 214.

92. Kisseloff, *The Box,* p. 81.

93. Farnsworth, *Distant Vision,* p. 172. See also Everson, *Story of Television,* p. 205.

94. Farnsworth, *Distant Vision,* p. 172. See also Everson, *Story of Television,* p. 204.

95. Eddy, quoted in Kisseloff, *The Box,* pp. 37–38.

96. "Spot News: Sight and Sound Broadcasts Due Soon," Philadelphia *Evening Public Ledger,* 15 November 1938, p. 2.

97. Lincoln Farnsworth interview with Donald G. Godfrey, February 13, 1990, Godfrey Papers. See also Farnsworth, *Distant Vision,* p. 175.

98. Letter to George Everson from Jesse McCargar, August 5, 1936, Godfrey Papers, Box 16, File 3.

99. Report to the Stockholders of Farnsworth Television Incorporated, August 9, 1937, Godfrey Papers, Box 9, File 1, p. 2.

100. "CBS-Farnsworth Deal,"*Business Week,* 17 April 1937, Madsen Papers, Box 171, File 5, p. 16.

101. Everson, *Story of Television,* p. 216.

102. "CBS-Farnsworth Deal," Madsen Papers, Box 171, File 5, p. 16. See also *Business Week,* 10 April 1937, p. 20.

103. Letter from E. K. Cohan, director of general engineering, CBS, to George Everson, February 15, 1936, Godfrey Papers.

104. "CBS-Farnsworth Deal," p. 16.

105. Correspondence from Donald K. Lippincott to George Everson, February 2, 1937, Godfrey Papers, Box 16, File 3, p. 2.

106. Seymour Turner had constructed the Philadelphia studio. Lippincott's comments are in correspondence to George Everson, February 2, 1937, Godfrey Papers, Box 16, File 3, p. 2.

107. Everson, *Story of Television,* p. 216. There was no mention of the volume of the equipment sold in the papers located to date.

108. Abramson, *History of Television,* p. 240.

109. Everson, *Story of Television,* p. 155.

110. Hugh Knowlton, a friend of George Everson, was a young man when he first met Everson under circumstances similar to Farnsworth. Everson had offered Knowlton a job as an office boy. Knowlton later graduated from Harvard Law School. Over the years he had gained a reputation as an astute New York lawyer, and by the late 1930s he was a partner in the firm Kuhn, Loeb and Company. Knowlton was an investment banker; vice president of the International Acceptance Bank Inc., 1926 to 1929; vice president of the International Manhattan Company, 1929 to 1931; and a law partner with Kuhn, Loeb and Company from 1932 to 1942 and 1946 to 1949. He worked in government service with the communications division of the United States Commercial Company, 1942 to 1943, as director of research and planning for Eastern Airlines, 1943 to 1945, and as a member of their board of directors. He was also a director at ITT. He authored *Transportation in the United States* (Chicago: University of Chicago Press, 1941). See *Who's Who in America,* vol. 25 (Chicago: A. N. Marquis Company, 1948–1949).

111. Bell Telephone Laboratories, created in 1925, was the research arm of AT&T. In the 1920s, AT&T had made significant contributions to radio including equipment such as the volume unit meter to measure sound and the sound mixers. They were also experimenting with largely mechanical television and sending still and moving pictures using AT&T wire-photo transmission. Sterling and Kittross, *Stay Tuned,* p. 100.

112. Everson, *Story of Television,* p. 156.

113. Everson reports that there were approximately 150 Farnsworth Television patents at this time. See Everson, *Story of Television,* p. 156. The actual number of patents filed by Farnsworth from 1927 through 1937 was ninety-one.

114. Letter from F. B. Jewett, AT&T vice president, to Hugh Knowlton, March 13, 1937, Godfrey Papers, Box 16, File 3.

115. Letter from Jesse McCargar to George Everson, August 5, 1936, p. 5. Also letter from McCargar to Everson, October 13, 1936, Godfrey Papers, Box 16, File 3, pp. 1–2.

116. "Television Deal Signed," *New York Times,* 26 July 1937, p. 8. See Abramson, *History of Television,* p. 238.

117. Everson, *Story of Television,* p. 158.

118. Report to the Stockholders of Farnsworth Television Incorporated, August 9, 1937, Godfrey Papers, Box 9, File 1, p. 1.

119. "AT&T, Farnsworth, Television," *Business Week,* 14 August 1937, p. 18. See also Abramson, "Pioneers of Television," p. 782; and Abramson, *History of Television,* p. 234.

120. Everson, *Story of Television,* p. 219.

121. "AT&T, Farnsworth, Television," p. 18.

122. Ibid.

123. "Cross-Licensing Pact Reached on Television Patents," *Philadelphia Record,* 27 July 1937, Farnsworth Papers, Box 27, File 2.

124. "Television," Beverly Hills *Citizen* 16:13 (2 September 1938): 11, 17. See Godfrey Papers, Box 12, File 4.

125. Donald G. Cooley, "An Interview with Philo T. Farnsworth," *Modern Mechanix* 16:2 (June 1936): 35–135.

126. Everson, *Story of Television,* p. 186.

127. Ibid., pp. 181–82. While this statement is no doubt true, it would be a misunderstanding to believe McCargar and Everson never profited from these ventures. They were two of the original stockholders, the stock grew in value, and it was bought and sold for both profit and money to support the laboratory.

128. "Registration Statement," Farnsworth Television and Radio Corporation, Registration no. 2-3939, Securities and Exchange Commission, Washington, D.C. Filed February 28, 1939, p. 31. It is interesting that in the listing of McCargar's accomplishments throughout his life, there is no mention of the Farnsworth corporations where McCargar had served as president, vice president, and a member of the board of directors for more than twenty years. "Last Rites for Jesse B. McCargar," p. 1.

129. "Registration Statement," p. 31.

130. Farnsworth, *Distant Vision,* pp. 193–95.

131. Schatzkin, part 4, p. 10.

132. Ibid. Reports on the date of this meeting differ. Schatzkin indicated it was in the summer. Pem Farnsworth, quoting a letter from Farnsworth to his mother, has the date fixed as late April 1937.

133. Letter from Philo T. Farnsworth to his mother dated April 25, 1937. Full text cited in Farnsworth, *Distant Vision,* pp. 199–200.

134. Everson, *Story of Television,* p. 219.

135. Letter from Bartley C. Crum to George Everson, January 25, 1937, Godfrey Papers, Box 16, File 3. Crum was a San Francisco attorney and a stockholder.

136. See Appendix A.

137. Letter from Elma G. Farnsworth to George Everson, September 26, 1938, Godfrey Papers, Box 16, File 3.

CHAPTER 6

1. UPI/Corbis-Bettmann Archive Photo U898199INP, January 27, 1940, Fort Wayne, Indiana. "Personalities in Science," undated clipping, Godfrey Papers, Box 12, File 3.

2. "Registration Statement," p. 2, and exhibit H-13, Lippincott Papers. According to the exhibit, only seven of the forty-nine Farnsworth patents had coinventors.

3. There is a slight difference here of patent numbers reported. "Registration Statement," p. 2, reports seventy-three patents pending. Exhibit H-14 reports seventy-four patents pending with forty-six of these being Farnsworth's; five of the forty-six were with coinventors.

4. List of his patents to date. "Registration Statement," exhibit H-17, Lippincott Papers.

5. "Farnsworth Television and Radio Corporation," Filed February 12, 1946, Securities and Exchange Commission, Philadelphia, Pennsylvania, p. 4. National Archives, General Correspondence 1927–46, File 89-6, Box 359, Envelope 6. See "Plan of Reorganization of Farnsworth Television Incorporated and Farnsworth Television & Radio Corporation," ITT Library Papers, Farnsworth Files. Also "New Television Company," *New York Times,* 22 December 1938, 35: 7.

6. "Certificate of Winding Up and Dissolution of Farnsworth Television Incorporated, a California Corporation," Farnsworth Television Incorporated; no. 133225, Secretary of State, California State Archives.

7. 1942 Annual report—Delaware Corporation, Farnsworth Television & Radio Distributing Corporation, p. 1. State of Delaware, Department of State, Division of Corporations, Dover, Delaware; hereafter referred to as Delaware Archives. A handwritten note on the papers indicated the Delaware organization was dissolved April 8, 1943.

8. Letter from E. A. Nicholas to the stockholders, July 19, 1939. Report of Farnsworth Television and Radio Corporation, from December 13, 1938 to April 30, 1939, p. 2, National Archives, Broadcast Bureau, Broadcast Facilities Division, Technical & Allocations Branch, Records Relating to the History of the Development of Television 1938–1965, Box 7, File Television, 1944 Allocations.

9. "New Television Company: Farnsworth Concern Proposed Plan to Its Stockholders," *New York Times,* 22 December 1938, 35: 7.

10. Edwin A. Nicholas was born December 13, 1893 in Cleveland, Ohio, and had a notable record of involvement in wireless, radio, and RCA. His career began as a messenger boy for the United Wireless Company. He had worked in ship-to-shore communications during the early part of the century. In 1915 he was working for the American Marconi Company as chief operator and inspector of the Great Lakes division. By 1924 he was called by David Sarnoff to be his personal assistant, working from the RCA office in New York. He advanced through the RCA organization working as the eastern district sales manager, then as manager of the radiola division of RCA, and later as the appointed vice president of the Radio-Victor Corporation. He took a two-year hiatus from RCA in 1929 to establish his own distribution company and was a licensed radiola distributor. In 1931 he was back again with RCA as the vice president of RCA Victor and later manager of its license division and a member of the corporate advisory board. The United Wireless Company was an early competitor in the United States. The assets of this company were eventually purchased by the British Marconi Company that resold

them in 1912 to the American Marconi Company. For further biographical information, see "E. A. Nicholas Wins Radio Citation," Farnsworth Employee's Victory Record, February 16, 1944, p. 8. Also see E. A. Nicholas résumé in the Clark Collection, Series 4, Biographies, Collection 55, Box 11, File E. A. Nicholas, National Museum of American History. "They Are Watching You Too," *World Wide Wireless* V (November 1924): 3–5. Sarnoff Corporation Library; see biographical information in the Nicholas obituary. "Ex-President of Farnsworth Dies," Fort Wayne *Journal-Gazette* 91:28 (28 January 1953): 1–2. Also see Gleason L. Archer, *History of Radio to 1926* (New York: American Historical Society, 1938), pp. 101, 103; also "E. A. Nicholas Appointed Distributor in Northern Illinois Section," *RCA News* XI (September 1930): 14, Sarnoff Corporation Library. See "Marconi Memorial Medal of Achievement: E. A. Nicholas," publicity release in George H. Clark Collection, Series 4, Biographies, Collection 55, Box 11, File–E. A. Nicholas, National Museum of American History.

11. Farnsworth Television and Radio Corporation, Annual report for year ended April 30, 1939, Securities and Exchange Commission, Box 2371; 450/71/27/07; 1939, pp. 8–9, 13.

12. "Registration Statement," Farnsworth Television and Radio Corporation, Registration Number 2-3939, Securities and Exchange Commission, pp. 1–2, 10. Filed February 28, 1939, Lippincott Papers. See "Plan of Reorganization," ITT Library Papers, Farnsworth Files, p. 1.

13. "New Television Company," p. 7.

14. "Plan of Reorganization," ITT Library Papers, Farnsworth Files, p. 3. The list of those holding outstanding stock included Nicholas, E. H. Rollins & Sons Inc., A. G. Messick, the Capehart Corporation, and the General Household Utilities Company. The list of underwriters included E. H. Rollins & Sons Inc.; Eastman, Dillon & Company; W. E. Hutton & Co; Hemphill, Noyes & Company; Hallgarter & Company; Riter & Company; H. M. Bylleshy & Company Inc.; Wm. Cavalier & Company; O'Melveny-Wagenseller & Durst; and Kuhn, Loeb & Company; see "Registration Statement," pp. 10, 16, and 18, Donald K. Lippincott Papers. The business of Hurley & Company also appears in a 1940 report verifying the citizenship of stockholders to the FCC. See letter from T. J. Slowie, Secretary of the FCC, to Farnsworth Television and Radio Corporation, December 23, 1940, National Archives, General Correspondence, 1927–1946, Box 359, File 89-6. "Registration Statement," pp. 16-18, notes 1-4, Donald K. Lippincott Papers. For a total list of the securities held by each director, see "Registration Statement," p. 16, Donald K. Lippincott Papers.

15. In the "Registration Statement," pp. 1–2, this figure is recorded at 600,000. The *New York Times* reported this figure at 690,000, see "New Television Company," p. 7. In "Report to the Stockholders of Farnsworth Television Inc.," December 20, 1938, the number is again at 690,000. Farnsworth Papers, Box 7, File 6. The "Plan of Reorganization," ITT Library Papers, Farnsworth Files, p. 2, also has the figure at 690,000.

16. "Television Issue Put on the Market," *New York Times,* 28 March 1939, 36: 1.

17. "Registration Statement," Lippincott Papers, p. 13. See "Communications," *Time,* 20 February 1939, p. 62. Also "Television I: A $3,000,000 'If,'" *Fortune,* April 1939, p. 174. Everson, *Story of Television,* p. 238.

18. Here it is noteworthy that these represent the gross-dollar reporting, and there were profits being made in the reorganization. Kuhn, Loeb, and Company rendered

their services at a cost of $210,750. See "Registration Statement," Lippincott Papers, p. S-7, note I. The trustees, W. W. Crocker and Roy N. Bishop, were to be paid $40,000 out of the first proceeds of the corporation. George Everson, Leslie Gorrell, and Philo Farnsworth were each paid $800 as the original partners. See "Registration Statement," Lippincott Papers, p. S-6, note E.

19. "Television Issue Put on the Market," *New York Times,* 28 March 1939, 36: 2.

20. Ibid.

21. The Capehart Company dates back to the late 1920s when entrepreneur Homer E. Capehart moved from manufacturing popcorn poppers to phonographs, radios, and jukeboxes. By 1929 the company was manufacturing "talking machines," and it was known as the Capehart Automatic Phonograph Corporation, with headquarters and manufacturing operations in Fort Wayne. It produced a number of expensive phonographs and radio-console combinations. Despite the fact that the 1930s were the Depression years, when others such as Philco were developing a low-price radio to increase their sales, Capehart stood stubbornly behind the company's quality product and its high-price structure. This pushed them close to bankruptcy. In the early 1930s, Capehart joined Wurlitzer, a producer of jukeboxes, and as a result Capehart was saved. Wurlitzer sold jukeboxes, which in turn sold records, which in turn created a demand for the Capehart phonograph. Despite his success with Wurlitzer, Homer Capehart was an entrepreneur and moved on to investments in land.

22. The announcement of the purchase was made in Fort Wayne the second week in March. See "Advent of Television Factory Emphasizes City's Advantages," Fort Wayne *News-Sentinel,* 13 March 1939, Vertical File–clippings, "Fort Wayne Industries–F," Allen County Public Library, Fort Wayne, Indiana; hereafter referred to as Allen County Public Library. The corporate records of the Capehart Corporation are filed with the Commission on Public Records, Indiana State Archives, Indianapolis, Indiana, Capehart Files. See also William B. Pickett, *Homer E. Capehart: A Senator's Life, 1897–1979* (Indianapolis: Indiana Historical Society, 1990).

23. Agreement between Farnsworth Television and Radio Corporation, Capehart Incorporated, February 1939, Proof no. 3. January 27, 1939, Farnsworth Papers, Box 6, File 4.

24. Reported in a review by certified public accountants, Ernst & Ernst, Chicago, p. 3.

25. The General Household Utilities plant was not as well known as Capehart, but it too had a history in radio manufacturing. It began in 1923 as the Indiana Manufacturing and Electric Company and by 1929 was building radios and refrigerators under the name of U.S. Radio and Television Corporation. In 1932 it merged with the Grigsby-Grunow Company, with a name change to General Household Utilities. Due to the Depression, it closed in 1937, thus when Farnsworth was reorganized it was an available manufacturing operation. See untitled chronological history of the Marion manufacturing plant, Marion Public Library, Indiana Room, Marion, Indiana. This one-page history has been copied and is contained in the Godfrey Papers, Box 18, File 6. See Douglas, *Radio Manufacturers,* vol. 2, p. 134. See "Plant History Traced Back to Middle 20s," unidentified newspaper clipping, Marion Public Library, Indiana Room, Marion, Indiana. Marion and Grant County, Industry–RCA File. See also Godfrey Papers, Box 18, File 6.

26. "Farnsworth Files for Stock," *New York Times,* 12 February 1939, III, 5: 4.

27. Sterling and Kittross report that five manufacturers had television sets available by the end of December 1938. By July 1939, ten more manufacturers had joined that growing list. Alfred R. Oxenfeldt, *Marketing Practices in the TV Set Industry* (New York: Columbia University Press, 1964), pp. 9–11, as cited in Sterling and Kittross, *Stay Tuned,* p. 149.

28. Abramson, *History of Television,* p. 251.

29. Sterling and Kittross, *Stay Tuned,* p. 149.

30. Philip Kirby, *The Victory of Television* (New York: Harper & Brothers Publishers, 1939), pp. 80–81. Similar figures appear in the *Development of Television Hearings Before the Committee on Interstate Commerce,* p. 13.

31. "21st Annual Report," Radio Corporation of America, December 31, 1940, RCA Annual Reports, 1939–1930 [sic], Sarnoff Corporation Library, p. 7.

32. This figure seems to assign a significant value to Farnsworth's patents, W3XPF, the studio building, and land. An inventory of the fixed assets of Farnsworth Television, in Philadelphia totaled $56,116.32. This included an itemization of the laboratory, transmitter, studio, and engineering equipment conducted May 1, 1939. See "Farnsworth Television Inc. of Pennsylvania Inventory," May 1, 1939, Godfrey Papers, Box 16, File 4. See also "Registration Statement," Lippincott Papers, p. S-5.

33. "Notes of Television," *New York Times,* 23 April 1939, X, 10: 7. Vogel's experience included sales and merchandising for General Electric and RCA.

34. "Named Vice President of Television Company," *New York Times,* 9 May 1939, financial section, 35: 7.

35. "B. R. Cummings Gets New Post," *New York Times,* 11 May 1939, 46: 4.

36. "News and Notes of the Advertising Field," *New York Times,* 29 June 1939, 41: 1.

37. "Named Sales Manager of Farnsworth Radio," *New York Times,* 8 July 1939, 27: 7.

38. Farnsworth Radio and Television Corporation, Annual Report, April 30, 1939, to Securities and Exchange Commission, pp. 8–10.

39. Everson, *Story of Television,* p. 239.

40. "Business Notes," *New York Times,* 9 September 1939, 28: 6.

41. "Farnsworth Radio: Book of Facts," Farnsworth Television & Radio Corporation, 1939. See copy in Godfrey Papers, Box 9, File 4.

42. "News and Notes from the Advertising Field," *New York Times,* 15 August 1939, 34: 2.

43. "Dealers Get Open House," *San Francisco Chronicle,* 25 August 1939, unidentified clipping, San Francisco Public Library Vertical Files.

44. "Television Makes Its Midwest Debut at Plant of Farnsworth Corporation Tuesday Afternoon," Fort Wayne *News-Sentinel,* 9 August 1939. See also "Initial Demonstration of Television Is Given Tuesday at Farnsworth Factory," Fort Wayne *Journal Gazette.* Both articles are from Allen County Public Library.

45. See the advertisement in *Radio Today,* June 1939, Farnsworth Papers, Box 6, File 4, p. 35.

46. "History and Business," Securities and Exchange Commission, Farnsworth Television and Radio Corporation, prospectus. Also National Archives, General Correspondence, 1927–1946, Box 359, File 89-6, p. 4.

47. Advertisement, "The Greatest Name in Television Is the Newest Name in Radio," *Saturday Evening Post,* 28 October 1939, pp. 32–33.

48. Ibid., p. 33.

49. Everson, *Story of Television,* p. 239. Also Farnsworth, *Distant Vision,* p. 208. George A. Freeman, Indiana radio pioneer, WIKI-FM, Madison, Indiana, indicated that although this sales organization was effective in prewar sales, eventual problems resulted from the fact that "Farnsworth was selling the same sets to giant retailers at discounted prices that [it] . . . was selling . . . to local mom & pop shops." The result was dissatisfaction among dealer representatives who couldn't move their product. "Clearly, the Farnsworth organization did not understand they had a partnership responsibility to their small retailers." Letter from George A. Freeman to Donald G. Godfrey, July 6, 1996. See Godfrey Papers.

50. Everson, *Story of Television,* p. 234.

51. See more than eighty volumes of "Addresses, Press Releases, Articles," "Addresses by David Sarnoff," and "Book of Newspaper Clippings" in the Sarnoff Corporation Library.

52. See Sterling and Kittross, *Stay Tuned,* p. 151. See also Barnouw, *Golden Web,* pp. 125–28; Barnouw, *Tube of Plenty,* pp. 90–92; and Abramson, *History of Television,* p. 252.

53. See, for example, "RCA, The Story of Television," circa 1951. This is a beautiful example of RCA public relations. This story is a pamphlet detailing the history of television with only slight mentions of other companies and not a single mention of Farnsworth. National Archives, Broadcast Bureau, Broadcast Facilities Division, Technical and Allocations Branch, Box 8, File–Television History.

54. "Television Display at the Fair Largely a 'Research Exhibit,'" New York *World-Telegram,* 23 October 1938 [sic]. This date was stamped on the article, obviously from a clipping service. In *David Sarnoff: A Newspaper History, 1917–1966,* Sarnoff Corporation Library. Also Farnsworth, *Distant Vision,* p. 213.

55. "Television Notes: Farnsworth Exhibit," *Broadcasting* 17 (November 1939): 65.

56. Farnsworth April trade paper advertisement, Godfrey Papers, Box 12, File 16. Emphasis in the original. This file contains a number of newspaper articles and photographs surrounding the promotional campaign tour.

57. Carlton Fitchett, "Television Debut Made 'Em Smile, Not Laugh," *Seattle Post-Intelligencer,* Wednesday, 4 October 1939, Part Two, p. 1.

58. "Tulsans Due for Glimpse at Television in Three-Day Showing at Brown-Dunkin," Tulsa *Daily World,* 24 September 1949, p. 2.

59. See photo and notes, Godfrey Papers, Box 12, File 16. The notes indicate the pictures were taken in Oklahoma City; however, the date of September 24 would place the event in Tulsa.

60. "Demonstration of Television Arranged Here," Richmond *Times-Dispatch,* 22 October 1940, p. 6.

61. "Communications," *Time,* 20 February 1939, p. 62.

62. Ibid.

63. Everson, *Story of Television,* p. 245.

64. "Agree on Patents," *New York Times,* 3 October 1939, 41: 4 and 32: 3. See "B-File," draft agreement dated September 29, 1939, Farnsworth Papers, Box 6, File 5.

65. "Agree on Patents," p. 4.

66. "Reduction of Royalties and Extensions," Letter of Agreement, September 15, 1939, between E. A. Nicholas and Edwin M. Martin, Farnsworth Television and Radio Corporation, and Otto S. Schairer and Lewis MacComnach, Radio Corporation of America. The author acquired a copy of this letter from Stephen Hofer, Chicago State University; see Godfrey Papers, Box 19, File 11. The dramatics of the signing of the agreement are reported by Everson and Pem Farnsworth. They report the RCA representative "had tears in his eyes as he signed." See Farnsworth, *Distant Vision,* p. 214. Also Everson, *Story of Television,* p. 246. The source of this account is unknown. It is likely Nicholas, but at this writing no primary documentation has been located. At the time of the signing, Mr. and Mrs. Farnsworth were in Maine preparing to make the move to Fort Wayne, and Everson was in New York. Abramson casts some doubt on this story based on Schairer's character, which he described as having, "very little sentimentality, hard boiled and not a soft man." Correspondence from Albert Abramson to Donald G. Godfrey July 17, 1996, Godfrey Papers.

67. Everson, *Story of Television,* p. 247. See also Abramson, *History of Television,* p. 254.

68. "Notes on Television," *New York Times,* 22 October 1939, IX, 10: 5.

69. See Appendix A.

70. *Business Week* reports the correct title of this committee to be the Temporary National Economic Committee. The *New York Times* reporting on the same events called the committee the Monopoly Investigating Committee. See *Business Week,* 28 January 1939, p. 17; and *New York Times,* 20 January 1939, 4: 5.

71. Sterling and Kittross, *Stay Tuned,* pp. 189–92. It was this FCC investigation that would eventually lead to the FCC's May 1941 "Report on Chain Broadcasting," which would force the sale of one of the NBC radio networks and loosen the stranglehold of the network over affiliate stations.

72. "Gain in Television Leads to Patenting," p. 5.

73. "Television at Hand Phila. Pioneer Says," *Philadelphia Inquirer,* 20 January 1939. Unidentified clipping in the *Inquirer* morgue. Everson, *Story of Television,* p. 226.

74. "Gain in Television Leads to Patenting," p. 5.

75. These titles all appear in various documents. He was active as a member of the board of directors and as director of research.

76. "Agreement Between Philo Farnsworth and Farnsworth Television Incorporated," July 1937, para. 2, Farnsworth Papers, Box 6, File 3.

77. "Agreement Between Philo Farnsworth and Farnsworth Television Incorporated," July 1937, para. 5, Farnsworth Papers, Box 6, File 3. See also Farnsworth Television and Radio Inc., Annual Report, April 30, 1939, Securities and Exchange Commission, pp. 6–7.

78. "Agreement Between Philo Farnsworth and Farnsworth Television Incorporated," July 1937, para. 6, Farnsworth Papers, Box 6, File 3.

79. Sterling and Kittross, *Stay Tuned,* p. 150.

80. Ibid., p. 149.

81. Abramson indicated the committee was originally created in 1928. See Abramson, *History of Television,* p. 128. However, its most significant work was in the mid-1930s to the early 1940s. See Abramson, *History of Television,* pp. 257–72.

82. Sterling and Kittross, *Stay Tuned,* p. 150.

83. Statement of David Sarnoff at the *Development of Television Hearings,* p. 47.

84. Bucher, part IV, pp. 981-A, 981-G, and 982. This record would reflect an appearance before the Senate Interstate Commerce Committee, April 1940, and FCC hearings March 20, 1941.

85. "Brief of Farnsworth Radio and Television Corporation," presented before the FCC by Edwin M. Martin, attorney for Farnsworth Television and Radio Corporation, February 9, 1940, p. 6, docket no. 5806, National Archives, Broadcast Bureau Facilities Division, Technical and Allocations Branch, Records in Relation to the History of the Development of Television 1938–1965, Television: Allocations, Box 7, File, Television: 1944 Allocations.

86. *Development of Television Hearings,* pp. 64–66.

87. Sterling and Kittross, *Stay Tuned,* p. 153. Abramson, *History of Television,* p. 269. These are the standards still in force at this writing.

88. Abramson, *History of Television,* p. 272. Also "RCA Sees Commercial Television Retarded by Defense Program," *New York Times,* 7 May 1941, 27: 3; and "RCA Studies Future of Video But Sees Rather Dim Future," *Broadcasting* 19 (12 May 1941): 92.

89. Sterling and Kittross, *Stay Tuned,* p. 209.

90. Inglis, *Behind the Tube,* p. 185.

91. Abramson, *History of Television,* p. 272.

92. Ibid.

CHAPTER 7

1. For the number of television stations on the air, see Sterling and Kittross, *Stay Tuned,* pp. 632–33. Also see Inglis, *Behind the Tube,* p. 185; and Abramson, *History of Television,* p. 272.

2. See Michael D. Murray and Donald G. Godfrey, eds., *Television in America,* pp. xix–xxiv. Stations were progressing technologically and in programming. In fact, the first commercial programming innovations at this time were extensions of these experimental stations—demonstrations, motion pictures, cooking, children's shows, and sports. Much of what has been written about programming in the early years of television makes it appear that everything emanated from the established networks and was passed on to local stations. In reality, there were no commercial television networks. It wasn't until after the war that the NBC and CBS radio networks even announced they would be organizing television networks. Most of the local stations programmed only a few hours each day to a small audience.

3. B. C. Gardner writes, "This is the first entry made in our new location in Ft. Wayne," September 13, 1939. See Daily Notes, Television Lab. Ltd., Vol. XIV, Farnsworth Papers, Box 56, Book 1.

4. See Chapter 6 for a listing of corporations with stations on the air. Ironically, the station Farnsworth started for Philco, WPTZ, was one of the stations still on the air.

5. Letter from Edwin M. Martin, patent counsel, Farnsworth Television and Radio Corporation, to John B. Reynolds, acting Secretary of the FCC, October 4, 1939, National Archives, General Correspondence, 1927–1946, Box 359, File 89–6. There is a series of letters about this transition. Interestingly, it appears Philco later set up its

operations for W3XE (the first station Farnsworth put on the air) at the same physical location as the old Farnsworth station.

6. Letter from E. A. Nicholas, president, Farnsworth Television and Radio Corporation to T. J. Slowie, Secretary of the FCC, October 21, 1940. National Archives, Box 359, File 89-6.

7. FCC Broadcast Station Inspection Report, filed June 9, 1941, by Ernest J. Galins, National Archives, Box 359, File 89-6.

8. Letter from T. J. Slowie, Secretary of the FCC to Farnsworth Television and Radio Corporation, December 31, 1941, National Archives, General Correspondence, 1927–46, Box 359, File 89–6, Farnsworth Television and Radio Corporation from June 14, 1935 to December 31, 1946.

9. Letter from B. Ray Cummings, vice president, Farnsworth Television and Radio, to T. J. Slowie, Secretary of the FCC, April 8, 1944, National Archives, General Correspondence, 1927–1946, Box 359, File 89–6, Farnsworth Television and Radio Corporation from June 14, 1935 to December 31, 1946.

10. "Farnsworth Acquires WGL from Westinghouse," *Farnsworth Employee Victory Record,* p. 2. Clipping circa 1944. ITT Library Papers.

11. Letter from Fred A. Barr, Patent Department, Farnsworth Television and Radio, to T. J. Slowie, Secretary of the FCC, August 5, 1941, National Archives, Box 359, File 89-6.

12. Letter from T. J. Slowie, Secretary of the FCC, to Farnsworth Television and Radio, December 31, 1941, National Archives, Box 359, File 89-6.

13. "Communications," *Time,* 20 February 1939, p. 62.

14. Farnsworth, *Distant Vision,* p. 217.

15. Player Papers, n.d., p. 65. See also Farnsworth, *Distant Vision,* pp. 217–19.

16. For additional comments from Farnsworth's wife on his health, see Farnsworth, *Distant Vision,* pp. 239, 245–46, 263, 276, 305–06, 311–12, and 331.

17. In oral history interviews with engineers and people who worked shoulder to shoulder with Farnsworth, I asked about his addictions. I can report that, right down to every person interviewed, there was not one who had anything but the highest of admiration for Farnsworth. The criticism for his being an alcoholic seems to come from those who really did not know the man. There was no hidden story here. As one of the interview subjects put it, "He was like the rest of us in the engineering world—he drank too much."

18. Farnsworth, *Distant Vision,* pp. 213, 217.

19. Letter from Carl Farnsworth to family, June 27, 1940, Player Papers, p. 35.

20. Letter from Carl Farnsworth to Laura Player, May 7, 1942, Player Papers, p. 35.

21. Letter from Philo T. Farnsworth to "Dear Folks," December 20, 1942, Player Papers, p. 37.

22. Neil Hitt, "It Was 22 Years Ago, on Telegraph Hill," San Francisco *Chronicle,* 23 January 1949, unidentified clipping, San Francisco Public Library Vertical Files. See also Everson, *Story of Television,* p. 240.

23. Farnsworth, *Distant Vision,* pp. 218–19.

24. Regarding Farnsworth's health, 1939–42, see "Life Sketch of Philo T. Farnsworth," revised October 11, 1988, Farnsworth Papers, Box 1, File 2.

25. Letter from Philo T. Farnsworth to Farnsworth Television and Radio, December 18, 1940, Farnsworth Papers, Box 20, File 7. In this letter that originally requests funding for the lab in Maine, note that Farnsworth calls the corporation "your corporation." Minutes of the board of directors meeting, February 25, 1942, Farnsworth Television and Radio Corporation, Farnsworth Papers, Box 7, File 1.

26. Letter from Philo T. Farnsworth to E. A. Nicholas, March 10, 1942, Farnsworth Papers, Box 7, File 2.

27. Letter from E. A. Nicholas to Philo T. Farnsworth, March 17, 1942, Farnsworth Papers, Box 7, File 2.

28. See Appendix D. "Certificate of Organization of a Corporation Under the General Law," State of Maine, Office of the Secretary of State, Bureau of Corporations, Elections and Commissions, Division of Corporations, Augusta, Maine. These corporate records are incomplete and primarily 1943 legal documents used in establishing the corporation. The names connected with this corporation were Agnes M. Greeley, Philip F. Thorne, and Harry C. Libby.

29. This was the name given the acreage by the family because of the large wild ferns.

30. Everson, *Story of Television* , p. 256.

31. Ibid., pp. 241 & 259.

32. Letter to Edwin M. Martin, secretary, Farnsworth Television and Radio, Fort Wayne from Philo T. Farnsworth, June 19, 1944, Farnsworth Papers, Box 7, File 2. Everson also notes that the wood products business was but a diversion for Farnsworth. See Everson, *Story of Television,* p. 257.

33. Farnsworth, *Distant Vision,* p. 227.

34. Letter to Hugh Knowlton from Philo T. Farnsworth, n.d. (circa 1942), Farnsworth Papers, Box 5, File 1. Farnsworth is staying in contact with this key figure and also selling stock certificates.

35. Handwritten letter from Philo T. Farnsworth to gentlemen [of the board] Farnsworth Television and Radio, n.d. (circa April 25, 1945), Farnsworth Papers, Box 21, File 3.

36. Minutes of the Farnsworth Television and Radio Corporation, board of directors meeting, September 19, 1945, Farnsworth Papers, Box 7, File 2. See also agreement between Farnsworth Television and Radio Corporation and Philo T. Farnsworth, 1945, Farnsworth Papers, Box 6, File 5.

37. See Appendix E for a brief history of the Farnsworth Television and Radio Corporation.

38. See *Brownfield Village,* October 24, 1947, and *Portland Herald,* newspaper clippings, Farnsworth Papers, Box 6, File 4. See also Everson, *Story of Television,* p. 260.

39. Letter from Elma G. Farnsworth to "Mother and Dad, Joe," October 28, 1947, Player Papers, p. 42.

40. Letter from Elma G. Farnsworth, December 17, 1847, Player Papers, p. 46. "Directive," E. A. Nicholas, president, Farnsworth Television and Radio Corporation, June 8, 1948, Farnsworth Papers, Box 6, File 8.

41. Player Papers, p. 47.

42. Farnsworth, *Distant Vision,* pp. 247–52. See also Player Papers, pp. 47–48.

43. Letter from Elma G. Farnsworth to her father, October 12, 1949, Godfrey Papers, Box 8, File 4.

44. Ibid., p. 2.

45. Ibid., pp. 2–3.

46. The board of directors for 1932 to 1938 controlled finances and were involved in the lab. The board of 1938 to 1949 acted more as an advisory board, providing overall approval and directing corporate management. They were not in the lab or involved in any aspect of manufacturing; finances were controlled by corporate management. In other words, McCargar was still around during the Fort Wayne corporate years, but he no longer held the strings. He served as board chair for many of these years. This is likely one of the reasons Farnsworth did not want to return to Fort Wayne and also the reason for McCargar's resignation when Farnsworth agreed to return. McCargar moved totally out of the Farnsworth picture at this time. He was sixty-seven years old and in poor health; he died in April 1954. In listing McCargar's career achievements there is no mention of his work for Farnsworth. See "Last Rites for Jesse B. McCargar, San Francisco *Chronicle,* 8 April 1954, 25:1.

47. Abe Fortas (1910–1982) was a Washington, D.C., lawyer from 1946 to 1965—the period he was briefly associated with the Farnsworth Corporation. He was Undersecretary, Department of the Interior, from 1942 to 1946 and an associate justice of the Supreme Court from 1965 to 1969. According to Fortas's biographer, his papers for the Farnsworth period did not survive. However, Fortas did have clients in the entertainment business and often sat on corporate boards while he was in private practice. See Laura Kalman, *Abe Fortas: A Biography* (New Haven: Yale University Press, 1990). There was no biographical information in the Farnsworth records on Abe Fortas, how he became a member of the board, or his role in Farnsworth activities.

48. "Farnsworth Revamped," *New York Times,* 29 November 1948, 36: 4.

49. Farnsworth Television and Radio, report no. 24, Vol. II, Roy D. Jackson, Business Management Counsel, Columbus, Ohio. "Good & Bad News Report," February 1949, Farnsworth-Everson Papers, Box 1, File 5.

50. Letter from George A. Freemam, Indiana broadcast pioneer, WIKI-FM, Madison, Indiana, July 6, 1996, to Donald G. Godfrey. See Godfrey Papers.

51. "Head of IT&T Replies to Ryan," *New York Times,* 3 December 1947, 43: 7 & 49: 2.

52. "Farnsworth Radio Files Stock with SEC; Trading Here Halts," *New York Times,* 14 January 1949, 35: 6.

53. Ibid., pp. 6 & 7.

54. "Halts Farnsworth Deals," *New York Times,* 14 January 1949, 37: 6–7. See also "Along the Highways and By-Ways of Finance," *New York Times,* 16 January 1949, III, 3: 2. There are several undocumented allegations relative to the Farnsworth corporate losses. The first asserts there was a secret deal between ITT and RCA that supposedly said ITT would stay out of the business of television if RCA would stay out of telecommunications. This rumor is false. There was no such secret deal that could be documented. In fact, ITT did compete with RCA as it continued manufacturing television sets under the Capehart name until 1956. The second allegation asserts there was a black market operation selling Farnsworth sets during the war and unusual activity at the Fort Wayne plant. See Farnsworth, *Distant Vision,* pp. 258–59; and Hofer, in letter from Stephen F. Hofer to Donald G. Godfrey, October 1997, Godfrey Papers, Box 19, File 11.

The father of Stephen F. Hofer, dissertation and *Journal of Broadcasting* author on Farnsworth, was an employee of Farnsworth Television and Radio in Fort Wayne. There was no documentation supporting either charge.

55. "Halts Farnsworth Deals," *New York Times,* 14 January 1949, 37: 6.

56. "Loss Figures Explained," *New York Times,* 27 January 1949, 36: 2.

57. The request for additional stock sales was withdrawn at the sale of the Farnsworth corporation to ITT. See "Farnsworth Asks to End Stock Sale," *New York Times,* 10 March 1949, 45: 4.

58. Report no. 1, submitted by R. D. Jackson, business management consultant, Columbus Ohio, October 27, 1948, pp. 1–4. In the exhibits to Securities and Exchange Commission, registration statement, form S–1, filed January 12, 1949. See Farnsworth Papers, Box 9, Book 1.

59. The News Sentinel Broadcasting Company took over operation of WGL-AM in October 1948 pending FCC approval that was granted June 9, 1949. See F.A.R. Liquidating Corporation, annual report, May 1, 1950, Delaware Archives. See also Jonathan D. Tankel, "Philo T. Farnsworth," in Donald G. Godfrey and Frederic A. Leigh, eds., *Historical Dictionary of American Radio* (Westport, Conn.: Greenwood Press, 1998), p. 152.

60. Report no. 1, pp. 2–3.

61. See Report no. 5, November 11, 1948, in Farnsworth Television and Radio Corporation, Exhibits to Registration Statement, Securities and Exchange Commission, report filed January 12, 1949.

62. Farnsworth Television and Radio, report no. 20, Vol. II. R. D. Jackson, January 14, 1949, Farnsworth-Everson Papers, Box 1, File 5. The report reads like this is a new idea. It was, however, the pattern already in existence.

63. Farnsworth Television and Radio, report Nos. 21 and 25, Vol. II. R. D. Jackson, January 14, 1949, and February 10, 1949, Farnsworth-Everson Papers, Box 1, File 5.

64. Farnsworth Television and Radio, report no. 21, Vol. II. R. D. Jackson, February 4, 1949, Farnsworth-Everson Papers, Box 1, File 5.

65. Farnsworth Television and Radio, report no. 25, Vol. II. R. D. Jackson, February 10, 1949, Farnsworth-Everson Papers, Box 1, File 5.

66. Letter from R. D. Jackson to George Everson, March 9, 1949, Godfrey Papers, Box 16, File 4.

67. Ibid.

68. Letter to Philo T. Farnsworth from R. D. Jackson, May 25, 1949, Farnsworth Papers, Box 21, File 6.

69. "IT&T Authorizes Farnsworth Deal," *New York Times,* 10 February 1949, 43: 5.

70. "Farnsworth Head Backs IT&T Offer," *New York Times,* 24 March 1949, 43: 6 & 46: 7.

71. Ibid., 46: 7.

72. Letter from Philo T. Farnsworth to Farnsworth stockholders, April 14, 1949, Farnsworth Papers, Box 8, File 6. See also "Farnsworth Sale Finally Ok'd by Stockholders," Fort Wayne newspaper clipping, 5 May 1949, Farnsworth Papers, Box 27, File 3.

73. "Farnsworth Head Backs IT&T Offer," *New York Times,* 24 March 1949, 43: 6. See also "Farnsworth President Raps Suit Challenging Firm Sale," Fort Wayne *Journal-Gazette,* 7 May 1949, Farnsworth Papers, Box 27, File 3.

74. "Operation Rescue," *New York Times,* 13 February 1949, III, 3: 3.

75. "Farnsworth Stock Holders Postpone Vote for 5th Time," Fort Wayne newspaper clipping, 30 April 1949, Farnsworth Papers, Box 27, File 4.

76. Letter from Philo T. Farnsworth to Farnsworth stockholders, April 14, 1949, Farnsworth Papers, Box 8, File 6. See also Godfrey Papers, Box 9, File 11.

77. "Farnsworth Sale Okayed," Fort Wayne newspaper clipping, 4 May 1949, Farnsworth Papers, Box 27, File 3.

78. "Sale of Farnsworth Reported Indicated," *New York Times,* 4 May 1949, 58: 2.

79. "Stockholders Vote Sale of Farnsworth," *New York Times,* 5 May 1949, 54: 3. The Liquidating Corporation was exactly as it denotes; it was to facilitate the sale and was dissolved the following year. See annual report, F.A.R. Liquidating Corporation, 3681–5, report filed May 3, 1950, Delaware Archives.

80. "Farnsworth Head Backs IT&T Offer," *New York Times,* 24 March 1949, 43: 6.

81. See "Radio Television," and "Farnsworth to IT&T," *Newsweek,* 21 February 1949 and 28 March 1949, 33: 8 & 13, pp. 56–59 and 65–66, respectively. This article also indicated that the first Farnsworth television set had been an admitted lemon (see p. 66). However, it says nothing further on the specific subject. At this writing no other reference was found relating to suggested inferiority of either the Capehart or Farnsworth models—both produced by the Farnsworth Television and Radio Corporation.

82. Robert Sobel, *I. T.T.: The Management of Opportunity* (New York: Truman Talley Books, 1982), p. 132.

83. Kevin Leinnger, "City Lost with Hi-tech Three Times," Fort Wayne *News-Sentinel,* 15 November 1983, 1A & 5A.

CHAPTER 8

1. Sobel, *I. T.T.,* pp. 140–41.

2. "Farnsworth to IT&T," *Newsweek,* 21 February 1949, 33: 8, p. 66.

3. Farnsworth, *Distant Vision,* p. 261.

4. "Ex-President of Farnsworth Dies," Fort Wayne *Journal Gazette,* 91 (28 January 1953), pp. 1–2.

5. See Farnsworth-Everson Papers, Box 1, File 8, and George Everson biography, Box 2, File 2. Everson served on the advisory board from 1949 to 1954.

6. "Production to Be Expanded," Fort Wayne newspaper clipping, 5 May 1949, Farnsworth Papers, Box 27, File 4.

7. The American divisions of ITT included the Federal Telephone and Radio Company, the Federal Telecommunications Laboratories, Capehart-Farnsworth, the Kellogg Switchboard and Supply Company and the Coolerator Company. Capehart-Farnsworth was considered a wholly owned subsidiary until July 1953 when it was merged, along with four other companies, "at which time . . . [it] became a division of IT&T." The other subsidiaries were the Coolerator Company (it manufactured refrigerators and air conditioners); the Federal Telecommunications Laboratories, Inc., the Federal Telephone and Radio Corporation (both manufacturing telephone, telegraph, and radio equipment); and the Kellogg Switchboard and Supply Company (manufacturing telephone equipment); see "IT&T Merger Authorized," *New York Times,* 11 July 1953, 19: 8. See also "Historical Data & Background: Farnsworth Electronics," rough

historical draft prepared for ITT lab brochure, May 16, 1958, ITT Library Papers, Historical File. For descriptions see also Farnsworth-Everson Papers, Box 1, Files 7 and 8.

8. "Historical Data & Background: Farnsworth Electronics," p. 3, ITT Library Papers, Historical File.

9. Sobel, *I.T.T.,* pp. 136–43. Television was but one of the "consumer durables," manufactured by ITT at this time. Also see pp. 141, 160–61 ,164, and 185.

10. Kevin Leininger, "City Lost with Hi-tech Three Times," Fort Wayne *News-Sentinel,* 15 November 1983, 5A, Allen County Public Library.

11. Anthony Sampson, *The Sovereign State of ITT* (New York: Stein and Day Publishers, 1973), p. 49. Sampson here also references the "Colderator" Company. He likely means Coolerator as referred to in other publications—it manufactured refrigerators, air conditioners, vacuums, and floor polishers.

12. Even with this, the third time under the Capehart name that people had tried and failed to manufacture high-end sets, there was still value in the Capehart name and reputation. This is apparently why it took two years from the split to the sale, since ITT was holding out for a better price. See Sobel, *I.T.T.,* p. 47.

13. See Letter from W. H. Harrison to George Everson, August 4, 1954, Godfrey Papers, Box 9, File 10.

14. *IT&T Newsletter,* 11: 10, May 15, 1956. Farnsworth Papers, Box 13, File 3.

15. This period would also include the federal subdivisions of ITT Laboratories when Farnsworth worked as a technical consultant for the general ITT system from 1958 to 1959; then Farnsworth Research was formed in 1959 and reorganized in 1962. Here Farnsworth remained until 1967. See "Career Data," Farnsworth-Everson Papers, Box 6, File 2.

16. Letter from W. H. Harrison, president of ITT, to George Everson, August 4, 1954, Farnsworth-Everson Papers, Box 2, File 4.

17. Agreement between Philo T. Farnsworth and Capehart-Farnsworth Corporation. May 4, 1951, Farnsworth Papers, Box 13, File 1.

18. "Inventor's Dream Leads to Plant," Fort Wayne *News-Sentinel,* 1958, Allen County Public Library.

19. Letter from George Everson to Philo T. Farnsworth, August 16, 1954, Farnsworth-Everson Papers, Box 2, File 1.

20. Letter from H. L. Hull, president, Farnsworth Electronics Company, to George Everson, December 16, 1954, Farnsworth-Everson Papers, Box 2, File 1.

21. Letter from C. A. McNeil to George Everson, January 6, 1955, Farnsworth-Everson Papers, Box 2, File 1.

22. House Memorandum from H. L. Hull to George Everson, April 19, 1955, Farnsworth-Everson Papers, Box 2, File 1.

23. Farnsworth, *Distant Vision,* p. 276.

24. Letter from H. H. Butner, vice president, ITT, to George Everson, October 4, 1955, Farnsworth-Everson Papers, Box 2, File 1.

25. "Drive on to Sell Industrial Video," *New York Times,* 30 November 1954, 41: 1.

26. "Capehart Gets U.S. Contract," *New York Times,* 19 July 1952, 23: 5. See also Farnsworth, *Distant Vision,* p. 261.

27. "Utah-Born Inventor of T-V Has New Reception Device," *Deseret News*, 16 November 1950; see Journal History of the church, CR 100/137, Reel #205. Farnsworth's

personal reference here to the different systems of color refers to the postwar debate over color standards and which system would be adopted for commercial use. It was the RCA standard that would finally be adopted in 1953; see Sterling and Kittross, *Stay Tuned,* pp. 296–98.

28. "Farnsworth Here: Declares Color TV Field Open," 15 September 1950, unidentified newspaper clipping, San Francisco Public Library Vertical Files. See also Terrance O'Flaherty, "Radio and TV: Inventor Farnsworth Back in S.F." The San Francisco *Chronicle,* 15 September 1950, Farnsworth-Meeks Papers.

29. "New Memory Tube to Clear TV Reception," San Francisco *Call-Bulletin,* 18 September 1950, San Francisco Public Library Vertical Files.

30. "Farnsworth 3-Dimensional Industrial T-V," *Farnsworth News* 3:1 (January 1957), p. 4, ITT Library Papers, Company News archival file.

31. "Father of TV, Utah Native, Sees 3D Video," Salt Lake *Tribune,* 30 June 1953, Journal History, CR 100/137, Reel no. 210. See "Father of TV Honored at Dinner in S.L." The Deseret *News-Telegram,* 1 July 1953; "Genius of the Airwaves," Deseret *News-Telegram* editorial, 1 July 1953; and "Utah's Own Genius—Father of Television," Salt Lake *Tribune,* editorial, 2 July 1953, Journal History, CR 100/137, Reel no. 210. This local press flurry was a result of Farnsworth's being honored by the Utah Broadcast Association. Speakers at the luncheon included Harold Fellows, president of the National Association of Broadcasters; Arch M. Madsen, president of the Utah Broadcast Association; and Earl J. Glade, Utah broadcast pioneer.

32. "Historical Data and Background: Farnsworth Electronics Company," pp. 4–6, ITT Library Papers, Historical Files.

33. "Inventor of TV Stumps Panel on Quiz Show," Fort Wayne *Journal Gazette,* 4 July 1957, Godfrey Papers, Box 12, File 2. "Dr. 'X' on Major TV Show," *Farnsworth News,* special edition, 11 July 1957, archival newsletter, ITT Library Papers, p. 2. See Farnsworth, *Distant Vision,* p. 263. Portions of this program were used in the 1997 documentary, "Big Dream, Small Screen: The Story Behind Television." A copy of the program itself is in the Godfrey Papers. The title "doctor" refers to Farnsworth's honorary doctorates bestowed upon him by the Indiana Technical Institute and Brigham Young University.

34. "Welcome to 'I've Got A Secret,'" Mimeographed directions given to guests of the program, Godfrey Papers, Box 9, File 12.

35. P. T. Farnsworth and F. R. Furth, "Controlled Nuclear Fusion Using Inertial Gas Confinement," December 22, 1966, unidentified papers, Godfrey Papers, Box 11, File 4, p. 1.

36. Farnsworth and Furth, p. 1.

37. Robert L. Hirsch, "Inertial-Electrostatic Confinement of Ionized Fusion Gases," *Journal of Applied Physics,* 38: 11 (October 1967), 4,522. This article contains information relating to key Farnsworth fusion patents. Hirsch indicates that this is the "one published paper on the IT&T fusion projects." Hirsch writes in a handwritten marginal note on the paper that reads, "P. T. F. did his publishing in the Patent Office."

38. W. J. Williams, "From Capehart to Farnsworth to ITT," ITT bicentennial presentation, March 18, 1994, p. 3, ITT Library Papers, Historical Files.

39. Gene Smith, "IT&T Voices Hopes on H-Bomb Power," *New York Times,* 4 January 1961, 10: 6.

40. "The Phone Company vs. the H-Bomb," San Francisco *Chronicle,* 4 January 1961, Godfrey Papers, Box 12, File 7, pp. 1 and 8.

41. Smith, "IT&T Voices Hopes," 1: 1 and 10: 6. "Fission" is an error. It was "fusion."

42. Ibid., 10: 6.

43. Hirsch, "Inertial-Electrostatic Confinement," p. 4,522. There were no data as to ITT's total investment on fusion, at this writing.

44. Smith, "IT&T Voices Hopes," 10: 6.

45. Because of the Cold War the idea of moving to New York was abandoned. However, a formal proposal was solicited from the Bechtel Corporation. They estimated the costs for such a move to be more than a million dollars. See letter from A. T. Krook, vice president Bechtel Corporation to Admiral F. R. Furth, vice president, International Telephone and Telegraph Corporation, October 26, 1962. The proposal to move accompanies this letter. See Godfrey Papers, Box 11, File 1.

46. Agreement between the Farnsworth Research Corporation and Dr. Philo T. Farnsworth, July 17, 1962, p. 3, Farnsworth Papers, Box 13, File 8. See Pem Farnsworth's notes on the contract in Farnsworth, *Distant Vision,* p. 290.

47. Agreement between the Farnsworth Research Corporation and Dr. Philo T. Farnsworth, pp. 4–7.

48. Research notes, n.d., circa 1960, Farnsworth Papers, Box 41, File 7. This note just appears among a lot of mathematical tabulations within the log book.

49. See Record+Inventory, Miniature Account Book, p. 55, Godfrey Papers, Box 4, File 1.

50. Philo T. Farnsworth, "Peace-Time Uses of Fusion Energy—As I See It," unpublished manuscript, Godfrey Papers, Box 11, File 4. See also Farnsworth Papers, Box 42, File 5.

51. Research notes, n.d., circa February 1962, Farnsworth Papers, Box 45, File 3.

52. Player Papers, p. 48.

53. Ibid., p. 50.

54. See letters from Elma G. Farnsworth to Laura Player, February 6, 1963; January 1964, Player Papers, p. 64. Also Farnsworth, *Distant Vision,* p. 297.

55. Farnsworth, *Distant Vision,* pp. 305–06.

56. "Examiner," Business Section, 5 December 1965, quoted in Player Papers, pp. 64–65. See also Farnsworth, *Distant Vision,* pp. 306–07.

57. Agnes and Claude Lindsay and Laura Player, oral history interview, Farnsworth Papers. See also Farnsworth, *Distant Vision,* pp. 311–12.

58. Letter from Philo T. Farnsworth to Harold S. Geneen, May 11, 1967, Farnsworth Papers, Box 23, File 3.

59. See note from R. L. Hirsch to Dr. R. T. Watson, September 1967, Godfrey Papers, Box 3, File 1.

60. Agreement between Farnsworth Research Corporation and Dr. Philo T. Farnsworth, July 17, 1962, pp. 5–6, Farnsworth Papers, Box 12, File 8.

61. Letter to Philo T. Farnsworth from Albert E. Cookson, September 5, 1967, Farnsworth Papers, Box 23, File 3.

62. Notes regarding September 12, 1967, phone call surrounding the Cookson letter to Farnsworth, September 5, 1967, Farnsworth Papers, Box 23, File 3.

63. "Career Data," Farnsworth-Everson Papers, Box 2, File 2.

64. Farnsworth's first honorary doctorate was from Indiana Technical College, 1952. The Brigham Young University award was in 1968. The documentary produced by Ted Capener and Bruce Christensen is in the possession of the Farnsworth family. Donald G. Godfrey interview with Ted Capener, 1998.

65. Farnsworth, *Distant Vision,* pp. 319–20.

66. Proposed prospectus, Philo T. Farnsworth and Associates, Godfrey Papers, Box 17, File 1, p. 4.

67. "The History of PTF Associates Inc.," Farnsworth Papers, Box 17, File 5. See also letters from L. W. Sahley to PTF Associates, February 20, 1969, Farnsworth Papers, Box 18, File 3.

68. Proposed prospectus, p. 6.

69. Engineers coming from Fort Wayne included George Bain, Kenneth R. Crowe, Gene Meeks, Ramon M. Bart, Cornelius Hart, Earl B. Keiser, Harold L. Heastan, and Edythe C. Heastan. See "Present Status and Prospects," Philo T. Farnsworth Associates, Inc., December 2, 1969, Godfrey Papers, Box 11, File 6.

70. "Investments in P. T. F. A.," Farnsworth Papers, Box 18, File 5. See also Godfrey Papers, Box 11, File 6.

71. See correspondence with Midwestern Securities Corporation, Farnsworth Papers, Box 23, File 6.

72. See for example the open letter from Philo T. Farnsworth to creditors. See Farnsworth Papers, Box 23, File 7.

73. "Present Status and Prospects," pp. 6–8.

74. Letter from Philo T. Farnsworth to Harold S. Geneen, president of ITT, December 17, 1968, Farnsworth Papers, Box 23, File 5.

75. Letter from Jack H. Vollbrecht, vice president of ITT, January 9, 1969, Farnsworth Papers, Box 23, File 5.

76. There are two spellings of this name in the Farnsworth papers, Buscines and Busignies—the latter is correct. Henri Busignies appears to have a good knowledge of Farnsworth's work at ITT. He was one of the scientists at ITT, New York who had worked on frequency modulation and opened early radio sales. In 1961 Busignies was ITT vice president and general technical director and one of ITT's "most important scientists." See Sobel, *I.T.T.,* pp. 103, 106, 121, and 183–85. "Notes on Call from Dr. Buscines [sic]," January 21, 1969, Farnsworth Papers, Box 23, File 5; the conversation appears to have been explanatory and cordial.

77. Ibid.

78. Letter from Philo T. Farnsworth to Harold S. Geneen, February 17, 1969, Farnsworth Papers, Box 23, File 5

79. Addenda, Letter from Philo T. Farnsworth to Harold S. Geneen, February 17, 1969, Farnsworth Papers, Box 23, File 5, p. 1.

80. Letter from Howard J. Aibel, vice president and general counsel, ITT, February 28, 1969, Farnsworth Papers, Box 23, File 5.

81. Letter from Philo T. Farnsworth to Cornell Remsen, ITT general patent counsel, June 6, 1969, Godfrey Papers, Box 11, File 6.

82. Letter from C. Cornell Remsen to Philo T. Farnsworth, November 3, 1969, Godfrey Papers, Box 11, File 6.

83. Letter from James Beisel, adjuster for the Travelers Insurance Company, May 19, 1969, Farnsworth Papers, Box 23, File 6.

84. Letter to Harold S. Geneen, ITT president, from Philo T. Farnsworth, February 17, 1969, Farnsworth Papers, Box 23, File 5.

85. Letter from Kenneth E. Dore, M.D., to the law firm of Besslin, Nygaard, Coke and Vincent, October 16, 1969, Godfrey Papers, Box 13, File 4. A copy of this letter was sent to Mr. John R. Anderson, Farnsworth's Salt Lake attorney. His father, Dr. Reese H. Anderson, was Farnsworth's Salt Lake physician (and brother-in-law), Elma G. Farnsworth's sister's husband. Marginal notes to "Pem & Phil" indicated a close relationship to the family.

86. Marginal notes to "Pem & Phil" on copy of letter from Kenneth E. Dore, M.D., to Besslin, Nygaard, Coke, and Vincent, October, 16, 1969, Godfrey Papers, Box 13, File 4.

87. "'Father' of Television, Philo Farnsworth, Dies," Los Angeles *Times,* 13 March 1971. "The Father of TV," Salt Lake City, *Deseret News,* 13 March 1971 Godfrey Papers, Box 12, File 7, p. 8A. "Philo T. Farnsworth Dies; Transmitted 1st TV Picture," Philadelphia *Evening Bulletin,* 13 March 1971, p. 10B.

CHAPTER 9

1. See Farnsworth Papers, Box 2, Files 2 and 3. The first was from Indiana Technical College, 1951, and the second from Brigham Young University, 1968.

2. "Phil's Teachings," handwritten note in an addendum of papers of Elma G. Farnsworth, Farnsworth Papers, Box 76, Files 5–7.

3. In 1998, a small Farnsworth museum was organized at ITT Industries, Cook Road, Fort Wayne, Indiana. The name Farnsworth appears throughout the business history of the city.

4. See Appendix A for a complete list of U.S. patents filed under Farnsworth's name. See also "Farnsworth," *National Inventors Hall of Fame* (Washington, D.C.: U.S. Department of Commerce, 1984), pp. 61–62. This pamphlet reports "over 300 U.S. and foreign patents." The number of Farnsworth's patents varies with differing lists, the variance likely due to how the patents were registered and who was compiling the list. For example, early Farnsworth television patents were listed under the names of Philo T. Farnsworth, Television Laboratories Inc., and the Farnsworth Television and Farnsworth Television and Radio Corporation. Later fusion patents were registered with ITT. Foreign patents for Farnsworth's work were also registered in Britain and Germany as well as other countries. See differing lists in Godfrey Papers, Box 13, File 7. Also, Allen County–Fort Wayne Historical Society, Farnsworth Papers.

5. "Philo T. Farnsworth, Inventor and Humanitarian," Unidentified typewritten page. Likely authored by Elma G. Farnsworth. See Godfrey Papers, Box 13, File 3.

6. "The Story of Television," RCA promotional material, National Archives, Broadcast Bureau, Broadcast Facilities Division, Technical and Allocations Board, Box 3, File—Television History.

7. Abramson, *Zworykin,* pp. 1–5.

8. See David Rapaport, "History Lesson," *Broadcasting* 122:2 (January 13, 1992): 108; Abramson letter in "Open Mike," pp. 46–47; and David Rapaport, *"Farnsworth v.*

Zworykin, Cont." *Broadcasting* 122:8 (February 17, 1992): 53. Also, letter to the editors of *Broadcasting* magazine, February 17, 1992, by Elma G. Farnsworth. It appears this letter was never published. The letter, however, was sent and a copy is in the Godfrey Papers, Box 13, File 1, along with the other published letters.

9. Oral history interview conducted with M. Phyllis Smith, editor, Special Projects Public Affairs, Sarnoff Corporation, May 22, 1997, by Donald G. Godfrey. Notes from the interview are in the Godfrey Papers, Box 18, File 9.

10. Abramson, "Pioneers of Television," p. 770.

11. In assessing the lasting importance of these differing patents, James Dove (a local television engineer) and Albert Abramson (engineer and author) were consulted.

12. Correspondence from Albert Abramson to Donald G. Godfrey, July 17, 1998. See patent no. 2,051,372, filed July 14, 1931, and granted August 18, 1936.

13. Correspondence from Albert Abramson to Donald G. Godfrey, July 17, 1998. See patent no. 2,087,683.

14. Jack Williams, "From Capehart to Farnsworth to ITT," audiovisual presentation before the Fort Wayne Engineer's Club bicentennial celebration event: "Engineering in Fort Wayne," March 24, 1994. Videotape presentation in the Godfrey Papers.

15. Commonly called "the Mormon Church," but often abbreviated as the L.D.S. Church.

16. David O. McKay, "Denial of God's Existence," *Conference Report,* October 1969, pp. 135–36.

17. M. Russell Ballard is a member of the Quorum of Twelve Apostles, one of the highest governing bodies within the Church. In this reference "elder" is a general term given senior Church authorities. M. Russell Ballard, "The Effects of Television," *Ensign* 19 (May 1989): 78.

18. The word active in the Church denotes "observing a full religious lifestyle of attendance, devotion, service and learning." Attendance at Sabbath day worship services; the payment of tithes and offerings; the observance of a health code that prohibits alcohol, coffee, tea, and tobacco; honesty; and the adherence to strict moral codes. It connotes continued learning and growth in family, church, and civic service; see Perry H. Cunningham, "Activity in the Church," *Encyclopedia of Mormonism,* vol. 1, ed. Daniel H. Ludlow (New York: Macmillan, 1992), pp. 13–15.

19. Philo T. Farnsworth, "Concerning the Nature of God," manuscript dictated by Farnsworth to Elma G. Farnsworth, February 6, 1966, Godfrey Papers, Box 13, File 2.

20. Oral history interview of Philo T. Farnsworth, conducted by Francis Jones, February 11, 1970. This interview was conducted as a part of a University of Utah graduate course in speech communication taught by Professor Christopher H. Sterling. See Godfrey Papers, Box 13, File 2.

21. Horatio Alger (1832–1899) was an eighteenth-century writer of inspirational success stories. His primary thesis was "rags to riches"—success in life was possible through hard work. The most famous of his stories was *Ragged Dick.* Russell Conwell's "Acres of Diamonds" was a contemporary proponent of the same success ideology.

22. Donald G. Godfrey and Alf Pratte originally coauthored a longer version of this essay on Elma G. Farnsworth. For the complete text see, Godfrey and Pratte, "Elma 'Pem' Gardner Farnsworth."

23. Everson, *Story of Television,* p. 170.

24. Carol McNalley, "The Women Around Us," Fort Wayne *Indiana Journal,* 18 (February 1955), Women's Page, n.p.

25. Everson, *Story of Television,* p. 170.

26. Farnsworth, *Distant Vision,* "A Word from the Author," n.p. Philo T. Farnsworth, speech to Indiana College, circa 1960, transcribed audio recording, Farnsworth-Meeks Papers. Included in the theology of Mormonism is the precept that marriage is an eternal union of the couple. "And they two shall be one," is a direct reference to scripture, see Mark 10:6–10, the *Holy Bible,* King James Translation. See Ludlow, *Encyclopedia of Mormonism,* pp. 855–59.

27. Elma G. Farnsworth, September 1987, p. 3, Farnsworth-Everson Papers.

28. Elma G. Farnsworth, handwritten pages, n.d., Farnsworth Papers, Box 61, File 4.

29. See early logs, Farnsworth Papers. See also Philo T. Farnsworth, *Log Book, III.* Farnsworth-Meeks Papers. For more examples of Pem's drawing, also see Farnsworth, *Distant Vision,* p. 95. In Farnsworth's first journal, it is of his own hand. Leslie Gorrell made the drawings for the first investment briefs.

30. See *Log Book III,* Farnsworth-Meeks Papers. Also Everson, *Story of Television,* p. 53.

31. Elma G. Farnsworth, handwritten pages, n.d., Farnsworth Papers, Box 61, File 4.

32. "Early Television Laboratories Inc. Personnel," lists personnel by name and salary. Farnsworth-Everson Papers.

33. Farnsworth's second son, Kenneth, died at thirteen months (1932). Their third son, Russell, was born in 1935; the fourth son, Kent, was born in 1948. Philo III was married by then, so two children were the most they had home at any one time.

34. The events surrounding the death of Farnsworth's father, son, and brother; his illnesses; and the fire that destroyed their home are detailed within chapters as they occurred chronologically.

35. Elma G. Farnsworth, handwritten pages, n.d., Farnsworth Papers, Box 61, File 4.

36. Correspondence from Elma Farnsworth to George Everson, January 4, 1932, Farnsworth-Everson Papers, Box 1/2. See also Agnes and Claude Lindsay and Laura Player, oral history interview, pp. 41–42, Farnsworth Papers.

37. Farnsworth, *Distant Vision,* p. 214.

38. Ibid.

39. For examples of articles resulting from these interviews see Warbis, "TV Inventor Finally Getting Public's Respect," p. 55; Lovece, *"Zworykin v. Farnsworth,"* pp. 96–98, 135–38; and Lovece, "Is It TV's 50th Birthday or Not?" *Channels* (June 1989): 9.

40. See recent editions of Sydney W. Head and Christopher H. Sterling, *Broadcasting in America: A Survey of Electronic Media,* 6th ed. (Boston: Houghton Mifflin, 1990) and compare with Sydney W. Head, *Broadcasting in America* (Boston: Houghton Mifflin, 1956). Giraurd Chester and Garnet R. Garrison, *Television and Radio* (New York: Appleton–Century–Crofts) also have no reference to Farnsworth in 1950 and 1957 editions. See also Barnouw, *Tube of Plenty.*

41. *Acceptance and Dedication,* p. 58. See Godfrey Papers, Box 13, File 5, for campaign letters surrounding the development of the stamp project.

42. Terrence O'Flaherty, "A Date to Remember," *San Francisco Chronicle,* 7 September 1977, Section TU Today, n.p. See Farnsworth-Meeks Papers.

43. See Godfrey Papers, Box 13, File 6. This fiftieth anniversary file contains press releases and photos.

44. See Godfrey Papers, Box 13, File 7. This file contains programs, press releases, and data on the hall of fame inductions.

45. Philo T. Farnsworth, typewritten manuscript, "The Future of Television," p. 1. This appears to be a speech prepared circa 1950, Godfrey Papers, Box 13, File 3. See also Utah Hall of Fame induction ceremony, July 1999, Godfrey Papers.

46. "Stop! Look!! Listen!" Deseret *News,* editorial, 19 February 1951. Journal History of the Church, CR100/137.

47. Farnsworth, "The Future of Television," p. 1.

48. Ibid., p. 3.

49. Ibid.

50. Farnsworth, handwritten notes in preparation of the manuscript, "The Future of Television," p. 2.

51. Philo T. Farnsworth, "Television and the American Home," p. 1. November 9, 1948. This is an unpublished article written for *House and Garden* magazine. It had a planned publication date of July 1950, but Farnsworth apparently did not follow through with corrections requested. See Godfrey Papers, Box 13, File 3.

52. Farnsworth, "Television and the American Home," pp. 3–4.

53. Homer H. Hickam, Jr., *October Sky: A Memoir* (New York: Random House, 1999). See also Ned Potter, "The Next Generation: Exciting Possibilities of Advanced Rocket Technology," ABC News, July 20, 1999, http://more.abcnews.go.com/onair/dailynews/wnt990720_potter_story.html. Also Linda A. Johnson, "Finding a Future for Fusion," The Associated Press, April 12, 1999. http://more.abcnews.go.com/sections/science/DailyNews/fusion990412.html.

54. Letter from Philo Farnsworth to George Everson, July 8, 1954, Farnsworth Papers, Box 1, File 2.

APPENDIX D

1. Letter to Edwin M. Martin, secretary, Farnsworth Television and Radio, Fort Wayne, from Philo T. Farnsworth, June 19, 1944, Farnsworth Papers, Box 7, File 2.

2. See product brochure, Godfrey Papers, Box 16, File 2.

3. Player Papers, p. 41.

APPENDIX E

1. For background information on Nicholas, see Chapter 6. Martin served in several capacities at Farnsworth from 1939. He headed "the legal, research, patent, public relations, and industrial relations departments." He also served as a member of the board of directors as well as the management team. See the *New York Times,* 24 February 1945, 22: 1, and 29 May 1947, 34: 3–4. Vogal was recruited from RCA and GE in 1939 to head sales and mechanizing. See the *New York Times,* 23 April 1939, X: 10: 7. Rogers came to Farnsworth management in 1939 with experience as treasurer of several corporations—Simmons Hardware Company, the United States Radio and Television Company, and the Crosley Corporation. See the *New York Times,* 9 May 1939, 35: 7. In

1939, Cummings took charge of engineering with "twenty years" of radio and television industry experience. See the *New York Times,* 11 May 1939, 46: 4.

2. "War Time Business," Farnsworth Television and Radio Corporation, Securities and Exchange Commission, p. 5. National Archives, General Correspondence 1927–1946, File 89-6, Box 359, Envelope 6. "Farnsworth: Research, Development, and Manufacturing," corporate brochure, n.d. ITT Library Papers.

3. See "Farnsworth Television and Radio Corporation Prospectus," February 11, 1946, Farnsworth Papers, Box 8, File 4.

4. The Huntington plant was added in 1945. See "Farnsworth Expanding Plant," *New York Times,* 6 October 1945, 20: 1. The Bluffton plant was actually leased to Farnsworth television. The lease expired in 1947, after the war. For a fiscal description of the plants and equipment, see Securities and Exchange Commission, Farnsworth Television and Radio Report filed February 12, 1946, pp. 7–8. National Archives, General Correspondence, 1927–46, Box 359, File 89-6.

5. For a description of such a black-out, see "Seattle Black Out," 7 March 1941, Milo Ryan Phono Archive, reel no. 4281, National Archives, Washington, D.C.

6. "Farnsworth Is the Firm That Developed Radar Jammer: Device Paralyzed Nazi, Jap Aircraft Detecting Equipment." This clipping has *New York Times,* 30 November 1945, handwritten on it. However, it likely comes from the Fort Wayne *News-Sentinel* or the *Journal Gazette.* Clipping was found in the Allen County Public Library.

7. Arthur M. Paulison, "Communications Apparatus," Fort Wayne *News-Sentinel,* 23 December 1944, Allen County Public Library.

8. Ibid.

9. "Farnsworth Net $647,237 in Year," *New York Times,* 13 July 1942, 23: 5.

10. "Output of Electronic Equipment Must Be Stepped Up 40%," *Farnsworth Employees Victory Record,* 2: 6 (September 16, 1943), p. 1, ITT Library Papers.

11. Official presentation of the Army Navy Production Award, Marion, Indiana, March 18, 1943. The program is in the Lippincott Papers. See also "March 18th Is Big Day for Marion Employees," *Farnsworth Employees Victory Record,* 1: 9 (March 4, 1943), p. 1, ITT Library Papers. The program notes Farnsworth's absence on medical leave.

12. "Farnsworth's Net Rises to $1,170,005," *New York Times,* 8 July 1943, 29 :1.

13. "Advertising Is Part of Post-War Plans to Build Future Jobs," *Farnsworth Employee Victory Record,* 3: 1 (January 17, 1944), p. 3, ITT Library Papers.

14. "Farnsworth Expands Budget," *New York Times,* 5 June 1940, 39: 2.

15. E. A. Nicholas, "Memorandum to Management," September 13, 1946, Farnsworth Papers, Box 6, File 7, p. 4.

16. Italics in the original. Advertisement draft, "Television by Bombardment," appearing in *Newsweek,* 15 November 1943, and *Collier's,* 27 November 1943. Slick drafts of these and other advertisements are in the ITT Library Papers.

17. "Farnsworth Television and Radio Reports 1943–44 a Record Year," *New York Times,* 21 July 1944, 24: 5 and 27: 1. See Letter to Baldwin B. Bane, Securities and Exchange Commission, Corporate Finance Division, from T. J. Slowie, Secretary of the FCC, February 11, 1946, National Archives, General Correspondence, 1927–1946, Box 359, File 89-6, Farnsworth Television and Radio Corporation from June 14, 1935, to December 31, 1946.

18. Annual Financial Report, 1945, Farnsworth Television and Radio Corporation, Station WGL, National Archives, Financial Reports of Broadcast Stations, Location 550, 18: 13: 2, Box 145, p. 2. Note: FCC regulations limited the number of stations a corporate licensee could own within a single community. As Westinghouse was the licensee of both WGL and WOWO in Fort Wayne, the smaller operation, WGL was up for sale. WOWO and WGL were licensed to Westinghouse in 1925 and 1936, respectively. Both operated from the same facility. WOWO was a 10 kW station, sharing time at night, operating at 1160 kHz on the dial. It was affiliated with NBC and Mutual networks. WGL was a 0.25 kW station, operating unlimited time, at 1370 kHz on the dial. It was affiliated with NBC. See Annual Financial Report, Westinghouse Radio Stations Inc., 1940, National Archives, Financial Reports of Broadcast Stations, Location 550, 18: 13: 2, Box 145, pp. 2–3.

19. "Vice President Cummings Predicts Great Future for Television Industry," *Farnsworth Employee Victory Record,* 3: 3 (May 5, 1944), pp. 3, 8, ITT Library Papers.

20. "Nicholas Outlines Position in Post War Television Picture," *Farnsworth Employee Victory Record,* 3: 9 (September 20, 1944), p. 2, ITT Library Papers.

21. "Head Up New Broadcast Division," *Farnsworth Employee Victory Record,* 4: 1 (January 1, 1945), p. 2, ITT Library Papers. When he took over, WGL-AM had nineteen employees, by the end of the year, fifteen staff members had been added. WGL-AM's reported net income for its first year as a Farnsworth station was more than $40,000. Annual financial report, 1945, Farnsworth Television and Radio Corporation, WGL-AM, pp. 10, 17.

22. D. D. Seely, "Historical Data & Background: Farnsworth Electronic Company," May 16, 1958, ITT Library Papers, Historical File.

23. Letter from Senator Homer E. Capehart to Paul Porter, FCC chairman, June 30, 1946, National Archives, FCC Docket Section, Box 2331, Docket No. 6796, Farnsworth Radio and Television. The letter urged progress on WGL's request for increased power. Capehart was elected to the Senate in November 1945. See Pickett, *Homer E. Capehart,* pp. 93–95. This is the same Capehart who had started the Capehart Corporation of the early 1930s.

24. The station still exists. It is owned by Kovas Communication, has a news-talk format and operates at same dial position and power—1250 kHz with a power of 1 kW. It is considered a class B, region 2 license.

25. "Engineering Statement Concerning the Application of the Farnsworth Television and Radio Corp. to Improve the Facilities of Station WGL," Fort Wayne, Indiana, October 5, 1945, A. D. Ring, Consulting Engineer. See WGL Files at the Federal Communications Commission. Note: These files are primarily technical in nature and were obtained from the FCC through the offices of Senator John McCain, Arizona. Copies of the actual documents have been placed in the Godfrey Papers, Box 18, File 4.

26. National Archives, FCC Docket Section, Box 2321, Docket No. 6796, p. 22 and exhibit A.

27. "Television Bringing the World to Your Home," Farnsworth Television and Radio Corporation booklet produced to communicate in common language "The Story of Electronic Television—How It Works—What It Means to You," pp. 1, 23, circa 1946, ITT Library Papers.

28. "Farnsworth Television and Radio Files for 219,571 Common," *New York Times,* 22 January 1946, 32: 6.

29. Letter from T. J. Slowie, Secretary of the FCC to Farnsworth Television and Radio Corporation, October 26, 1945, Farnsworth Television and Radio Corporation from June 14, 1935, to December 31, 1946, National Archives, General Correspondence, 1927–1946, Box 359, File 89–6.

30. In granting the license of W9XFT, see correspondence from T. J. Slowie, Secretary of the FCC, April 3, 1946; June 26, 1946; November 20, 1946; and November 26, 1946; National Archives, General Correspondence, 1927–1946, Box 359, File 89–6, Farnsworth Television & Radio Corporation from June 14, 1935, to December 31, 1946. These applications were a part of hundreds filed with the FCC as the war was ending. See Sterling and Kittross, *Stay Tuned,* p. 228. See also *The 1946 American Television Directory* (New York: American Television Society, 1946), pp. 86–87. The directory is in the Thomas T. Goldsmith Papers, Library of Congress, Box 113, File–A History of TV 1930–1947.

31. Ernest E. Williams, "Industrial Fort Wayne, no. 3 in a Series: The Farnsworth Television and Radio Corporation," Fort Wayne *News-Sentinel,* 13 December 1947, Allen County Public Library.

32. "Farnsworth Announced Television Plans," Fort Wayne *News-Sentinel,* 11 June 1946, Allen County Public Library.

33. Farnsworth Television and Radio Corporation, Securities and Exchange Commission, p. 5, National Archives, General Correspondence, 1927–1946, File 89–6, Box 359, Envelope 6.

34. In order to get a more accurate picture of the Farnsworth corporation's profit and loss, the "net" is the figure sought from most of the sources cited in this section. It should be noted that even these reported "nets" were not always consistent—this was not due to fraudulent accounting, but rather portrayed the detail and different growth pictures to assorted audiences. Where there were significant differences they have been noted; however, for the most part the figures could all be calculated and recalculated to reflect the "net" reported in the *New York Times.* It is the figure reported herein as most accurately reflecting the corporate financial pictures.

35. "Farnsworth Television and Radio," *New York Times,* 21 August 1941, 21: 5.

36. "Farnsworth Net $647,237 in Year," *New York Times,* 13 July 1942, 23: 5.

37. "Farnsworth Gets Loan," *New York Times,* 15 July 1942, 28: 2.

38. See "Letter to Stockholders from E. A. Nicholas, December 6, 1943." Here he provided a six-month report and gross figures for the previous year, Farnsworth Papers, Box 8, File 3. Note the differences in the gross figure reported here versus the gross reported in the 1946 Securities and Exchange Commission report in the table.

39. See "Stock Exchange Notes," *New York Times,* 24 September 1943, 37: 1; and 29 October 1943, 30: 6.

40. "Stock Trading Sought," *New York Times,* 11 January 1944, 26: 8.

41. "Transactions on the New York Stock Exchange," *New York Times,* 30 October 1943, 22: 5.

42. Now that Farnsworth corporate stock was being traded publicly, the Securities and Exchange Commission required quarterly financial reports be published.

43. "Farnsworth Net Declines Sharply," *New York Times,* 15 December 1943, 39: 1.

44. Ibid.

45. See "Farnsworth Stock Sold," *New York Times,* 16 April 1944, 31: 8. He was allocated 5,000 shares in 1939 agreements. See "Registration Statement," Farnsworth Television and Radio Corporation, Registration no. 2–3939, p. 10.

46. "Transactions on the New York Stock Exchange," *New York Times,* 30 May 1944, 27: 4. See Appendix G.

47. "Farnsworth Television and Radio Corporation," *New York Times,* 3 March 1944, 25: 2.

48. "Farnsworth Television and Radio Reports 1943–44 a Record Year," *New York Times,* 21 July 1944, 24: 5.

49. Minutes of the Farnsworth Television and Radio Corporation, Board of Directors Meeting, November 28, 1944, Farnsworth Papers, Box 7, File 2.

50. Annual report, Farnsworth Television and Radio Corporation, April 30, 1945, Farnsworth Papers, Box 8, File 3.

51. "Farnsworth Television and Radio Corporation," *New York Times,* 25 July 1946, 31: 2.

52. E. A. Nicholas, "Memorandum RE: Shortage of Cabinet Supplies," September 20, 1946, Farnsworth Papers, Box 7, File 2.

53. Minutes of the board of directors meeting, Farnsworth Television and Radio Corporation, September 20, 1946, Farnsworth Papers, Box 7, File 2. Purchase of Thomasville of North Carolina was proposed for $575,000. The purchase was not approved until the January 22, 1947, meeting along with a $200,000 loan authorized to make the purchase.

54. Securities and Exchange Commission, Farnsworth Television and Radio Corporation report, filed February 12, 1946, National Archives, General Correspondence 1927–47, Box 359, File 89–6, p. 5.

55. E. A. Nicholas, memorandum to management, September 13, 1946, p. 1.

56. Minutes of the board of directors meeting, Farnsworth Television and Radio Corporation, January 22, 1947, Farnsworth Papers, Box 7, File 2.

57. Despite these cuts, a corporate memorandum indicated a continuing and aggressive advertising campaign.

58. E. A. Nicholas, memorandum to management, September 13, 1946, pp. 8–9.

59. Annual Financial Report, Networks and Licensees of Broadcast Stations, WGL-AM, December 31, 1946, National Archives, Location 550, 18: 13: 2, Box 145, p. 10. Net loss for the station was $9,279.

60. "Farnsworth Forms Subsidiary," *New York Times,* 4 October 1947, 29: 8.

61. Farnsworth Television and Radio Corporation, *New York Times,* 16 December 1946, 39: 4.

62. Annual Financial Report, Networks and Licensees of Broadcast Stations, WGL-AM, December 31, 1946, National Archives, Location 550, 18: 13: 2, Box 145, p. 10 and schedule 7.

63. Minutes of the board meeting, Farnsworth Radio and Television Corporation, October 8, 1947, Farnsworth Papers, Box 7, File 5.

64. Ibid.

65. Minutes of the board meeting, Farnsworth Radio and Television Corporation, "A Special Meeting of the Board," October 17, 1947, Farnsworth Papers, Box 7, File 5.

66. Minutes of the board meeting, Farnsworth Television and Radio Corporation, October 22, 1947, Farnsworth Papers, Box 7, File 5.

67. Minutes of the board meeting, Farnsworth Television and Radio Corporation, "Special Meeting of the Board," April 22, 1948, Farnsworth Papers, Box 7, File 5.

68. "RCA Buys Farnsworth Plant," *New York Times,* 18 December 1948. See also Bucher, part IV, chapter LXXV, pp. 2,340–341.

69. "Two Way Radio for Rail Usage Hailed after Switch Yard Test," *Dallas Morning News,* 13 November 1946, clipping found in National Archives, General Correspondence, 1927–1946, Box 359, File 89-6, Farnsworth Television and Radio Corporation from June 14, 1935, to December 1936.

70. "Railway Test Successful: Farnsworth Communications System Is Demonstrated," Fort Wayne *Journal Gazette,* 24 February 1946, Allen County Public Library.

71. Ibid. See also Press Release, Detroit, Toledo, and Ironton Radio Company, n.d., National Archives, General Correspondence, 1927–1946, Box 359, File 89–6, Farnsworth Television and Radio Corporation from June 14, 1935, to December 31, 1946.

72. The Hell Gate Power Generating Station was located in the Bronx. The station has long since been decommissioned and demolished. The property is vacant and belongs to Consolidated Edison. It is bounded by 132nd Street on the south, 134th Street on the north, the East River on the east, and Locust Avenue on the west. See correspondence from Joe Petta, Consolidated Edison's Media Relations Group, to Donald G. Godfrey, January 7, 1999, Godfrey Papers. "Farnsworth Utiliscope Marks Industrial Television's Debut," Fort Wayne *News-Sentinel,* 7 January 1947, Allen County Public Library.

73. "Farnsworth Expands Research, Manufacturing Plant Facilities," Fort Wayne *News-Sentinel,* 5 March 1947, Allen County Public Library.

74. George Ryder, "Master Diorama! Double Talk? Nope, Means Television's Here;" also "Here's How Television Really Looks," Fort Wayne *News-Sentinel,* 19 April 1947, Allen County Public Library.

75. Correspondence between the Farnsworth Television and Radio Corporation and the Federal Communications Commission clearly indicates movement toward continued research and development in specialized equipment, mobile land communication, railway communication, and various transmitters. See National Archives, General Correspondence, Box 109, Farnsworth Television and Radio File, Correspondence with the FCC from January 1, 1947, through December 31, 1956.

76. "Television Sets Displayed in San Francisco," San Francisco *Chronicle,* 26 August 1947, unidentified clipping, San Francisco Public Library Vertical Files.

77. "Video Set Shown by Farnsworth," *New York Times,* 3 September 1947, 37: 2 and 32: 4.

78. Ibid., 37: 2.

79. Ibid., 32: 4.

80. Ibid., 37: 2.

81. See Sterling and Kittross, *Stay Tuned,* p. 294.

82. There is some historical folklore asserting that the Farnsworth corporation never manufactured televisions. A part of this accusation is due to ignorance. The Capehart name at this point belonged to the Farnsworth corporation. The Capehart television

sets were manufactured by the Farnsworth Television and Radio Corporation. The models called Capehart were the more expensive in the line and received the most attention. On the few Farnsworth television sets left in existence you will see Capehart as the trademark name.

83. "Video Sets Seen Headed Upward," *New York Times,* 17 August 1948, 35: 1.

84. Sterling and Kittross, *Stay Tuned,* pp. 290–92.

85. For figures on "Television Receiver Ownership," see Sterling and Kittross, *Stay Tuned,* p. 657.

86. Ibid., p. 254.

87. Ibid., pp. 294–96, 657–58.

88. Ibid., pp. 632–33.

APPENDIX F

1. Sobel, *I.T.T.,* p. 131.

2. Ibid., p. 132. Sobel goes on to describe Farnsworth as uninterested in business and, "almost no talent in the boardroom." Sobel insinuates that Farnsworth's management skills were partly responsible for the economic state of the corporation. In this inference he's obviously unfamiliar with Farnsworth's limited involvement in the management of the company that bore his name. Nicholas was the president of Farnsworth Television and Radio during the war and in the postwar years. Farnsworth himself was ill, living in Maine, and, as discussed previously, making his contributions from a small lab in Fryeburg, Maine.

3. Ibid., p. 131.

4. Sampson, *Sovereign State of ITT,* p. 69.

5. Ibid. See also Sobel, *I.T.T.,* pp. 151–55.

6. "IT&T Man Heads Farnsworth Corporation," New York *Times,* 7 May 1949, 20: 7. For a brief background on Stone, see Sampson, *Sovereign State of ITT,* pp. 61–66. Stone resigned to accept a position as president of the American Cable and Radio Corporation and Wilson was brought in at that time. See "IT&T to Receive $500,000 in Capehart-Farnsworth Dividend," *New York Times,* 7 December 1950, 53: 4.

7. "North America," ITT Information Department, 11: 2 (January 13, 1956), Godfrey Papers, Box 14, File 3, p. 1.

8. At Hull's resignation he served as president of Lipton Industries from 1956 to 1957 and formed Hull Associates in 1957. See obituary by Kean Heine, "Harvard L. Hull, 81 Scientist and Inventor," *Chicago Tribune,* sec. 1, 6 October 1968, p. 8.

9. "New President of Farnsworth Receives Enthusiastic Welcome," *Farnsworth News,* November 1956, p. 3, Godfrey Papers, Box 14, File, 4.

10. Ibid.

APPENDIX G

1. "New Television Sets," *New York Times,* 30 January 1950, 28: 3. See also "Air Force Buildings Leased," *New York Times,* 25 January 1950, 39: 3.

2. "Capehart Reports $3,000,000 Orders," *New York Times,* 24 August 1950, 38: 1. See also "IT&T to Receive $500,000 in Capehart-Farnsworth Dividend," *New York Times,* 7 December 1950, 53: 4.

3. Brochures, the Capehart Warranty, and a price list for 1950 can be found in the Farnsworth–Allen County Papers, Box 2. The Capehart, Service Bulletin, VII: 112, October 15, 1950, p. 1, claims these two films were "the first motion pictures of this type produced." It is an interesting note on nonbroadcast training film production history.

4. "TV Receiver Sent to Tokyo," *New York Times,* 29 May 1951, 33: 6.

5. Fred D. Wilson, "Philo Farnsworth Got Idea for Television When 15," Camden, New Jersey, *Courier-Post,* 4 June 1952. Unidentified newspaper clipping, The *Philadelphia Inquirer,* library. Note: this article was written under the author credits of Wilson, who was the president of Capehart-Farnsworth at the time of authorship. Obviously, this was a reprinted press release. The narrative link between Farnsworth's youthful experiences and the quality of Capehart television sets is awkward and stretched. An interesting footnote to this article appears in the last paragraph, subtitled, "Set Still Okay." "One of the First Television receivers placed on the market in 1939 is still operating and giving good picture quality. This set is located in the New Jersey residence of Dr. Thomas T. Goldsmith Jr."

6. "TV Sets Cut $20 to $40," *New York Times,* 5 August 1952, 34: 1. The average cost of a black-and-white television receiver was quoted at $138 by Sterling and Kittross, *Stay Tuned,* p. 657.

7. "Minutes of Management Advisory Board, Capehart-Farnsworth Company, January 21, 1954, Farnsworth-Everson Papers, Box 2, File 1.

8. "Minutes of Management Advisory Board," Capehart-Farnsworth Company, March 3, 1954, Farnsworth-Everson Papers, Box 2, File 1.

APPENDIX H

1. Letter from H. L. Hull, president of Farnsworth Electronics, to George Everson, June 6, 1956, Godfrey Papers, Box 9, File 10.

2. Historical data and background, Farnsworth Electronics, p. 3. May 16, 1958, ITT Library Papers, Historical File.

3. Untitled manuscript from the Capehart & Farnsworth Chronology File, p. 4, ITT Library Papers. This is a seven-page paper outlining the history of Farnsworth Electronics. Page numbers are handwritten in the bottom right-hand corner.

4. "New President of Farnsworth Receives Enthusiastic Welcome, *Farnsworth News* 2: 5 (November 1956), p. 3, ITT Library Papers, Company newsletter archival file.

5. Historical data and background, p. 3, ITT Library Papers.

6. Ernest E. Williams, "Farnsworth Plans $3 Million Plant on Camp Scott Site; Its Fourth Here," Fort Wayne *News-Sentinel,* 11 July 1957, p. 1, Allen County Public Library.

7. Bill Disbro, "City Shares in Farnsworth Success Story," Fort Wayne *Journal-Gazette,* 14 July 1957, Allen County Public Library.

8. Farnsworth, *Distant Vision,* p. 262.

9. Henry P. Steier, "Bomarc Guidance Spawns New Testing Techniques," *American Aviation,* 21:16 (December 12, 1957), p. 32. See also "Farnsworth Supplied More Equipment for Bomarc Missile," *The International Review of International Telephone and Telegraph Corporation,* 12: 1 (May 1957), p. 27, Godfrey Papers, Box 14, File 9.

10. Sobel, *I.T.T.,* pp. 158–61. Also Sampson, *Sovereign State of ITT,* p. 69.

11. Sobel, *I.T.T.,* p. 161. Sampson, *Sovereign State of ITT,* p. 69.

12. "Reorganization Plan Announced by IT&T," *Farnsworth News* 3: 2 (February 1957), p. 2, ITT Library Papers, archival newsletter. Note to the reader: the citation data in these newsletters are not always consistent. Volume and number information appears sporadically and is cited when available.

13. "Farnsworth Purchases Camp Scott Property," *Farnsworth News* (March 1957), p. 2, ITT Library Papers, archival newsletter.

14. "President's Message," *Farnsworth News* (Spec. ed., July 11, 1957), pp. 8–10, ITT Library Papers, archival newsletter. Reports on the numbers of employees vary widely from 1954 to 1958. The lowest cited is 1,400; most vary to 2,000. The Haggerty report cited is likely to be the most accurate and is pinpointed in time and corporate growth.

15. General Edmond H. Leavey, "From the IT&T Ink-Well," *Farnsworth News* (Spec. ed., July 11, 1957), p. 3, ITT Library Papers, archival newsletter.

16. "International . . . U.S. Group Activities," *Farnsworth Electronics,* p. 2. This quote is from a publication attached to a "House Memorandum from W. R. Hechman, March 24, 1958. However, it appears to be a separate memo titled, "International . . . Group Activities," Historical Files, ITT Library Papers.

≈

A Selected Bibliography

BOOKS

This bibliography focuses on the general literature and the environment that surrounded the life, career, and industry of Philo T. Farnsworth. Specific documentation is provided in the notes.

Abramson, Albert. *Electronic Motion Pictures: A History of the Television Camera.* Berkeley: University of California Press, 1955; reprint, New York: Arno Press, 1974.

———. *The History of Television: 1880–1941.* Jefferson, N.C.: McFarland & Company, 1987.

———. *Zworykin: Pioneer of Television.* Chicago: University of Illinois Press, 1995.

American Television Society. *The 1946 American Television Directory.* New York: American Television Society, 1946.

Archer, Gleason L. *Big Business and Radio.* New York: Arno Press, 1971.

———. *History of Radio to 1926.* New York: American Historical Society, 1938; reprint, New York: Arno Press, 1971.

Arrington, Leonard J., and Davis Bitton. *The Mormon Experience: A History of the Latter-day Saints,* 2nd ed. Urbana: University of Illinois Press, 1992.

Barnouw, Erik. *The Golden Web: A History of Broadcasting in the United States, 1933–1953.* New York: Oxford University Press, 1968.

———. *A Tower of Babel: A History of Broadcasting in the United States to 1933.* New York: Oxford University Press, 1966.

———. *Tube of Plenty: The Evolution of American Television.* New York: Oxford University Press, 1975; 3rd ed., 1990.

Bilby, Kenneth. *The General: David Sarnoff and the Rise of the Communications Industry.* New York: Harper & Row, 1986.

Binns, Joseph J. "Vladimir Kosma Zworykin." *Those Inventive Americans.* Washington, D.C.: National Geographic Society, 1971.

Bogart, Leo. *The Age of Television: A Study of Viewing Habits and the Impact of Television on American Life.* New York: Frederick Ungar Publishing, 1958.

Burns, R. W. *British Television: The Formative Years.* London: Peter Peregrinus/Science Museum, 1986.

———. *Television: An International History of the Formative Years.* London: IEE/ Science Museum "History of Technology Series 22," 1997.

Chester, Giraud, and Garnet R. Garrison. *Television and Radio.* New York: Appleton-Century-Crofts, 1950 and 1957.

Cunningham, Perry H. "Activity in the Church." In *Encyclopedia of Mormonism,* edited by Daniel H. Ludlow. vol. 1. New York: Macmillan, 1992.

Douglas, Alan. *Radio Manufacturers of the 1920s,* 3 vols. Vestal, N.Y.: Vestal Press, 1991; reprint, Chandler, Ariz.: Sonoran Publishing, 1995.

Dunlap, Jr., Orrin E. *The Future of Television.* New York: Harper & Brothers, 1942; revised 1947.

Eckhardt, George. *Electronic Television.* Chicago: Goodheart Willcox, 1936; reprint, New York: Arno Press, 1974.

Eddy, William C. *Television: The Eyes of Tomorrow.* New York: Prentice-Hall, 1945.

Everson, George. *The Story of Television: The Life of Philo T. Farnsworth.* New York: W. W. Norton, 1949; reprint, New York: Arno Press, 1974.

Farnsworth, Elma G. *Distant Vision: Romance & Discovery on the Invisible Frontier.* Salt Lake City, Utah: Pemberly Kent Publishers, 1989.

Fessenden, Helen M. *Fessenden: Builder of Tomorrows.* New York: Coward-McCann, 1940; reprint, New York: Arno Press, 1971.

Fisher, David E., and Marshall Jon Fisher. *Tube: The Invention of Television.* Washington, D.C.: Counterpoint, 1996.

Godfrey, Donald G., and Frederick Leigh (eds.). *Historical Dictionary of American Radio.* Westport, Conn.: Greenwood Press, 1998.

Halloran, Arthur H. *Television with Cathode Rays.* San Francisco: Pacific Coast Publishing, 1936.

Head, Sydney W. *Broadcasting in America.* Boston: Houghton Mifflin, 1956; 3rd ed. Boston: Houghton Mifflin, 1976.

Head, Sydney W., and Christopher H. Sterling. *Broadcasting in America: A Survey of Electronic Media,* 6th ed. Boston: Houghton Mifflin, 1990.

Hickam, Homer H. Jr., *October Sky: A Memoir.* New York: Random House, 1999.

Hilliard, Robert L., and Michael C. Keith. *The Broadcast Century: A Biography of American Broadcasting,* 2nd ed. Boston: Focal Press, 1997.

Inglis, Andrew F. *Behind the Tube: A History of Broadcasting Technology and Business.* Boston: Focal Press, 1990.

Jenkins, C. F. *The Boyhood of an Inventor.* Washington, D.C.: Jenkins Laboratories, 1931.

Kalman, Laura. *Abe Fortas: A Biography.* New Haven: Yale University Press, 1990.

Kirby, Philip. *The Victory of Television.* New York: Harper & Brothers Publishers, 1939.

Kisseloff, Jeff. *The Box: An Oral History of Television, 1920–1961.* New York: Penguin Books, 1995.

Knowlton, Hugh. *Transportation in the United States.* Chicago: University of Chicago Press, 1941.

Lessing, Lawrence. *Man of High Fidelity: Edwin Howard Armstrong.* Philadelphia: Lippincott, 1956.

Lewis, Tom. *Empire of the Air.* New York: Harper-Collins, 1991.

Ludlow, Daniel H. (ed.). *Encyclopedia of Mormonism.* New York: Macmillan, 1992.

McArthur, Tom, and Peter Waddell. *The Secret Life of John Logie Baird.* London: Century Hutchinson, 1986.

Maclaurin, William R. and R. Joyce Harmon *Invention & Innovation in the Radio Industry.* New York: Macmillan, 1949; reprint, New York: Arno Press, 1971.

Murray, Michael D., and Donald G. Godfrey (eds.). *Television in America: Local Station History from Across the Nation.* Ames: Iowa State University Press, 1997.

Myrick, David. *San Francisco's Telegraph Hill.* Berkeley: Howell-North Books, 1972.

Horace Newcomb (ed.), *Encyclopedia of Television.* Chicago: Fitzroy Dearborn Publishers, 1997.

Nye, R. Glen. *Farnsworth Memorial II,* 2nd ed. Washington, D.C.: Family Publication, Library of Congress, No. 74-81077, n.d.

Oxenfeldt, Alfred R. *Marketing Practices in the TV Set Industry.* New York: Columbia University Press, 1964.

Pardon, T. Earl. *The Sons of Brigham.* Provo, Utah: Brigham Young University Alumni Association, 1969.

Pickett, William B. *Homer E. Capehart: A Senator's Life, 1897–1979.* Indianapolis: Indiana Historical Society, 1990.

Ramirez, Ron, and Michael Prosise. *Philco Radio: 1928–1942.* West Chester, Penn.: Schiffer Publishing, 1993.

Runyon, Steven C. "The West Coast's First Television Station: KCBS, Los Angeles." In Michael D. Murray and Donald G. Godfrey (eds.), *Television in America: Local Station History from Across the Nation.* Ames: Iowa State University Press, 1997.

Ryder, David Warren. *Great Citizen: A Biography of William H. Crocker.* San Francisco: Historical Publications, 1962.

Sampson, Anthony. *The Sovereign State of ITT.* New York: Stein and Day Publishers, 1973.

Scott, Patricia Lyn. *The Hub of Eastern Idaho: A History of Rigby Idaho, 1885–1986.* Rigby, Idaho: City of Rigby, 1976.

Shiers, George. *Early Television: A Bibliographic Guide to 1940.* New York: Garland Press, 1997.

Shiers, George, with May Shiers. *Bibliography of the History of Electronics.* Metuchen, N.J.: Scarecrow, 1972.

Sobel, Robert. *I.T.T.: The Management of Opportunity.* New York: Truman Talley Books, 1982.

Sterling, Christopher H., and John M. Kittross. *Stay Tuned: A Concise History of American Broadcasting,* 2nd ed. Belmont, Calif.: Wadsworth, 1990.

Tankel, Jonathan D. "Philo T. Farnsworth." In Donald G. Godfrey and Frederic A. Leigh (eds.), *Historical Dictionary of American Radio.* Westport, Conn.: Greenwood Press, 1998.

Varian, Dorothy. *The Inventor and the Pilot: Russell and Sigurd Varian.* Palo Alto, Calif.: Pacific Books, 1983.

Woal, Michael, and Linda Kowall Woal. "Forgotten Pioneer: Philco's WPTZ." In Michael D. Murray and Donald G. Godfrey (eds.), *Television in America:*

Local Station History from Across the Nation. Ames: Iowa State University Press, 1997.

Zworykin, Vladimir K. "The Early Days: Some Recollections." In Lawrence W. Lichty and Malachi C. Topping (eds.), *American Broadcasting.* New York: Hastings House, 1975; reprinted from *Television Quarterly* 1: 4 (Nov. 1962) pp. 69–72.

PERIODICALS AND NEWSPAPERS

Newspapers systematically checked for Farnsworth entries (1927–1975).

New York Times
Fort Wayne *News-Sentinel* and *Journal-Gazette*
Philadelphia *Evening Public Ledger,* the *Record,* the *Bulletin,* and the *Inquirer*
Salt Lake City *Tribune,* the Deseret *News-Telegram,* and the *Deseret News*
San Francisco *Examiner,* the *Chronicle,* and the *Call Bulletin*

Selected publications. The archives and corporate collections with reference to Farnsworth are full of partial and unidentified newspaper and magazine clippings.

Abramson, Albert. "Pioneers of Television—Philo Taylor Farnsworth." *SMPTE Journal* 101:11 (November 1992): 770–84.

———. Letter in "Open Mike." *Broadcasting* 122:6 (February 3, 1992): 46–47.

Arvin, W. B. "See with Your Radio." *Radio News* 7:278 (September 1925): 384–87.

"Baird Television Limited Progress in Transmission: Sir Harry Greer on Committee's Report." *Manchester Guardian* 18 (21 June 1935), 6.

"Baird Television Limited: Progress in the Invention: Company's Practical Experiences. Television Committee's Report. Sir Harry Greer's Address." *London Times,* 21 June 1935, 25a–c.

Baudino, Joseph E., and John M. Kittross. "Broadcasting's Oldest Stations: An Examination of Four Claimants." *Journal of Broadcasting* 21 (Winter 1977): 61–88.

Bigelow, Suzanne. "Philo Farnsworth: Television's Frustrated Genius." *This People* 10:1 (Spring 1989): 24–27.

Blair, J. L. "Television, or Seeing by Wireless." *Discovery* 6:142 (April 1925): 143.

Brolly, A. H. "Television by Electronic Methods." *Electrical Engineering* 53 (August 1934): 1,153–160.

Carlisle, Norman. "Farnsworth of Television." *Coronet* (October 1946): 126–27.

Carskadon, T. R. "Phil, the Inventor." *Collier's,* 3 October 1936, 19–30.

"CBS-Farnsworth Deal." *Business Week,* 17 April 1937, 16.

Chapple, H. J. B. "Television's Magic Power." *Tele Vision* 4 (February 1932): 465–67.

Cooley, Donald G. "An Interview with Philo T. Farnsworth." *Modern Mechanix* 16:2 (June 1936): 35–135.

Cremer, Robert. "A Tinkerer Who Became the Father of Video," *San Francisco Examiner and Chronicle,* 17 January 1978, Sunday Television Report.

Dinsdale, A. "Television by Cathode Ray: The New Farnsworth System." *Wireless World* 28 (18 March 1931): 286–88.

———. "Television in America Today." *Journal of the Television Society* 1 (September 1932): 137–49.

———. "Television Takes the Next Step." *Science and Invention* 19 (May 1931): 46–47, 72–73.

"Dr. Ernest Alexanderson, Radio Pioneer, Dies at 97." *New York Times,* 15 May 1975, 46.

"Dr. Farnsworth, TV's Father, Was a Star NRI Student at 15." *NRI Journal* 28 (3, May/June 1971): 11.

"Electron Multiplier, An." *Electronics* 7 (August 1934): 242–43.

"European Version of Farnsworth's Television Camera." *Radio-Craft* 8 (February 1937): 455.

Farnsworth, Elma (Pem). "Philo Farnsworth Inventor: A Memoir," *Video Eighties Magazine,* Winter 1983, 28–35.

Farnsworth, P. T. "An Electrical Scanning System for Television: Another Vacuum-Tube Development." *Radio-Craft* 2 (December 1930): 346–49. See also *Radio Industries* 5 (November 1930): 386–89.

———. " An Improved Television Camera." *Radio-Craft* 8 (August 1936): 92, 113.

———. "Scanning with an Electric Pencil." *Television News* 1 (March–April 1931): 48, 51–54.

Farnsworth, Philo T., and Larry Lubcke. "The Transmission of Television Images." *California Engineer* 8:5 (February 1930): 12–33.

———. "The Transmission of Television Images." *Project Engineering* 2 (September 1930): 21–23.

Farnsworth, Philo Taylor. "Television by Electron Image Scanning." *Journal of the Franklin Institute* 218:4 (October 1934): 411–44.

"Farnsworth Television Receiver." *Radio Engineering* 16 (September 1936): 14–15.

Federal Communications Commission. "The Evolution of Television, 1927–1943." *Journal of Broadcasting* 4:3 (Summer 1960): 199–207.

Gietsen, Phil. "Dr. Philo Taylor Farnsworth." *Videocity* 2:3 (1972): 30–38.

Godfrey, Donald G., and Alf Pratte."Elma 'Pem' Gardner Farnsworth: The Pioneering of Television." *Journalism History* 20:2 (Summer 1994): 74–79.

Halloran, Arthur H. "Farnsworth's Cold-Cathode Electron Multiplier Tube Uses Neither Grid Nor Filament." *Radio* 16:10 (October 1934): 6, 14, 18.

———. "Scanning Without a Disc." *Radio News* 12 (May 1931): 998–99.

Hergenrother, Rudolph C. "The Farnsworth Electronic Television System." *Journal of the Television Society* 1 (December 1934): 384–88.

Herndon, C. A. "Motion Pictures by Ether Waves." *Popular Radio* 8:107 (August 1925): 113.

Hewel, H. "Details of American Cathode-Ray Television System." *Fernsehen* (in German) 2 (April 1931): 123–28.

Hirsch, Robert L."Inertial-Electrostatic Confinement of Ionized Fusion Gases." *Journal of Applied Physics* 38:11 (October 1967): 4,522.

Hirsch, Robert L., Gerald Kulcinski, and Ramy Shanny. "Fusion Research with a Future." *Issues in Science and Technology* 13:4 (Summer 1997): 60–64.

Hofer, Stephen F. "Philo Farnsworth: Television's Pioneer." *Journal of Broadcasting* 23:2 (1979): 153–65.

Kaufman, S. "Demonstrates High-Definition Television." *Radio News* 17 (November 1935): 265, 308.

———. "Farnsworth Television: How Cathode Rays Are Used in Both Transmission and Reception." *Radio News* 17 (December 1935): 330–31, 375.

"Latest Continuous-Film." *Radio-Craft* 10 (August 1938): 83, 112.

Lee, Bart. "The Radio History of Telegraph Hill." *Journal of the California Historical Radio Society* 20:2 (August 1996): 12–13.

Lippincott, Donald K., and H. E. Metcalf. "Cold Cathode Tube." *Radio Engineering* 14 (November 1934): 18–19.

Lovece, Frank. "Is It TV's 50th Birthday or Not?" *Channels* (June 1989): 9.

———."Zworykin vs. Farnsworth." *Video* 9 (September 1985): 96–98, 135–38.

May, Dennis. "Philo T. Farnsworth: The Father of Television." *BYU Today* 43:3 (May 1989): 32–36.

Minton, James. "Tom Swift in San Francisco: Philo T. Farnsworth and his Electric Television." *San Francisco Monthly* (November 1972): 27–29.

Mitchell, W. G. W. "Developments in Television." *Journal of the Royal Society of the Arts* 79 (May 22, 1931): 616–42.

"Mormon Youth Aims to Simplify Television." *Science and Invention* 17 (April 1930): 1,081.

"Mr. Philo Farnsworth: A Twenty-Three-Year-Old San Francisco Experimenter, with a New Television Receiver Which He Has Made." *Tele Vision* 3 (July 1930): 231.

"New Television System Uses Magnetic Lens," *Popular Mechanics* 62 (December 1934): 838–39

Ormond, Clyde."Telecaster." *Outdoor Life* 113:1 (January 1954): 334–35.

"Oscillight Television Receiver." *Popular Mechanics* 64 (December 1935): 901.

"Philo T. Farnsworth Dies; Transmitted 1st TV Picture." Philadelphia *Evening Bulletin,* 13 March 1971, 10B.

Postman, Neil. "Electrical Engineer: Philo Farnsworth." *Time 100* 153:12 (Spec. issue, 1999): 92–94.

Rapaport, David. "Farnsworth vs Zworykin, Cont." *Broadcasting* 122:8 (February 17, 1992): 53.

———. "History Lesson." *Broadcasting* 122:2 (January 13, 1992): 108.

"Retrospect on Television in 1934." *Journal of the Television Society* 1 (December 1934): 388.

Rogers, Adam. "2000: The Power of Invention: How We Live." *Newsweek* 130:4 (1997), 45.

Ropp, T. "Philo Farnsworth: Forgotten Father of Television." *Media History Digest* 5:2 (Summer 1985): 42–58.

Ropp, Thomas. "The Real Father of Television." *Arizona Republic Magazine,* 6 May 1984, 4–11.

Schatzkin, Paul. "Farnsworth: TV's Inventor: RCA Battles, Sarnoff, the Philco Years, and the Philadelphia Demonstration," part 2. *Televisions* 5:2 (1977): 17–19.

———. "Farnsworth: TV's Inventor: Refinanced, Relocated and Bought Out, Sarnoff Pays," part 4. *Televisions* 5:4 (1978): 10–20.

———. "Farnsworth: TV's Inventor: To England for Cash, On the Air in Philadelphia, Last Days of the Lab Gang," part 3. *Televisions* 5:3 (1977): 15–18.

Schatzkin, Paul, and Bob Kiger. "Philo T. Farnsworth: Inventor of Electronic Television." *Televisions* 5:1 (1977): 6–8.

Shiers, George. "Ferdinand Braun and the Cathode Ray Tube." *Scientific American* 230:3 (March 1974): 92–101.

———. "Television 50 Years Ago." *Journal of Broadcasting* 19:4 (Fall 1975): 387–99.

Steier, Henry P. "Bomarc Guidance Spawns New Testing Technique." *American Aviation* 21:16 (December 12, 1957): 32–33.

Stern, Robert H. "Television in the Thirties." *American Journal of Economics and Sociology* 23 (1964): 285–301.

"Television: A Survey of Present Day Systems." *Electronic* 7 (October 1934): 300–05.

"Television at Hand." *Electronics* 9 (December 1936): 14–15.

"Television News Shorts." *Radio-Craft* 8 (December 1936): 326.

"Television News Shorts." *Radio-Craft* 8 (March 1937): 518.

"Television News Shorts." *Radio-Craft* 8 (April 1937): 583.

"Television Progress." *Electronics* 7 (September 1934): 272–73.

"Television Rumors from Here and Abroad." *Radio News* 17 (October 1935): 198, 252–53.

"Television Scanning by Cathode Ray: Amplification by Electron Multiplication." *Wireless World* 36 (March 1, 1935): 208–09.

"Television Transmitters Planned." *Electronics* 8 (September 1935): 28–29.

"Video Set Shown by Farnsworth." *New York Times,* 3 September 1947, 37:2 and 32:4.

Vogel, T. "The Quality of Images In Different Television Systems." *Technique Moderne* (in French) 29 (November 1937): 284–309, 319.

Warbis, Mark. "TV Inventor Finally Getting Public's Respect." *Electronic Media,* 19 June 1989, 55.

Wilson, Mitchell. "The Strange Birth of Television." *Reader's Digest* 62:379 (February 1953): 19–22.

GOVERNMENT DOCUMENTS

Acceptance and Dedication of Statue of Philo T. Farnsworth, Presented by the State of Utah, Proceedings in the Rotunda of the United States Capitol, May 2, 1990. Washington, D.C.: Government Printing Office, 1991.

Development of Television, Hearings Before the Committee on Interstate Commerce. U.S. Senate, 76th Cong., 3rd sess., April 10–11. Washington, D.C.: Government Printing Office, 1940.

"Farnsworth." Pages 61–62 in *The National Inventors Hall of Fame.* Washington, D.C.: U.S. Department of Commerce, 1984.

Report of the Federal Trade Commission on the Radio Industry: In Response to House Resolution 548. 67th Cong., 4th sess. Washington, D.C.: Government Printing Office, 1924; reprint, New York: Arno Press, 1974.

Sarnoff, David. *Statement at the "Development of Television" Hearings Before the Committee on Interstate Commerce.* U.S. Senate, 76th Cong., 3rd sess., on S. Res. 251. April 10–11, 1940.

Securities and Exchange Commission Reports, Farnsworth Television and Radio Corporation, 1939 through 1943 and 1946.

UNPUBLISHED DOCUMENTS

Bucher, Emil E. "Black and White Television." "Radio and David Sarnoff." "Television and David Sarnoff." Unpublished manuscripts, Sarnoff Corporation Library, Princeton, N.J., n.d.

Everson, George. Unpublished autobiography, Arizona State University Library Special Collections, Box 4, File 1.

Farnsworth, P. T. "Conflicts Between Quantum Mechanics and Relativity." Published bound paper, Farnsworth Electronics, Fort Wayne, Ind., n.d. (circa 1952).

Hofer, Stephen F. "Philo Farnsworth: The Quiet Contributor to Television." Unpublished Ph.D. dissertation, Bowling Green University, 1977.

———. "Philo Farnsworth: Television's Pioneer." Unpublished paper delivered at the Broadcast Education Association Convention, n.d.

Parker, William N. "Early Philadelphia Television." Unpublished paper, May 13, 1986, W3XE file, Theater Collection, Free Library of Philadelphia. Philadelphia, Pennsylvania.

Wolkoniwicz, John Paul. "The Philco Corporation: Historical Review and Strategic Analysis, 1892–1961." Unpublished masters thesis, Massachusetts Institute of Technology, June 1981.

FILMS

"Big Dream, Small Screen: The Story Behind Television," Television Documentary. Windfall Films production for *The American Experience,* WGBH Educational Foundation. PBS Home Video, 1997.

Williams, Jack. "From Capehart to Farnsworth to ITT," audiovisual presentation before the Fort Wayne Engineer's Club bicentennial celebration event: "Engineering in Fort Wayne," March 24, 1994. Videotape presentation.

ORAL HISTORY INTERVIEWS

Complete citations for these interviews are in the endnotes. Interviews were conducted by the author unless otherwise indicated.

Abramson, Al. 1997.

Clark, Nathan C. Oral history interview conducted by Richard Searle, Sierra Club History Committee, San Francisco, Calif., 1977.

Eberhardt, Edward H. 1995.
Everson, George. 1977, by Elma G. Farnsworth.
Farnsworth, Elma G. 1987, 1996, 1997.
Farnsworth, Elma G., and Philo T. Farnsworth II. 1981, by Steven C. Runyon.
Farnsworth, Kent. 1989, by Anthony Whittaker.
Farnsworth, Lincoln. 1990.
Freeman, George. 1996.
Hirsch, Robert L. 1997.
Lindsay, Agnes and Claude, and Laura Player. 1985, by Timothy Larson.
Lubcke, Harry R. 1974, by Steven C. Runyon.
Meeks, Gene. 1995.
Nevin, Scott. 1995.
Player, Laura. 1997.
Reitan, Ed. 1997.
Rhodes, Dean. 1998.
Rutherford, Tobe. 1974, by Elma G. Farnsworth.
Schroeder, Alfred C. 1997.
Smith, M. Phyllis. 1997.
Turner, Seymour "Skee." 1977, by Elma G. Farnsworth.
Vassilatos, Jerry. 1997.

INTERNET SOURCES

Consumer Price Index Inflation Calculator CPI, 1998. http://www.jsc.nasa.gov/bu2/inflateCPI.html
Philadelphia: A New Company. http://www.comnetinc.com/tvhphila.htm
Philo Taylor Farnsworth. http://www.oldradio.com/archives/people/Philo_Farnsworth
Philo Taylor Farnsworth. http://www.invent.org/book/book-text/41.html
Popular Mechanics. http://popularmechanics.com/popmech/sci/time/M3412_94D.html
Radio in a Nutshell. http://www.ctvcson.com/ch/radio_is.html
RCA Oral History Collection. http://ieee.org/organizations/ history_center/oral_histories/oh_rca_menu.html
Schatzkin, Paul. "The Farnsworth Chronicles." http://www.songs.com/philo/
U.S.News On Line. http://www.usnews.com/issue/980817/17phil.htm

ARCHIVES AND MANUSCRIPT COLLECTIONS

Allen County Public Library. Vertical Files—clippings, "Farnsworth," "Fort Wayne Industries–F," and "Fort Wayne Industries–International Telephone and Telegraph," Allen County Public Library, Fort Wayne, Indiana. Newspaper clippings collection for Fort Wayne and vicinity.
California State Archives, Secretary of State, Department of State Corporation Division, Sacramento, California. Contains files of incorporation relative to Farnsworth's activities in California.

Delaware Archives, Department of State Division of Corporations, Dover, Delaware. Incorporation papers for Farnsworth corporations.

DuMont Papers. Allen B. DuMont Papers, The Library of Congress and the National Museum of American History, Washington, D.C. References to Farnsworth exist within these papers, but not extensively.

Farnsworth–Allen County Papers. Farnsworth Papers, Allen County Historical Society Library, Fort Wayne, Indiana. This collection is small but contains the most complete list of patents as well as technical data.

Farnsworth-Everson Papers. Philo T. Farnsworth and George Everson Papers, Special Collections, Arizona State University Library, Tempe, Arizona. This is George Everson's collection. It is one of the two most important collections on Farnsworth, second only to the collection at the University of Utah. Everson was Farnsworth's first financier and lifelong friend.

Farnsworth-Meeks Papers. Philo T. Farnsworth and Gene Meeks Papers, Special Collections, Arizona State University Library, Tempe, Arizona. Meeks was a work associate of Farnsworth's in Fort Wayne and Salt Lake City. There are only a few files, photocopied clippings, and an original Farnsworth log book.

Farnsworth Papers. Philo T. Farnsworth Papers, Manuscript Division, Special Collections, University of Utah Marriott Library, Salt Lake City, Utah. Papers acquired from the family. This is the most extensive collection of Farnsworth material. A number of papers from this collection appear duplicated in other collections. There is a great deal of crossover between this collection and those at Arizona State University.

Federal Communications Commission, WGL-AM. These are primarily license files. Copies of these papers are filed with the Godfrey Papers.

Godfrey Papers. Donald G. Godfrey Papers, Special Collections, Arizona State University Library, Tempe, Arizona. Donald G. Godfrey acquired these papers during his research. There are primarily photocopy materials. The collection does duplicate some of the Everson and Farnsworth papers. It has not all been cataloged.

Hyde Papers. Rosel H. Hyde Papers, Special Collections and Manuscripts, Harold B. Lee Library, Brigham Young University, Provo, Utah. This collection contains a wealth of information on the Federal Communications Commission. There are a few files dealing with Farnsworth's Philadelphia experimental television station.

Indiana State Archive, Commission on Public Records, Indianapolis, Indiana. Incorporation papers for Capehart and Farnsworth corporations.

ITT Library Papers. ITT Aerospace/Communication Division Library Papers. Fort Wayne, Indiana. This corporate library has a generalized collection of Farnsworth information.

Jefferson County Historical Society. Jefferson County Historical Society and Farnsworth TV Pioneer Museum, Rigby, Idaho, General Files. This collection is primarily one of displayed artifacts. There are a few press clippings.

Journal History of the Church. The Church of Jesus Christ of Latter-day Saints, Historical Department, Church Archives. Salt Lake City, Utah. The church maintains a news clipping service. There were no Farnsworth papers located in the archives, but the name Farnsworth does produce a lot of information from various news sources.

Lippincott Papers. Donald K. Lippincott Papers (Banc MSS 79/39C), The Bancroft Library, The University of California, Berkeley, California. This collection is largely Lippincott's personal history. It is at present unorganized. There are a few materials relating to Farnsworth. Lippincott was Farnsworth's patent attorney and personal friend.

Madsen Papers. Arch Leonard Madsen Papers, Manuscripts Division, Special Collections, University of Utah Marriott Library, Salt Lake City, Utah. Madsen was the CEO of the Bonneville International Corporation, a friend and supporter of Farnsworth & Associates. There are references and some correspondence with Farnsworth.

Marion Public Library. Indiana Room, Marion & Grant County, Industry Files, Marion Public Library, Marion, Indiana.

National Archives. National Archives, RG 173, Federal Communications Commission, Office of Executive Director, Washington, D.C. Records include information on Philco Radio and Farnsworth Television as well as their experimental stations.

National Museum of American History. Curator's Collection, Electrical Collections, Division of Information and Technology, Society, National Museum of American History, Washington, D.C. This collection contains a rare log book of Farnsworth's earliest experiments.

Pennsylvania Historical Society, Philadelphia, Pennsylvania. The historical society has a valuable newspaper and photo collection, particularly for Philco.

Pennsylvania State Archives, Department of State, Corporation Bureau, Harrisburg, Pennsylvania. Contains Pennsylvania papers of incorporation.

Philadelphia Free Library, Business, Science and Industry Collections. Newspaper clipping files from the area.

Player Papers. Laura Farnsworth Player Papers, Special Collections, Arizona State University Library. This is a single volume of Farnsworth family history.

San Francisco Public Library. San Francisco History Room, Vertical Files–Farnsworth, San Francisco Archives, San Francisco Public Library. Contains several small files of newspaper clippings on Farnsworth as well as microfilms of local papers.

Sarnoff Corporation Library, Princeton, New Jersey. Contains RCA and broadcast history collection. Contains an extensive Sarnoff collection including newspaper clippings, corporate newsletters, press releases, and historical books.

Theater Collection, Free Library of Philadelphia, Philadelphia, Pennsylvania. Information collected by the Woals on the Farnsworth station is deposited here.

Varian Correspondence. Varian Papers at the electronics museum, Los Altos Hills, California.

≈

Index

≈

Other books by Donald G. Godfrey

American Electronic Media: Television, Cable, Radio and the Future.
With John Craft and Fritz Leigh.
The Diaries of Charles Ora Card: The Canadian Years, 1886–1903.
With B. Y. Card
A Directory of Broadcast Archives.
Historical Dictionary of American Radio.
With Fritz Leigh.
Reruns on File: A Guide to Electronic Media Archives.
Television in America: Pioneering Stations.
With Michael Murray